Sales Promotion

Sales Promotion

Tony Yeshin

THOMSON

Australia • Canada • Mexico • Singapore • Spain • United Kingdom • United States

THOMSON

Sales Promotion

Tony Yeshin

Publishing Director
John Yates

Publisher
Jennifer Pegg

Editorial Assistant
Natalie Aguilera

Production Editor
Fiona Freel

Manufacturing Manager
Helen Mason

Marketing Manager
Leo Stanley

Typesetter
The Partnership Publishing
Solutions Ltd, Glasgow

Cover Design
P. Fielding

Printer
Zrinski d.d., Croatia

For more information, contact
Thomson Learning
High Holborn House
50–51 Bedford Row
London WC1R 4LR
or visit us on the World Wide Web
at:
http://www.thomsonlearning.co.uk

ISBN-13: 978-1-84480-161-9
ISBN-10: 1-84480-161-6

This edition published 2006 by
Thomson Learning.

*British Library Cataloguing-in-
Publication Data*
A catalogue record for this book
is available from the
British Library

Contents

Chapter 4
Developing the theory of sales promotion   56

Chapter 5
The strategic dimensions of sales promotion   70

Chapter 6
Developing the sales promotion plan   86

Chapter 7
Identifying sales promotion objectives   112

Chapter 13
The evaluation of sales promotion   233

Chapter 14
Integrating sales promotion activities   251

Chapter 15
International sales promotion   270

Acknowledgements

I would like to thank all of the academics who have developed the papers referenced in this text. Their work has enhanced our understanding of the important aspects of sales promotion. They have raised the profile of the important tools within the armoury of marketing communications.

I would also like to thank my former clients and colleagues in the sales promotion industry who have enabled me to put many of these principles into practice.

But a very special thank you is reserved for Ed Mutton for the kind words included in his foreword to this text. To receive the plaudits from the most important professional body in the area is praise indeed.

Foreword

At last! A scholarly in-depth acknowledgement that sales promotion as a marketing discipline is alive and well.

It is fashionable to hide promotional marketing under all manner of names, experiential and integrated to name but two, or to be in denial by insisting, for example, that direct marketing is different from sales promotion.

The fact is that sales promotion is at the centre of all below-the-line activity and increasingly the driver of above-the-line spend in integrated promotions. In a recent analysis, 97% of all direct mail included an element of sales promotion.

The increasingly complex array of routes to market involving every aspect of digital technology and the sophistication of experiential creativity must not and does not mean that the core techniques and basic principles of sales promotion are no longer relevant. It almost certainly means that they need the reinforcement of a book like this.

A glance through the contents page will confirm this message. First, the breadth of the topics covered, and second, the analytical treatment of each part. So much so, that the most senior practitioner will find it compulsive reading, while the student will discover a friend for life.

With the shift of emphasis in marketing from the passive to the active, from the stand-alone advertisement to the integrated brand experience, this book addresses the future expansion and diversity of our industry in terms of the fundamental verity of basic principles.

I welcome it as a timely contribution to the industry.

Edwin Mutton
Director General
Institute of Sales Promotion
December 2005

Preface

As someone who has been both a practitioner and an academic, I have long sought a text that approached the subject of sales promotion from both perspectives. For anyone studying the subject it is important to understand the practitioner approach but also to ensure that their studies are underpinned with solid reference to the very considerable number of academic papers that have been written.

My objectives in writing this text have been twofold. Firstly, to fulfil the above requirement. But equally important has been the desire to correct the notion that sales promotion is, as many writers on the subject would have it, merely a short-term expedient solution to a variety of marketing problems. With the level of expenditure on sales promotion growing rapidly, it is important to recognise the strategic role that these tools can fulfil.

Whether I have succeeded in meeting these objectives is for others to judge, but I sincerely hope that those reading it find it a satisfying and rewarding introduction to this increasingly important area of marketing communications.

Additional material can be found on the accompanying website at www.thomsonlearning.co.uk/yeshinsp. This material includes additional case studies, useful web links and PowerPoint slides.

Tony Yeshin
December 2005

Dedication

This text is dedicated to my wife and family. Their support for my endeavours is what makes it all worthwhile.

1 Understanding sales promotion

Chapter overview

Sales promotion is an increasingly important tool within the overall armoury of marketing communications. Recent years have seen recognition of the roles that sales promotion can play in achieving a variety of marketing objectives. However, there remains the misconception that sales promotion is, at best, a short-term device designed to encourage an increase in sales. This chapter defines the scope and compass of sales promotion and seeks to outline the importance of sales promotion not only in a tactical sense, but also in terms of the strategic contribution that it can deliver.

Learning outcomes

- To understand the nature of sales promotion
- To examine the reasons for the growth of sales promotion activities
- To consider the classification of sales promotion
- To reflect on the changing nature of sales promotion.

The changing nature of sales promotion

Sales promotion, perhaps more than any other area of marketing communications (other than direct marketing) has witnessed both dramatic growth and change over recent years.

Yet as recently as 1992 Van Waterschoot and Van den Bulte[1] argued that sales promotion was just a minor part of the communication mix. However, most practitioners would agree that the tools within the field of sales promotion can not only achieve specific objectives, but also do so more rapidly than any other area of marketing communications.

Moreover, in contradiction to Van Waterschoot and Van den Bulte[1], it is now recognized that more money is spent on the various forms of sales promotion than any other single tool within the marketing communications armoury.

These facts alone demand a re-appraisal of the role and contribution of the techniques of sales promotion: a fundamental objective of this text.

The value of sales promotion

One of the difficulties facing those examining the field of sales promotion is that of assigning a true value to the level of expenditure. Unlike advertising, for example, where it is possible to gain reasonably accurate expenditure figures (based on MEAL data), there are few published sources for sales promotion.

Whilst it is possible to identify advertising spend levels for individual brands from the above source, individual expenditures on sales promotion are more difficult to come by. The reason for this is simple: the data are only known to the company mounting the activity – and they are unlikely to want publication of this information. Take, for example, a promotion offering a free gift to consumers. In order to identify the true cost of the offer, it would be necessary to identify:

1   the number of packs containing the offer
2   the cost of the item offered
3   the levels of redemption
4   direct costs associated with the offer, e.g. cost of banding the item to the pack or costs of mailing the gift to redeemers, etc.
5   the cost of point-of-sale material used to support the promotion in-store
6   trade incentives offered to encourage trade support of the activity
7   ancillary materials produced for the sales force to introduce the promotion to distribution channels
8   sales force incentives designed to motivate the selling-in of the promotion
9   trade advertising, if any, used to announce the promotion
10 possible consumer advertising to create awareness of the promotional offer, etc.

Obtaining all of the above essential information would be extremely difficult, if not impossible. The consequence is that data for expenditure levels, where available, tend to be aggregated and based on an estimation of the value of the overall activity.

A major study which attempted to quantify the levels of expenditure was conducted jointly by the Institute of Sales Promotion and the Advertising Association in 1988. At that time, it was estimated that the overall value of UK sales promotion expenditure was of the order of £2.5 billion. By comparison, in the same year, the Advertising Association estimated advertising expenditure to be at a level of £6.57 billion. Extrapolating that data, Mintel (1996)[2] have suggested that expenditure in the field has increased to around £4900 billion by 1995 (vs. £10.98 billion on advertising in the same year).

Similarly, an estimate by the Institute of Grocery Distribution suggested that around £7 billion was spent in 1997 on food retail promotions alone.

A more recent study of the promotions market, conducted by Mintel (2000),[3] estimates that around £8.6 billion was spent on sales promotion in 1999. They also calculate that between 1987 and 1996 total expenditure on sales promotion doubled.

Mintel's updated estimates of the value of sales promotion is reproduced on the following page:

In the USA, a similar rate of growth in promotional expenditures has been wit-

Table 1.1

Year	£m	Index	£m at 1990 prices	Index
1987	2,500	100	3,153	100
1989	2,800	112	3,094	99
1991	3,400	136	3,211	102
1993	3,750	150	3,360	107
1995	4,900	196	4,142	131
1997	6,300	252	5,044	160
1999 (est.)	8,600	344	6,550	208

Source: Mintel Special Report on Sales Promotion, January 2000

nessed: 'Expenditure on sales promotions have increased considerably in recent years by packaged goods manufacturers, and the amount spent on consumer promotions currently exceeds that of advertising.'[4] Mela, Jedidi and Bowman (1998)[5] suggest that 'Consumer and Trade promotions now account for 50 per cent of many manufacturers marketing budgets'. According to Carol Wright (1997),[6] companies normally spend between 15 per cent and 30 per cent of the retail price of a product on marketing. Sales promotion as a tool is by far the largest by value and it has been increasing by 12 per cent annually compared with advertising growth of only 7.6 per cent.

Justin Bateman (1998),[7] in an article in *Marketing Week*, attempted to estimate the percentage of volume sold on promotion for a number of different product categories. These ranged from 60 per cent for frozen desserts, around 58 per cent for mincemeat, 45 per cent for yogurts and dairy desserts, 40 per cent for deodorants and body sprays and 35 per cent for disposable nappies.

A more recent estimate for the USA provided by Ailawadi, Neslin and Gedenk (2001)[8] suggested that sales promotions accounted for 74 per cent of the marketing budgets of US packaged goods firms.

Together, these various attempts to dimensionalize the sales promotion industry leave little doubt that the growth has been both rapid and substantial.

The reasons for growth

Several factors, both internal and external, have contributed to the rapid growth of sales promotion:

- Consumers, confronted with a decline of their purchasing power, have become more price sensitive and react positively to promotional activities.
- Distributors, more concentrated and powerful, demand more promotions from manufacturers to help them build store traffic.
- Competition for market share intensifies and competitors use consumer and trade promotions more frequently.
- The effectiveness of mass media advertising has declined because of rising costs,

media clutter and similarity amongst competing brands.

- Companies, more concerned with a slowing down of sales, are more concerned with short-term results.

Unlike some other tools of marketing communications, which work over the longer term, sales promotion produces rapid results. Used appropriately, there is little doubt that sales promotion activities create a greater level of immediate response than almost any other marketing communications activity. The impact of an effective promotion on buying behaviour is rapid, with the impact on sales being seen almost immediately. Without doubt, if a short-term uplift in sales is the requirement, sales promotion techniques will, invariably deliver.

By comparison with other forms of marketing communications, sales promotion is comparatively easy and inexpensive to implement. Pound for pound, the return on investment is often substantially higher than in other forms of activity.

Further, the outcome of sales promotion activity is directly measurable. The impact of such activity is easily observed in terms of a direct-sales response. There is no argument as to the impact of other variables, or waiting to observe some form of effect in the longer term.

The over-riding reason for the continued growth of sales promotion is because the techniques deliver results. This is especially true in the increasingly competitive retail environment in which most brands operate. Moreover, because most markets are mature, sales are more likely to come from increasing market share in comparison to competitors, rather than from growth in the sector. Sales promotion provides the means of stealing share from competitors.

Since the impact of sales promotion is, primarily, geared to the short term, it is inevitable that the area should enjoy considerable growth at times of economic recession. Pressure on personal levels of disposable income tends to make consumers significantly more price sensitive, and price-oriented sales promotions reflect this consumer pressure. Moreover, consumers have become increasingly price and value sensitive. Instead of simply purchasing a particular brand, many consumers use the basis of price in order to make their purchasing decisions. In many categories, consumers have become increasingly used to the offer of some form of incentive. Increasing numbers of brands are effectively forced to continue providing such incentives to satisfy the needs of consumers. However, it is also true that this growth has been influenced by changing attitudes amongst marketers.

In an increasingly competitive retail environment, and with the concentration of buying power into relatively few hands, manufacturers have turned to sales promotion to achieve on-shelf differentiation between their own products and those of their competitors. The opportunity for real product differentiation is diminishing as a result of the convergence of technology. As soon as one manufacturer improves his product offering, he is likely to be followed rapidly by his competitors offering the same, or a similar, benefit. The variety of sales promotion techniques provides manufacturers with a comparatively easy method of distinguishing their product from that of the competition within the retail environment.

The retail trade has also imposed other pressures on manufacturers to focus their attention on promotions. Rising sophistication on the part of retailers and, importantly, direct access to brand sales data collected at the point of purchase, have resulted in retailers demanding higher levels of promotional support from their suppliers in return for continued distribution and display levels. Retailers are now more aware than ever before of the financial contribution that an individual brand can make towards its overall profitability. In their efforts to improve their own margins, they bring pressure to bear on manufacturers to increase their rate of sale by the use of sales promotional devices. Manufacturers have little choice but to agree or face the possibility of having their product removed from the fitment.

Moreover, since the appeal of retailer products is often based on price, sales promotion has provided manufacturers with the ability to adjust the retail price to the consumer (in the short term) and minimize the differential.

Buzzell *et al.* (1990)[9] detail the progressive shift of power from manufacturers to retailers, with the large chains becoming the dominant players. They identify several factors stimulating the growth in the use of sales promotion:

- They are useful in securing trial for new products and in defending shelf space against anticipated and existing competition.
- The funds manufacturers dedicate to them lower the distributors' risks in stocking new brands.
- They add excitement at the point of sale to the merchandising of mature and mundane products.
- They can instil a sense of urgency among consumers to buy while a deal is available.
- Sales promotion costs are incurred on a pay-as-you-go basis, which can spell survival for smaller, regional brands that cannot afford large advertising programmes.
- Sales promotion allows manufacturers to use idle capacity and to adjust to demand and supply imbalances or softness in raw material prices while maintaining the same list prices.
- They allow manufacturers to discriminate among consumer segments that vary in price sensitivity.

To these might be added senior management's concern for meeting short-term volume targets, which are more readily achieved through the use of sales promotion activities. Moreover, many young managers seek rapid career advancements that, similarly, can be achieved by reaching or exceeding pre-established sales targets. The overall result is a preference for boosting sales through promotions rather than in the development of long-term activities to strengthen the consumer franchise via advertising.

Undoubtedly, a major influence has been the desire for short-term sales achievement in its own right. The consequence of the adoption of mass production techniques in many industries has, in many instances, heightened the level of competition for market share. Sales promotion techniques are often seen as a means of achieving these increases in sales volume with the benefit of improved market share and, importantly, the ability to utilize excess manufacturing capacity.

Stewart and Gallen (1998)[10] echo this view that some of the drivers of sales promotion are the need for short-term results, competitive action resulting in the sales promotion dilemma (no one firm dares pull out), escalating media costs and media fragmentation, and the change in the balance of power from the manufacturer to the retailer.

However, another possible driver of sales promotions is a consequence of ineffective planning, implementation, and evaluation processes, which have evolved over recent decades, rather than the actual sales promotion tools themselves.

In many companies, the performance of product management may be monitored by their ability to deliver volume sales. Since sales promotion, potentially, has an immediate impact on consumer sales, there has been a tendency for product managers to turn to these techniques in order to achieve their sales objectives. At the same time, pressure on margins has made for a closer attention to the detail of the achievement of cost-effective sales volume. Since the results of the application of many promotional devices can be predicted with a high degree of accuracy, product management can be confident in their volume forecasts. Similarly, with the increasing costs of other forms of marketing communications, especially that of advertising, management has turned to areas that are perceived to be more cost effective; especially for the achievement of short-term sales. The progressive fragmentation of audiences and the increases in media costs have altered the balance in favour of sales promotion techniques that are more likely to deliver demonstrable results.

A further factor is the growing belief of product and sales management in their ability to handle the techniques of sales promotion. Unlike other areas of marketing communications, sales promotion is rarely subjected to the same level of internal debate as would be the case with, say, advertising. This enables product managers to be more 'independent' and self motivated in the determination and implementation of sales promotional activities.

The growth of specialist sales promotions agencies has also contributed to the increased recognition of the importance of the area and the growth in the credibility that the application of sales promotion techniques has enjoyed. Historically, sales promotion has been viewed as an adjunct to other marketing communications techniques. Today it is recognized that the use of sales promotion has an important impact on marketing strategy.

Flanagan (1988)[11] reiterates some of these reasons for the growth in sales promotion activities:

- Media costs are continuing to escalate to the point where manufacturers are exploring alternative means of achieving their objectives.
- Companies are increasingly concerned with achieving short-term results, which can be obtained with sales promotions that, when properly applied, do not detract from the brand's image.
- Sales promotions provide account-specific programmes that respond to the increasing power of the retailer and their need to create 'events' that help them stand out from their competitors.
- Sales promotions enable both retailers and manufacturers to interact with the market to gain immediate results at the point of purchase.
- Activities can be focused into small regions or even a group of retail outlets to take advantage of specific opportunities.

According to Hardie (1996)[12] price promotions have been taking up a growing proportion of the marketing budgets of fast-moving consumer-goods manufacturers. He attributes the shift in expenditures from above-the-line advertising to promotional activity to several factors:

- The proliferation of different types of items stocked in supermarkets, often with negligible product differentiation, and the maturing of markets have made markets more competitive with the result that marketers have turned to short-term promotions in order to achieve share targets.
- The increasing power of the retailers and the growth of private label have forced manufacturers to make more use of promotions (both as a result of retailer pressure and the need to meet the threat of lower priced products).
- The availability of electronic point-of-sale scanner technology (EPOS) means that it is both easier to implement promotions and to measure their immediate effects.
- The increasing pressure for marketing accountability has increased this trend. Promotions, particularly those that are price based, produce large and measurable sales increases, at least in the short term.
- Pressure from sales forces who are often evaluated and compensated on the basis of volume sales has encouraged the use of such activities.

The definitions of sales promotion

The definitions of what sales promotion is and does are more divergent than, perhaps, any other form of marketing communications.

The Institute of Sales Promotion (2004)[13] defines the activity as follows:

> A planned and implemented marketing activity that both enhances product or service appeal and changes customer behaviour positively in return for an additional benefit for purchase or participation.

Shimp (2000)[14] suggests that 'a promotion is any incentive used by a manufacturer to induce the trade and/or consumers to buy a brand and to encourage the sales force to aggressively sell it. Retailers also use promotional incentives to encourage desired behaviour from consumers. The incentive is additional to the basic benefits provided by the brand and temporarily changes its perceived price or value'.

Kotler *et al.* (1999)[15] define sales promotion as 'short-term incentives to encourage purchase or sale of a product or service'.

Schultz, Robinson and Petrison (1992)[16] provide a more strategic definition of sales promotion. They suggest that: 'Sales promotions are marketing and communications activities that change the price/value relationship of a product or service perceived by the target, thereby (1) generating immediate sales and (2) altering the long-term brand value.'

The Direct Marketing Association (1994)[17] similarly argues that: 'Sales promotion activities that communicate distinctive brand attributes and contribute to the brand development and reinforcement of brand value are consumer franchise building promotions.'

Alan Toop (1994),[18] writing in *Marketing* suggests: 'Sales promotion conducts an interactive relationship with its audience … . It invites participation, invites consumers to enter, to apply, to collect.'

These fundamental contradictions in definition have resulted in considerable confusion of the role and purpose of sales promotion and has led many, including serious academics, to conclude that the techniques offer little in the way of brand sustenance, lead to no lasting uplift in the value of post-promotion sales and, perhaps more seriously, can result in serious damage to brand perceptions.[19,20,21]

Sales promotion encompasses all promotional activities other than advertising, personal selling and public relations. Blattberg and Neslin (1990)[22] consider sales promotion as 'an action-focused marketing event whose purpose is to have an impact on the behaviour of the firm's customers'.

Several important aspects of sales promotions should be highlighted to complete this definition. First, sales promotions involve some type of inducement that provides an extra incentive to buy and this represents the key element in a promotional programme. This incentive is additional to the basic benefits provided by the brand and temporarily changes its perceived price or value. It is also primarily seen as an acceleration tool designed to speed up the selling process and maximize sales volume.

For example, Nestlé mounted a two-level promotion on its confectionery product Kit Kat. Purchasers were invited to register on line and were invited to use on-pack codes to bid or buy a wide range of merchandise valued at over £5 million.

Others classify sales promotions as active or passive. Promotions such as coupons require active search on the part of consumers, whereas in-store promotions such as 'two-for-one' involve a limited search, restricted to the store environment. Sales promotions have also been divided into price- and non price-oriented categories. The end benefit of price promotions for the consumer is a lower purchase price (e.g. coupons), whereas other promotions focus on other benefits (e.g. value for money, like 'two-for-one' promotions).

Part of the problem stems from the definitions themselves. Adrian Broadbent (1998)[23] writing in *Marketing Business* says of sales promotion that:

> This marketing discipline has developed further in recent years than any other, as brand owners have begun to recognise the value of effective and quantifiable promotional activity in getting rid of mass volumes of stock.

He infers, along with many others, that this is the sole role of sales promotion.

Chandon (1995)[24] produced a useful summary of consumer research in the field of sales promotion. He identified more than 200 studies that had been conducted in the decade prior to the publication of his paper.

He suggests that 'the numerous definitions of sales promotion have in common the idea that sales promotions are a temporary and tangible modification of supply'. He also raises the question as to whether, as many definitions suggest, the term 'sales promotion' should encompass the variety of individual techniques, or whether it is more appropriate to consider each of them separately.

Gupta *et al.* (1997)[25] highlight the fact that since empirical research in the area of promotions typically focuses on identifying the short-term effects of promotions, most people see sales promotion as being purely tactical.

Peattie and Peattie (1994)[26] support this notion. They argue that the 'tendency to bundle all the different types (of promotion) together for study and discussion ... has encouraged:

1 a limited view of what promotions can achieve
2 an overly rational–economic view of their effects on consumers
3 a tactical and short-term view of promotion
4 a negative perception about the impact that promotions may have on brands and brand positioning.'

In a subsequent paper, Peattie *et al.* (1997)[27] argue that preconceptions result from the overwhelming tendency to view promotions as only those that are price-based, money-off deals and coupons, excluding other forms of promotional activity that add value to the brand. As they state: 'As our understanding of sales promotion increases, it is becoming increasingly clear that it is inappropriate to research and write about promotions by lumping together all of the different elements ... and assuming that the findings relating to the type of promotion tool will apply to sales promotion in general.'

This point is reiterated by Peattie (2002),[28] who argues that the tendency has been to generalize about sales promotions inferring that they are about money-off and coupon offers.

She contends that many of the criticisms levelled at sales promotions reflect this underlying assumption. Much of the research that has been conducted has generally considered the short-term effects of sales promotion on sales patterns and has rarely investigated the more long-term and communications-oriented impact of sales promotions on customers.

This author is certainly of the latter view. To be meaningful, the disaggregation of sales promotion techniques into their component parts provides a far better understanding of the differing roles of the individual promotional devices. To lump them all together is to imply, quite wrongly, that all promotions, irrespective of their specific execution, can achieve the same goals.

The need for a more strategic focus of sales promotion is underpinned by various authors, as the following quotes illustrate:

> Sales promotion has come a long way from the time when it was 'simply a short term inducement to increase sales'.
>
> Robinson and Hauri (1995)[29]

> Promotions are no longer simply short-term initiatives to lift sales, they are increasingly being used to reinforce brand values.
>
> Gay (1997)[30]

This author believes that there is a fundamental problem, either with the specific definitions of sales promotion or, more likely, their interpretation. Much of the work that has been conducted by academics tends to view promotions as being some variation on the theme of money off. Whether this takes the form of direct financial incentives, delayed incentives, such as money off next purchase or free product, there is the consistent interpretation that promotions are all of a similar form.

In some respects, there is support for this belief in terms of the implementation of sales promotion activity. By far and away the bulk of all promotions do take this form. However, not only does this denigrate the role of sales promotion as a tool within the marketing communications armoury, it becomes a self-fulfilling prophecy. If marketers continue to believe that sales promotion is a short-term expedient solution to a particular marketing problem, they will fail to address the longer-term and more strategic dimensions of sales promotion. Moreover, it fails to recognize that individual techniques of sales promotion can be designed to fulfil very different objectives. Whilst many are, undeniably, short term in their focus, others can be designed to achieve a long-term perspective for the brand. The Walkers Crisps 'Books for Schools' promotion is one instance of a long-term device (first introduced in 1990 and still running at the time of writing), which is designed to impact on consumer perceptions of the brand and which, unequivocally, has achieved that aim.

There is much support for the notion that other forms of sales promotion, such as collect devices, competitions, sponsorship and other activities can, in certain instances, achieve similar objectives to those of advertising. Used appropriately, these forms of sales promotion can enhance the brand in a positive manner and add emotional value to the brand-purchasing decision.[31,32,33]

One of the aims of this text is to encourage planners to think more strategically about the application of sales promotion executions and, associated with that, consider the broader dimensions of the impact of sales promotion. Used properly in a manner that is consistent with the desired image associated with the brand, it is entirely possible to plan sales promotions that either support and enhance that image or, in some instances, provide the opportunity to refocus consumer attitudes towards the brand in question.

The classification of sales promotion

Sales promotions can operate on three levels:

1   They communicate. They can gain customer attention at the point of purchase by providing additional information that may be relevant to the purchasing decision.
2   They provide incentive. Sales promotion offers some form of direct inducement, either immediate or delayed, which changes the perceptual base of the purchasing decision.
3   They advance the purchasing decision. They invite the consumer to engage in an immediate transaction.

It is argued by Raghubir et al. (2004)[34] that promotions may have three forms of impact on the consumer:

1   Economic – monetary or non-monetary gain derived from the nature of the promotional offer. The amount of the monetary offer may be combined with a potential decrease in transaction time, or simplifying the purchasing decision process.

2 Informational – the communication of information about a brand that is unknown to the consumer.

3 Emotional – the feelings/emotions aroused by exposure to the promotional offer.

Sales promotion can, broadly, be classified into four main categories, dependent on the source and the intended target audience:

1 Manufacturers using sales promotions to motivate the trade

2 Manufacturers offering incentives to motivate the consumer

3 Manufacturers directing promotions towards their own (and intermediary) sales forces

4 Retailers offering promotions to the consumer.

This is reinforced by Stewart and Gallen (1998)[10] who state that sales promotions can be divided into trade promotions, such as those directed at retailers (e.g. margin allowances, slotting and case allowances) and consumer promotions, which include activities such as premiums, coupons and money off. Consumer promotions can be further divided into price-related trial promotions and non-price (mainly usage) promotion. Examples of price-related promotions are sampling, coupons, and money off, whereas non-price promotions include warranties, premiums, contests and sweepstakes.

Ingold (1995)[35] similarly makes a distinction between four types of promotions:

1 Consumer promotions, in which a direct, indirect or hypothetical benefit (samples, coupons, rebates, cash refund offer, etc.) is proposed to consumers to stimulate the purchase of a product. Manufacturers, generally, offer consumer promotions through the distribution channel.

2 Trade promotions are proposed to retailers or wholesalers, generally taking the form of money allowances, to persuade them (a) to carry the brand, (b) to carry more units than the normal amount, (c) to promote the brand by featuring display or price reductions or (d) to push the products in their stores.

3 Commercial promotions are promotional activities organized by distributors and targeting their own customer base, generally using the financial support given by manufacturers.

4 Sales force or network promotion, where the objective is to stimulate all the partners involved in the selling activities (sales force, wholesalers and retailers) through individual incentives.

This can be seen in diagram form below.

Figure 1.1

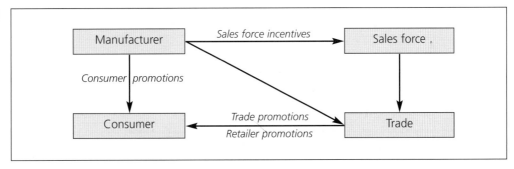

Promotions may have very different targets and objectives:

1 Some promotions may be specifically targeted towards the end user or consumer, and are designed to fulfil a 'pull' strategy. They specifically encourage consumers to select one brand over another because of the added value provided by the promotional device.

2 Other promotions target members of the distribution chain. These may be designed to encourage them to place additional efforts behinds the brands that they are stocking and, hence, fulfil a 'push' strategy.

3 Different forms of promotion appeal to different groups of consumers.

4 The conventionally used demographic variables together with those associated with lifestyle and attitudes will exert a significant impact on the acceptability of a particular promotional execution.

5 Several authors distinguish between promotional types as to whether the execution is value adding or value increasing. The distinction is an important one:

   a Value-adding promotions are those that operate beyond the basic proposition. The price charged for the product, and the quantity provided, remain unchanged. The promotion offers some new dimension in the form of a free gift, a self-liquidating offer, a contest, a competition or some other execution.

   b Value-increasing promotions affect the fundamentals of the product proposition and, generally, are associated with a change of the price, quantity or both.

6 Sales promotions differ in terms of the objectives that they can fulfil. Whilst some have a deliberate short-term impact, others are designed to achieve longer-term objectives, sometimes associated with changes in the perception of the product image.

Daugherty *et al.* (1993)[36] have provided a similar, but more comprehensive, overview of consumer and trade-sales promotions.

Figure 1.2

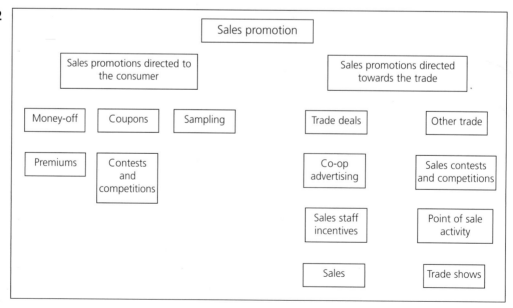

The scope and compass of sales promotion

A complication in dealing with a single discipline is determining the limits. What elements should properly be considered and what should not? Within the field of sales promotion, this is a difficult issue to deal with. Although, increasingly, specialist companies exist within the field of sales promotion, the nature of their activities varies considerably.

A major attempt was made by the Institute of Sales Promotion in conjunction with the Advertising Standards Authority to define more precisely which activities should be included within the sales promotion armoury (1988). Their conclusion was that practices were too varied amongst users to enable any precise definition. For example, whilst some clients included discounting activities within the remit of sales promotion, others regarded them as a separate activity determined and implemented by the sales and marketing departments.

Even those activities that can be clearly defined as sales promotion are sometimes created and implemented by companies specializing in other disciplines. At what point, for example, should a brand-based competition be included as a public relations activity as a result of its being placed in a media environment? Since some forms of advertising feature promotional offers, should these be included or not? Should sponsorship be defined as a separate activity or included within the compass of sales promotion, etc.?

The distinction between advertising, promotions and direct marketing is increasingly becoming blurred. However, on the whole, sales promotions agencies speak to brand managers, whilst advertising agencies have the ear of the marketing manager/director.

Undeniably, a tangible offer made directly to the consumer should be considered as part of the armoury of sales promotion. However, it may be presented as part of a direct mail piece, or an advertising campaign.

Even the professional bodies recognize the confusion. As a recognition of the increasingly diverse range of activities undertaken by its members, the IPA is currently considering an alternative name to reflect this.

The changing face of sales promotion

Undeniably, the nature of the practice of sales promotion is changing rapidly. Whereas once, perhaps, the practitioners of sales promotion could be accused of coming up with solutions and then attempting to locate a problem that was appropriate, today's sales promotion practitioners are characterized by the strength of strategic thinking and effective planning. Moreover, to achieve the latter demands thorough integration of the sales promotion plan into other aspects of the marketing programme to ensure benefits to the brand in the longer term.

The biggest single problem remains that sales promotion is accused of being a short-term tactical device. This denies both the strategic role of sales promotion and the benefits that it can deliver to the brand in the longer term.

In most markets brands are, essentially, similar to each other and, for the most part, the consumer accepts several of them as alternatives for each other. The consequence is that there is little inherent in the product or its packaging to differentiate one offering from another. In the crowded environment of the supermarket, a sales promotion device may provide the differentiation that serves to encourage the consumer to purchase the product. Indeed, this may be of paramount importance since, according to the Point of Purchase Advertising Institute (POPAI), 70 per cent of supermarket purchase decisions are actually made in-store.

It could be argued that there is a major contrast between advertising and public relations, both of which are designed to impact on awareness, information gathering and, sometimes, evaluation phases. For the most part, sales promotion works directly on the decision-making stage. The reason sales promotion is so effective in the short term is because it alters the consumer's perception of the value that the brand provides (especially when compared with its competitors).

However, some authors argue that, similar to the other tools of marketing communications, sales promotion operates across all phases of the explanatory models.

Peattie and Peattie (1994)[26] propose that the attention, interest, desire and action (AIDA) model developed by Strong and conventionally applied to advertising, can be seen to be appropriate in the context of sales promotion.

In terms of attention, the very nature of sales promotion is designed to secure the attention of the audience at the point of purchase. Promotions specifically attract consumers and ensure that featured products stand out on the retailer's shelves. For example, Weetabix offered a prize competition in which £5 million worth of prizes were on offer. The promotion took the form of a virtual game. Each pack contained a competitor number that was required for the consumer to log on to a dedicated website. Consumers were invited to choose one of a series of races and the 'winners' would be invited to a prize village. Apart from a range of prizes including Plasma TV sets, MP3 Players and training days with a British Olympian, the promotion also included a self-liquidating offer of an inflatable supporter's chair for four pack tokens plus £5.99.

Promotions affect the intrinsic nature of the product proposition. As such, they may serve to add interest to the brand. For a brand with which the consumer has become overly familiar, the promotional deal may invite them to take a new look at what is on offer. Nestlé Aero for example have a *Charlie and the Chocolate Factory* promotional tie-in providing the opportunity to win a trip to a USA chocolate factory and five golden tickets to be won. This is a movie tie-in that links directly to the values of the brand.

The particular offer may make the product more desirable to the audience. Mars Kids Mix is a cross-promotion of various fun-size products including Maltesers, Starburst and Milky Way.

Promotions have an immediacy at the critical moment of purchase decision. As such they may well encourage consumers to take specific action in the form of a purchase of the promoted brand. Pringles has joined forces with the new Star Wars movie for an on-pack promotion. If a light sabre sticker is found under the seal of packs, the winners will receive a Star Wars-related prize. The top prize is a trip to California for 2 days' training with the film's stunt team. The 'instant win' nature of many prize competitions may positively affect the consumer's desire to purchase the brand.

It remains true that most sales promotion activity remains focused on the short term. There has, historically, been comparatively little concern about the relationship between sales promotion and the other strategic dimensions of the marketing plan.

Indeed, even when research is used to contribute to the sales promotion planning process, it is concerned much more with pre-evaluating the likely impact of the promotion than with the strategic fit between this activity and other dimensions of the brand.

Against the background of the changing attitudes towards all aspects of marketing communications, it is important to recognize that, with possibly a very few exceptions, companies rarely use sales promotion in isolation of other marketing communications techniques. For this reason, sales promotion must be seen within a broader context. Effective implementation of sales promotion demands a thorough consideration of the need to integrate the activity with other aspects of the marketing communications plan.

Mintel (1996)[2] argues that the UK sales promotional industry has been so successful that consultancies have achieved a status paralleling that of the traditional advertising agencies.

This change in both role and status has come about for a number of reasons. In the first instance, several of the agencies specializing in sales promotion have extended their range of provision and are, therefore, more able to respond to the variety of client needs. Rather than remaining constrained by the traditional practices of sales promotion, they are now major contributors to the overall brand welfare.

There has been an increasing recognition, by both clients and practitioners, of the strategic contribution possible with the appropriate use of sales promotion techniques. They are, therefore, able to respond both to the short-term requirements by clients for sales increases, as well as contributing to the relationships between consumers and their chosen brands in the longer term.

The increased provision and flexibility of former sales promotion specialists has enabled a greater contribution to integrated activities that encompass a wider use of marketing communications (several campaigns utilize advertising, public relations activity, and direct marketing, as well as on- or off-pack promotions, point of sale, etc.). Sales promotion agencies are well placed to ensure that activities are planned and co-ordinated to achieve an integrated impact on the target market.

The consequence has inevitably been a blurring of the distinctions between the various practitioners that, in turn, makes it increasingly difficult to define precisely those activities that are properly contained within the sales promotion arena and those that lie outside.

Case study

WALKERS CRISPS
Agency: The Marketing Store

Background

The children's snacks market has seen almost continuous growth over recent years and in 2003 sales were around £450 million. Although the market is highly competitive, Walkers is the dominant brand with around 46 per cent share of value. However, the brand was facing increased pressure not only from other brands but also from, particularly, private label products.

Objectives

The brand owners sought a promotion that would enhance the brand equity and help it stand out in a very crowded market place. Additionally, it was desired that the promotion assist in building loyalty towards the brand.

Strategy

Comic Relief was identified as a key opportunity to promote the brand. It was recognized that the charity event was already enjoying a high profile and would provide the means to create distinctive packaging and in-store displays. Additionally, the brand would be linked with a number of high-profile personalities already linked to the charity event.

Campaign summary

The promotion consisted of several distinct elements:
- The brand guaranteed a donation of £1 m to Comic Relief that was not linked to purchase.

- Walkers introduced a limited edition baked-bean flavour for which every single pack sold contributed 1p to Comic Relief.
- 5-pack multipacks of baked-bean flavoured crisps and Monster Munch snacks were developed each of which contained a free whoopee cushion. The pack design clearly communicated the baked-bean imagery. Each multipack sold contributed an additional 5p to Comic Relief.
- The promotional message ran across the full range of Walkers Crisps and snacks (750 million packs) under the creative umbrella 'Whoopee! Walkers are giving a guaranteed £1,000,000 to Comic Relief'. Walkers wanted to ensure that the consumer understood that the £1000 000 was not linked to purchase.

A heavyweight TV campaign featured the three designs of whoopee cushions to drive repeat purchase of the multipacks and raise awareness of the link between Walkers and Comic Relief.

Results

- The campaign met Walkers' objectives and delivered funds to Comic Relief in a way that captured the hearts and minds of the general public.
- Consumer regard for the Walkers brand reached an all-time high during the promotional period.

The promotion was the ISP silver award winner of the 2004 Fundraising and Cause Related Marketing; it was also a highly commended campaign for the 2004 Free Items at the Point of Purchase and the MCCA awarded it the best communication campaign featuring sales promotion, 2004.

Questions

1 Identify the factors that have contributed to the growth of sales promotion activities over recent years.
2 Why is it considered important for sales promotion to adopt a strategic focus?
3 What are the main impacts of sales promotion on the consumer?
4 Identify the different targets and focus of sales promotion.
5 Consider what elements should be included under the heading of sales promotion.

2 The roles and limitations of sales promotion

Chapter overview

This chapter examines the advantages that the use of sales promotion offers relative to other forms of marketing communications. It indicates the many positive impacts that it can have. However, since the area remains one of considerable contention, particularly amongst academics, it also outlines the various criticisms that have been levelled against sales promotion.

The importance of identifying the strategic context for sales promotion is undeniable and it is imperative that those planning to implement sales promotion activities consider the wider implications of their plans rather than simply the desire to achieve short-term sales volume.

Learning outcomes

- To consider the advantages of sales promotion
- To examine the specific benefits that the application of sales promotion executions can deliver
- To identify the criticisms that have been made against sales promotion
- To understand the negative impacts that follow the wrong use of sales promotion techniques.

The contribution of sales promotion

Undeniably sales promotion offers manufacturers a series of benefits that few other forms of marketing communications activity can deliver. Price promotions enable manufacturers to adjust to variations in supply and demand without changing list prices. Often price promotions can help even out peaks and troughs in consumer demand to lower average operating costs. By reducing prices during periods of comparatively slow sales, manufacturers can entice more consumers to purchase their products.

However, sales promotion represents a range of different tools that can influence consumer (or trade) behaviour and can enhance the appeal of products and services. It would be wrong to assume that there is one thing called 'sales promotion'. In fact, each of the different tools can be used to achieve different objectives. These tools differ in a number of important respects:

1 Promotional target – some promotions are specifically designed to influence the trade. Their role is to encourage intermediaries to provide support to the pro moted brand. This may appear in the form of lower on-shelf prices, in-store display or other constructs. These emphasize a 'push' strategy.

    Other promotions are designed to appeal directly to the consumer and represent a 'pull' strategy. Here, direct or indirect incentives are offered to encourage the consumer to select the promoted brand at the point of purchase.

2 Benefits offered – whilst some promotions seek to add value to the brand proposition, others increase value. Value-added promotions offer some form of additional item that enhances the value of the brand. These may take the form of premium items, such as free gifts that can be either instant (i.e. included with the product) or delayed (requiring a succession of purchases in order to qualify for the gift). Other value-added promotions can take the form of competitions, such as instant win or delayed competitions. In some instances, the promotions may be 'continuous' and promote loyalty to the brand or service over time. For example, Patak's offer a chance to win an Indian Summer holiday and 50 sets of floor cushions across their range of Indian Food products.

    Value-increasing promotions alter the relationship between price and quantity. As such, they can be instant promotions, as in money off or increased quantity for the same price, or delayed, as in some forms of coupon offer.

3 Promotional appropriateness – some promotional formats are better suited to some markets than others. Whilst most forms of sales promotion can be used in the market for fast-moving consumer goods, it would be difficult, if not impossible, to apply some executions to consumer durable products.

4 Promotional appeal – different promotional offers appeal to different consumer groups. Whilst the vast majority of consumers would be attracted to a money-off offer or free additional product, research indicates that not everyone is similarly attracted to a coupon offer. Equally, by comparison, fewer consumers are likely to enter a competition. What is important is finding the most appealing promotion to the identified target groups and the execution most capable of achieving the desired objectives.

The benefits of sales promotion

Because sales promotion costs are variable with volume they enable small regional businesses to compete against brands with large advertising budgets. Whilst a small manufacturer may not be able to afford the high costs associated with media-based activity, those companies will be able to afford on-shelf promotional activity. The same point applies equally to new products targeted at segments too small to warrant large-scale advertising spend. Sales promotions may well be the only marketing communications support a new product introduction receives. Particularly in those markets where the underlying product proposition is familiar to potential purchasers, a store-based promotion may be all that is required to induce desired levels of trial and off-take. This is, similarly, important from a retailer perspective. By inducing consumer trial of new products and clearing retail inventories of obsolete products, price promotions reduce the retailers' risk in stocking new brands.

According to Peattie (1998),[1] sales promotion can:

1   attract new customers from competitors
2   induce existing customers to buy more
3   persuade customers to switch to the brands of products with higher profit margins.

Sales promotions encourage different retail formats, thereby increasing consumer choice. In almost any product category, there will be more on-shelf differentiation by virtue of the divergent promotional techniques being employed than for any other reason. And, because different items are on promotion weekly, consumer choice is enhanced and shopping for otherwise mundane products becomes more exciting. According to Blattberg and Neslin (1990),[2] in many frequently purchased product categories, more than 50 per cent of the total sales volume is sold on promotion. Promotions have, therefore, become the key influences in many product categories, because they are a mechanism to bring the product to the attention of the consumers. Promotions are also designed to directly influence behaviour, which is immediately observable, whereas advertising is often considered to affect attitudes, an antecedent of behaviour.

Peattie and Peattie (1994)[3] have demonstrated that promotions have been shown to affect consumers directly in a variety of ways, leading to:

- re-timed purchasing
- brand switching
- increased volume of purchasing
- product-type substitutions
- store substitutions.

Sales promotions may increase consumer demand by encouraging trial in new categories and improving the attention-getting power of advertising. Often advertising and promotions are linked together to ensure the maximum impact of the message upon the desired target audience. Buying on deal is a simple rule for time-pressured consumers. If there are no other factors on which to base a purchasing decision, price may well have a significant bearing on the brand chosen.

Sales promotion can encourage repeat purchase of a product. In some instances and depending on the promotional execution used it can influence purchasing behaviour and establish new patterns of purchase. Following initial sampling of a product or service, promotions can be used to encourage repeat purchase and usage. At the time of writing, Huggies are offering a free 'Heffalump' from the Disney film for points from promotional packs. Redemption requires four proofs of purchase and may establish a pattern of purchase for the brand relative to its competitors.

Sales promotion can help build more frequent or multiple purchases. Sales promotion can be used to increase the amount of product bought or to increase consumption of the product. In some instances consumers can be persuaded to purchase a larger pack size (10 per cent extra free) or multiples of the product (two for the price of one). In turn, they can be encouraged to use the product more frequently by providing the consumer with 'new' usage opportunities or by identifying new uses for the product. One device that is regularly used is recipes that present the consumer with new ways in which the product can be used. Currently, for example, Campbell's soups are offering recipes on pack in which the chosen soup variety is the key ingredient.

Sales promotion can secure trial of a new product or service. Because sales promotion is generally used to offer a short-term incentive to the prospective purchaser, such activities can, generally, achieve product trial. This can be of a new product, an existing product that has been reformulated, or may be used to encourage non-category users to try a previously unused product. Increasingly, consumers are invited to obtain samples of new or improved products via television commercials or the Internet.

Sales promotion can energize the sales of a mature brand. Consumers tend to forget the salient features of a particular brand after a time. In some respects it recedes into their memory. In this context, an appropriate sales promotion can effectively re-introduce the brand to them. It can give new life to such a brand and ensure that consumers are made more aware of its presence.

Sales promotion can be used to familiarize consumers with new packaging. In those instances where a manufacturer introduces new packaging, sometimes to avoid 'look-alike' products, at other times to introduce some specific benefit of new packaging such as easy re-sealing or easier pouring, there is a way to ensure a transition between the old and new formats. Sales promotion can be specifically designed to enhance the awareness of the new form of packaging and ensure that the consumer is not confused by the changes.

Because of their speed of implementation, promotions can be used to offset the effects of competitive actions. Strong promotional activity at the point of purchase can serve to minimize the impact of a competitor's advertising or promotional campaign.

Sales promotion can build upon existing events. There are many 'events' in the calendar that can be exploited by promotional activities. Many companies introduce special promotions to tie in with, for example, Easter, Valentine's Day (perfume brands), or to exploit the seasonality inherent in the nature of the brand purchase (e.g. special promotions on ice cream products during the summer months).

Sales promotion can be used to even out peaks and troughs in the sales pattern. Most products experience periods of high sales followed by declines as a result of traditional patterns of buying behaviour. Sales promotions can be used to encourage consumers to purchase during periods of decline, thus smoothing out the patterns of purchase.

Some forms of sales promotion can be used to enhance the image of the brand to potential consumers. The use of techniques such as competitions, lotteries and charity-related promotions can be used to add both physical and emotional value to brands and broaden their appeal.

Often, sales promotion is used to reinforce the advertising proposition. By selecting a promotional execution that reflects the theme of the advertising campaign, the activity can remind the consumer of the advertising proposition. An excellent example of such activity was a campaign run by Kleenex. Clearly, amongst other uses, tissues are used by people who are suffering from colds. At a time of increased pollen levels, many people suffer from hayfever. The brand offered a free hayfever survival kit in exchange for six proofs of purchase from special Kleenex tissues packs. Similarly, Flora Pro-Activ is offering a free cholesterol-lowering guide

Short-term sales promotional activity may serve to encourage the retail trade to bring forward their purchases, reducing the incidence of out-of-stock situations on retail shelves. Promotions also encourage the trade to provide temporary displays, price cuts and or advertising features, all of which may contribute towards increasing sales to consumers. Such activities often are used to add excitement at point of purchase to otherwise mundane products.

Brand activities can ensure that the product is featured in-store at the time when the consumer is making the purchasing decision. Following negotiations with the trade, a brand can obtain special pricing, featuring, sampling or other activities at a prominent in-store location. A key feature of sales promotion activity is its ability to increase merchandising space for the brand. If the retail trade anticipate increased off-take they will allocate more shelf space, which provides greater prominence for the brand.

Sales promotion can improve levels of distribution. By providing the retail trade with some form of direct incentive, they may be encouraged to stock a previously un-stocked product.

Sales promotion can be used to modify trade inventories. A major benefit of sales promotion is its ability to help the trade reduce stocks of an existing product. By offering some form of incentive to the end consumer, the rate of sale may be increased, hence reducing the inventory. The opposite can also be achieved encouraging the trade to increase their stocking level to take advantage of some special invoice price or other incentive offered to them.

Sales promotion can be used to motivate the sales force. The success of any promotion is, substantially, dependent on the support of the sales force, whether this be internal to the company or one hired for the specific purpose of selling-in to the trade. In many instances, companies offer incentives to the sales force to achieve a series of targets, such as volume sales, levels of display, opening new points of distribution, etc.

Sales promotion can be used to motivate intermediaries. By the same token, the support of the intermediaries in the distribution channel may need to be motivated to promote the sales of the promotion.

In the short run, the increased use of sales promotion has given marketing managers a means to meet the expectations top management have of ever-increasing sales and profitability from brands. Sales promotion is more effective in an immediate sense, thus being more visible to the top management. However, this trend has generated concerns that overemphasis on short-term brand performance might hurt brands in the long run.

The last two decades have seen budgets moving funds from advertising to sales promotions such as couponing. This trend continues for several reasons. Brand managers face – and make – increasing demands for brand performance. The benefits of sales promotions are easier to observe than the benefits of advertising. Finally, the number of deal-prone consumers increases as products become more mature. The manager who uses targeted promotional strategies has unique opportunities to protect both the short-term and the long-term viability of brands.

If a marketing strategy ignores sales promotions there is a strong likelihood that it will fail. Sales promotions, after all, enjoy an advantage over advertising in that they are extremely flexible and easier to implement or change at short notice. Within a strategy such promotions allow response to competitor behaviour, easier market penetration and trial, and a better chance of coping with disaster.

Within the retail marketing mix, sales promotions have one of the strongest impacts on short-term consumption behaviour. Sales promotions are beneficial to retailers in several aspects: first, promotional variables, such as in-store display and 'two-for-one' are often used to trigger unplanned purchases; second, sales promotions encourage consumers to purchase non-promoted merchandise and finally, sales promotions accelerate the number of shopping trips to the store. In addition, it has been argued that sales promotions encourage consumers to stockpile, leading to a reduction of the retailer's inventory costs. In a study conducted by Ailawadi *et al.* (2001),[4] they concluded that promotion has a stronger direct impact on share than advertising for the average packaged goods brand.

Carefully planned promotions can provide substantial gains in the short term and the long term. In addition, as Ghosh (1997)[5] makes clear, the availability of scanner data and sophisticated database technology lets us reach target groups within our overall market. We can attract some promiscuous customers for a short-term lift or we can target loyal brand customers with offers that will help tie them in to our products.

We can use data collected from coupons, competition entries and other promotions to build a database. These promotion-prone customers represent a way of targeting promotions without alienating loyal customers or giving too much warning to our competitors. Indeed, the wedding of sales promotion and direct marketing (enacted with the database as priest) should now be inevitable. There is little point – when you have the technology – running promotions that don't provide you with customer information.

Chandon *et al.* (2000)[6] indicate that one of the benefits of sales promotions for the consumer is the monetary savings they provide (the savings benefit). However, sales promotions may also enable consumers to upgrade to higher-quality products by reducing the price of otherwise unaffordable products (the quality benefit), which will often lead to a higher price being paid. Because they signal the availability of the brand at the point of sale and advertise its promotional status, sales promotions can also reduce consumer search and decision costs and, therefore, improve shopping convenience (the convenience benefit). Furthermore, sales promotions can enhance consumers' self-perception of being smart or good shoppers and provide an opportunity to reaffirm their personal values (the value expression benefit). Because they create an ever-changing shopping environment, sales promotions can also provide stimulation and help fulfil the consumer's needs for information and exploration (the exploration benefit). Finally, sales promotions are often simply fun to see or use (the entertainment benefit). It is worth noting that the last of these five benefits can be achieved above and beyond any monetary savings.

The disadvantages of sales promotion

In contrast to the many advantages offered by sales promotion, it has to be recognized that there are a number of disadvantages. However, as mentioned earlier, one must be careful to distinguish between the 'genuine' disadvantages and those that reflect the narrow definitions of the discipline. Much of the academic research that has been conducted is premised on the fact that sales promotion is a short-term device. The inevitable consequence is that such research, predominantly, looks at those promotional executions that are short term in their application. This ignores the opportunities for sales promotion to contribute to the longer-term health of the brand and its potential role to impact positively upon brand image.

A key objective of much sales promotion activity is to encourage brand switching and to counter the franchise-building effects of competitive brands' advertising. Few manufacturers deny that increasing promotional expenditures have, in some instances, diminished the strength of brand franchises and brand loyalties and have resulted in an increasing level of 'promiscuous' buying on the part of consumers.

A major critic of sales promotion is Andrew Ehrenberg (1991)[7] who, along with colleagues, states that in contrast to some of the other marketing communications tools, sales promotion predominantly works on a short-term basis. In addition to this, unlike advertising or public relations, promotions may have no lasting impact on the brand. Their research indicated that 'Consumer promotions have large immediate sales effects, but do not appear to be brand building'. In a study of 25 grocery brands across four countries the authors found the following:

- For an established brand, sales do not remain high once the promotion is over. The benefit is only very short term and post promotional sales only show a 1 per cent increase.
- Buyers coming in because of price promotions had bought the brand before.
- Price promotions only reach a limited percentage of the customer base, typically 10–20 per cent.

They concluded that promotions provide no sustained impact on sales, i.e. promotions offer temporary effect only. Equally, they found that there is no discernible after-effect on consumer loyalty because the majority of extra buyers in a sales blip will have already bought the brand previously (80–90 per cent during the last 12 months).

In an earlier paper, Ehrenberg (1994)[8] had already argued that price-related promotions are picked up only by a brand's existing customers. He suggests that an average of 93 per cent of those buying during a price promotion had already bought the brand before.

These views are reflected in the comments of John Philip Jones (1990),[9] an equally strident critic of sales promotion. He condemned the use of sales promotion generally stating that:

- a promotion rarely stimulates repeat purchase
- the consumer sales effect is limited over the time period of the promotion itself
- a promotion causes a 'mortgaging' effect, it brings forward sales from a later period
- they devalue the image of the promoted brand in the eyes of the consumer.

Moreover, he states, 'As a rule, promotions can never improve a brand image or help the stability of the consumer franchise.'

However, this view is contradicted by Anschuetz (1997),[10] who asserts that the flip side of 'double jeopardy' is that brands bought by households have greater strength on nearly every measure of brand health. With increased brand popularity comes greater frequency of brand buying, a greater number of heavier buyers in the brand's franchise, and a greater level of loyalty as measured by the levels of repeat buying and greater share dominance.

It is certainly true that, in the desire to achieve short-term results, many promotions are developed independently of the overall brand strategy and may, therefore, impact negatively on the desired brand image. Unless the promoting company ensures a consistency between the nature of the promotional device and the product position, there may be a conflict that undermines the effectiveness of image-building advertising for the brand.

It must be recognized that inappropriate use of sales promotion in an attempt to boost performance in the short run can have detrimental consequences in the long run. Increased use of coupons by current users or loyal consumers might damage brand image and promote price-oriented behaviour, resulting in lower brand loyalty levels and in lower brand profitability in the long run. Therefore, rather than complementing each other, advertising and sales promotion might end up working against each other: advertising building brand franchise and sales promotion eroding brand franchise. Avoiding this problem requires designing a carefully targeted promotional strategy based on a thorough analysis of the composition of the target market.

There is a great deal of evidence that frequent price promotions make both trade customers and consumers significantly more price sensitive, not just towards the brand on offer but towards all brands in the category. Some consumers become unwilling to make any purchase unless the product is on special offer. Some consumers may infer that a promoted item is not selling well, is about to be discontinued, or has been reduced in quality to finance the incentive. Some retail accounts may claim promotion allowances without providing the appropriate levels of support, thereby increasing the costs of sale to the manufacturer without the benefit of expanded consumer exposure. Although it is difficult to quantify, it is believed that some part of the promotional allowance may, in certain instances, be retained by the retailer rather than passed onto the consumer.

Dodson *et al.* (1978)[11] indicate that whilst sales promotions have the capacity to boost short-term sales, they will not influence consumers once these promotions have been removed. Moreover, they suggest that promotional pricing will lower customers' evaluation of a brand because they use price as a measure of quality.

Similarly, various authors have indicated that by altering the 'deal' offered to consumers, promotions will result in their lowering the reference price for the brand, which causes post-promotional dissatisfaction once the deal is removed and the price returns to normal (Lattin and Bucklin 1989, Kalwani *et al.* 1990, Bawa and Shoemaker 1987).[12, 13, 14]

A research study conducted by Hoek and Roelants (1991)[15] found that sales during the promotion period increased markedly for each discounted product. When the discount period ended, sales declined for each brand; however, in most cases sales remained above the weekly sales level recorded before the promotion commenced. In general, sales of competitors' products declined during the discount week. It was found that in some cases they increased, although never to the levels recorded by the promoted brand. Whilst it is possible that chance variations in sales could have caused sales of competing products to rise, these might also have occurred because of an 'out of stocks' situation – this is where a supermarket cannot maintain sufficient stock levels of a brand to meet the consumers' demand for it. When this occurs, consumers who would ordinarily have purchased the brand may instead purchase a substitute brand, thus causing sales of competing products to rise, rather than decline.

Several studies suggest that increasing use of sales promotions, such as couponing, at the expense of advertising, tends to reduce brand profitability. It is claimed that such promotions unnecessarily subsidize current brand users and teach consumers to wait for deals, thus promoting information searches and price-oriented behaviour. Of greater concern is that sales promotion can negate advertising's impact by eroding brand image or the loyalty levels for brands (Low and Mohr 1992).[16]

Certainly, some consumers tend to stock up during a promotional period rather than purchasing during the normal cycle with the result that the brand enjoys a short-term increase in sales and market share. However, this may be achieved at a lower margin and, in effect, be obtained at the cost of future 'full price' volume. Promotions are important in changing the timing rather t han the level of purchasing because customers tend to buy earlier or stockpile during a promotion and then buy less afterwards (Doyle and Saunders 1985).[17]

The overuse of sales promotion within the marketing communications mix may reduce the overall profitability of the brand. This is evidenced by a comprehensive Product Impact of Market Strategy (PIMS) study conducted in 1991. A total of 749 businesses involved in consumer goods and services were assessed on the basis of the differing advertising and sales promotion ratios. The companies that used dominant sales promotion activity within their communications programmes achieved a return on investment (ROI) of some 18.1 per cent. Those with a more balanced ratio enjoyed a ROI of 30.5 per cent (see PIMS website).[18]

To these may be added several other criticisms that have been levelled at sales promotion.

Escalation of sales promotions

Because of the very success of sales promotions, promotion after promotion may be launched. This is neither desirable for the manufacturer nor the distributor. There is the risk that a promotional war will erupt as a direct result of frequent response of competitors to each other's promotional activities.

Brand confusion

If there are too many promotions, the brand image is weakened and promotions can conflict with the brand positioning strategy. Certainly, as mentioned above, it is important in the planning of promotional activity to ensure that there is a consistency between the actions implemented and the overall brand strategy. It would be totally inconsistent, for example, for a premium priced brand such as, for example, an expensive perfume product, to implement promotions that cheapened the brand in the eyes of the consumer. Offering money off or extra product free is inconsistent with the desire to position such a product as aspirational.

Jorgensen and Zaccour (2003)[19] argue that excessive retailer promotions, although they enhance current local demands for the product, tend to erode the brand image and consumers' brand loyalty.

Much of the debate surrounding sales promotion is the extent to which they create negative brand associations. On the one hand, writers such as Dodson *et al.* (1978)[11] argue that the use of sales promotion lowers a consumer's brand evaluation. In contrast, Davis *et al.* (1992)[20] and Neslin and Shoemaker (1989)[21] suggest that if such effects are present, they are very short lived.

Speculation

If a growing number of purchases are made during sales promotions, consumers may change their buying behaviour by postponing their purchases. This is potentially counter-productive as the intention of sales promotions is to increase consumer purchases during normal periods. The anticipation effect is then prevalent. It is important to distinguish between consumers who wait for sales promotion periods and those who respond in the intended manner.

Difficulty of price comparison

The increase in the level of sales promotion activity increases the difficulties in establishing a 'fair' price for the brand and of comparing prices (Lambin 2000).[22]

In a further paper by Dekimpe *et al.* (1999),[23] the authors used research to estimate the permanent versus transitory effects of promotions on sales. A key finding of their research is that permanent effects of promotions are largely absent. This implies that promotions do not structurally change sales over time and that their long-term profitability depends only on the magnitudes of response and cost parameters.

However, an examination of much of the work cited above supports the notion that the research is something of a self-fulfilling prophecy. Many of the studies are restricted to a consideration of the impact and effects of price-based offers. It is freely acknowledged that money-off promotions, particularly when overused, can have a negative impact on brand image and have no lasting impact on the brand, other than, perhaps, a negative impact on profitability. What is lacking in much academic research, other than a very limited amount of work, is an examination of alternative promotional executions.

One of the most coveted forms of promotion is a programme that can stand the test of time, returning year after year. There are many examples of such longevity including the Pepsi Taste Challenge. Originally introduced by the brand in the 1970s it continues to attract consumers. Similarly, the Walkers Books for Schools promotion has equally been run successfully on a number of occasions. What is important about both of these promotions is not only have they achieved short-term success for the brands involved, they have equally delivered a long-term impact on brand-image dimensions.

However, in order to maintain interest, these promotions need to be re-examined on a regular basis to keep them from going stale. Once such a promotion has been created, the programme builds equity and the company acquires proficiency in execution. Having a pre-existing promotional structure creates a lot of efficiencies because the company doesn't have to re-invent its activity each year.

Case study

FIAT PANDA
Agency: Arc Worldwide

Background

The UK car market is highly competitive, with many marques competing for the consumer's attention. The purchase of a car requires that purchases are planned and need to be budgeted for. At times when consumer confidence falters (as has been the case in the UK over the past couple of years) car purchases tend to be deferred. Traditionally, the car manufacturers use heavyweight television campaigns and other promotional activities to support new car launches.

The campaign

With no TV support, the launch of the new Fiat Panda was dependent on strong and innovative communication. The Panda had nostalgic appeal to its mainly female target audience, but lacked charm and personality. This was addressed by creating an animal theme to deliver warmth, personality and emotional engagement. The core proposition was 'New Fiat Panda – everything it does is loveable'.

Compelling visuals of animals, depicted in black and white like a panda, were used to highlight the features of the new model – a giraffe for headroom, a shark for agility and a tortoise for protection.

Dealerships held 'open door' weekends and the campaign was supported with direct mail, electronic direct mail and in-dealer point of sale.

Convoys of Pandas displaying different animal heads toured cities and helicopters towed cars within cages. Consumers completing a test drive received a voucher entitling a child to a free visit to the zoo and the opportunity to enter a prize draw for a 4-day cruise to the Bay of Biscay, France.

Close to 2000 test drives were taken and 4626 prospects attended the 'open door' weekends. Fiat met 60 per cent of its annual volume within the first 3 months of the campaign.

The campaign received a gold award in the automotive section of the 2005 ISP Promotion Awards.

(The above is adapted from an article that appeared in the Special Supplement to *Promotions and Incentives* magazine, June 2005)

Questions

1 What are the specific benefits of sales promotion compared with other forms of marketing communications?

2 Identify the disadvantages of sales promotion and consider whether all of the criticisms levelled at sales promotion are justified.

3 What are the dangers of the inappropriate use of sales promotion?

3

The context for sales promotion

Chapter overview

Sales promotion does not exist in a vacuum. The successful implementation of sales promotion programmes demands a comprehensive understanding of the surrounding environment. This chapter examines some of these important issues.

Amongst these are a consideration of the market place, the competitive environment, the target audience and the important dimensions of branding.

Learning outcomes

- To consider the context for sales promotion
- To examine the issues relating to the marketing place and, in particular, the growth of private label products
- To reflect on the nature of the competitive environment
- To understand the nature of the target audience and their motivations to purchase
- To examine the nature of branding.

Understanding the market place

Over recent years we have seen quite fundamental changes in the retail scene. Most significant amongst these has been the growing power of the major retailers. The progressive number of mergers and takeovers has resulted in a comparatively small number of substantial retailers dominating their market sectors. In turn, this consolidation of retailing is shifting the centre of power away from brand owners. The level of concentrated buying power has given the advantage to many large operators in mass-market retailing: Boots, Toys "Я" Us, Tesco, ASDA (now part of Wal-Mart) and, most recently, the absorption of Safeway into Morrisons. As a consequence, manufacturers must increasingly submit to the demands of these powerful retailers, or risk the consequence of being de-listed from their shelves. At the same time, these leading retailers have consolidated their hold on key consumer markets by becoming more efficient.

Using all of the tools of marketing communications, retailers have created their own brand personalities that automatically invest their own-label products with the same image. Their brand power is combined with heavyweight activity of both advertising and in-store support. These represent a major threat to manufacturers' brands. However, this is a particular area where sales promotion offers can reduce the impact of private label.

The growth of private label

There are four key reasons why retailers are motivated to develop own-label sales:

1 To increase margin
2 To build store loyalty
3 To mask price comparisons
4 To generate greater supply chain efficiency.

Private label brands are no longer dependent on major manufacturers to supply their products. New manufacturing facilities have been specifically built to produce own-label products. Cott's, the supplier of Virgin Cola together with many supermarket brands, is a prime example of this development. However, several major brand manufacturers also produce private-label products on behalf of the larger retailers.

In an increasing number of sectors, whilst the products are not perceived as commodities, there has been a failure on the part of the major manufacturers to differentiate their products sufficiently to prevent a switch to private label.

The growth of the international own-label market allows the manufacturers to achieve considerable economies of scale. Many retailers now have an international presence and can market the same own-label products in several countries.

As technology becomes cheaper and more accessible, manufacturers of private label can invest in higher technology production facilities. In addition to this, there has been a fundamental shift in consumer attitudes towards private-label products.

Many brands with high levels of advertising and promotional investment have been subjected to considerable private-label attack both in generic form and from look-alikes. It would appear that the scale of the advertising and sales promotional spend is no longer seen as a deterrent to private-label attack: examples are Coca Cola and Procter and Gamble.

According to Quelch and Harding (1996)[1] several factors suggest that the private-label threat is serious and may stay that way regardless of economic conditions.

The improved quality of private-label products

Ten years ago, there was a distinct gap in the level of quality between private-label and brand-name products. Today that gap has narrowed; private-label quality levels are much higher than ever before, and they are more consistent, especially in categories historically characterized by little product innovation. The distributors that contract for private-label production have improved their procurement processes and are more careful about monitoring quality.

The development of premium private-label brands

Many retailers have introduced premium-priced products that, in some instances, are more expensive than their branded comparisons. Tesco, for example, has its 'Finest' range of superior quality meals.

The creation of new categories

Private labels are continually expanding into new and diverse categories. In super-markets, for example, private labels have developed well beyond the traditional staples to include health and beauty aids, paper products such as nappies, and soft drinks. Private-label sales have also increased in categories such as clothing and beer. With that expansion comes increased acceptance by consumers. The more quality private-label products on the market, the more readily consumers will choose a private label over a higher-priced name brand. Gone are the days when there was a stigma attached to buy-ing private labels.

To these can be added a new trend. Retailers are increasingly using the tools of sales promotion in order to promote their own label ranges against those of the manufac-turers. Indeed, in some instances, they are emulating the style of promotions that, tra-ditionally, have been offered by the major brands. For example, Sainsbury's Rice Pops (and other own-label cereal products) promotion, where kids go free, with an accom-panying adult, to Legoland Windsor.

Taken together, these trends may seem daunting to manufacturers of brand-name products. But they tell only part of the story. The increased strength of private labels does not mean that we should write an obituary for national brands. Indeed, the brand is alive and reasonably healthy. It requires only dedicated management to thrive. It is important to consider the following points.

The purchase process favours brand-name products. Brand names exist because consumers still require an assurance of quality when they do not have the time, oppor-tunity, or ability to inspect alternatives at the point of sale. Brand names simplify the selection process in cluttered product categories; in the time-pressured, dual-income households, brands are needed more than ever.

A study published in 1997[2] reinforces previous findings that manufacturers' brands continued to attract significant market share despite their higher prices. From an analy-sis of the AGB Superpanel data, involving over 10 000 respondents, the study found that consumers were continuing to pay a significant premium for branded products, as the table overleaf shows.

Despite a significant increase in the power and competitive position of the main supermarket chains, the leading premium brands in most packaged grocery categories have proved remarkably successful in maintaining both their position and sales (Buck 2000)[3].

Using Taylor Nelson Sofres data from the AGB superpanel, Buck demonstrates that recent years have seen both an increase in the strength of the major supermarkets, and a corresponding increase in the share held by supermarket brands. In 1975, the top four supermarket groups held 22 per cent of the packaged groceries market. By 2000, the figure for the top four approached 70 per cent. Similarly, supermarket (private label) sales have shown a similar pattern. Their sales have more than doubled to around

Table 3.1

Average prices in Tesco stores			
Category	Premium brand	Tesco own-label	Tesco value label
Instant coffee	185p	139p	57p
Baked beans	33p	23p	10p
Cola	65p	30p	13p
Washing up liquid	136p	82p	20p
Muesli	202p	156p	132p
Yoghurt	184p	161p	95p
Average Index	100	69	35

Source: AGB Superpanel

40 per cent of the market in the early 2000s. There remain very few packaged grocery categories into which private-label products have not made deep inroads.

Both studies support the belief that, although many consumers suggest that there is little to choose between branded and private-label products, the perceptual values continue to be vitally important. The consequence is that major brands continue to hold significant shares of their market sectors.

Brand-name goods have a solid foundation on which to build current advantage. The strongest national brands have built their consumer equities over decades of promotion and through the delivery of consistent quality. From year to year, there is little change in consumers' rankings of the strongest national brands. Brand strength parallels the strength of the economy. Sales of premium-quality, premium-priced brands are on the rise.

National brands have value for retailers. Retailers cannot afford to cast off national brands that consumers expect to find widely distributed; when a store does not carry a popular brand, consumers are put off and may switch stores. Retailers must not only stock but also promote, if necessary at a loss, those popular national brands that consumers use to gauge overall store prices.

Excessive emphasis on private labels dilutes their strength. What could be more convenient, some retailers argue, than to have consumers remember a single store name? The problem is that stretching a store name (just like a manufacturer name) over too many product categories muddies the image. Many consumers rightly do not believe that a store can provide the same excellent quality for products across the board. Sethuraman (1992)[4] concluded from a study of panel data that when the price difference between major brands and private label is greater than 20 per cent, the consumer is likely to regard the private-label product as being of inferior quality

Similarly Garretson et al. (2002)[5] reported that while value-consciousness is a commonality among consumers who seek price savings, the perception of price in terms of its relationship to product quality had the opposite effect. For these consumers, the lower average prices of the private labels cause such products to be regarded as less attractive. Quite likely, the low price on private labels signals inferior quality for consumers. In contrast, these same buyers viewed national brands on price promotion more favourably. For these consumers, price promotions may represent a way to achieve savings without feeling that quality was being sacrificed.

Consumers demand choice. Stores that concentrate on the promotion of private-label products at the expense of manufacturer brands, often de-listing some of the latter, have found that the consumer simply goes elsewhere to shop, at stores where the brand choice they expect is available.

Quelch and Harding (1996)[6] recommend that national-brand manufacturers take the following seven actions, whether they currently make private-label products or not, to stem any further share gains by private labels:

1 Invest in brand equities. For most consumer goods companies, the brand names they own are their most important assets.

2 Innovate wisely. Too many national-brand managers launch line extensions. Most are of marginal value to customers and dilute rather than enhance the core-brand franchise.

3 Use fighting brands sparingly. The purpose of a fighting brand is to avoid the huge contribution loss that would occur if a leading national brand tried to stem share losses to private labels by dropping its price. The fighting brand gives the price-sensitive consumer a low-cost branded alternative. However, the fighting brand can end up competing with the national brand for consumers who would not have switched to private-label products anyway.

4 Build trade relationships. The best consumer goods companies should know more about their consumers and their categories than any private-label manufacturer. Indeed, they should also know more than their trade customers, who, though closer to the end consumer and inundated with scanner purchase data, have to plan assortments of products and allocate shelf space for 250 to 300 categories with only the resources that 1 per cent after-tax profit margins will permit. Manufacturers must leverage their knowledge to create a win–win proposition for their trade accounts. Retailers and national-brand producers can maximize their profits jointly without excessive emphasis on private labels.

5 Manage the price spread. Many consumer goods manufacturers have increased prices ahead of inflation (the easiest way to add bottom-line profit in the short term) and then offered periodic reductions off their artificially inflated list prices to distributors and consumers who demanded them. As long as some still paid full price, this price discrimination was thought to be profitable. Over time, however, such a high proportion of the typical brand's volume was being sold at a deep discount that the list prices no longer had credibility.

6 Exploit sales promotion tactics. National-brand manufacturers cannot prevent retailers from displaying copycat private-label products alongside their brands with 'compare and save' signs heralding the price gaps. However, they can use sales promotion tactics to enhance the merchandising of their brands.

7 Manage each category. Categories differ widely in private-label penetration, the price–quality gap between private labels and national brands, and the relative profitability and potential cannibalization cost of any private label or value brand.

The competitive environment

The importance of understanding the competitive environment cannot be overstated. By appreciating the nature and timing of competitive activity, the company can be better prepared to provide promotional activity that provides a distinctive advantage in the market place.

Many manufacturers adopt very specific timings in terms of their promotions. In effect they introduce promotions on the basis of a 'promotional cycle'. By monitoring their actions, it will be possible to predict their future activity. Equally, some manufacturers tend to favour particular promotional executions. Similarly it will be possible to plan promotions for the brand to offset the likely activity that they will introduce.

Understanding the target audience

In order to introduce effective sales promotions, it is important to understand both the nature of the audience and their motivations to purchase. In a paper by the research company ACNielsen (1993)[6] it is suggested that:

> ...by understanding exactly who their customers are, and what factors motivate them to buy, [manufacturers] will have the insight into their consumers' shopping patterns necessary to target their marketing with a new level of precision.

The first thing to understand about consumers is that they all have different motivations for purchase. This has particular significance in the context of sales promotion.

Figure 3.1

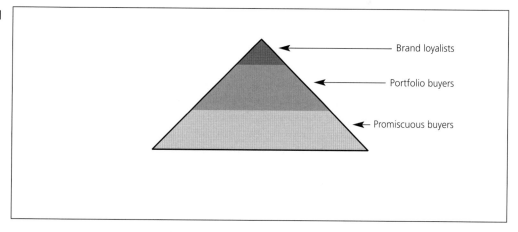

Brand loyalists

Portfolio buyers

Promiscuous buyers

Purchasing motivations

Loyal brand users

Every brand has a percentage of devoted loyalists. These are consumers who purchase the product on a very regular basis. However, it must be remembered that very few consumers are absolutely loyal to a particular brand. Even diehard loyalists may purchase an alternative brand if their preferred brand is out of stock or if there is an appealing promotional offer. It is estimated that these consumers probably represent no more than 20 per cent of the consumers for a particular brand. Although based on the Pareto principle (also known as the 80:20 rule) these consumers may account for as much as 80 per cent of the volume of a brand.

Equally, competitors will possess some consumers who are intensely loyal (and where promotions will have a very limited impact). Even in everyday purchases, some consumers will choose to purchase a particular brand that they perceive to be superior even though another competitive brand is less expensive. This is particularly true of the carbonated soft drinks market where some consumers are exclusively loyal to Coca Cola whilst others show the same preference towards Pepsi. Competitors will also have some consumers who may prefer their own brand, but who will be open to persuasion as a result of an appropriate offer. These can be termed value seekers and their presence is evident in many market categories.

In various papers by Andrew Ehrenberg (1997, 1988, 2000)[7,8,9] the point is made that habit or inertia may result in a consumer re-purchasing a brand on a regular basis. It is not because they have made a study of the relative prices and performance of competitive brands, but rather that it has become their habit to purchase a particular brand. In the main this pattern of purchase is seen in low involvement purchases particularly amongst those consumers who are short on time, since the process eases the task of shopping.

However, many of those consumers who state that product x is their favourite brand will be induced to purchase an alternative, often as a direct result of some promotional offer. The consequence is that companies must continue to promote even to those consumers who define themselves as loyal to their product, to avoid the risk of their migrating to a competitive brand.

From a promotional perspective the need is to develop promotions designed to reinforce existing patterns of behaviour and to provide customers with a reward for continuing to use the brand. Some promotions will be used to encourage them to use more of the brand or to use it more often and in some instances, where appropriate, to use other products from the same manufacturer. Appropriate devices may be loyalty-based promotions designed to reinforce the value of the brand.

To this group of consumers, although price promotions may 'work' in the sense that they will encourage them to buy more of the product (stockpile) they may also raise doubts about the brand and encourage a closer focus on price which, in turn, will make them more likely to consider alternative manufacturers' products. Moreover, if the brand has a high percentage of loyal brand users, such incentives may serve to increase purchase even where no incentive was needed to do so. The consequence is that the promotion may actually result in the brand losing money. Nonetheless, since all brands operate in a highly competitive environment, price-based activity may be necessary to offset competitive activities in an attempt to prevent those loyal users from being attracted away to other brands because they offer a price advantage.

Portfolio buyers

The next group of consumers are those who have been previously referred to as portfolio buyers, that is, they tend to purchase from a limited range of brands within the category. These consumers are similarly motivated to respond to promotional offers. They represent the largest group of consumers who tend to choose products from a self-defined list of alternative brands that can satisfy their own or their family needs.

In some instances, this might reflect the nature of the usage occasion since particular products may be seen as more appropriate to specific occasions. For example, one brand of cake might be chosen for everyday consumption whilst another will be chosen when they are entertaining. In other instances, purchases may be dictated by the need for variety. It would be somewhat boring, for example, to eat the same breakfast cereal every day.

Clearly, it is amongst this group that promotional activity can have the greatest level of impact. Portfolio buyers are, substantially, motivated to buy on the basis of price, although they are, generally, open to offers against a smaller range of products. Other promotional offers will also have an appeal to this group.

Encouraging stockpiling on the part of the consumer may be an advantage to the brand in a number of ways. In some instances, particularly where the rate of consumption can be increased, it is likely that if the consumer has the particular product in the household, they will tend to use it more often. By the same token, if the consumer feels that they already possess adequate quantities of the product to satisfy their immediate needs, they will be unlikely to purchase a competitor's product in the near future. It is important to consider issues such as the frequency of usage and the frequency of purchase in this context. Stockpiling may offer another benefit, albeit in the short term. Most companies establish specific volume targets which will need to be met if the company is to achieve its overall goals. Encouraging consumers to purchase additional quantities of the brand at one moment in time will serve to bring forward future purchases and hence enable the company to achieve its targets.

This is reinforced by the findings of Ailawadi and Neslin (1998)[10] who demonstrated that promotions induce consumers to buy more and consume faster. In a subsequent paper the same authors (2001)[11] argue that a company's promotional policy influences its ability to attract and retain customers by inducing more of them to:

- switch to the firm's brand
- repeat purchase it more often

or

- consume larger quantities.

Promiscuous buyers

Finally, there are those consumers who switch between brands on the basis of their perceptions of which offers the best value at a moment in time. Clearly, price-based and value-added promotions are significant motivators of this group. Often these consumers have limited amounts of money and, therefore, cannot afford to purchase the more expensive brand, although others will be motivated by their perception that they are getting the best value for money from the cheaper products, including private label. In most product categories such consumers are a comparatively small group, although there is evidence that their numbers are growing.

Consumers' decisions to purchase a product are based on their perceptions of the product's value, defined as the trade-off of the product's perceived quality relative to its perceived price, i.e. perceived monetary sacrifice. Manufacturers and retailers can reduce a product's perceived monetary sacrifice by offering a price reduction on the product. Assuming that price reductions do not affect a product's perceived quality, price promotions should enhance the perceived value of the product to this group of consumers.

Non-users

The final group that needs to be discussed are those people who are non-users of the product category. There may be a variety of reasons for this behaviour. For some, the reason may simply be that of price; products within the category are perceived to be too expensive and hence do not represent good value for money. For others there is simply a lack of need for the products offered. Yet others will never have tried the product and perceive the purchase as a form of risk. Here again, promotions can induce some potential consumers to enter the category.

As a result Mela, Jedidi and Bowman (1988)[12] argue that 'sales promotions have the potential to impel people to try a product for the first time, to change their views regarding a brand and to attract a diversified consumer base. The use of long-term sales promotion strategies can, therefore, enable advertisers to cultivate the loyalty of, and retain their customers.'

The extent to which consumers are open to deals is also an important factor. Some consumers, even brand loyalists, will be more or less likely to respond to a promotional offer. Some, in response to a temporary price reduction, will simply incorporate it within their normal purchasing cycle; others will take advantage of it to stockpile their favourite brand. Work by Fraser and Hite (1990)[13] suggests that the majority of consumers are responsive towards promotional activity. They go on to say that 'promotional incentives are effective in capturing brand choices, encouraging purchase acceleration and stimulating category demand. Many customers use and expect deals, and many more are induced to alter purchase behaviours by deal offers.'

Anschuetz (1997)[14] argues that the key to brand success is to broaden brand appeal to more and different kinds of households. He suggests that the brand must integrate its target audience to include as many categories as possible.

Similarly, according to Matthew Hooper (1998)[15] sales promotions can attract a different audience and encourage people to try a product for the first time. You have the opportunity to change people's perceptions of a brand and then, through on-going activity, you can keep those customers.

Categorizing customers

Various attempts have been made to divide consumers into discrete groups in order to define specific targets for promotional activity. One such categorization is that provided by ACNielsen (1997).[16] In similar work conducted by Fearne et al. (1999)[17] they also identified five similar clusters or groups of consumers in terms of their responsiveness to promotional activities. The findings of the two studies have been merged in order to provide more texture to the definitions.

'Branded everyday low price seekers'

These customers are not well off. A promotion on a well-known brand will not cause them to switch. They are fiercely loyal towards brands, although not to retail outlets, and are prepared to shop around for the best deals on preferred products. They will often visit a number of stores in order to find their favourite products at the right price. They are mostly downmarket C2DEs, often in their later family life stage, house-wife not working, driven by brands and low prices. They represent approximately 19 per cent of all shoppers.

'Low price fixture ferrets'

These consumers are loyal to stores, but not to brands. They are generally downmarket DEs with young families and low disposable income. They are extremely price con-scious. They like to budget but the children stop them from shopping around. They favour low price rather than EDLP and like coupons and store loyalty schemes togeth-er with price reductions and free items. In the main they reject bulk buys as these often require too much initial outlay. They account for around 23 per cent of grocery expenditure.

Promotions appeal to them more than average, with some 20 per cent of their pur-chasing related to offers. As a result they are quick to switch brands and also tend to spend a lot of their purchasing on private-label products.

'Promotion junkies'

These consumers respond extremely well to promotions. They do not need the pro-motion but they love hunting out the bargains. Their aim is to get the lowest possible shopping bill. They are predominantly upmarket ABs, in the pre- or family life stage, working housewife, enjoy shopping, price aware but not budget conscious, prepared to invest time and effort in seeking out promotions, brand and store disloyal.

They represent around 18.4 per cent of households and around 25 per cent of everything this group buys is on offer. The most appealing promotions are also the most aggressive: price cuts, extra quantity and multi-buys are favoured over competi-tions and coupons.

'Stockpilers'

They are hoarders, although only on preferred brands. They do not have money wor-ries; however, they take pride in the advantage gained by bargains. These consumers are affluent ABs, in the later or post-family stages, are not budget conscious, but are both store and brand loyal.

They favour multi-buys and bulk offers on their preferred brands, but tend not to switch brands for the sake of a promotional offer. This group represents around 21 per cent of all households.

'Promotionally oblivious'

This group contains habitual and myopic shoppers who are very habitual in their shopping patterns. They are financially comfortable and are both brand and store loyal. They comprise mainly middle market C2s, post-family, full time or retired, one- or two-member households, habitual, old fashioned, comfortable standard of living, not innovative.

The main characteristic of this group is their indifference to promotions and offers. As a consequence only 14 per cent of their total spending tends to relate to offers of any sort. They account for around 18.3 per cent of households.

Leo Burnett, the advertising agency, has identified four types of consumer buying strategies:

1   Long loyals – The consumer is committed to one particular brand regardless of price or any other factors.
2   Rotators – The consumer shows regular patterns of shifting between preferred brand, motivated by variety rather than the price of the product.
3   Deal sensitives – The consumer shows patterns of shifting between brands on availability of special offers or incentives.
4   Price sensitive – The consumer purchases the cheapest option regardless of brand.

Similar research conducted by Meer (1995)[18] identifies four distinct categories of consumers:

1   Brand loyals express strong brand preferences and report acting on those preferences regardless of price considerations.
2   System beaters also have brand preferences but are committed to buying their favourite brands at lower than regular prices.
3   Deal shoppers focus on price, not brand.
4   The uninvolved have neither strong brand preferences nor a strong low-price orientation.

Comparatively few consumers actively search for the keenest price on their regular purchases. Instead, for the most part, they form impressions over time as to which retail outlet offers the best combination of value for money/product quality that they seek. This should not imply that they remain loyal to one outlet. Rather, they use the outlet that most closely fits their particular needs at the time.

By the same token, relatively few consumers are aware of the actual prices charged for specific products. Various researchers have indicated that price awareness may be as low as 50 per cent. Zeithaml (1982)[19] indicated that price knowledge appeared to be considerably lower than necessary for consumers to have accurate internal reference prices for many products. Similarly, in research conducted by Dickson and Sawyer (1990),[20] 21.1 per cent of shoppers interviewed immediately after making their purchases failed to even offer a price estimate of the item they had chosen; they simply had no idea of the price! A further 31.8 per cent gave a price estimate that was inaccurate.

However, Vanhuele and Dreze (2002)[21] demonstrate that the accuracy of consumers' price knowledge depends on both the shopping environment (e.g. category clutter, promotion activity) and consumers' idiosyncrasies (e.g. brand loyalty, in-store price search behaviour). These findings are important to managers who make pricing decisions in a competitive multi-product environment.

Although most consumers do not possess an accurate knowledge of price that permits accurate recall or recognition, they possess a working knowledge of prices that is accurate enough for the consumers to make good purchase decisions.

Having determined the nature of consumer response, we can determine more precisely which consumers we wish to reach with promotional activity:

- What are we trying to achieve with the promotional offer?

  Promotions inevitably have different objectives. We may, for example, seek to reward existing brand purchasers; or attract users of competitive brands, etc. Defining the specific objectives that a promotion must meet is an important requirement of the planning process.

- Who are the consumers who will be targeted by the promotional offer?

  Depending on the overall goals, we need to identify which group of consumers is the main goal of the activity. This will affect the nature of the promotional offer since existing users will need less reason to continue to purchase the brand than other potential consumers.

- What are the underlying reasons for their purchasing behaviour?

  Understanding how and why consumers purchase within the brand category will, again, affect the nature of the promotional offer designed either to reinforce existing purchasing behaviour or attempt to change it.

Schultz *et al.* (1993)[22] identify a variety of consumer segments that provide the basis for identifying the relevance and impact of particular promotional types. We have already seen that consumers can be readily divided into relatively discrete groups depending on the discerned patterns of purchasing behaviour. It is vitally important to consider the role of promotions in this context, since the promotional device must be appropriate not only to the target group but the responses that are desired from them.

Table 3.2

	Coupons	Special packs	Sampling	Contests/ sweepstakes	Continuity	Refunds	Price-offs	Premiums	Trade deals
Current Loyals Reinforced	Strong	Strong	Limited	Strong	Strong	Strong	Strong	Strong	Strong
Extra sales	Moderate	Strong	None	Strong Depends	Strong	Moderate	Strong	Moderate	Strong
Crossover sales	Moderate	Strong	–	Strong Depends	Strong	Moderate	–	Strong	–
Competitive loyals / Intense loyals	None	None	Limited	Limited	None	None	None	Limited	None
Value seekers	Limited	Limited	Strong	Strong	Moderate	Limited	None	Moderate	Limited
Inertia	Limited	Limited	Strong	Strong	Moderate	Limited	None	Moderate	Limited
Switchers Value	Strong	Strong	None	Strong	Strong	Strong	Strong	Strong	Strong
Variety	Strong	Strong	None	Strong	None	Strong	Strong	Strong	Strong
Distribution	Moderate	None	Strong	Limited	Moderate	Limited	None	None	Moderate
Price buyers	Strong	Limited	Limited	Limited	Limited	Strong	Limited	Limited	Strong
Non-users Price	Limited	None	None	None	None	Moderate	None	None	Limited
Value	Limited	None	Limited	Limited	Limited	Moderate	None	Limited	Limited
Lack of need	None	None	None	None	None	None	None	None	None

Source: Schultz, Robinson and Petrison (1993)

Consumer response to promotions

In both their 1996 and 2000 Special Reports, Mintel[23,24] include the results of specially commissioned research studies amongst consumers. The latter study was somewhat broader, although there is considerable overlap, enabling direct comparisons to be made in several important areas.

Table 3.3

Promotion type	% 1995	% 1999	% change
Multiple purchase promotion (2 for price of 1, 3 for 2)	59	56	-3
Buy one product, get different product free	26	47	+21
Extra product free	45	42	-3
Loyalty card points	17	38	+21
Free sample	–	34	–
Money-off coupons	29	30	+1
Linksave (buy one item, get another at reduced price)	–	24	–
Multi-packs at reduced price	31	23	-8
Introductory trial price	–	19	–
Free gift with purchase	13	17	+4
Free gift (voucher/token collect)	12	13	+1
Cause related promotion	13	12	-1
'Try for free' (send off for refund)	11	10	-1
In store demonstration/sampling	–	9	–
Instant win promotion	11	7	-4
Self liquidating offer	5	6	+1
Competition	5	4	-1
None of these	12	11	-1
Don't know	1	2	+1

Sample size: 1995 = 989, 1999 = 1458

Source: Mintel Special Report on Sales Promotion, 2000

Further analysis of these figures provides interesting information as to the appeal of particular promotions in socio-demographic terms.

Table 3.4

	Multi-purchase	Different product free	Extra free	Loyalty cards	Free sample
All	56	47	42	38	34
Men	51	38	40	33	28
Women	60	55	44	44	39
15–19	37	49	26	23	43
20–24	56	50	50	35	37
25–34	70	53	49	43	39
35–44	63	58	44	42	37
45–54	64	45	47	44	34
55–64	54	40	44	45	28
65+	38	34	34	31	24
AB	63	45	50	50	29
C1	60	45	45	42	38
C2	55	46	39	34	30
D	51	52	38	34	39
E	40	48	33	25	34
Lifestage:					
Pre-family	53	49	42	31	36
Family	69	56	47	46	40
Empty nesters	60	49	44	41	35
Post-family	44	36	38	36	25

Source: Mintel Special Report on Sales Promotion, 2000

Table 3.5

	Coupons/ vouchers	Linksave	Banded pack	Trial price	Free gift
All	30	24	23	19	17
Men	23	20	21	16	16
Women	37	28	25	22	18
15–19	29	17	13	6	33
20–24	28	23	18	18	26
25–34	29	30	32	24	17
35–44	28	27	23	25	18
45–54	23	25	24	26	15
55–64	36	24	25	19	14
65+	30	19	19	10	7
AB	29	29	22	18	16
C1	31	24	25	22	20
C2	27	21	23	19	16
D	32	24	24	19	18
E	35	21	19	15	12
Lifestage:					
Pre-family	25	22	21	14	27
Family	32	30	28	29	15
Empty nesters	31	22	23	21	18
Post-family	32	21	21	14	10

Source: Mintel Special Report on Sales Promotion, 2000

Table 3.6

	%
Loyalty card schemes are a good idea to reward regular shoppers	35
I prefer 'no frills'	30
Promotions give you value for money	27
The chances of winning a competition are very slim	24
They encourage you to try new products or brands	22
Saving tokens/packet tops isn't worth the trouble	15
They make shopping more fun	9

Source: Mintel Special Report on Sales Promotion, 2000

Behavioural research on sales promotions has tended to focus on the demographics of deal-prone consumers. (Bawa and Shoemaker 1987, Blattberg *et al.* 1978, Narasimhank 1984)[25, 26, 27] and the identification of personal traits such as 'coupon proneness', 'value consciousness', or 'market mavenism' (Feick and Price 1987, Lichtenstein *et al.* 1990, Mittal 1994).[28,29,30] These studies offer a coherent portrait of the demographic and psychographic characteristics of deal-prone consumers. However, because of their focus on individual variables, these studies do not examine the nature and the number of the specific consumer benefits of sales promotions. As a result, most analytic and econometric models of sales promotions simply assume that monetary savings are the only benefit that motivates consumers to respond to sales promotions (Blattberg and Neslin 1990).[31]

Understanding the brand

In many ways, an understanding of brands underpins much of what we attempt to achieve within the field of marketing communications since, of course, the brand is at the centre of all such activity. Ultimately, the key responsibility of brand management is to sustain and develop the product or service for which they are responsible in such a way that it can respond positively to all eventualities. The stewardship of the brand remains the singular goal of management since it is the profitability of those brands that will determine the eventual survival of the companies that own them.

Branding itself is a comparatively recent process evolving from the essential need for manufacturers to distinguish their products and services from the commodity sectors within which they operate. There is considerable debate as to when the process of branding began. It has been suggested by Griffiths (1992)[32] that Sunlight Soap was one of the first true brands. William Lever recognized that consumers were dissatisfied with the characteristics of unbranded soap products then available. They were inconsistent in quality, smelt unpleasant, offered no consistency in weight, and no packaging. Products were produced by a crude process of mixing tallow and the remnants of raw alkali in large cauldrons into large bars that were to be sliced into lengths by the grocer. The Sunlight brand remedied these defects. In February 1884, Lever registered the brand name and in 1885 created a formula comprising a mix of coconut and cottonseed oil, resin and tallow. The formula remained unchanged for many years. By the 1890s the company was producing nearly 40 000 tons of soap. The process followed by Lever encapsulates some of the roles of branding.

As Adam Lury (1998)[33] puts it, 'The practice of branding, although over 2000 years old, is primarily a 20th century phenomenon. Indeed, it is one of the most important phenomena of the century. It ranks with the decline of imperialism, the growth of feminism and the arrival of the atomic age.'

Major brands represent significant commercial value to their owners. The following table, representing the 20 largest UK brands, reveals that even the 10th is worth over £300 million.[34]

Table 3.7

Top 20 UK Brands – 2004[35]		
Brand	Sales to June 04 (£m)	% change 2002/03
1 Walkers crisps	530–535	12
2 Birds Eye	515–520	-1
3 Kellogg's	495–500	4
4 Cadbury	480–485	9
5 Heinz	435–440	1
6 Coke/Diet Coke	385–390	0
7 Muller	375–380	1
8 McVitie's	340–345	-1
9 Bernard Matthews	340–345	1
10 Stella Artois	305–310	11
11 Pampers	265–270	11
12 Warburtons	250–255	18
13 Hovis	250–255	11
14 Nescafé	245–250	-3
15 Andrex	230–235	7
16 Kingsmill	210–215	14
17 McCain	210–215	0
18 Whiskas	210–215	8
19 Weight Watchers	210–215	21
20 Nestlé cereals	205–210	8

Marketing based on A.C. Nielsen figures

The importance of brands (and their sustenance) is exemplified by the fact that many of the brands that occupy positions of leadership today were introduced as long as 100 or more years ago. Coca Cola, Hovis and Heinz were all first launched in the late 19th century, whilst Cadbury's Dairy Milk is a product of the early 1900s. Only nine of the top 50 UK brands have been launched since 1975.

The significance of developing a strong brand is underpinned by a study conducted by Buzzell and Gale (1987),[35] which indicated that strong brands achieve significantly more profit than their weaker counterparts. Their research of some 2600 business revealed that products with a market share of 40 per cent are capable of generating a return on investment three times greater than those with a share of 10 per cent. Moreover, according to the *Financial Times*,[36] 'Companies which base their businesses on brands have outperformed the stockmarket in the past 15 years.'

According to Brandt and Johnson (1997)[37] the strongest brands are those that have developed unique, meaningful differences that set them apart in the mind of the consumer. These discriminators can be functional or emotional, or a combination of the two. Biel (1991),[38] however, recognizes that the functional/physical differences between brands have diminished significantly and it is, therefore, the emotional differences that operate as the real discriminators: 'The key to remember is that brand success and brand equity live in the heart and mind of individual consumers.'

Branding definitions

A brand is defined as a name, term, design, symbol, or any other feature that identifies one seller's good or service as distinct from those of other sellers. A brand name may identify one item, a family of items, or all items of that seller (Bennett 1998).[39]

De Chernatony and McDonald (1992)[40] argue that 'a successful brand is an identifiable product, service, person or place, augmented in such a way that the buyer or user perceives relevant unique added values which match their needs most closely. Furthermore, its success results from being able to sustain these added values in the face of competition'.

Clifton and Maughan (2000)[41] defines brand as 'a mixture of tangible and intangible attributes, symbolised in a trade mark, which if properly managed, creates influence and generates value'.

We will see below how the process of branding creates a unique identity for a product or service in the mind of the consumer and, with it, a level of distinctiveness that sets it apart from all of its competitors. Reassurance derives from the fact that the consumer can readily identify the maker of the product and consider the company reputation and, importantly, in the context of marketing communications activity, it provides the sense of focus for the promotion of the brand.

The advantages of branding

Advantages to the manufacturer and the consumer

By branding a product, the manufacturer can obtain legal protection for its composition and other features in order to avoid the problems of being copied by competitors. It creates a unique identity in the market place that assists in the process of attracting consumers who, over time, will establish patterns of loyalty to the product and, in turn, will enable the company to enhance its profitability. In many instances, branding enables manufacturers to charge a premium price for their products by associating a desirable image with it for which consumers may be encouraged to pay a higher price. It assists the manufacturer to plan his inventory more efficiently and to ensure the rapid processing of orders. Finally, it helps in the process of segmenting markets by providing distinctive product offerings designed to satisfy the needs of smaller groups of consumers.

A critical element of the debate is an understanding of the fact that, for the most part, consumers are unable to differentiate between competing products. Sampson (1993)[42] indicates that 'most markets have a convergence of brands. They look alike, taste the same and have the same formulation. Brand choice is no longer about the rational product attributes. It is, and increasingly will be, all about brand personality'. In most instances the core product offered by a manufacturer may be indistinguishable from that of his competitors. Indeed, given the nature of technology, the specific product advantages that one manufacturer has over his competitors will often be readily and rapidly duplicated by them.

In countless 'blind taste' tests, consumers are unable to identify the identity of the brands and, often, select as 'the best' a product that they decry once the brand names are revealed. The perennial example of Coca Cola vs. Pepsi[40] serves to illustrate. In a direct comparison of the brands with the identities concealed, the preferences expressed were:

Prefer Pepsi	51%
Prefer Coke	44%
Equal/Can't say	5%

Once the brand identities were revealed, the following preferences were expressed:

Prefer Pepsi	23%
Prefer Coke	65%
Equal/Can't say	12%

During the 1980s, the Stella Artois 'reassuringly expensive' campaign captured the spirit of the times and resulted in the brand becoming number one in the premium lager market. As Duckworth (1996)[43] indicates: 'Interestingly, the brand comes last in blind taste tests! Add the brand name and it becomes first choice – a clear demonstration of the power of brand potency overcoming the limitations of product reality.' The brand has continued to use this platform as the basis of their promotional activity.

The consumer also benefits. Branding provides the potential buyer with a reassurance of quality. Consumers can reasonably expect that a branded product will, other things being equal, offer a consistency over time. They enhance the process of shopping since the consumer can rapidly identify products and services with which they are familiar. Finally, they enable consumers to identify new products in which they might be interested.

Economic benefits:
- Brands promote competition (consumers gain from brands competing strongly for their patronage)
- Brands improve consumer value (whether branding brings higher or lower prices, it still ensures value for money)
- Brands insure consumer risks (brands provide 'insurance' satisfaction to consumers in that they can rely on the brand's consistency and quality assurance standards)
- Brands provide consumers with choice (competition implies a variety from which consumers can make their individual selections to match their needs most closely).

Functional benefits:
- Brands require, and thus create, horizontal differentiation. It offers assortments of added values – services and psychological
- Brands require, and thus create, vertical differentiation (consumers want goods of the best quality they can afford and they would like choices of different levels of quality to suit different needs and situations)

- Brands provide reliability and thus reassurance (the brand/consumer relationship provides reassurance that the manufacturer will look after the consumers' best interest since it is also in the interest of any manufacturer who intends to build the brand over the longer term)
- Branded products are fit for the use for which they are advertised (consumers do not buy brands for the sake of buying, but to solve a problem or to meet a need)
- Manufacturer brands are more widely available
- Brands subsidise consumer usage of media and sporting, arts and other events through advertising and sponsorship.

Psychological benefits:
- Brands simplify consumer problem solving and information processing
- Brands help consumers feel good about their purchases
- Brands have social benefits for consumers.

Similarly, Davis (2002),[44] identifies a series of benefits that derive from successful branding:
- Strong brands command higher price points and higher margins
- Brand loyalty drives repeat business
- Strong brands lend immediate credibility to new product introductions
- Strong brands embody a clear, valued and sustainable point of difference
- Strong brands offer internal focus and clarity within an organization
- Customers are more likely to be forgiving if a company makes a mistake when the customers have a consistently positive experience with the brand
- Brand strength is a lever for attracting the best employees and keeping satisfied employees.

Successful brands are those that create a distinctive image or personality. By associating particular attributes with a brand, the product is differentiated in the minds of the consumers. Attributes may be real and tangible, such as product performance, value for money, or other aspects of quality, or emotional and intangible, providing status or being associated with trendiness.

A slightly different perspective is offered by Southgate (1994)[45] who identifies branding as initially being purely a defensive device to make it harder for the competition to steal one's products. In fact, branding is both defensive and aggressive. A strong brand will actively communicate with potential customers on a variety of levels providing them with all manner of reasons to buy a product or service.

Differentiation is the first step in creating a brand (Agres and Dubitsky 1996).[46] Differentiation can take many forms, from the clear-cut, physical or functional to the emotional and 'distinguishing but irrelevant differentiators such as the colour of the packaging or stripes in toothpaste' (Barnard *et al.* 1998).[47] The overriding objective is to gain competitive advantage by building sustained customer loyalty towards products or services, meeting the demands of closely defined markets precisely.

Developing and managing a brand's image is a fundamental part of a firm's marketing programme (Roth 1992).[48] Many practitioners have long advocated the use of a clearly defined brand image as a major basis for achieving market success. A well com-municated brand image enables consumers to identify the needs satisfied by the brand (Park *et al.* 1986)[49] and thereby differentiate the brand from its competitors (Reynolds and Gutman 1984).[50] In fact, developing a brand image strategy has been prescribed as the first and most vital step in positioning a brand in the market place. As a long-term strategy, a consistent and effective brand image helps build and sustain brand equity. Moreover, brand images can provide a foundation for extending existing brands.

The brand name

Branding and packaging are the overt and tangible aspects of a product and serve to distinguish a manufacturer's product from that of his competitors. In the crowded retail environment, it is these aspects of the product that assist the brand in standing out from the crowd.

Most brand names are made up of letters and numbers and, in some instances, may also include an additional graphic design that is unique to that product. In most instances, manufacturers will register these logo designs to ensure legal protection of their mark and to avoid the risks of 'passing off'. Bass Beer with its red triangle logo became the first registered trademark in the UK.

Brand image

If, for one moment, we strip away the brand marks of Levi, Kellogg's, Cadbury, Mercedes, and Johnson & Johnson, to name but a few, we are left with commodity products shorn of all of the brand values that are associated with those names. All of the investment made by those companies over many years into the creation of image values through the use of marketing communications is lost. It is the function of mar-keting communications to establish a series of defined images and values in the minds of consumers that are instantly recalled on exposure to the brand name. Consumers buy brands. Thus, the loyalty that the brand identity can create in the market place is fundamental to the ability of a company to offset competitive activities.

The brand values are equally important to the company in terms of its longer-term extension of activities. Many brand names have positive values associated with them that extend beyond the particular product with which the name is identified. These intangible values can be used by the company to extend its portfolio into other areas. Within the soap and detergent markets, two brands stand out as examples of the pos-itive values of branding. 'Fairy' and 'Persil' have both been used as brands that have taken their owners into extended categories by the association of related new prod-ucts with the positive values built up around those names.

However, the brand image is made up, as we have seen, of a combination of func-tion and emotional value. Sampson (1993)[42] states: 'It is not sufficient to measure the rational attributes of a brand alone. That gives only a partial picture. The emotional attributes must also be measured to obtain the complete picture. And it is the emo-tional benefits that usually account for brand choice, to a larger degree than rational ones.'

Brands and consumer perceptions

Brands continue to maintain a considerable price premium, despite expressions to the contrary. It was anticipated that pressure on disposable income during the recession would force consumers progressively towards cheaper products.

Identifying and building brand values

The process of identifying and building brand values is interactive with that of marketing communications. As we have already seen, the environment of the message that is communicated to the potential consumer is just as important as the nature of the message itself. In this instance, sales promotion can be used to enhance the values of the brand or to associate particular values with it. For example, the Discovery range of seasonings, which have a distinctly 'South American' feel, are running a promotion offering free dance lessons to purchasers. These take the form of Salsa, Tango and Latin, all of which reinforce the 'origin' of the products.

The consequence of manufacturer failure

Three major manufacturer-led factors have contributed to the weakening of brand positions.

Firstly, many manufacturers have increasingly sought to compete on price, both with each other and with retailers' own products. This has served to erode the distinctive characteristics that, historically, set brands apart from their private-label equivalents. The overuse of price-based promotional techniques has resulted in a focus on price as a purchase discriminator.

Secondly, partly to fund promotional activity and partly to improve overall short-term profitability, some manufacturers have withdrawn other forms of marketing communications support. It is clear that if manufacturers fail to reinforce brand images, particularly with advertising, consumers will rapidly forget the underlying reasons why they chose the brands in the first place. The only factor that remains is the comparative price of the products on the shelves. In this circumstance, the private-label products will always win!

> The barrage of coupons and price specials has trained a generation of consumers to buy on price. Product proliferation and the seemingly endless stream of brand extensions and line extensions have blurred brand identity. As store brands improve in quality and as consumers gain confidence in their store chains, store brands are posing a strong challenge to manufacturers' brands.
>
> (Kotler and Armstrong)[51]

The brand response

The central issue for manufacturers is to create a brand with a sustainable differential advantage and provide it with a distinctive personality that customers can relate to.

The concern is no longer brand versus own label, but brand versus brand. Manufacturers must constantly improve their brands to stay ahead of the competition. In this context, the role of marketing communications is to communicate the added value of the brand versus any other, including retailer own label and look-alikes.

There are a series of important facets of the sales promotion plan. The most important dimension is an understanding of the way in which consumers behave and the reasons for their particular behaviour.

A consideration of brand loyalty factors

An important dimension of sales promotion, which is sometimes overlooked, is the fact that certain forms of activity reward all users with the incentive, irrespective of whether or not they would have purchased the product anyway. It has to be remembered that the consumers for any product or service make up a continuum ranging from:

Loyal users $\longrightarrow$ Promiscuous buyers.

Loyal users would be those consumers who purchase regularly or on all occasions, whilst promiscuous buyers will be those who usually purchase only in response to some form of incentive. Most promotional techniques are indiscriminate in this context and tend to reward all purchasers. Thus, whilst a promotional device may be attractive in terms of attracting new users, it will also be received by those users who would have purchased the brand without the incentive. When costing out the benefits of promotional activity, this factor must be taken into account. Although comparatively few brands can boast a high level of loyalty, this may account for 15 to 20 per cent of purchasers and, on the Pareto principle, these customers may account for up to 80 per cent of all product purchases. By definition, therefore, the incremental benefit of the promotion may only be the remaining 20 per cent of purchases that might not otherwise have been bought.

There are a number of other factors that need to be considered in the determination of promotional strategy.

Level of involvement with purchase

There is some evidence that where consumer involvement with the product category is low, promotions that have an immediacy of impact will work better than those that impact over time. Thus, clearly identified money-off promotions or the offering of bonus free product will have a high level of impact compared with money off next purchase and similar offers. In this regard, it is important that the discount or offer is clearly 'flagged' to the consumer. Since many consumers are not aware of absolute prices, an on-shelf offer that effectively reduces the price, but is not clearly identified to the consumer as such, will have far less impact.

Purchase frequency

It is important to understand the nature and frequency of purchase for the target consumer. Ideally, incentives should be timed to coincide with the patterns of purchase of the heavy user, so that they are encouraged to buy within their normal rate. If a phased incentive (with, say, on-pack vouchers that need to be saved) has too short an interval, even heavy users will not be able to buy sufficiently often to achieve their goal. Petrol promotions in the past, which have offered vouchers for items, or collectable free gifts (World Cup Coins, Car Badges and so on) can result in considerable consumer irritation if insufficient time is allowed for them to complete their set.

By the same token, a differential impact can be achieved by addressing the issue of pack size. It is reasonable to assume that regular users will, in the main, tend to buy a larger pack size. If an incentive is offered on a smaller size, it will tend to attract more new users than existing.

Coupon distribution

We have already seen that all recipients of a promotional incentive will be rewarded, irrespective of whether or not they would have purchased the product at the 'regular' price. By targeting discount offers, for example, by including the coupon in a newspaper or magazine advertisement, or by the use of direct mail, it can be more effective in attracting new users than those who are loyal to the brand.

Brand franchise

Much has already been said about the potential risks of short-term promotional incentives undermining the desired imagery of a brand. Careful consideration needs to be made of the likely impact which a promotion will have on overall consumer perceptions, as much on the assessment of its ability to achieve short-term volume goals. Too great a reliance on price-based offers will tend to encourage consumers to focus on the price, not only of the preferred brand, but also of potential competitors, sometimes to the detriment of the brand.

Case study

KELLOGG'S
Agency: Blue Chip Marketing

Special K, as the leading cereal brand targeted at shape-conscious women, was being threatened by the launch of Nestlé's Fitnesse. This new brand was aiming to revolutionize the market and steal share directly from Special K.

Kellogg's research identified walking as the next big 'shape management' trend. Its defence strategy was to exploit this trend with the objectives of re-enforcing Special K's credentials, driving sales and delivering added value to consumers.

The 10 000 Steps Challenge encouraged consumers to take 10 000 steps every day and, to help them to do this, they were offered an exclusive Special K pedometer (worth £12) for just £3.99 plus two tokens.

The pedometer was multi functional and came with a personal achievement tracker and tips on shape management from a Reebok Master Trainer. Consumers could also download a personalized shape-management programme from the Special K website.

The campaign featured on 11 million packs with full media and online support.

Response to the offer was unprecedented with 700 000 applications – better than a successful free-mail-in.

The campaign received a gold award in the Free and Self-Liquidating Promotions section of the 2005 ISP Promotion Awards.

(The above appeared in the Special Supplement to *Promotions and Incentives* magazine, June 2005)

Questions

1 What are the reasons for the growth of private-label products?

2 How can an understanding of the nature of the target audience affect the selection of promotional executions?

3 How do consumers differ in terms of their likelihood to purchase specific brands on a regular basis?

4 Why do brands matter? What benefits do they offer?

5 Why is an understanding of brand dimensions an important consideration in the planning of promotional activity?

4 Developing the theory of sales promotion

Chapter overview

One of the difficulties within the field of sales promotion is the very limited amount of academic underpinning that is available to evidence the use of sales promotion techniques. Although there are a considerable number of academic papers on the subject, few develop specific theories or models that can assist in the general development of sales promotion activities. This chapter brings together a number of diverse theories that have been developed, sometimes in other areas, that apply to sales promotion and help us to understand the application of the techniques.

Learning outcomes

- To consider the nature of the communications process
- To examine the implications of the product life cycle
- To reflect on models that assist in the understanding of promotional activity.

The communications process

Before we can begin to examine the models that relate to the development of sales promotion, we must first understand how communication itself takes place. We can begin by examining a simple model that identifies the fundamental elements of communication.

Figure 4.1

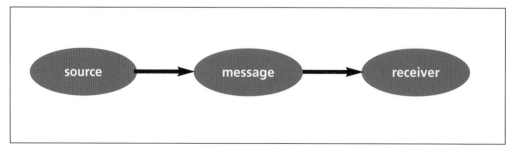

Whilst this model is over-simplistic, it depicts the three basic elements of communication: the first is the source of the message that, in this context, is the advertiser; second, there is the message itself, designed to deliver specific information to the third part of the equation, namely the receiver. Whilst the basic elements are present, the model fails to communicate the depth of the process since it ignores other important factors that come into play.

A somewhat better understanding is provided by the more detailed model shown below. This model introduces a number of new elements that serve to demonstrate the complex nature of communications.

Figure 4.2

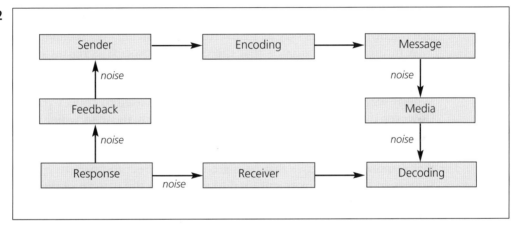

When we send any form of communications message, we need to encode it into some form of symbolic representation. Although much sales promotion communication is explicit, there are times when the company uses other devices designed to convey some form of impression to the reader or viewer. For example, competitions may provide an indication of the sort of prizes that can be won or communicate some global prize value. At other times, different forms of promotional offer are conveyed in some form of 'shorthand' that needs to be understood by the receiver of the message. The message will need to be placed into some form of medium or carrier that the sender believes will be seen or heard by the receiver. This might be television, a newspaper, radio or any other medium such as a leaflet or in-store poster available to the sender.

It is important to recognize that the message is only one of the many that the intended receiver will be required to deal with. It is estimated that the average person is exposed to around 1300 commercial messages in a normal day (White 1998).[1] The inevitable consequence is that the promotional message becomes confused with the others. This is what we refer to as 'noise': the general clutter of information within which the message is placed and through which it must penetrate in order to achieve effective impact on the desired audience.

The consequence is that the intended message may well be incompletely communicated or confused by this surrounding 'noise'. Moreover, whatever message is received will be impacted by the recipient's preconceptions related to the sender or the message or both. If the receiver regards the company as reliable and trustworthy then the message will be interpreted in that context. However, the opposite might also be true, particularly if the receiver has previously had some negative experience with the same company or product.

For example, in some bonus pack offers the manufacturer may offer as much as 100 per cent extra product free. This will only be believed if the consumer feels that the brand itself has credibility. Ong *et al.* (1997)[2] suggest that:

> …consumers view high volume bonus packs with scepticism. The higher the extra amount added 'free' the less believable the offer.

They add that 'occasionally, bonus packs offer 100 per cent more free. While offers like these may catch the attention of consumers and impress them, there is a chance that the manufacturers may be inadvertently sacrificing the credibility of their brands'.

A further complication is that the decoding process is reliant upon the receiver understanding the signs and symbols used by the advertiser. For the most part, we grow up with an understanding of the 'language' used by advertisers. We are mostly familiar with the 'shorthand' and symbols that are used to convey particular meaning. However, this is not true of all cultures, particularly those in which advertising is not the norm, or where the chosen signs and symbols may deliver alternative meanings.

Marklin (1969)[3] says: 'A response which is not rewarded leads to an extinction of that response.' He argues that cues are used to direct the pattern of response of consumers and the reinforcement used to strengthen the pattern of the cues.

Stuart Henderson Britt (1978)[4] reinforces the above comment: 'The less time elapsed between the message and the reward it offers, the higher will be the level of audience members' recall of that message, that is, delaying the reward will hinder learning of the message.'

This of course is particularly important in the context of coupon offers. If the product purchasing cycle is long, that is there are long gaps between purchases, there is a high chance that the initial offer will be forgotten in the intervening period.

However, Stern (1994)[5] argues that the standard communication model proposed by information theorists (sender, message, addressee – in which the message is decoded on the basis of a Code shared by both the virtual poles of the chain) does not describe the actual functioning of communication.

> The existence of various codes and subcodes, the variety of sociocultural circumstances in which a message is omitted (where the codes of the addressee can be different from those of the sender) and the rate of initiative displayed by the addressee in making presuppositions and abductions – all result in making a message (insofar as it is received and transformed into the content of an expression) an empty form to which various possible senses can be attributed. Moreover what one calls 'message' is usually a text, that is, a network of different messages depending on different codes and working at different levels of signification.
>
> (Stern 1994)[5]

The particular response that the receiver makes will itself be dependent on a variety of factors. Some advertising simply conveys information to the consumer; other forms are intended to elicit some form of invitation to purchase or to take some other specific type of response. Clearly, the response of the receiver to the message will be of considerable importance to the sender. Accordingly, the sender will often build in some form of feedback mechanism in order to understand the nature of the response that, in turn, can be used to refine the message if it fails to deliver the desired response.

Chandon (1995)[6] has developed a model to depict a framework for promotional analysis:

Figure 4.3

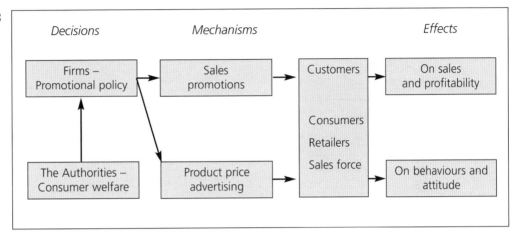

The product life cycle

The principle of the product life cycle is well established and has particular relevance to the application of sales promotion principles. Strang[7] conducted a study of some 57 consumer goods companies in order to define the specific role of sales promotion in the context of achieving a company's objectives. His results are depicted below:

Table 4.1

How companies choose between advertising and sales promotion

	Impact on budget allocation	
	Increase advertising	*Increase sales promotion*
Stage in product life cycle		
Introduction	❖	❖
Growth	❖	❖
Maturity		❖
Decline		❖
Other decision factors		
Increase profit performance	❖	
Market dominance	❖	
Regional brand		❖
Promotion oriented competitors		❖
Distribution vulnerability		❖

Adapted from Strang, R., Marketing and Sales Promotions, special report from *Sales and Marketing Management Magazine*, no date

This can be depicted graphically in the more familiar representation of the product life cycle diagram:

Figure 4.4

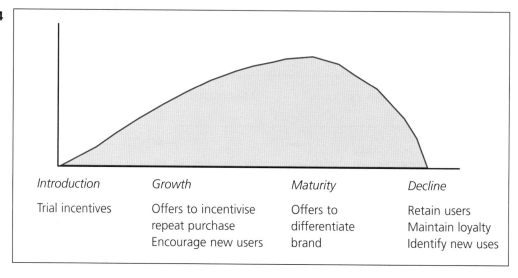

Introduction	Growth	Maturity	Decline
Trial incentives	Offers to incentivise repeat purchase Encourage new users	Offers to differentiate brand	Retain users Maintain loyalty Identify new uses

The stimulus–response model

The stimulus–response model, derived from cognitive psychology, suggests that all activity is based on these two key dimensions, although studies have shown that other factors impact.

The overall model is depicted as follows:

Figure 4.5

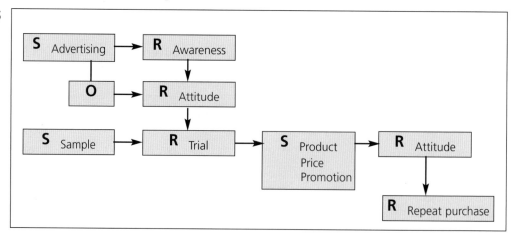

There are a number of important dimensions to this model. The initial role of advertising is to create an awareness response (as depicted on the first level). As a consequence of repeated exposure to the advertising message, together with some internal processing and product use (depicted by O), the result is the formation of an attitude towards the company, the brand or the product.

Work within the field of psychology suggests a series of further dimensions that have significance in the area of sales promotion activity. It is suggested that behaviour is influenced by the level of either reward or punishment that is associated with it. If the stimulus is positive, such as a sample, a reduction in price or similar promotional device, the result will be trial. This can be reinforced through the use of the tools of marketing communications, further resulting in the strengthening of the attitude and, ultimately, leading to repeat purchase.

The principle of just noticeable difference

One particular theory has particular application to the field of sales promotion. Although developed a long time ago, the theory still retains its relevance today. This is the principle of the just noticeable difference (JND) developed by Karl Weber.[8]

Weber's law asserts that consumers differ in their ability to detect differences between stimulus values. Accordingly, it is necessary to ensure that any consumer offer is sufficiently meaningful for it to be both noticed and responded to by consumers. If the difference is too small it will simply not be noticed by the consumer. In the context of sales promotion offers the imperative, therefore, is to make the offer at a sufficiently large level for the consumer both to notice it and to respond to it.

Various experiments have taken place based on Weber's law that appear to indicate that price reductions of at least 15 per cent are usually needed to attract consumers towards a promotional offer. The same principle has relevance in other contexts. If, for example, the manufacturer wishes to change the price/value relationship without it being noticed by the consumer, then it will be important to ensure that the changes made are below the JND.

The AIDA model

Again, a well-established, although somewhat simplistic model used to describe the role of advertising has been used by Peattie and Peattie (1995)[9] and Gupta *et al.* (1997)[10] to describe the impact of sales promotion.

Both sets of authors relate sales promotional activity to the attention, interest, desire and action (AIDA) model of marketing communications. They suggest that promotions work effectively against each stage of the somewhat simplistic model.

Peattie and Peattie assert that promotions are specifically designed to be attention grabbing. They are designed to help products stand out in today's competitive retail environment. This is especially important given that a major retail supermarket, for example, will stock around 50 000 products all trying to gain the attention of the consumer.

Promotions are designed to create novelty and excitement and to inject them into products that have become familiar and sometimes mundane. They suggest that in the financial-services market, competitions, in particular, have been shown to create considerable interest amongst both customers and staff, which is especially important in a price-competitive market with an intangible product.

Desire is encouraged by the offer of additional benefits. These may take a variety of different forms, but all are specifically designed to add value to the purchase of the product and make it more desirable than those of competitors, even those with similar product attributes.

Promotions differ from much advertising in that they seek a direct response from the consumer. The action phase is a particular facet of sale promotions that stimulates both sales volume and the rate of consumption (Ailawadi and Neslin 1998).[11] They argue that promotions can go beyond simply prompting action to create interaction and involvement with a product or service. Consumers might be invited to suggest new ways of using the product, for example, or to rank its attributes thus creating a dialogue between the consumer and the manufacturer. Kellogg's for example, asked consumers to vote for or against changing the name of their Rice Crispies brand.

Promotions provide the opportunity to develop relationships with the consumer. Various loyalty card schemes such as those run by Tesco and Boots establish patterns of loyalty between the consumer and the retail outlet. Moreover such schemes can be used both to identify and target specific groups of customers.

Similarly, Gupta *et al.* (1997)[10] argue that, in terms of attention, promotions provide the vehicle for grabbing the eye of the consumer with the immediacy of the words used, such as 'free', 'extra', 'bonus', 'money off', etc.

Promotions provide a level of interest and immediacy to almost any product or service, sometimes going beyond the inherent interest in the product itself. The consumer is often motivated by the desire to achieve the benefit of the incentive offered, which results in an immediate response to take action.

Techniques that reduce the purchase price of the product or service are the most commonly used. These methods are often successful when tackling short-term objectives, but rarely on brand share; often the promotional intensity within the product category will also be high, resulting in most competitors providing similar incentives. This, in turn, results in little or no change in the market share.

According to Guiltinan and Paul (1991)[12] several factors impact on the nature of consumer response to sales promotional activity.

Figure 4.6

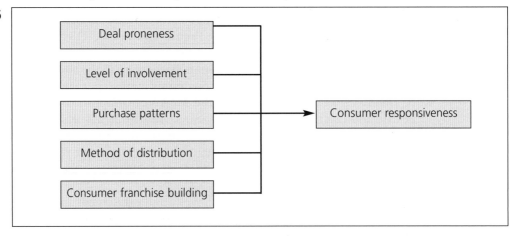

Deal proneness

Consumers can be segmented in terms of the extent to which they are likely to seek out and respond to sales promotion activity.

Level of involvement

The consumer's level of involvement in the search process will have an impact on their likely response to promotional offers.

Consumer purchasing patterns

Understanding the rate of purchasing frequency amongst groups of consumers is important in determining both the specific nature and scale of the promotional offer, and the likely response amongst different groups of consumers. Clearly, offers should be available for a sufficient period to enable consumers to respond during their normal purchasing cycles. However, if the duration of the promotion is extended too far, all potential new buyers will have had an opportunity to purchase with the consequence that additional sales will primarily come from regular consumers who will use the opportunity to stockpile whilst the incentive is available.

Method of distribution

Consumer response to promotional offers will depend on the degree of effort involved on the part of the consumer. Those which require limited effort, for example on- and in-pack coupons, will tend to have higher redemption rates simply because consumers do not need to expend much effort in acquiring these offers. Equally, since they are already pre-disposed towards the product, limited decision making is required. Where the promotional objective is to attract new users, different distribution methods will need to be employed to ensure that the offer is more precisely targeted to non-users or users of competitive brands.

The impact of promotions on sales are complex and go beyond just affecting sales, even if this is the main objective according to Lambin (2000):[13]

- Internal transfer effect – loyal buyers take advantage of an offer but would have bought the brand in any case
- Anticipation effect – sales go down just before a promotion comes into effect because consumers wait for the promotion to buy. This is particularly true when the periodicity for sales promotions is regular.
- Decay effect – sales go down after a special promotion because consumers have stocked up on the product.
- Cannibalization effect – there are purchasing transfers among different sizes and varieties within a range of products during sales promotions.
- Brand switching effect – this is what was intended. Additional sales are achieved through a switch from some other brand to the brand under promotion.
- Trial effect – whatever the tool, it induces consumers to use the product. This is especially important for new products.
- Retention effect – here the positive effects of the promotion survive the period of activity and can keep the product at a higher level of sales after the promotion period.

In research conducted by Raghubir and Corfman (1999),[14] they analysed pre- and post-promotional evaluations within a product category. They found that promotions are often used as a source of information on the product when the consumer is not an expert. Hence, price promotions may often shape the consumer's expectation of the brand. In those categories where promotions are uncommon, offering a price-based promotion is likely to result in a far lower brand evaluation. Finally, price-based promotions will also lower the brand evaluation if it has not been promoted in this way previously, due to consumer perceptions of lower-priced goods.

The operant conditioning theory suggests that on-going, price-based, sales promotional activities within the product category conditions both loyal and non-loyal consumers to be more price sensitive and leads to lower price expectations as the norm (Mela *et al.* 1997, Ehrenberg *et al.* 1991).[15,16]

Scarcity theory suggests that consumers curb consumption of products when supply is limited because they perceive smaller quantities to be more valuable. Promotions can have a positive impact on household inventory levels, which increase with the consequence that consumption increases also (Ailawadi and Neslin 1998).[17]

Gardener and Trivedi (1998)[17] suggest that consumer satisfaction with a promoted brand leads to increased repeat purchasing after that promotion has been withdrawn. However, other researchers have found that consumers revert to their pre-promotion purchasing behaviour after the promotion has finished (Bawa and Shoemaker 1987, Ehrenberg *et al.* 1994).[18,19] Yet others have suggested that promotions can have a negative effect on the brand (Gaudagni and Little 1983, Neslin and Shoemaker 1989).[20,21]

Peattie *et al.* (1993)[22] similarly argue that if some trialists can be retained, this will be reflected in long-term benefits through increased market share. These authors propose a model to apply dimension to the benefits of targeting promotions.

Jones (1990)[23] argues that 'there is little truth that promotions encourage repeat purchases, especially those associated with price reduction'. He adds 'they lack the customary stress on building a consumer franchise that features the brands' competitive benefits or builds warm, non-rational associations with it'. He concludes that promotion can only induce volatile demand, whereas franchise building is about creating stable demand.

Gupta *et al.* (1997)[10] have developed a varying parameter model of purchase incidence and quantity, examining the stockpiling behaviour of households within the context of frequent promotions. They conclude that:

> … increasing expectations of future promotions lead to:
> A reduced likelihood of purchase incidence on a given shopping trip
> An increase in the quantity bought when a purchase is made.

They assert that this strategy is consistent with the consumer learning to wait for especially good deals and then stockpiling when those deals occur.

Huff and Alden (1998)[24] state: 'Price orientated promotions increase sales and market share, entice trial and encourage brand switching. Non-price promotions add excitement and value to brands and may encourage brand loyalty.'

Certainly, the earliest model used in most of the literature is that of AIDA, variously attributed to St Elmo Lewis (1898)[25] and Strong (1925).[26] It was Lewis's contention that sales people needed to pursue a sequence of actions in order to achieve success. It was somewhat later that the model and its sequence of events were applied to advertising.

In the ensuing decades a great many similar models were described in the literature, sometimes changing the words used or adding or deleting stages (Barry and Howard 1990, McDonald 1992).[27,28]

The AIDA model proposed a simple hierarchical structure to identify the stages of the communications process. Originally proposed at the turn of the century to explain the process of personal selling, it was rapidly adopted as a model to explain the process of communications in advertising.

The basic tenet was that, in order to have effect, the first task of any campaign was to gain the attention of the viewer or reader. From the outset, it was recognized that a

Figure 4.7

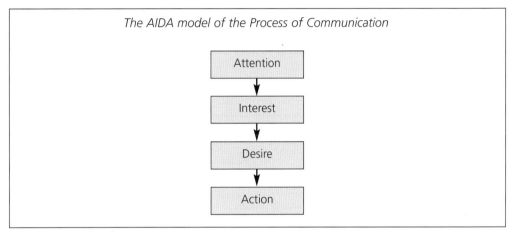

The AIDA model of the Process of Communication

fundamental aim of communication was to cut through the surrounding clutter and arrest the attention of the potential purchaser. Moreover, it suggested that the process of communications required the audience to pass through a series of sequential steps and that each step was a logical consequence of what had gone before. The principle of sequential activity or learning is used commonly in many marketing models, and is often referred to as a hierarchy of effects. The attention phase is the key to the process, since whatever follows will be of little value if the attention of the audience has not been achieved.

The second stage is the stimulation of an interest in the proposition. In most cases, it would be reasonable to assume that if the first requirement (attention) had been met, the second would follow on almost automatically. Indeed, if the communications message has been properly constructed, this will be true. However, in some instances, particularly where an irrelevant attention-getting device has been employed, the potential consumer does not pass fully to the second stage.

The third stage is to create a desire for the product or service being promoted. Often, this will take the form of a 'problem–solution' execution, in which the advertiser seeks to position his product as the answer to a problem that he has previously identified. Soap powder advertisements often follow this sequence of events, although many other examples can be found from contemporary marketing activity. Personal care, hair care, and do-it-yourself products are other areas where this approach is currently employed.

The fourth and final stage of the AIDA model is the stimulation of some form of response on the part of the audience (the action stage). Most advertisements have a specific call to action and many are linked with promotional offers designed to induce a purchase of the product or some other desired end result.

This sequential pattern (or something like it put in different words) is treated as common sense: it only says that people need to be aware of a brand before they can be interested in it and that they need to desire it before they can take action and buy it.

The market for any product category is made up of various consumers who differ in terms of their responsiveness to promotional offers. As we have seen in Chapter 3, some consumers remain loyal to a particular brand and tend to purchase that brand whenever it is available. At the other end of the spectrum, some consumers demonstrate absolutely no brand loyalty and will purchase any product that is on special offer.

McAlister (1986)[29] developed a segmentation model to depict the various types of consumer in terms of their propensity to purchase deals.

Figure 4.8

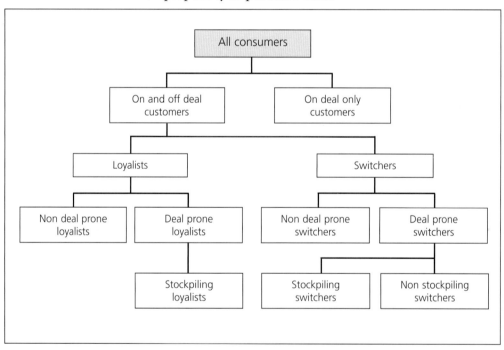

Although these purchase patterns are derived from a single product category, they nonetheless provide a framework for the consideration of consumers and their reactions to promotional offers. However, it must be recognized that consumers may be more or less responsive to promotional offers depending on the particular category of market being considered.

McAlister makes the primary distinction between those consumers who only purchase when a brand is on special offer and those who continue to purchase irrespective of whether a promotion is available.

Even amongst loyal brand consumers, a distinction can be made between those who respond to deal offers and those who do not. Switchers are those consumers who alternate between brands even when no promotions are available.

The other point to be made is to distinguish between those consumers who have a tendency to stockpile to take advantage of a particular promotional offer and those who do not (possibly because they are constrained by the high initial outlay that stock-piling involves).

The importance of this form of segmentation is that it potentially enables manu-facturers to calculate the levels of profitability deriving from a particular execution if they can identify the various groups of consumers relating to their brand and their propensity to purchase the brand when it is on offer.

Pringle and Thompson (1999)[30] argue that it is the new values that the consumer is looking for in order for them to make their choices, instead of the usual functional, eco-nomic, emotional and psychological values.

> You have the opportunity to change people's perceptions of a brand and then, through on-going activity, you can keep those customers.

(Miller 1997)[31]

Case study

PROCTER & GAMBLE UK – ARIEL DETERGENT
Agency: Lifestyle Incentives Ltd

Background

The UK detergents market is currently worth over £840 million. Within the market two major players each have several brands competing for the consumer's attention. Both Unilever and Procter & Gamble maintain stables of brands offering different formulations to satisfy consumer needs. Amongst these Ariel washing powder is a specially formulated detergent that keeps whites looking whiter for longer.

For the 2 years prior to the promotion Ariel had run advertising campaigns featuring Tim Henman to demonstrate the product's ability to keep whites 'championship white' wash after wash. However, these campaigns had failed to make inroads into the key competitor's target audience.

Objectives

The brand required a promotion to generate incremental trial and sales of Ariel in Tesco stores. It would build on the association of Ariel with tennis and the Lawn Tennis Association and would be designed to make significant inroads into the key competitor's core market.

It would be required to build on previous 'championship whites' campaigns and create a point of difference for Ariel in a market of perceived parity.

Strategy

The promotion would aim to make Ariel synonymous with keeping tennis whites white, building on research that indicated consumers perceive this as a torture test for any detergent.

It would extend the alliance with the Lawn Tennis Association that would emphasize the brand's strong juxtaposition with playing tennis.

The promotion would be aimed to target AB mothers with children aged 5–12 who research indicated had a high interest in tennis and would create an added value in-store promotion offering a reward for every purchase of Ariel.

Campaign summary

As noted, the promotion was exclusive to Tesco outlets. The offer to Tesco customers was a free tennis lesson from an LTA licensed, qualified coach in return for the purchase of any Ariel product. To claim their tennis lesson consumers were asked to mail their till receipt and a C5 stamped addressed envelope to the offer address. In return they received a booklet containing a voucher for one free introductory tennis lesson lasting one hour and valued at up to £25. The book also included a directory of over 200 participating coaches nationwide.

On receipt of the booklet the consumers telephoned their chosen coach to book a lesson stating that they had an Ariel Free Tennis Voucher. The promotion was launched during the first week of Wimbledon when the interest in tennis reaches its peak.

A full range of in-store support material was developed including end-aisle displays with hanging banners, shelf barkers, and A5 leaflets.

Radio advertisements and in-store POS invited consumers to purchase any Ariel product in Tesco and claim a free tennis lesson.

Results

- The campaign resulted in a 38 per cent sales uplift of Ariel in Tesco stores.
- There were 107 450 free tennis lesson redemptions over the 10-week promotional period.
- The promotion was a key part of the 2003 'championship whites' campaign that resulted in Ariel becoming the UK's market leading washing detergent for the first time in 4 years.
- Market share increased by 5%.
- Data collected from the redemption process added 100 000 new names to Ariel's database.

The promotion was the ISP Bronze Award winner 2004 in the other FMCG category. It was also given the award of the best and most effective long-term communication campaign by the Marketing Communication Consultants Association. The relationship with tennis has been continued in 2005 with an on-pack offer on the brand of Free Mini Tennis Lessons.

Questions

1 Why is it important to establish a theoretical framework for sales promotion?
2 How does an understanding of the communications process assist in the development of effective promotions?
3 Why is it important to consider the brand's position in the product life cycle in the context of planning promotions?
4 What factors affect consumer response to promotional offers?

5 The strategic dimensions of sales promotion

Chapter overview

All too often sales promotion is considered as a short-term tactical tool. This is to deny its more complete role as a strategic component of marketing communications. Whilst it is undeniably true that sales promotion can fulfil a variety of short-term objectives, the failure to recognize its strategic contribution often results in an undermining of the position and image of the brand.

This chapter considers the strategic role of sales promotion and the contribution that it can make to the longer-term brand-building process.

Learning outcomes

- To examine the reasons why sales promotion has been regarded as a short-term tactical tool
- To consider the role of strategy
- To examine the strategic use of sales promotion
- To investigate the development of sales promotion strategy
- To review the long-term effectiveness of sales promotion.

In contrast to what might be expected from many of the widely used definitions of sales promotion, the reality should be that sales promotion should be considered as part of the longer-term strategy for the brand. Rather than simply using sales promotions to create short-term uplifts in sales, they should contribute to the longer-term aims of the brand: reinforcing brand image, encouraging consumer loyalty towards the brand, and developing strong relationships with the consumer.

Considered in this light, sales promotion can make a strong contribution towards the strengthening of the brand position. By selecting promotional executions that add value to the brand and that communicate image values, such activities can add to consumer perceptions of the brand values. Moreover, if there is a consistent theme for promotional activity, successive promotions can build on previous executions. In order to achieve this objective it is important that sales promotion reflects other forms of marketing communications activity. In other words, it must be fully integrated with the overall marketing communications programme.

The increased use of sales promotion

Recent years have seen a significant increase in the use of sales promotion techniques. There are several reasons for the change:

1   The increase in strength of retailers.

    As a direct consequence of growth of retailers, both organic and as a result of mergers and acquisitions, a smaller number of retailers now control a greatly increased percentage of the retail trade. In the retail grocery trade, for example, the major retailers, i.e. Tesco, ASDA, Sainsbury's and Morrisons, now control almost 70 per cent of sales. In the field of electrical retailing a similar concentration of power into very few hands, i.e. Dixons, Curry's and Comet, has seen an increased level of pressure on manufacturers. The consequence is that these few retailers have a dominant impact on whether manufacturer brands are successful or not. The trade requires (and often demands) incentives to stock and display a product.

    Retail stores have now become the newest battleground in the war of consumer goods manufacturers to win consumers. Manufacturers are discovering the need to reach potential buyers directly at the time and place at which the buying decision is made: the point of purchase (Jones 1990).[1]

2   Reduction in product differentiation.

    Most products offer little that is different from their competitors in real and tangible terms. Sales promotional activity may be a major point of difference between one brand and its rivals, at least in the short term.

3   Reductions in the levels of brand loyalty.

    Various studies (Ehrenberg 1993, Mela *et al.* 1997)[2,3] suggest that the levels of brand loyalty have declined significantly. This is a direct consequence of the essential similarities between brands, but equally a result of the increasing use of price-oriented promotions that serve to accelerate the levels of consumer price sensitivity.

    However, according to Buck (2000),[4] despite a significant increase in the power and competitive position of the main supermarket chains, the leading premium brands in most packaged grocery categories have proved remarkably successful in maintaining their position and sales. He analysed sales from Taylor Nelson Sofres data in 26 leading grocery categories and compared them to data from a previous study conducted in 1975. Out of the 26 categories, 19 of the brand leaders in 1975 were still brand leaders in 1999 and half of these had succeeded in increasing their market share in spite of significant private-label growth across all categories.

4   Short-term focus of brand activity.

Most brand activity is designed to achieve short-term volume increases motivated both by internal structures and responsibilities and external factors such as reporting to the City and Investors who demand a short-term return on their investments.

Griffith and Rust (1997)[5] contend that many companies aspire to matching the price points of competitors rather than maximizing brand profitability. The consequence of this form of price competition is often damaging to the company.

5   Increased recognition that consumers are more responsive to promotional offers than other forms of activity.

Consumers have become more price and value sensitive according to research carried out by Mela *et al.* (1997).[3]

It is argued by Jones (1990),[1] amongst others, that promotions cannot establish a consumer franchise for a brand, nor can they overcome inherent weaknesses in the product. At best, they serve to delay the unavoidable collapse of the brand. Moreover, they do so at considerable cost since the profitability of the brand is eroded until the point is reached where they are no longer affordable and the brand can no longer provide a justification for purchase.

Against this, however, there are many examples of instances where promotions have been used to achieve the specific objective that these authors indicate they cannot meet!

Kleenex, for example, have used sales promotion to reinforce the relevance of their brand. Over a period of seven years, they have mounted a series of promotions under the general theme of 'Hay Fever Survival'. These promotions have included a survival kit for two proofs of purchase, a guide-book, pollen-filtered cars as prizes in competitions and hay-fever free holidays.

McDonald's have used sales promotion consistently to reward their target audiences. They regularly use movie tie-ins and similar devices to extend the imagery derived from the films to encompass their brand. This activity is not restricted to the UK, but extends across all of the regions in which the company operates.

Coca Cola is another company that uses sales promotion activity on a regular and consistent basis. Whilst they are involved in a variety of sports promotion (their association with the Olympic movement goes back to the 1930s according to Mark Prendergast),[6] they regularly use links to football to promote their brand. Both advertising and sales promotion have used a broadly consistent football theme over a number of years, although this does not preclude their use of other activities to achieve their promotional goals.

Similarly, Tango successfully integrated its above-the-line campaign with promotional activity in 1995. The Tango Doll competition is arguably the first ever self-liquidating telephone promotion. It was claimed that the activity resulted in a sales increase of 34 per cent.

Other promotions have demonstrated the potential to enhance the brand franchise. Examples would be the Pepperami Fanimal and Levi's Flat Eric.

Similarly, the various frequent flyer schemes operated by the airlines are an ample demonstration of the fact that promotions can generate loyalty to the brand in the longer term.

The short-term approach towards sales promotion

Undeniably, many authors have condemned sales promotion but, in the main, their criticisms relate to the implementation of short-term, often price-reducing promotions. For example, Alexander Biel[7] writing in *Admap* argues that:

> I am concerned that this short-term orientation has destructive long-term effects. A major question that marketers must confront is whether excessive emphasis on promotion actually erodes brand value.

Similarly, Ehrenberg *et al.* (1997)[8] state that:

> The general short-term, immediate action, tactical nature of sales promotion contrasts with the longer term image and brand building capability of advertising.

They add:

> While price clearly matters, it is not everything. Consumers do not always strive to pay less, nor are they uniquely motivated by price.

Mitchell (1999)[9] makes the point that there are significant problems associated with continually cutting prices as 'an item's price is pregnant with meaning and symbolism'. Ambler (1999)[10] reinforces this view with the statement that 'price promotions have a long term detrimental effect to the brand's acceptance in the market'.

Jones (1990)[1] produced an indictment of promotions suggesting that companies, faced with saturated markets, have been guilty of misguidedly channelling money away from above-the-line advertising and fighting with fury for market share using promotions as the main tactical weapon. He concluded that promotions devalue the image of the promoted brand in the consumer's eyes and rarely stimulate repeat purchase. Moreover, he argues that:

> ... as a general rule, promotions can never improve a brand image or help the stability of the customer franchise. It is suggested that this should be left to consumer advertising as it can lead to a growing perceived differentiation of the advertised brand from rival brands.

However, whilst his accusations could reasonably be applied in the area of price promotions, there are a wide variety of promotional tools that serve to add value to a brand and, hence, achieve the opposite effect.

Another critic of sales promotion, Larry Light (1998),[11] similarly equates sales promotion to price reduction and argues that:

> Excessive emphasis on sales promotion can increase sales value while it damages brand value. Sales promotion which emphasises the price of the brand hurts the quality image and brand loyalty and increases price sensitivity.

This view is reinforced by Raghubir and Corfman (1999)[12] who state that there is evidence 'when consumers buy a product on a price promotion, they are less likely to repeat the purchase when the offer finishes'. There is no relationship being built and the product's value will not be enhanced.

However, Lisa Campbell (1996)[13] writing in *Promotions and Incentives Journal*, states that:

> Over using price promotion can corrode the bonding agent that make people adhere to one brand. Used carefully, however, they can be effective in recruiting stable users from floating shoppers ... It's not the tool we should be blaming, but the users.

These papers preclude any consideration of the use of sales promotion in anything other than a tactical role and, therefore, denigrate the entire work of agencies and others striving to achieve strategic goals with the use of sales promotion.

The role of strategy

Head (1998)[14] identifies the role of a strategy. It provides:

- a definition of the base point
- a definition of the end point
- a description of the process of making the transition
- criteria against which progress can be measured
- a platform from which detailed plans can be produced.

Above all, the strategy provides the framework against which research and measurement can take place.

It is, therefore, important to consider the role of sales promotion within the overall brand-building process. Schultz *et al.* (1992)[15] have suggested an alternative definition to provide a more strategic focus for the consideration of sales promotion activity:

> Sales promotions are marketing and communications activities that change the price/value relationship of a product or service perceived by the target, thereby:
> i.   generating immediate sales and
> ii. altering long-term brand value.

Whilst recognizing that sales promotions can fulfil their role of generating short-term sales volume, this definition promotes the need to consider the longer-term issues relating to the brand. For this reason, it is important to consider the wider implications of the impact of sales promotion on brand values. Moreover, it is important to assess the broad framework before identifying a specific promotional solution.

Marc Drake[16] of Taylor Nelson and Associates suggests that 'brands need to have an overall communications strategy. Not only will this help benefit the consistency and reinforcement of the overall brand message, but will help each individual function achieve its objectives by creating increased awareness'.

The strategic use of sales promotion

A contrasting view of sales promotion is provided by two authors. Davies (1992)[17] writing in *Management Decisions*, suggests that sales promotion, well co-ordinated and executed with other activities of an integrated marketing communications plan, has a strategic value and can build long-term brand value. This view is reinforced by O'Malley (1993).[18]

Similarly, Aaker (1991)[19] argues that 'sales promotions, whether they involve soda pop or automobiles, are effective – they affect sales in an immediate and measurable way ... Promotions which simply offer a discount or rebate are the most likely to cheapen the brand and thus adversely affect the brand image. There are ways to engage promotions to enhance rather than tarnish brand equity'.

He suggests that promotions can enhance brand equity by reinforcing and strengthening key associations and brand awareness. Much has been written about promotions that seek to align brands with charitable enterprises, such as the Walkers Books for Schools promotion, amongst others. We will develop this thinking in Chapter 10.

As Gay (1997)[20] states: 'promotions are no longer simply short-term initiatives to lift sales, they are increasingly being used to reinforce brand values'.

Peattie *et al.* (1997)[21] conducted research to identify specific strategic applications of sales promotion. They concluded that sales promotion has the potential to:

1 improve brand awareness
2 stimulate product trial
3 smooth seasonal demand patterns
4 act as a communications channel between a company and its customers
5 reinforce advertising themes
6 reinforce POS communications efforts
7 provide PR opportunities
8 reduce rivals' promotional efforts.

Lee (2002)[22] suggests four reasons for using sales promotions:

1 reaction to competitor promotions
2 inertia: this is what we've always done
3 meeting short-term (sales) objectives
4 meeting long-term objectives.

Most sales promotions fall into the first three of these categories and this is especially true of promotions based on price offers. He argues that sales promotions can form an important element of promotional strategy but this means that those promotions have to be planned. However, he indicates that, in the main, we do not treat sales promotions strategically but use them as panic measures.

Lee, however, does offer some hope for sales promotions enthusiasts: '... price-oriented promotions are used primarily to meet short-term objectives, while non-price promotions are used mostly for actioning long-term results'.

Sales promotions can make a contribution to meeting longer-term objectives (can form a core element of marketing strategy) but only when we eschew the simple option of cutting price. The lesson is to use sales promotions at a higher level in the overall promotional mix. With this approach the sales promotion becomes more integrated with the main brand strategy. Rather than seeing the sales promotion as a panic measure, it becomes a support to brand objectives and, rather than offering a discount, we offer a prize or some other incentive: we give the consumer added value.

According to Flanagan (1988)[23] with sales promotion it is necessary to focus on the strategic planning part of the business. The craft of sales promotion is driven by the planning processes more than it is by any creative considerations. Flanagan argues that concentrating on the planning process will help greatly in using some of the powerful techniques of sales promotion that do not rely on product discounting, such as value added, continuity, cause-related and special event promotions.

One attempt to add dimension to the strategic use of the tools of marketing communications is that summarized by Biel (1999).[24] In his paper he presents the results of an analysis of Profit Impact of Marketing Strategy (PIMS) data to identify the outcome of three different advertising/promotion strategies. A sample of 749 consumer businesses together with 314 non-durable businesses were examined with three different strategic approaches:

1   Those using sales promotion as their dominant strategy, i.e. companies spending 77 per cent on sales promotion.

2   Those using a mixed strategy, spending between 36 per cent and 50 per cent on advertising.

3   Those using advertising as the dominant strategy, allocating two-thirds of their funds to media advertising.

The findings demonstrated that the greatest return on investment was achieved among those companies employing advertising as their lead strategic tool.

Table 5.1

	Average R.O.I
Advertising emphasis	30.5
Mixed strategy	27.3
Sales promotion emphasis	18.1

However, whilst these findings are, broadly, valid they fail to reflect the real market situation. Few manufacturers actually use sales promotion as their exclusive marketing tool. The reality is that manufacturers use a combination of advertising, sales promotion and the other tools of marketing communications to achieve their brand objectives. Moreover, the integration of these activities can serve to enhance the values associated with the brand.

Push vs pull strategies

One issue to be resolved prior to any form of promotional planning is the broad approach to be taken. In this regard it is necessary to distinguish between 'push' and 'pull' strategies.

Sales promotions can reflect both push and pull strategies. A push strategy is one in which the effort of the manufacturer is directed towards the distribution channels to motivate and encourage them to promote the product or service to the end user. In contrast, a pull strategy is one in which activity is targeted directly towards end users who are motivated to take products from the distribution channel. The alternatives can be seen in the following diagram:

Figure 5.1

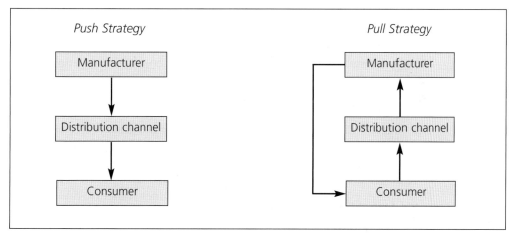

Most manufacturer activity consists of both push and pull elements used simultaneously.

The promotional devices associated with a push strategy include:

- promotional allowances
- incentive programmes
- point of sale
- co-operative advertising
- contests and competitions directed to the trade
- merchandise allowances
- retrospective bonuses
- management assistance such as staff training
- category management
- trade shows, etc.

Techniques associated with a pull strategy might include:

- sampling
- money-off incentives

- coupons
- contests and competitions
- premiums, etc.

Consumer franchise building

It is important to make a distinction between promotions that simply provide a short-term incentive to purchase and those which are designed, in some way, to support brand attributes or benefits. The latter would be considered to be franchise building since they are used to maintain a brand's image.

Stewart and Gallen (1998)[25] suggest that consumer franchise building (CFB) is the basis of building strong brands. The basis is that the ratio of advertising to sales promotion is the major determinant of a brand's CFB ability.

Similarly, Richards (1998)[26] argues that customer loyalty is the major key to long-term brand success. The author argues that the consumer's relationship with the brand is a far more important basis for the development of a long-term commitment than the simple provision of short-term incentives.

Bunyard (1999)[27] argues that whilst advertising is effective at sustaining brands, it is less successful in building business growth. He suggests that a high level of sampling prior to exposure to the advertising message is an important contributor to the changing of consumer expectations regarding the brand.

Quester and Farrelly (1998)[28] also emphasize that the best promotions are those that reinforce positive activities, such as consumer franchise-building promotions.

Davies (1997)[29] argues that customer loyalty should be a key consideration within any marketing strategy. As markets mature it becomes increasingly difficult and costly to recruit new users to the brand. It, therefore, becomes imperative to ensure that those who are attracted to the brand remain with it and that their commitment builds rather than depletes over time.

The development of sales promotion strategy

In order to select the appropriate sales promotion strategy it is important to follow a series of steps, as follows:

1 Consider the corporate framework within which promotional activity takes place.

   For sales promotion to contribute effectively, it must be considered within the framework of the overall strategy for the brand. Failure to recognize this, and considering sales promotion in isolation, may result in there being a conflict between the sales promotion plan and the brand strategy.

   De Chernatony and Dall'Olmo Riley (1998)[30] considered the role of brands and the implications for marketing communications. They conclude that brands are important for both companies and consumers, but stress that the way that brands are handled, particularly in their use of marketing communications, needs to be considered in the context of their longer-term value to the organization. This is important to ensure that there is no conflict between promotional activity and the longer-term images desired for the brand.

Davis *et al.* (1992)[31] are amongst those who support the notion that promotions need not have a negative impact on brand evaluation. They re-measured brand evaluations after a 3-month period and saw no evidence that the memory of the promotion lingered to drive down brand evaluations and concluded that there was no negative effect on repurchase probabilities.

As Miller (1998)[32] stresses, finding a synergy between the brand and the promotion is vital. Adding value to a brand via sales promotion can be very effective, but it requires lateral thinking from the agencies.

2   The prevailing economic conditions.

Promotions have different effects dependent on the economic environment in which they are operated. At times when money is tight, promotions that offer extra value in the form of money off or extra product free are more likely to achieve the overall objectives. However, at times of economic growth consumers may seek other elements from promotional offers. At such times promotions that offer added value in the form of free gifts or competitions may enhance the enjoyment of purchase.

3   Identify the overall promotional objectives.

What objectives is the promotion intended to achieve? Can these be met within a single execution or does it require several devices to be used in tandem? Only by determining the specific objectives in advance will it be possible to identify promotional executions to meet those objectives.

4   Identify the specific target audience(s) for the promotion.

Is the promotion designed to reach consumers, the trade, the sales force or all of them? Promotions have different impacts on different groups of consumers, for example. Understanding the nature of the target audience will enable the selection of promotional executions that meet the specific needs of those target groups.

Moreover, promotions designed to appeal specifically to the trade will be different from those that appeal to consumers. Equally, it is important to consider how the promotion will be received by the trade. Unless they actively support the promotional activity, it is unlikely to achieve the desired success.

Hallberg (1995)[33] describes the Pareto principle as the idea that 80 per cent of a brand's volume is accounted for by 20 per cent of its buyers. The Pareto principle can be applied to sales promotion. Brand benefits invariably derive from the top third of category buyers. A brand's greatest potential for increased profitability derives from the ability to increase penetration and share amongst this high profit, heavy category buyer.

5   Consider the nature of the product, usage patterns, position in the market place and the stage in the product's life cycle.

It is important to consider the patterns of consumption and the reasons underlying the purchasing decision. If the company can develop a deep understanding of the nature of purchases in its category it will be more able to utilise promotions strategically to achieve broader based goals.

Products that are bought on a frequent basis are more likely to respond, for example, to promotions that reward loyalty. If the interval between purchases is extended, it is more likely that consumers will forget a promotional offer associated with the first purchase.

There is a particular need to break inertia purchasing; many consumers purchase the same product out of habit. These consumers need a relevant incentive to get them to switch. This is especially important if consumers can be encouraged to appreciate the benefits of new brand since they will be more likely to remain with it after the promotion is over.

Sometimes, in this context, it will be desirable to reinforce existing purchasing decisions. Many products, especially those that are purchased on a regular basis, will tend not to be re-evaluated. The consequence is that the underlying reason for purchase will not be remembered. Promotions can be designed to reinvigorate the brand in the minds of existing consumers or to provide them with a further rationale for continuing to purchase the brand.

According to Graeff (1995):[34] 'The relationship between the product and the consumer must be identified at the early stages of developing promotional strategies.' In order for a promotion to work effectively, it must fit with consumer perceptions of the brand and be relevant to them.

The stage that the product occupies in the life cycle will also be an important determinant of the effectiveness of promotional activity. Different executions will be associated with different stages in the life cycle and should be selected appropriately.

Similarly, Swait and Erdem (2002)[35] argue that consistency within the marketing mix (for example, selling an upscale product through an upscale retailer) and promotion mix (implementing sales promotions in conjunction with the overall communication strategy to enhance rather than dilute brand equity), as well as between the individual components, is generally considered essential for successful marketing strategy.

6   The cost of the activity.

It is equally important to consider the financial consequences of the promotional activity. This is particularly important in the context of the overall profitability of the brand. A company may choose to sacrifice short-term profits in order, for example, to gain market share. This raises the important issue of whether promotions need to generate profit within the period of the promotion itself. This will be determined by a consideration of the overall objectives.

If the company has decided to use sales promotion they have to predict whether the increased profits as a result of the promotion they are running are high enough to warrant the expense of running the promotion. Failure to do this could mean a waste of both time and money for the company.

However, sacrificing short-term profit in order to encourage sampling of the brand may achieve longer-term benefits. The consumer may need the additional incentive in order to move from their present brand. If they can be persuaded of the benefits of the new brand they may decide to remain with it after the promotion is over. Whilst this is an obvious need in the case of a new brand, it may be equally relevant to overcome consumer resistance to an established product.

Hardy and Magrath (1990)[36] identify a series of possible promotional strategies that can leverage expenditures:

1   Concentrate spending regionally in order to create special promotions by territory
2   Enter into promotional alliances in order to develop a synergy that enhances the promotional value to the consumer
3   More promotional spending closer to the point of purchase in-store
4   Piggyback promotions on an existing event

To these can be added two further possible promotional strategies:

5   Encourage consumers to trade up in pack size
6   Provide and associate new values with the brand.

Ehrenberg *et al.* (1991)[37] have demonstrated that the majority of consumers who purchase products during periods of price promotion are, in fact, already users of the product and are simply taking advantage of the reduced price.

In a paper presented by Leigh McAlister and James Lattin (1983)[38] the authors identify different types of brand purchaser and suggest the viability or otherwise of promoting to each of the segments. Their results are summarized below:

Table 5.2

Segment	Likelihood of promotional profitability
Brand loyal consumers – do not use deals	Never profitable
Brand loyal consumers who use deals to stock up on their favourite brand	Never profitable
Brand loyal, but will switch brands as a response to a promotional offer	Occasionally profitable
Brand loyal who will stock up on favourite brand, but will switch for a better offer	Occasionally profitable
Brand switchers who are not loyal and do not use respond to offers	Never profitable
Brand switchers who purchase on the basis of promotional offers	Occasionally profitable
Brand switchers who use an offer to select the brand and to stock up	Occasionally profitable
Consumers who only purchase on the basis of a promotional offer	Always profitable
Consumers who only purchase on the basis of a promotional offer and stock up	Always profitable

McAlister and Lattin (1983)

Several studies have concluded that constant use of promotions serves to weaken consumer perceptions of the brand. If the product is almost continuously on promotion, consumers will avoid paying the full price. Since promotions, particularly those that are price-oriented, focus the consumer's attention on the price, the inevitable consequence is that this will become the sole focus of consumer purchasing behaviour, over-riding other product dimensions.

Whilst a number of studies have suggested that sales promotion is unlikely to achieve sustainable competitive advantage, there are some notable exceptions, e.g. BA Airmiles, Tesco ClubCard, etc. The essential ingredient is the extent to which the organization utilizes integrated marketing communications to ensure consistency in both the execution and the message delivered to the target audience.

There is a responsibility to adopt a strategic approach towards sales promotion rather than a tactical one, as has been prevalent for some time. Internal factors, however, such as organizational structure and reward mechanisms, tend to mitigate this. Most companies reward their marketing departments (and others) on the basis of their achieving short-term sales targets. This, inevitably, results in the predominant use of short-term tactical promotions that are capable of generating immediate and mostly short-term sales volume.

Sales promotions must be consistent with the longer-term organizational goals. This involves close participation by senior management in the identification of promotional objectives and the internal evaluation of executions. All too often the determination of sales promotion campaigns is left to comparatively junior members of the marketing team. Sadly, many have little regard for the longer-term sustenance of the brand values and look to promotional activities that, as noted above, are consistent with the creation of short-term sales volume.

Whilst sales promotion has, traditionally, been regarded as the province of FMCG, it is increasingly evident within services and business-to-business marketing. The unique benefits attached to the use of sales promotion mean that the techniques are increasingly being adopted across the entirety of the marketing arena.

For example, the *Sunday Times*, a newspaper that regularly uses sales promotion techniques linked up with J.W. Spear (the owners of Scrabble) to run a 'scratch and win' game over several weeks. Each issue contained a series of numbers on the game card which were to be scratched off to reveal letters. Players then used these letters to make words on the special 'Scrabble' Board. A total of £75 000 was offered as prizes.

Similarly, *Classic FM Magazine* offered a free CD attached to the front cover of Driving Classics, whilst *Glamour* magazine offered a free summer bag. Banks offer incentives to new university students to sign up for their current accounts. These range from free rail cards to CDs and other gifts.

Long-term effectiveness of promotions

We can make a series of descriptive statements about the long-term effectiveness of sales promotion:

1   Sales promotions can enhance the brand or cause it damage. What determines the impact will be the nature of the promotion selected to fulfil the defined objectives.

2   Repeated price promotions tend to undermine the image of the brand. Price promotions result in consumer orientation towards price rather than other aspects of the brand proposition.

3   Consumers tend to associate frequent price reductions with reduction in product quality.

4   The consequence is that consumers tend to plan purchases against expected price reductions.

5   There is a significant difference between promotions specifically designed to achieve short-term impact and those that are considered as part of a longer-term strategy.

6   Other forms of promotional activity are more likely to offer the opportunity to enhance brand imagery and create positive associations in the minds of consumers.

7   Some forms of sales promotion can alter consumer perceptions of the brand and its values.

8   Sales promotion is an important facet of the communications armoury. It enables a brand to achieve both short-term and longer-term goals.

Case study

JEEVES
Agency: Triangle Communications Ltd

Background

Ask Jeeves is a web search engine that aims to provide unique functionality by enabling users to ask a question and receive an answer in plain English.

Promotional objectives

The primary objective of the promotional campaign was to encourage frequency of usage amongst existing users of the website. There was also a desire to build a database of participants.

Promotional strategy

- To develop a promotion based on the unique functionality of the Ask Jeeves website.
- Encourage usage of the site.
- Promotional activity directed towards all online search engine users.

Campaign summary

Users of the Ask Jeeves website were offered the opportunity to win £1 million if they asked a question that exactly matched a pre-identified question. Once they had registered on the site they were able to ask a maximum of fifty questions each day. Every question asked was entered into a weekly draw that provided the opportunity to win one of the runners-up prizes, which included holidays, a car and tickets to Wimbledon tennis.

The more questions each participant asked, the greater the chance of winning one of the prizes on offer. The promotion itself was run on a fully dedicated microsite accessed from the main site.

Existing Ask Jeeves users were e-mailed with details of the promotion on the launch day.

Brand support

The campaign was provided with media support on commercial radio and in London newspapers. An e-mail campaign was also mounted in support of the promotion.

Results

- The number of questions logged on the Ask Jeeves site increased by 32 per cent during the promotional period.
- The number of visits to the site increased by 7.4 per cent.
- Over 1000 people registered on the site.

The promotion was awarded a gold in the Interactive Media Promotions in the 2002 ISP Awards.

(The above case study is adapted from articles that appeared in *Promotions and Incentives* magazine.)

Questions

1 Identify some companies (other than those mentioned in the text) that use sales promotion on a regular basis.

2 Why are strategic issues important in the context of sales promotion?

3 What do Peattie *et al.* mentioned above suggest are the strategic applications of sales promotion?

4 Why do we need to distinguish between 'push' and 'pull' strategies?

5 What are the factors to consider in the development of a sales promotion strategy?

6 Developing the sales promotion plan

Chapter overview

An important aspect of developing sales promotion activities is the plan itself. There are several important factors to be considered and no plan can work effectively unless it results from a comprehensive analysis of the situation in which the brand finds itself.

This chapter considers the various elements of the plan and suggests a format to be adopted. Whilst this is not the only approach that can be taken, it is a format that has served the author well over several years in the development of sales promotion programmes.

Learning outcomes

- To consider the dimensions of the sales promotion plan process
- To examine methods of determining the sales promotion budget
- To consider the use of sales promotion agencies
- To identify the methods used for selecting a promotional agency.

Developing the plan

Since the sales promotion plan is an integral part of the overall marketing plan it is important that the marketing plan forms the basis of all sales promotion planning. In most instances the marketing plan will be developed independently of the sales promotion plan but the imperative is that all sales promotion activity seeks to fulfil the overall objectives contained within the marketing plan.

As with all forms of marketing communications, the development of a sales promotion plan is a sequential process and all aspects must be considered before it becomes possible to identify an appropriate promotional solution.

There are several stages to the overall planning process.

Figure 6.1

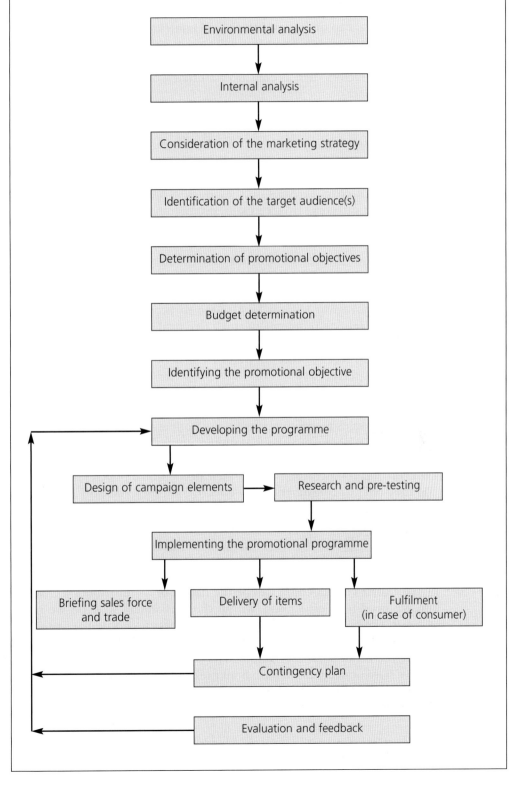

Environmental analysis

It is important to understand the broad context in which promotional planning is to take place. Although a great deal will already be known about the brand and its position in the market place, it must be recognized that the market itself is somewhat fluid. Changes in factors such as consumer attitudes, competitive activity, retail changes, etc. may all impact on the brand position.

Not only do we need to understand the position we occupy in the market, we also need to consider how we wish to be perceived by consumers. Sales promotion can contribute to strengthening or changing that position and can also be used to modify consumer perceptions.

We need to develop our understanding of the customer dynamics: who are our customers, what characteristics do they possess and what are their specific needs from our product category? How can sales promotions contribute to an improvement in our position?

A significant factor will be the nature of the purchasing profile: why do consumers buy the products they do, why do they purchase our products or those of our competitors? Understanding considerations such as the frequency of purchase will impact on our ability to run particular forms of promotional activity. A product that is purchased on a regular basis is best suited to promotions that reward high frequency. Setting redemption requirements for a free mail in, for example, will be affected by the regularity of purchase. If the product is purchased only infrequently, the amount of time taken to collect proofs of purchase may be so long as to be impractical from the consumer's perspective.

Equally, given the ability of promotions to target marginal consumers (those who are less likely to be exposed, for example, to media advertising) it is important to recognize that sales promotion may be the perfect vehicle for attracting such consumers to the brand. Moreover, these consumers are potentially very profitable to the brand.

We also need to consider competitor dynamics. Not only do we need to understand who are the competitors, but also their promotional policies. What sort of promotions do they offer to consumers? How effective are they and how can we utilize sales promotion to achieve a greater level of impact on the target market? What we don't want to do, in an ideal situation, is to run a promotion that is very similar to those run by competitors. This will only serve to blur the differences between our product and theirs. If we can identify a promotion that is different, we can establish a distinctive edge in the market place.

A further consideration will be the nature of the distribution chain. What channels do we need to consider and, within those channels, who do we need to motivate? Clearly, markets differ significantly between particular product categories. Understanding the nature of the channels of distribution and our relationships with them will be an important guiding factor in promotional development. For example, do we have or need to establish better relationships with the major chains? What is the role of wholesalers and do we need to motivate their staff to give greater support to our brands?

Internal analysis

According to Ailawadi *et al.* (2001)[1] a company's promotional policy influences its ability to attract and retain customers by inducing more of them to:

1 switch to the firm's brand
2 repeat purchase it more often, or
3 consume larger quantities.

There will be a number of internal factors that affect our ability to implement promotional activity effectively. We need to consider, for example, where our product is in the product life cycle. Products at different stages of the product life cycle react differently to the various promotional executions. In turn, this will affect the objectives that we establish for promotional activity.

The stage of the product life cycle for a brand captures consumer demand and competitive intensity in the marketplace. In the two early stages of a product's life cycle (introduction and growth), advertising is used to inform consumers about features and benefits, to strategically position a brand and to build awareness. Previous research (Farris and Buzzell 1979)[2] found that advertising spending was positively related to the introduction and growth stages of the product life cycle and negatively related to the maturity stage. During the mature phase of the product life cycle, intense competition can also lead managers to shift funds away from advertising and into promotions as they attempt to take market share from competitors.

As brands progress through the product life cycle, managers plan to allocate proportionately less of their marketing communications budget to advertising and more to consumer and trade promotions. In addition, lower relative price brands and family brands typically receive an allocation that emphasizes sales promotion relative to advertising. These product/market factors appear to be commonly used guidelines that managers rely on in making their allocation decisions.[3]

We need to consider the various production issues involved in the implementation of a sales promotion. Are there, for example, specific production factors that need to be taken into account? In many instances, the primary vehicle used to communicate promotional offers will be the packaging. Does this impose limitations on what we can do? Is the surface area of the product label capable of carrying sufficient detail to communicate effectively to the target audience? It is likely that there will be other limits imposed by packaging. Can we, for example, band several products together or do we require to order in special packaging in order to offer the consumer an increased volume of product for the same price? What impact will this have on the ability to maintain current production levels? Some companies possess special machinery to ensure that they are able to cope with what might be considered as 'special production runs'. In other instances, such promotions can only be mounted at a significant cost to output.

What are the time factors involved in designing new labelling or obtaining alternative packaging? Can we insert a free gift item inside the packaging? Do we have machinery that can cope or will we need to make special arrangements? Are there restrictions on what we can do, imposed by the regulatory bodies for our specific sector? Some professional bodies preclude specific forms of promotional offer and so on.

Connolly and Davidson (1996)[4] stress the importance of packaging design in consumer motivation. Pack design offers the opportunity to set the brand apart from the normal design codes that have been adopted for the category. They conclude that packaging design is a crucial element within the marketing mix. This has significant implications for promotional activity, since the pack is often used as a main (sometimes the only) communication device for a promotional message. The ability to incorporate a promotional message without compromising the identity of the brand is a critical component of the original pack design. Successful brands continue to communicate their over-riding brand values whilst providing incentives to induce consumer purchases. Coca Cola is particularly successful in this respect.

Then we need to consider the way in which the promotion will be sold in to the trade. What is the nature of our sales force and what is their role? Many companies maintain a slender sales force that visits retail outlets only on an infrequent basis. Is it possible for them to establish contact with all outlets within the necessary timeframe to ensure that the promotion is universally available? Perhaps we need to employ the services of some external sales force from a broking agency, or a field force company to assist in the process of delivering and erecting point-of-sale material.

Consideration of marketing strategy

The point has already been made that sales promotion activities must be consistent with the overall marketing strategy. Not only do we need to understand what the marketing strategy is designed to achieve, we must consider the role of sales promotion within the overall strategy. It is likely that there will be advertising support running behind the brand? Can we develop promotions that reinforce the advertising message and that are consistent with the overall brand platform?

The target audience

Turning to the target audience, we need to identify clearly which customers we intend to motivate. We may choose to target all consumers for the brand or, alternatively, we can select a smaller segment of those consumers. We might, for example, wish to target non-users of the brand or to reward existing customers. These alternative targets will require different promotional executions and different methods of distributing the promotion to ensure that it reaches the right people.

We need to identify the underlying reasons for the behaviour of the chosen target audience in order to ensure that the promotional execution is appropriate to either the reinforcement of that behaviour or changing behavioural patterns if that is the requirement.

Finally, we need to define what are we intending to achieve with the promotion. What is the desired outcome and how will the chosen execution deliver it?

Objectives

As with other forms of marketing communications, it is important to set precise objectives for the activity. Is the promotion expected to increase trial and sampling or reward loyal users? Not only must the objectives be specific they should also be measurable. What level of trial is to be generated: 10, 20 or 30 per cent or higher? If no value is given to the objective, it will be extremely difficult to determine whether the goal has been achieved on its completion!

Walters (1989)[5] suggests that priority should be given to promoting products that have received little promotion for some time, as this increases the likelihood of both retailer support and consumer participation.

Krishna (1991)[6] makes the point that the consumer's perception of the frequency of deals is an important factor in determining the impact of those deals. Whereas others, such as Gurumurthy and Little (1987),[7] have shown that the more frequent the level of promotional deals, the smaller the market share gained by those brands, she argues that perception of frequency is the main determinant of promotional success.

We will consider the nature of sales promotion objectives in more detail in the following chapter.

Budget determination

Although the specific budgets can only be identified once the promotional execution has been determined, it is important to identify the scale of the budget (appropriation) that will be allocated to the activity.

Promotions broadly fall into three distinct categories:

1   Fixed budget promotions: where the total cost of the promotional activity is known in advance. Some promotions, such as money off or free product, have absolutely fixed costs. It is possible to calculate in advance the value of the discount or the cost of the free product and multiply this by the total number of packs that will carry the offer. To this can be added the ancillary costs such as trade and sales force incentives, point-of-sale material, sales aids, etc.

2   Partially fixed cost promotions: where many of the costs are known in advance, but where some costs are variable with the volume sold on promotion. With a competition format, for example, the value of the prize structure can be pre-determined, but the costs of handling entries will be dependent on the number received.

3   Promotions with totally variable costs: some promotions such as those involving coupon distribution will be totally dependent upon the number of consumers redeeming the coupon. Although estimates can be made, based on previous experience or pre-testing, the outcome will only be known once the promotion has been completed and the final redemption levels isolated. The same is true of promotions that involve the consumer collecting proofs of purchase in order to redeem a free gift.

Predominantly, sales promotion activity is volume related, hence the ability to predict the sales impact is vitally important. Two facets are important:

1   The understanding of the buying process

2   Previous experience of the response to promotional activity either on the same brand or with other brands within the company's portfolio. This knowledge will enable a more accurate prediction of the likely levels of participation in the proposed promotional activity.

According to Low and Mohr (2000),[3] manufacturers continue to allocate almost 75 per cent of their marketing communications budgets to these short-term activities. The advertising vs sales promotion budget allocation is defined as the relative budget amount allocated to advertising compared to the budget amount allocated to sales promotions (consumer and trade). Since advertising and sales promotion can be used to achieve similar marketing objectives in different ways, managers are faced with a difficult decision when allocating funds between them.

There are many reasons for the interest in the factors that determine promotional expenditure. For example, if a linkage could be established between market conditions and promotional expenditure, then management would be able to predict the necessary adjustments that would be required to suit changing market dynamics. Similarly, modelling promotional expenditure may permit a firm to predict the promotional activity of competitors.

The marketing literature suggests that there are at least five generic methods of determining the appropriation for the promotional budget. Stewart (1996)[8] identifies the objective task method, the percentage of sales method, comparative parity, the marginal approach and, finally, the 'all you can afford' approach. While some of the above methods may be superior to the percentage of sales method, the latter does offer some advantages. First, it is extremely simple to implement. All that needs to be known is an appropriate measure of revenue and an acceptable percentage for the firm. Second, it ensures that sufficient sales have been generated to cover the costs of promotional activity. Finally, in mature markets, many changes are predictable (or at least there is less uncertainty); consequently, it may be more appropriate to use a 'formula' to determine the size of the promotional budget in these markets. However, it should be said that the percentage of sales method has a serious logical flaw, in that it suggests that sales determine promotional expenditure, rather than vice versa.

Identifying the promotional strategy

As White (2002)[9] argues, once objectives have been determined, the type of promotion can be decided on and a budget developed that should deliver the desired result and ROI . The detailed planning should be developed with the aid of a database of past results for both the brand and the company.

Having determined the objectives, the next stage is to identify the potential solution. We have already seen that a number of promotional techniques can achieve similar objectives. Selecting the appropriate promotional technique is a vital part of the process.

Manufacturers use many different kinds of consumer promotions (coupons, direct-mail, free-standing inserts, on-pack, peel-off, in-pack premiums, rebates, contests, and price packs) to attract customers to their brands. In planning promotion campaigns, brand managers in major consumer packaged-goods firms face decisions about which promotional vehicle to use in a particular product category. As Zhang et al. (2000)[10] state, an important aspect of this choice is to decide whether to use immediate or delayed value promotions. Peel-off coupons, FSI coupons, direct-mail coupons and price packs provide consumers with an immediate benefit upon purchase or a front-loaded incentive. However, in-pack coupons, on-pack coupons, contests and loyalty programmes require repeat brand purchases and reward the consumer on a future purchase occasion, i.e. a rear-loaded incentive.

The multi-period sales promotion design problem involves designing a series of promotions mailed periodically to a group of potential customers. Here the aim is to maximize the multiple purchases of a group of people over time. Another way of looking at this problem is that we are trying to increase customer lifetime value by creating dynamic, customized incentives to encourage a customer to more frequently make purchases.

Sales promotions, in general, are meant to stimulate stronger target market response than would otherwise occur without the promotions. They can originate with the manufacturer and be directed at the retailer or consumer or be targeted at the consumer by the retailer. Manufacturer-to-retailer promotions or trade promotions are often in the form of cash, advertising or trade allowances. Manufacturer-to-consumer promotions might consist of coupons, mail-in refunds or free samples. Retailer-to-consumer promotions often take the form of discounts, free gifts and contests.[11]

Porter (1993)[12] argues that any offer, special promotion, price reduction, etc. offered by mail order may be more effective when coupled with some 'conditions' that allow the customer to earn the offer, e.g. completing a survey, a scratchcard, etc.

All sales promotions are, in one way or another, restricted. The promoter may limit the amount of product carrying the offer, the time during which the offer is available or the people entitled to claim the offer. Tan and Chua (2004)[13] suggest that the restriction need not be communicated explicitly to the potential consumer: offering a price discount will be limited but the retailer or brand owner does not have to say so and can simply withdraw the offer and return to full price.

Experimentation and research are both important in this respect. In some instances the company may not have previous experience in the running of a particular form of promotional activity yet does not want to risk everything on the outcome of an untried execution. Test markets (both real and simulated) and market research can contribute to the gaining of an understanding of the ways in which particular promotions affect the brand without the risk of endangering the brand position.

Developing the promotional programme

Pre-costing the promotion must be an important element of the process. Perhaps, with the usage of market-research techniques, it will be possible to identify the likely take-up of a consumer free gift offer or coupon promotion.

At the very least it will be important, for budgetary reasons, to be able to anticipate the likely costs of the exercise. In the case of merchandise offers, it will be important to ensure that adequate quantities of the items are available to meet expected levels of consumer demand (avoiding consumer disappointment), and at the other end of the spectrum, not to over-order and thereby be left with unused stocks of the free gifts.

Feary (1998)[14] states that ensuring the right mechanics are selected to optimize consumer response mean that the sales generated are incremental and will not compromise future sales. Moreover, expected sales can be forecast accurately enabling supply chain efficiencies to be achieved. If the response of the consumer to different promotional mechanics is understood, then the most appropriate promotion can be selected for each product. Continuous evaluation techniques allow the impact of different activities to be isolated and the relative merits calculated.

Design of campaign elements

Creativity and timing are both important dimensions of the plan. The aim is to develop executions that achieve visibility for the brand in a crowded retail environment. The promotion must ensure that the offer is noticed and the brand stands out from its competitors. Often, it is the specific execution of the promotional offer that will make the difference.

Research and pre-testing

Pre-testing is important to determine the likely take-up of a promotional offer. Whilst the principle remains firmly established, the reality is that comparatively few promotions are tested prior to implementation.

There are several aspects of pre-testing to be considered:

1 Exposing the promotional concept to members of the target audience
2 Comparing alternative propositions
3 Relating proposed activity to the known outcomes of previous promotional campaigns.

In some instances focus groups comprising members of the target audience may be used to assess the relative merits of alternative promotional executions. Their reactions to different propositions will guide the planning process and ensure that the chosen execution is the most likely to achieve the desired objectives.

Quantitative research may also be used in order to assess the likely levels of participation and, in turn, enable a more accurate costing to be undertaken prior to the promotion being fully implemented. There are several options in this context.

If the scale of the promotion warrants, the company may organize a test market within a selected area of the country. All of the elements of the promotion will be introduced to a limited area to assess the level of impact. Only if the results are positive will the promotion be introduced on a national basis. Alternatively the promotion may be mounted in a limited number of retail outlets. These store tests enable a similar assessment of the likely impact. In both instances, it is important to remember that it is essential to gain the co-operation of the retail trade. The tests will only be valid if the stores that accept the promotion are representative of the national picture.

Implementing the programme

Control mechanisms must be established at the outset to ensure the smooth implementation of the promotion. How will the company respond to changes in the levels of consumer demand: is there sufficient manufacturing capacity, for example, to cope? What happens in the event that the promotion goes wrong: are there adequate monitoring procedures to identify what is going on in the market place, etc.?

Briefing sales force and trade

If the campaign is to achieve the maximum effectiveness, it must be sold in to the trade. This involves ensuring that the sales force is properly equipped to achieve this aspect of the campaign. Meetings will be needed between the marketing department and the sales department to identify the specific requirements. Sometimes companies will convene a special meeting of the sales force to explain the promotion and its objectives. Often, some form of incentive will be developed for the sales force to reward them for achieving specific targets. Certainly, the sales force will require special material in the form of sales aids to ensure that they can explain the workings of the promotional mechanics and its benefits to the trade.

In turn, the sales force will arrange meetings with key trade customers to ensure that the requirements are fulfilled. This may involve the provision (and, in some instances, the erection) of special point-of-sale material to support the promotion.

These activities will require a considerable amount of pre-planning and sufficient time must be allowed for this important part of the promotional cycle to be fulfilled.

Delivery of items

Where the promotional offer involves the provision of merchandise arrangements must be made to ensure that adequate stocks are available to meet anticipated consumer demand.

Similarly, promotional support materials must be available for delivery to the trade prior to the commencement of the promotion.

Fulfilment

It is rare that a company will handle the fulfilment of consumer offers. Usually a specialist handling house will be appointed who will deal with consumer requests or collate competition entry forms and the like. Again, this requires pre-planning and represents a cost against the promotional offer that must be included in the budget.

Contingency plan

Whilst great care will be taken in the development of a promotional programme, it is impossible to predict some aspects. Accordingly, pre-planning is essential to identify what will be done in order to correct any difficulties that occur during the implementation of the activity.

It is rare that a plan will be implemented without changes. Bear in mind that the plan itself is determined in isolation of the market conditions that obtain at the time of implementation. Often it will be necessary to change elements of the plan to meet unforeseen circumstances. There may be some change in the competitive environment, for example, that needs to be responded to. A new brand introduction, especially if offered at a lower price, might impact negatively on the effectiveness of the planned promotion. Alternatively, some competitive action might similarly negate the power of the promotion. Not only must such market changes be responded to, it is vital that there is money within the budget to enable the necessary changes to take place.

Evaluation and feedback

Finally, once the promotion has been implemented, the results must be carefully measured. These will add to the database of knowledge held by the company and will be useful in the planning of subsequent activities.

Stewart and Gallen (1998)[15] similarly identify the stages required in the promotional planning process:

1 Define the problem and set objectives. The marketing problem is defined and promotional objectives are set that are consistent with the company's overall goals and objectives.
2 Appraise the overall situation. Consider the specifics within the context of the overall problem.
3 Determine tasks and identify means. The various tasks necessary to achieve the promotion objectives are determined and the promotional tools to achieve the tasks are identified.
4 Identify alternative tasks and promotional mixes. Different ways to combine the promotional tools are identified.
5 Estimate the expected results. Estimates are made of how well each alternative mix will achieve the promotion objectives.
6 Review the alternatives and identify the specific plan.
7 Implement the agreed promotional plan.
8 Obtain feedback and audit the results of the promotional activity.
9 Adapt the programme if necessary.

Pre- and post-promotion sales dips have been the subject of increased attention in academic papers (Neslin and Stone 1996, Van Heerde *et al.* 2000).[16,17] A reason for this is that they are potential indicators of consumer stockpiling and deceleration. Stockpiling is the propensity of consumers to increase their inventories above normal levels either by purchasing the category earlier or by purchasing greater-than-normal quantities. Deceleration is the willingness of consumers to deplete their inventories below normal levels by holding out for an anticipated promotion. These behaviours are important because they reflect sophisticated planning by consumers. From managers' perspectives, such behaviours influence profitability because they decrease the incremental sales generated by promotions.

Consider the role and function of planning within sales promotion

Once the province of advertising, it is increasingly recognized that the role of the planner is equally valid within the context of sales promotion. As it is increasingly acknowledged that the impact of sales promotion activities is as much on the image of the brand as it is on short-term sales, so too there is a recognition that the wider implications of activities need to be considered prior to implementation.

The planning function is designed to gain an insight into the behavioural patterns of the consumer and provide guidance to the appropriate selection of promotional mechanics.

Budgeting for sales promotion

Various methods of budget determination have been suggested and the issue is one of deciding which approach is right for the situation.

The determination of the marketing communications budget cannot be considered in isolation. It is merely a part of the overall budgeting process that affects all aspects of the company's operation. Ultimately, any company must ensure that it remains in profit (at least in the longer term) if its business is to remain viable. As such, there will be a number of demands on the company's income and capital reserves. It may be necessary to improve the quality of production, which will require a significant investment in plant and machinery; to augment the sales force in order to achieve better distribution for the products it manufactures; to invest in research and development to ensure that the brand portfolio is maintained and is successful in a competitive environment, and so on.

Sales promotion, in this context, is part of the overall marketing budget. Inevitably, companies must consider the variety of demands for expenditure from a wide range of different sources, and demands for expenditure on advertising and other forms of marketing communications must compete with all these other areas. Arguably, the most important 'competitor' for funds comes from the desire to maintain a competitive price at the point of purchase. Inevitably, if prices are reduced, either to the retailer or the end consumer, there will be a consequence for the overall level of revenue. In many companies, the source from which expenditure is most likely to be withdrawn is that of advertising and other forms of marketing communications.

As noted earlier it is unlikely in the majority of instances that sales promotion will operate in isolation of other forms of marketing communications activity. Accordingly, it is essential to consider the totality of the marketing communications effort in the budgeting process. A balance must be achieved between the expenditure on sales promotion and that on other forms of marketing communications. Ultimately, the consideration must be the extent to which the marketing communications programme is capable of achieving the desired objectives.

A major consideration will be the level of competitive activity and the extent of pressure from the distribution channels. In general, sales promotion will tend to receive a larger share of the overall budget in those situations where a brand's competitors are heavy users of sales promotion and where there is pressure from distributors for promotions within the product category.

The anticipated levels of response from both consumers and distributors are important in the determination of likely costs. Unlike some other forms of marketing communications, the cost of sales promotion activity is directly related to the level of sales.

A key task is that of determining an effective approach to the setting of a budgetary level. It should be clear that the determination of the correct level of expenditure must depend on proper analysis of the situation, rather than the use of 'norms', rule of thumb or 'gut-feeling'.

The following section sets out most of the ways used to determine the budget.

Marginal analysis

Several attempts have been made to transfer the learning from the principles of economic theory to that of budget determination. In essence, the principles of marginal analysis suggest that a company should continue to increase its marketing communications expenditure until the point where the increase in expenditure matches, but does not exceed, the increase in income that those expenditures generate.

This can be shown graphically, as follows:

Figure 6.2

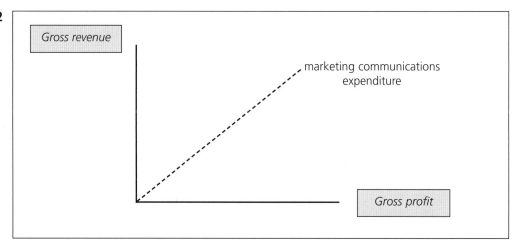

Unfortunately, the application of the theory of marginal analysis does not transfer readily into real-world situations. The first problem to deal with is the fact that the theory assumes that sales are a direct function of marketing communications expenditures. Whilst it is possible to postulate situations in which this might be the case, for example, in the area of direct marketing, even here this may be somewhat wide of the mark. The level of expenditure is only one of the variables that need to be considered. The theory makes no attempt to consider either the location of the activity in terms of, for example, media placement or the copy content of the advertisement or sales promotion tool. It simply assumes that every pound spent is likely to achieve the same impact on the market. Clearly, other marketing activities will have an impact on the level of achievement that will render the formula almost incalculable.

Importantly, most marketing communications activities rely on a built-in time lag. Even in the area of direct marketing, where a more precise correlation can be established between patterns of expenditure and achievement, it will be necessary to make an allowance for other indirect variables. The nature of the message, its placement, the competitive environment and other factors will all have to be allowed for if the theory is to stand up in practice. Certainly, until the advent of rapid response computer programmes the amount of detail that would need to be built in to such a calculation proved unwieldy at best.

Several attempts have been made to build econometric models against which to 'test' different levels of expenditure. Suffice it to say that at best they provide some guidance as to the likely impact of the proposals in the real world.

Percentage of sales

Probably the most widely used method of budget determination is the calculation of a ratio between past expenditure and sales, sometimes referred to as the advertising/sales ratio. The calculation itself is quite straightforward. The previous year's expenditures are calculated as a percentage of total sales and the resultant figure is used to calculate the budget for the coming year. Thus, if £12 million worth of sales was achieved against a communications budget of £300 000, the percentage would be 2.5%. Assuming that the sales forecast for the coming year was £15 million this would yield a budget of £375 000. Whilst the process is a quick and easy one, there are flaws in the argument.

In the first place, the data used will be considerably out of date by the time it is implemented. Since we do not have a full picture of current year sales, we must rely on, at best, the latest 12 months for which we have information on which to base our calculations for next year's activity. Secondly, it creates a situation in which the budget only increases against an expectation of higher sales. If sales are expected to decline, then the future communications budget must be reduced to bring it into line with the defined ratio. The inherent danger is that a brand that is under threat and losing volume actually reduces its budgets rather than increasing them. Thirdly, it fails to recognize that marketing communications activity can create sales volume for a brand. The application of the principle, in fact, operates in reverse, with sales being the determinant of expenditure levels.

However, it does demand a close examination of the relationship between the costs of marketing communications, the price charged for the product and the level of profit that is likely to be generated. This is particularly important when considering the specific nature of the ratio to be applied to the calculations. It may be possible, for example, to examine competitive ratios to determine whether the company is operating at, or near, the norm for the product sector.

The most important consideration, however, remains the basis on which the ratio itself is established. Many companies set a norm that is rigorously applied. In some cases, it becomes the established company practice and though it may have been determined after a full consideration of the competitive environment, the conditions obtaining at the time of setting the 'norm' will have changed considerably over time. The problem with this approach, therefore, is that there is a tendency to ignore many of the other important variables that may have a direct bearing on the possibility of achieving the desired objectives. Unless the ratio is regularly and consistently reviewed, it may become irrelevant to the contemporary situation that the brand faces.

Percentage of product gross margin

This approach is, essentially, similar to the previous one except that the gross margin rather than the level of sales is used as the basis of calculating the future level of expenditure. Here, a percentage of either the past or expected gross margin (net sales less the cost of goods) is used.

It has particular relevance to brands with comparatively low production costs set against high unit prices. The manufacturers of such products will be concerned with maintaining the size of the margin, as much as with unit sales volume. The consequence will be to enable such brands to spend more on marketing communications than would necessarily be the case with an A/S ratio in order to maintain their premium price in the marketplace.

As with other ratio methods, it is extremely easy to apply once the specific relationship has been established. But it carries with it many of the same advantages and disadvantages discussed above in the context of the percentage of sales approach.

Residue of previous year's surplus

This method is entirely based on prior performance whereby the excess of income over costs in the previous year is designated as the budget for the following year. Although simple in principle, it clearly demands that a surplus is achieved in order for monies to be spent in any future period. It fails to recognize the need for investment in growth brands or, for that matter, the impact of competitive activities.

Percentage of anticipated turnover

This approach is based on the allocation of a fixed percentage of future turnover to the marketing communications budget.

Unit–case–sales ratio method

This method, sometimes referred to as the case rate, requires that brand volumes for the next year are estimated and a fixed sum per unit is allocated towards marketing communications expenditure. It is then a simple process of multiplying the expected sales volume (in units or cases) by the fixed allocation to arrive at a total communications budget. In some instances, comparisons are made between the company's own case rate and those of its competitors to explore the relationships between them.

Obviously the approach is a simple one, but it begs the question as to how the case rate itself is calculated. In some instances it may be based on past experience. Usually it is a company or industry norm. Here again, as with other ratio-based approaches, expenditure patterns reflect past achievement or anticipated sales. As such it tends to benefit growth brands and disadvantage those which are declining. It ignores the fact that a brand that is suffering in the market place may need to increase its levels of expenditure to arrest the decline, rather than reduce the budget which would be the automatic result of applying the method.

Competitive expenditure

Another approach, frequently used, is to base the brand's expenditure levels on an assessment of competitors' expenditures.

Often a calculation is made of the level of category expenditure and a percentage, usually related to a brand's share of market, is chosen as the basis of calculating that brand's expenditure levels. In other instances, an attempt is made to achieve parity with a nominated competitor by setting a similar level of expenditure to theirs. At the very least, this approach has the benefit of ensuring that brand expenditure levels are maintained in line with those of the competition. However, it suffers from the obvious difficulty of being able to determine an accurate assessment of the level of competitive spend.

Whilst it is obviously possible to obtain a reasonable fix on advertising spend from published information the same is not true of sales promotional spend, and other categories of marketing communications. Expenditure figures for sales promotions are rarely published.

Moreover, it fails to recognize that the expenditure patterns of a competitor may well be dictated by a totally different set of problems and objectives.

Objective and task method

This method is based on a more realistic examination of the specific objectives that the marketing plan needs to meet and was established as an attempt to apply a more scientific approach to budget determination. The basis of the approach was a paper commissioned by the American Association of National Advertisers and published in 1961.

It offers the benefit of being able to monitor the campaign achievement against the targets set and provides a more accurate guide to budgetary determination for the future. The limitation on the accuracy of the method is the ability to access sufficient information to ensure that all of the relevant variables can be considered. Although the original paper dealt specifically with the task of establishing advertising budgets, the method is equally applicable to other areas of marketing communications.

Experimentation

A guiding principle for budget determination, as with other aspects of marketing, is the need on the one hand to protect the company investment whilst, on the other, ensuring that sufficient new and innovatory approaches are taken to drive the brand forward. It is for this reason that most major marketing companies utilize an experimental approach at various times. Having established the overall marketing communications budget by the normal or most appropriate means, it is possible to create a mini 'test market' for the purposes of experimenting with a variation. By isolating, say, one region of the country, it is possible to experiment with alternative budget constructions. In many cases and in the absence of definitive data it is useful to determine the impact of, for example, an increased level of media expenditure or of a particular sales promotion technique.

The benefit of this approach is that the main sources of business are 'protected' in the sense that they receive the 'normal' support levels. Hence, the position of the brand is not unduly prejudiced. By 'hot housing' a different approach, real experience can be gained and the budgetary process enhanced with the additional knowledge. It is an attempt to apply an empirical approach and, thus, a more scientific method to the process of budget determination. However, it is important to restrict the number of 'experiments' in order to ensure that the data are readable against the norm and that the individual variables can be properly assessed within a real market environment.

What we can afford

This approach is based on a management assessment of either the brand itself or the overall company position. In effect, management determines the level of profit desired, or the return on investment, and the marketing communications budget is the amount that remains after calculating that level. Of course, it fails to recognize the contribution of marketing communications itself and ignores other environmental factors, such as competitive pressure, which might mitigate against the profit level being achieved. Although this is a somewhat arbitrary approach to the budgetary process, it has to be recognized that the issue of affordability plays an important part within any financial procedures. There will always be competing demands for funds within the company: to support the activities of other brands within the portfolio, to fund areas such as production capability, to finance research and development, etc. It is a fundamental role of management to determine company priorities and to allocate funds accordingly.

One important dimension of budget planning is the concept known as 'lost revenue analysis'. In this context it is important to identify the break-even point of the promotional activity. This requires a calculation of the number of units that need to be sold to cover the cost of the activity.

As Paul Polman (1997),[18] the then UK MD of P&G, stated:

> Two thirds of promotions actually lose money and many only break even. Marketers are investing vast amounts of money in an area that doesn't enlarge market share, appeals only to a minority of consumers, encourages consumer disloyalty and reduces market value.

Similarly, Abraham and Lodish (1990)[19] argue that following an analysis of 100 separate sales promotions, only 16 per cent are profitable.

Campbell and Dove (1998)[20] pursued a similar analysis of AGB Superpanel data. The repeat purchase rate was around 40%; however, the percentage of first purchase of a product under promotion was only 10%.

In a paper by Roger Strang (1975),[21] the author attempts to identify the reasons for the differences in the levels of advertising and sales promotional expenditures:

1 Lower levels of promotion relative to advertising are associated with those brands that:

- have a higher profit contribution rate above the company average
- have a high level of brand loyalty
- have a strong competitive differentiation
- have a high degree of perceived risk associated with purchase
- are in the growth and maturity stages of the product life cycle
- have a large market share.

2 Higher levels of promotion relative to advertising are associated with brands that:

- have a profit contribution rate below the company average
- have little brand loyalty

- have little competitive differentiation
- are directed towards children
- are purchased with little planning
- are at the introductory or decline stage of the product life cycle
- have a marked seasonal sales pattern
- have a small market share
- face promotion-oriented competitors
- are in a market where private labels are important.

Although it remains difficult to be precise in estimating the incremental sales resulting from sales promotion activities, Abraham and Lodish (1990)[19] attempted to provide a model based on scanner data. They argue that the traditional wisdom has been that a successful promotion is one where the company sells a lot of its products to the trade and that a promotion for an established brand can be used to attract and retain new users for the brand.

Their work, based on the performance of different brands in 65 product categories, suggests that the productivity of promotional spending is poor. They claim that only 16 per cent of the trade promotions they studied were profitable. They assert that the cost of selling an incremental dollar of sales was greater than one dollar!

For many years attempts have been made to identify the major determinants of promotional expenditures across industries. Ailawadi *et al.* (1994)[22] conducted a major study in order to isolate the important variables. They concluded that the ratio between promotional expenditures and sales are not a function of share and growth. However, the method continues to be favoured as a measure of budget determination despite being less sophisticated than other approaches because of its ease of implementation.

Under-funding a promotion in order to contain costs or to fund several smaller promotions ignores the fact that there is a critical level required to ensure interest in the deal. A research study of 108 successful and 108 unsuccessful promotions carried out by Hardy (1986)[23] revealed that under-funding was one of the major causes of failed promotions.

According to Low (1999)[24] the most common way that brand managers set budgets is to start the same as last year.

Sales promotion budgets are set and allocated as part of the annual brand planning process. In many firms, a brand team approach is used involving managers from sales, trade marketing, manufacturing and market research as well as brand managers. Managers first establish the overall strategic direction for the brand and set marketing objectives, based on an extensive situational analysis. This is followed by the preparation of financial projections based on forecasts and projections for the coming year.

He asserts that inherent in the budget allocation process is the conflicting nature of the accountabilities of the various people involved in the process. Marketers want to see their brand thrive and prosper over the long term. However, they are also required to meet quarterly and annual profit expectations of senior management. The sales force is, generally, compensated on the basis of volume sold and, inevitably, will press for an increase in sales promotional budget allocation.

The legal and regulatory framework

The field of sales promotion is governed by a number of both voluntary and legal requirements. The major practitioner bodies have jointly established guidelines for the implementation of sales promotional activities. The British Code of Sales Promotion Practice is published by the Committee of Advertising Practice (CAP) and the Institute of Sales Promotion (ISP) and provides an indication of best practice for the structuring of all forms of promotion. Both of these are available online and are an essential basis for the planning process.

Promotional activity is also embodied in a number of Acts of Parliament and other directives. Amongst these are the Gaming Act of 1968 and the Lotteries and Amusements Act of 1976, which specifically set out the requirements for competitions and lotteries; the Trading Stamps Act of 1964, which requires that any vouchers offered must have a cash value printed on them; the Financial Services Act of 1986 and the Sales of Goods Act, to name but a few.

Under normal circumstances, it is the Local Trading Standards Officer that polices pricing and trading issues, and investigates claims of unfair or illegal promotional practice. Price claims are the most frequent of the promotions issues. The various controls provide that:

> Any price offer should be clear and not contain hidden extra charges; the promoter should avoid implying that the price is less than it really is; and where there is some form of restriction on the nature of the offer, for example, money off next purchase, both parts of the offer should be made clearly and distinctly in the same typeface and size; where some form of comparison of value or worth is made, then this must be justified in a way that consumers can understand.

Trading Standards

We have seen that an alternative to money-off promotions is to provide additional 'free' product. These extra value claims must be justifiable and conform to the same basic rules as for price claims. It is important to note that in some product categories there are restrictions that govern the packaging sizes that must be used, e.g. the Weights and Measures (Miscellaneous Foods) Order 1997 largely prohibits extra value on a wide range of food products.

It is vitally important that the codes of practice and legal frameworks are adhered to closely. Apart from the adverse publicity that may attach to an 'illegal' promotion (programmes like *Watchdog* often feature promotional activity that, it feels, acts against the consumer's interests), it must be remembered that the Local Trading Standards Officer has the power to demand the removal from distribution of any packs that carry an illegal offer.

The rules governing the implementation of promotional activity are currently under review. A green paper on Commercial Communications, published by the EU, is designed to ensure a greater degree of harmonization between the member states: 'People have realised the importance of making a realistic estimation of consumer take-up and getting promotions legally checked.' The Hoover case highlights the necessity of getting promotions checked by the relevant experts. According to Susan Short, secretary-general of the ISP, even before the Hoover row erupted, the ISP was taking at least 10 calls a week requesting legal and copyrighting advice from people launching sales promotions. After Hoover, that number increased to 25 per day.[25]

The ASA even revised its code of practice as a result of the Hoover affair. It now states that no promotion should bring the industry into disrepute.

During 1999 the High Court handed down a ruling that potentially could have resulted in the banning of instant-win promotions. In the case of Russell vs Fulling and Page, the Court found that a scheme in which retailers handed out scratchcards with an instant-win prize in fact constituted an illegal lottery since such mechanics would only be acceptable providing there was a genuine, realistic and unlimited free route to entry. The situation was clarified by the CPS in August 1999, which reinstated the position that had previously operated in which companies could operate instant-win promotions, providing there was a clear opportunity for consumers to play without making a purchase.

Using sales promotion agencies

Whilst it is entirely possible to mount sales promotional activity in-house, in the majority of instances it is likely that companies will turn to specialist expertise to assist in the development of sales promotion solutions. The last 20 years have seen the emergence of several specialist agencies and consultancies in the field, who have built up a substantial body of knowledge and experience that can be brought to bear in the identification of a sales promotion solution.

In its annual survey of sales promotion consultancies, *Marketing Magazine*[26] lists the top 45 sales promotion companies, with turnovers ranging from £23.5 million (Proximity turnover 2003, 267 employees) to £165 000 (GCAS sales with five employees). Clearly, therefore, the range of agencies is enormous and so too are the variety of services that might be provided to their client companies. These will depend on the specific requirements of the client base but are likely to include:

- strategic and advisory inputs
- the development of consumer and trade promotions
- promotional design and artwork production
- copywriting services
- print design and buying
- the sourcing of merchandise
- the design and development of sales literature
- promotional administration, implementation and evaluation.

Somewhat more specialized services might include:

- project management
- event management
- sponsorship

- staff motivation schemes
- co-ordination between suppliers
- locating and negotiating with third party contracts.

Several companies operate exclusively within one or more of these latter areas.

At the top end, agencies including Proximity, The Carlson Marketing Group, The Marketing Store and Haygarth Group (ranked 1 to 4 in 2004) offer a totally integrated promotional facility and the ability to provide almost all related facilities in-house. At the other extreme are a series of smaller consultancies, which aim to provide a responsive and fast service to their clients, but which have relatively few internal resources. For the most part they maintain low staff levels and tend to buy in all or many of the services required.

Between these are the specialist agencies that operate in a niche promotional area. Some will specialize in sports sponsorship, others in conference organization and management, some in event creation and management, some in field sales operations, etc.

Selecting promotional agencies

The identification of a partner with whom to work is an important process since the company will want to secure the best talent at the best possible price. The starting point in any agency selection process must be the definition of the services that the client requires them to provide. Different agencies fulfil different specialist roles and it is important to isolate which services will be required. The range is certainly broad enough to provide the flexibility to meet any circumstances. Agencies work both in the strategic and the tactical context. The process itself follows a series of distinct stages, as follows:

1 Identify a list of agencies to be considered.

Since there are a wide variety of agencies that might be considered, it is important to identify the specific requirements at the outset. Agencies sometimes specialize in particular forms of promotional activity and it is necessary to determine whether the particular services are appropriate to the client's needs. For example, an agency skilled in the development of specialist areas (for example, pharmaceutical promotions) may not be relevant to the development of effective consumer-based promotions.

The trade press will be an important starting point for the review, providing up-to-date information on the performance of likely agencies. Similarly, it will be important to contact current and previous clients in order to obtain the views of others who have worked with them.

The scale of the agency will need to reflect the scale of the company and the nature of the promotional inputs it requires. Do they have the necessary scale of resources to deal with the company's requirements? Can they operate in a variety of countries, if appropriate?

A further issue will be that of remuneration. Agencies derive their profit in two ways. By charging a fee and making a mark-up on the services they provide. Charges usually relate to the scale of activity in which they are involved. Some will work on ad hoc assignments or on a project basis, whilst others will only operate against a retainer income. The company needs to be satisfied that the method of remuneration is consistent with the way in which it wishes to do business.

Whilst comparatively few promotions agencies can boast a truly global network, this does not preclude their involvement in global or pan-European promotional activity. A critical issue is finding a way through the minefield of legal and other restrictions. The diversity of regulations that apply even within member states of the EU make the area one of great difficulty. There are, obviously, several ways around the problems. Some practitioners draw on the resources of the legal profession, although this is a potentially expensive route. Those that have links within other countries can seek advice from them on the rules governing implementation. A third route, often overlooked, is the fact that, by definition, a company seeking to develop a promotion for broadscale implementation will itself have operations in each country in which the promotion is designed to run. These offices can often provide the necessary input, to ensure not only that the proposed activity is legal but, perhaps even more importantly, that it takes account of the local differences in culture and practice.

2   Arrange a credentials presentation.

Agencies will be happy to meet with a prospective client and present a series of case histories of promotions run for other clients. The past work and experience of the agency will be important considerations. Some agencies offer specialist skills and knowledge and may well have worked within the market sector on a previous occasion.

Apart from seeing what they have achieved, it is also an important opportunity to meet with the agency personnel. As with any form of agency/client relationship the 'people skills' are an important factor and it is important that you visit a number of agencies to get to know the personalities involved; relationships with agencies are dependent on people factors. These meetings will provide them with the opportunity to set out their credentials and, hopefully, to identify the personnel who would be working on your business, should they be appointed.

Such a meeting will also enable an assessment of their staff and the nature of the service the agency provides to its clients. To what extent will the company deal with the management of the agency or will it be serviced by less senior employees? What specific qualities and experiences will the team bring to the relationship? In addition, since this area, as much as any other within the marketing communications business, depends on the relationship between people, what are their interpersonal skills and is it likely that a positive chemistry will be established between them and the company?

3   Check out agency background, client lists and, if possible, references from existing clients.

The credentials meeting will provide a great deal of useful information upon which decisions can be based. Not only will it be possible to see their current work, it will also be possible to identify their clients. Some of these may be contacted later to identify their levels of satisfaction with the agency and its ability to deliver effective promotions on time and on budget, both of which are important considerations.

It is also advisable to check out whether agencies are members of the professional body (in the UK this is the ISP) together with any awards that they have received for previous promotions developed for their clients.

4   Define a shortlist of candidates.

It will now be possible to select a small number of potential candidates for the business. It is advisable to restrict this number to about three or four, both because of the time involved in seeing presentations as well as the recognition that these presentations cost the agency considerable sums of money to develop.

In some instances, the selected agencies will expect to be paid a rejection fee in the event that they are not chosen to handle the business. If this is the case, the scale of the rejection fee will need to be identified.

5   Provide them with a comprehensive brief of promotional requirements.

The agency can only develop effective promotional solutions if it is in full possession of all the relevant information that will guide the creative process. Agencies will mostly be prepared to sign a non-disclosure document to protect any confidential information that they will require.

Most often the brief will take the form of a written document, although there should also be opportunities for the agency personnel to meet with the company to discuss any further issues and to indicate their need for additional information. Again, these sessions will provide a useful guide to the nature of the agency, the executives with whom the company will work and to explore the interpersonal relationships that might follow.

6   View the presentations.

The agency responses to the brief will provide useful guidance to various facets. Have they demonstrated a clear understanding of the nature of the brief and provided a rationale for their proposals? Have they costed out their proposals fully? Did they discuss the implementation and evaluation of their proposals? What will be the basis of their remuneration? Different agencies operate in different ways and it is important that the company understands how the agency will derive their income from the outset.

Will the agency charge a fee, for example, and will the fee be related to the specific promotion or will it be part of a retainer over an extended period of time? Will the agency mark up the costs of materials that it purchases on your behalf and, if so, at what rate?

Whilst it is important that the agency is appropriately recompensed for the work involved in developing a promotion, nothing is more disconcerting for a client than to discover at some later date that the agency has charged unrealistic mark-ups for such things as promotional items, print costs, etc.

Mishon (1998)[27] highlights the changing basis of promotional agency remuneration. Where, previously, agencies derived their income from relatively low fees together with a mark-up on promotional items, there has been a progressive shift towards total fee income. The difficulty remains, however, that promotions continue to be the domain of relatively junior members of the marketing department whose concern more often relates to the price of the service rather than the quality and relevance of what is provided.

7   Evaluate the presentations against identified criteria.

In order to ensure consistency in the evaluation of the presentations, it is important to define specific criteria for the purpose. Does the proposal fit with the strategic direction of the brand? Is it likely to enhance consumer perceptions or does it conflict with the current brand position? What is the agency expected to deliver and how will they charge for their services? How will they operate the account: for example, who will be the direct contacts between the company and the agency?

8   Select the agency and establish a written contract.

Once the agency has been selected, it is important to agree a contract for their services. This will cover many of the points covered above, but also provide for such things as the agency remuneration in the event that the promotion does not run. The agency will have to put in a great deal of work and if the promotion is cancelled for some reason will expect to be paid for that work.

At the same time, it is important to consider issues such a copyright and exclusivity of the promotional execution. This may become important if the company is happy with the promotional execution, for example, but feels that the agency does not provide the appropriate levels of service and wishes to appoint an alternative agency to handle subsequent implementations.

Equally it is important to communicate with the losing agencies to explain why they have not been awarded the business. They too will have put in a great deal of effort in developing their recommendations and deserve to understand the reasons behind the company's decision to place the business elsewhere.

Finally, if a rejection fee has been agreed for the unsuccessful agencies, it is important that this is paid as partial recompense for their efforts.

A survey of some 47 client users of sales promotion conducted by *Campaign Magazine*[28] identified several important factors in the selection of a sales promotion consultancy. Critical to the decision-making process were three dimensions:

The need to maintain regular contact with clients	87%
Have a proven track record in the client's sector	85%
Principals and directors are readily accessible	81%

Somewhat further down the list of priorities were the following:

They are conveniently located	55%
They offer a wide range of services	39%

Case study

THE HOOVER DEBACLE

Arguably the most written-about sales promotion, the consequences of which resulted from the implementation of a flawed device, is that mounted by Hoover. In 1995 the company offered free flights to New York to any consumer purchasing a Hoover model costing more than £100. The initial response was no less than spectacular. Not only were retailers inundated with consumers purchasing the Hoover brand, advertisements were appearing in newspapers offering slightly used vacuum cleaners from purchasers who had done so simply to take advantage of the offer.

The fundamental problem was the calculation of the likely redemption levels. Their estimates were wildly inaccurate anticipating 5000 responses against the actual redemption levels of above 600 000! The company had made the simple mistake of comparing the free offer with others that had provided two flights (or holidays) for the price of one.

Moreover, they contracted the offer with a small travel agency that simply could not fulfil the demand and that subsequently went bankrupt. This left the company responsible for fulfilling the massive demand for free flights.

Newspapers and television were quick to publicize the failings of the promotion with regular articles featuring dissatisfied consumers who had made the required purchase but who were unable to secure their flight tickets. The negative publicity continued for several years after the promotion was eventually withdrawn, re-invigorated with the outcomes of the many court cases that were pursued by unhappy customers who sought compensation.

It is estimated that the promotion eventually cost the company around £48 million. In addition, those responsible for creating and implementing the promotion left the company, their careers in tatters, whilst the impact on the image of the company was devastating. Many retailers reported that they were unable to sell their stocks of the brand and refused to order any more.

The lack of understanding of the mechanics of the promotional offer and the requirements for its implementation cost the company dearly. Important conclusions can be drawn from the Hoover disaster.

1 It is vital to gain a clear understanding from the outset of the likely uptake of a promotional offer.

2 The mechanics of the promotion must be fully checked in advance to gain a clearer estimate of the implications.

3 It is possible to take out insurance policies to cover the costs of unexpected redemptions.

4 Companies must ensure that they have a contingency plan in place to deal with the unwanted publicity that inevitably follows disasters of this nature.

The important point to note is that there is nothing fundamentally wrong with the promotional offer itself, simply the implementation. Indeed, BT Broadband recently offered a similar 'free flights' offer to new subscribers.

Questions

1 Why is it important to have a structure for the sales promotion plan?
2 What are the important areas that require investigation prior to the development of a promotional solution?
3 Why is the determination of a budget an essential ingredient of the planning process?
4 What are the methods that might be used to identify an appropriate budget?
5 Why is a consideration of the legal and regulatory factors essential prior to the implementation of a promotional plan?
6 What role do promotional agencies play and what services might they provide?

7 Identifying sales promotion objectives

Chapter overview

Sales promotion can achieve a great deal within the context of a marketing plan. However, to maximize its impact it is essential that the planner is clear as to the objectives that require to be fulfilled. Not only are there fundamental differences between the various objectives that might be set, each of these can be fulfilled by the use of different sales promotion techniques. Matching the technique to the objective ensures that the most effective campaign can be implemented.

Learning outcomes

- To understand the role of objectives within the sales promotion context
- To consider the role of objective setting
- To identify the different consumer objectives that sales promotions can meet
- To identify the different trade objectives that sales promotion can meet.

Although sales promotion has an important role in the context of ensuring the speedy achievement of sales objectives, to consider sales promotion in this way is somewhat limiting. It is clear that the techniques available are capable of fulfilling a wide range of different objectives.

The necessity of setting objectives and goals in the creation and implementation of promotional activities is widely agreed. Generally accepted formats for goal-setting usually involve setting consumer-based communication goals. Promotional communication goals may be more necessary than ever with increasing competition and increases in non-advertising promotional techniques, such as couponing and other point-of-sale techniques. As marketing continues to focus on making customers rather than sales, there is increased attention on how all marketing efforts build and maintain relationships with customers.

First and foremost, communication-based goals centre on the consumer's hierarchy level (i.e. the potential buyer's current stage in the purchase process) rather than on sales measures alone. While no one would deny the importance of sales and profitability, by themselves they tell us nothing about what led to the sale or whether or not a particular customer is satisfied. As Jones (1994)[1] states, without a customer focus, a company has no idea of which aspects of a promotional campaign (e.g. advertising, merchandising, promotions) were successful. Not knowing what works also means that a success may not be reproducible.

The last 15 years have seen a substantial increase in the share of marketing budgets taken by promotions, as the spread of scanners has enabled weekly analyses of sales and demonstrated the ability of promotions to create short-term sales 'spikes', which advertising typically cannot match. This has fed the need of brand managers to provide short-term results to meet increasingly tough targets.

An important distinction needs to be made between the words 'objectives' and 'strategy'.

The objectives define the desired outcomes of the sales promotion programme, i.e. what the specific promotion is designed to achieve. Moreover, it is important that whatever the objective is, it should be capable of measurement. It is important to understand that if the objectives are not given dimension, then it will be impossible to determine whether they have been met, at the end of the promotion. It is not sufficient to state that the promotion will increase sales (by how much?) or take share from competitors. Since sales promotion is a tool of the overall marketing programme, it is important that the sales promotion objectives are related to the marketing objectives. These are specific goals or targets that the marketing programme seeks to achieve. As such they might specify targets of profit, sales, margins, market share, etc. It is imperative that the sales promotion aspects of the plan relate directly to these marketing goals.

Sales promotion strategy represents the means by which the objectives will be met. It states how the objective will be met but does not include the specific details of the sales promotion that will be mounted.

A further word that is used is 'execution'. Sales promotion execution is the specific detail of the promotion that will be implemented. In other words it describes the promotional offer made to the consumer or the trade in detail.

However, before exploring the nature of objectives, it is important to establish the key principles behind the establishing of the objectives themselves:

1   Sales promotion objectives must be defined clearly and succinctly.

It is vital to define precisely what is expected of the campaign and over what duration it will be run. Few promotions are open-ended and a time scale must be established for the fulfilment of commitments. Promotions that, for example, are designed to establish consumer loyalty will cause consumer alienation and will, almost certainly, fail if the time scale is too far beyond normal consumer purchase patterns. Equally, establishing a promotional period that is too short for the consumer to achieve the goal with their regular level of purchases will similarly result in consumer hostility. Whilst this may not be expressed, it may, nonetheless, result in consumers deciding to abandon the particular brand (or promotion) in favour of one that is perceived as being more achievable. By the same token, however, promotions should not be allowed to continue for too long a period of time as they will lose the enthusiasm of the retail trade.

2 Sales promotion objectives must be capable of measurement.

Some numerate value must be attached to the objective. Is the campaign, for example, designed to achieve a 40 per cent level of trial, or re-purchase amongst 25 per cent of existing users? Not only will this establish the parameters for the campaign, it will also enable a proper evaluation once the campaign has been completed. By monitoring the results, it will be possible to determine whether the objectives have been met or exceeded, over what time scale the results have been achieved and the cost effectiveness of the expenditure.

Apart from the immediate benefit of evaluation, the process will add to the sum of knowledge to ensure the efficient use of resources and the selection of the most appropriate techniques in the future. This is an important facet of promotional planning. Many companies build up a 'database' of experience in the promotional field. Previous experience of the impact of specific promotional formats will enable them to predict, with a reasonable degree of accuracy, the likely outcome of a new implementation of that format.

3 Sales promotion objectives must be achievable.

There is an inevitable temptation to set grand objectives for any form of marketing communications activity. Whilst it obviously makes sense to establish real targets, it is also important that they are felt to be realistic within the constraints of the budget available, the organization's structure and the competitive environment. A promotion that, for example, sets unrealistic targets for the number of sales force contacts will, inevitably, fail. By the same token, a reduction in the on-shelf price of a particular product will only achieve consumer impact if it is meaningful. Reducing the price by one or two pence is unlikely to result in large increases in the levels of offtake.

4 Sales promotion objectives must be realistically budgeted.

Few companies have a bottomless financial pit. Almost all activity will be constrained by budgetary limitations. It is imperative that the objectives are related to the financial resources and not set at an unrealistic level.

By the same token, it is important that the organization is aware of the likely cost impact of the achievement of the objectives. All promotions cost money and if the level of consumer demand for the promotional offer exceeds the level of affordability the consequence will be disappointed consumers and a failure to meet the requirements of the campaign. The alternative if consumer demands are to be satisfied is that the cost of mounting the promotion will far exceed the available budget. The Hoover experience is a perfect example of such an outcome. More recently, Walkers Crisps offered a free mail in of a pedometer. According to *Promotions and Incentives* magazine (2005)[2] the company based its cost estimates on a redemption level of 700 000. By the end of the promotion the actual redemption level is expected to be over 2 million. Although consumer demand for the free item has been met, it has resulted in long delays in consumer fulfilment and satisfaction.

A considerable level of consumer alienation will inevitably follow the withdrawal of a promotional device if substantial numbers of consumers have collected vouchers or other proofs of purchase but been unable to collect sufficient to redeem the incentive offered.

To these broad principles can be added further guidelines to assist in the development of effective sales promotion activity:

1 Appealing to the target audience.

   We have already seen that gaining an understanding of the target audience is an essential component of promotional planning. As part of this understanding, we also need to identify which promotional executions appeal to the defined target audience.

2 Easy to understand.

   The promotional execution should be readily understood by the target consumers. Overly complicated rules and incomprehensible instructions will limit the appeal of the promotion and result in a shortfall in consumer participation.

3 Cost effective to implement.

   The promotion should be capable of achieving the objectives within the budgetary constraints. It is important to understand the nature of redemptions to eliminate (as far as possible) those consumers who would have purchased the product without the promotional incentive. Whilst this cannot be achieved fully, it will be important to ensure that the cost of the promotion allows for this element of 'wasted' costs.

4 Simple to administer.

   By the same token the promotion must be easy to implement. In most instances promotions involve third parties that handle consumer and trade redemptions, reimburse retailers (in the context of coupons) and so on. The process needs to be considered in advance to ensure that it is as straightforward as possible.

5 Consistent with the brand image.

   Promotions must seek to build upon the existing brand image and, where possible, to enhance it. Promotions that are incompatible with the desired brand positioning and image will undermine consumer perceptions.

6 Capable of integration into other activities.

   Promotions should be capable of complete integration. Whether this involves consumer advertising or other forms of marketing communications activity, they should be capable of adaptation into appropriate executions to maximize their impact. An example is Nescafé Cappuccino's running of an on-pack competition offering the opportunity to win a £10 000 spending spree with Trinny and Susannah who feature in the brand's TV commercials.

7   Provides unique benefit to associate the promotion with the brand.

In order to enhance consumer perceptions of the brand, ideally any promotion should be capable of providing some point of difference to enable the brand to differentiate itself from its competitors. In some instances it might be possible to offer the consumer some form of branded merchandise as part of the offer that will endure after the promotion itself has been completed. Over many years, various manufacturers have offered 'container premiums' such as the Ariel Soap Powder container or other forms of reusable packaging. Similarly, Coca Cola have offered branded glasses that live on to remind the consumer of the brand long after the promotion is over.

8   Not susceptible to immediate competitive response.

Obviously, money-based offers are simple for competitors to match speedily. Mounting a promotion that is not only distinctive, but which differentiates the brand from its competitors restricts the likelihood that competitors will be able to match the promotion rapidly.

Undeniably, used properly, the extensive range of sales promotional techniques enables companies to fulfil a wide range of objectives. Below, we will consider some of the objectives that specific sales promotion campaigns can achieve. As has previously been established, some sales promotions can be designed to achieve defined consumer objectives, others trade objectives while some executions are designed to achieve both.

Consumer objectives

Promotional activity can be used to create a sense of urgency in consumers, persuading them to stop comparing alternatives and buy earlier, or in greater quantities than would otherwise have been the case. If consumers believe that a price reduction will only be available for a comparatively short period, they may be induced to 'bulk buy' to the obvious benefit of the brand. This is an increasing facet of the retail environment with some major supermarkets, for example, offering periodic 'three for the price of two' offers to achieve this objective. It is for these reasons that temporary promotions often produce greater sales increases than equivalent price cuts.

A further application of the technique is to place price offers or coupons within a specific advertising campaign. This can serve to enhance the impact of the advertising message and convey a brand benefit as well as price information. The mobile telephone market is a good example of this application of the promotional device.

Promotions may also be used to convey specific brand information by stimulating trial use. The consumer is informed of a specific product benefit, perhaps through advertising, and their interest in the feature or benefit is heightened at the time of usage. It is important to recognize that sales promotions enable manufacturers to communicate directly with those consumers who are specifically stimulated by an 'offer' and encourage the switching between brands. Particularly in today's pressured purchasing environment it has to be recognized that many consumers use promotional pricing as a simple rule of thumb for making the purchase decision.

According to White (2002)[3] promotions can fulfil a wide range of objectives. Arguably the main ones are to:

- Encourage trial by new buyers
- Encourage loyalty among existing buyers
- Counter or pre–empt competitive threats (e.g. by stocking retail shelves, or consumer cupboards, before a competitive launch or new campaign).

In addition, some types of promotion can be used, for example, to

- Build and work a customer database
- Ensure that the brand is adequately stocked and displayed by retailers.

Consumer objectives might include those outlined below.

Promoting trial amongst new users

A key area of sales promotion rests in its ability to generate product trial and sampling, either of an existing or a new product. A properly constructed promotional offer will have an immediacy of impact that will attract the potential consumer. Here, the key requirement is to overcome consumer objections to using the product, most often associated with risk. By reducing the consumer's level of risk, the desired levels of trial can be achieved. Most commonly, price-oriented promotions are used for this purpose, although an alternative expression of price reduction (additional free product) will have a similar impact.

Targeting a specific market

Sales promotions can be used to appeal to specific segments of the overall market. These might be segmented on the basis of geography, or use demographic or psychographic approaches to encourage take-up of the promotional offer.

Rewarding existing customers

Sales promotion can be used defensively to restrict the levels of competitive encroachment. In an increasingly competitive market, manufacturers seek to restrict the number of their customers defecting to a rival brand. It may be possible, for example, to use promotional activity to encourage multiple purchases by existing users of the product. By ensuring that they have adequate quantities of their brand the promotion takes the consumer out of the market for a period of time and restricts the possibility of their purchasing an alternative product.

Attract new users to the brand

An alternative approach is to encourage non-users of the brand to try it or to attract users of a competing brand. Here, sales promotion can provide an additional incentive to try the product.

Stimulate repeat purchase of the product

The generation of repeat purchase and, in the longer term, the establishment of consumer loyalty to a product, is a major facet of sales promotion activity. Such promotions can be targeted specifically to recent trialists, for example, to encourage them to purchase on another occasion. Long-term promotions are frequently used to provide an overlay to the purchase that provides the consumer with a valid reason (over and above the specific product benefits and performance) to purchase the brand on a number of separate occasions. However, it is important to recognize the work of Ehrenberg *et al.*,[4,5] mentioned previously, in this context.

Encourage more frequent purchase

A similar requirement will be that of increasing the rate and frequency of purchase. This objective may be achieved by the presentation of new usages for the product or the suggestion of new use occasions. Kellogg's ran a television campaign that suggested that 'breakfast' cereals are also appropriate for consumption at other times of day.

Sales promotion offers the potential to identify new uses for the product. Devices such as recipe cards are commonly used to encourage the consumer to use the product in new and different ways.

Sometimes the desired objectives may be fulfilled by overcoming the consumers' 'out-of-stock' situation.

Several major newspapers, including the *Telegraph* and the *Times* have, at various times, distributed money-off vouchers to encourage consumers to purchase the particular title at reduced price for an extended period of time. The *Daily Telegraph*'s and *Sunday Telegraph*'s offer during the year 2000 lasted for 14 weeks. This enabled consumers to purchase the newspaper for 20p on weekdays and for 35p at weekends. For consumers participating for the full duration of the campaign, a saving of £32.20 could be made against the regular cover price. By extending the duration of the promotion the owners hoped that the campaign would encourage a regularity of purchase that would be continued even after the promotional offer was withdrawn.

Encourage multiple purchases

Various offers such as banded packs (three for two; buy five and receive an extra product free, etc.) are all designed to encourage the consumer to make multiple purchases on a single buying occasion. Research has demonstrated two major benefits associated with such promotions.

In the first place, there is evidence that the consumer will use more of the product since they are confident that they have more in stock. By encouraging multiple purchase of a product, the manufacturer will also achieve more frequent usage because the product will be there when the consumer requires it. Findings from a field experiment conducted by Chandon and Wansink (2002)[6] together with scanner data demonstrate that stockpiling causes people to consume products at a faster rate.

Equally, having several items in their store, consumers are taken out of the market for an extended period of time and, hence, are unavailable to competitors.

Encourage the consumer to trade up in size

Often, particularly at the time of the introduction of a new product, the manufacturer will make available a smaller size of the product for trial purchases. Subsequently, however, they will wish to encourage the consumer to purchase larger quantities. This will be encouraged through the use of a variety of promotional techniques.

At the very least, the manufacturer will ensure that purchases of the product are brought forward. As with promotions that encourage multiple purchases, this may also be accompanied by a greater frequency of use simply because the product is immediately available to the consumer. In addition, as with the increasing of the frequency of purchase, the manufacturer removes the consumer from competitive attack for a period of time.

To introduce a new product

sales promotional techniques, because of the immediacy of their impact, are conventionally used at the time of a new product introduction. Often, either through the use of successive promotional executions or the specific nature of the execution, the manufacturer will provide incentive for the consumer to pass through the various initial stages of the product life cycle.

Many new products are introduced to the market each year. However, the vast majority of them fail! Estimates suggest that as many as 90 per cent of all new products fail during their first year. In many instances, these failures are attributed to the lack of promotional support given to the product after introduction. For any new product it is vital to encourage a sufficient level of trial and subsequent re-purchase amongst those who have bought the product previously.

Sales promotion can make a unique contribution in this respect, providing an incentive to encourage initial purchase and to minimize the risks involved in making that purchase. Subsequently, consumers may be encouraged to make repeat purchases as a direct result of the incentives provided, with the objective being to establish a level of loyalty to the product or, at least, to ensure that the brand is included within the consumer's purchasing repertoire.

This approach is commonly seen in the partwork market. Publishers invariably offer the first issue of a collectable magazine at a specially reduced trial price in order to induce the initial purchase. The price is raised for subsequent purchases, although the price increase may be gradual in order to establish a pattern of repeat purchases. When the item achieves its 'going' price, many people will have become sufficiently interested in the series to continue with their collections.

To overcome seasonal variations in sales

Many brands exhibit a distinct seasonality in which sales fluctuate as a result of patterns of purchase. Promotions can be used to make the brand more attractive at times when seasonal purchasing is likely to decline and even out the spread of sales across the year.

Brand switching

A primary goal of many sales promotions is to encourage consumers to change their purchase patterns from a competitive product to the one being promoted. Often some incentive is required to advocate a change in the brand being considered for purchase. Indeed, many promotions specifically target competitive brand users in order to increase share of market. Providing the incentive is sufficient, such promotions can be very effective.

According to Gupta (1988),[7] who conducted research within the coffee sector, more than 94 per cent of the sales increase from promotions comes from brand switching. Purchase acceleration in time accounts for less than 14 per cent of the sales increase, whilst stockpiling accounts for less than 3 per cent.

To increase the level of enquiries and to build lists

An increasing concern amongst manufacturers is the desire to build accurate lists of actual and potential consumers. Promotions can be designed specifically to ensure that consumers provide this information. Traditionally, a variety of sales promotions have used a mail-in or phone-in facility as the means by which the consumer gains access to the promotion incentive. However, comparatively little use was made of such information. Today, as the costs of conventional media increase, companies are seeking more cost-effective ways of reaching their target audiences. Access to lists of names and addresses enables the subsequent communication to these named individuals with a minimum of wastage.

H. J. Heinz, for example, has developed a sophisticated database of brand users and is increasingly using direct mail as a means of maintaining contact with those consumers.

To reinforce other aspects of marketing communications activity

Promotions may become part of the overall communications programme for a brand and serve to reinforce the positioning of the product in the minds of consumers. Many perfume companies offer comparatively expensive free gifts (sometimes of branded merchandise) in order to associate the values of these items with the purchased brand.

Other promotions can be used to reinforce the brand's proposition to the consumer. Kimberly-Clark, for example, use the device of the Andrex Puppy, which has been a consistent feature of their advertising as a strong component of promotional campaigns.

Building brand equity

It is increasingly recognized that sales promotion can contribute to the strengthening of brand equity by encouraging consumers to interact with the brand. The overall desire of such promotional activity is to create positive associations with the brand. This may be achieved in a variety of ways, but one that is commonly employed is to associate the brand with some charitable organization or some other cause in order to create positive attitudes towards the promoted brand. Tesco, for example, has used the device of 'Computers for Schools' on a number of occasions in order to stimulate the use of their store and to foster positive feelings about the organization.

Respond to competitive activity

In some instances, sales promotion is used defensively in order to protect the brand from competitive encroachment. If a company becomes aware of competitive activity that is likely to result in a decline in its sales it may introduce some form of counter-promotion to enhance the value of the brand and make switching to competitors less attractive.

Trade objectives

In the same way that sales promotions can be targeted specifically towards the consumer, although there is an inevitable trade impact, various techniques are available specifically to target the trade.

Promotions will be designed to provide either general or specific support to the trade.

Some of the objectives which can be fulfilled by such activities are feature pricing; the provision of displays and display incentives; and in-store demonstrations, which will allow the trial of a product and will often be accompanied by some additional incentive to the consumer, e.g. discounted price, to purchase the product.

Other in-store support may provide the opportunity to build on special events, for example, a new store opening, some form of themed activity in which the brand can participate (e.g. Italian week, cookery week, etc.); seasonal activity to promote sales (e.g. spring cleaning event, mid-summer sales, etc.); cross-promotion, where two products are sold together – Safeway mounted a large campaign in which a branded product was sold together with an appropriate Safeway own-label product at a discount (e.g. Dolmio sauce with Safeway pasta).

Trade objectives might include those outlined below.

To introduce new products

Incentives might be offered to the trade to encourage them to stock new products. These might include a special reduced price designed to increase their margin, deals such as sale or return to eliminate the risks involved in the stocking of products that are 'untested' by the retailer, or the provision of special point of sale. Co-operative advertising together with in-store sampling might also be offered as trade incentives.

Increase distribution

Critical to the success of any product is its ability to gain widespread distribution. Put simply, if the product is not available to consumers at the point of purchase, they are unlikely to go to a specific store that stocks it. Rather they will select an alternative from the same product category. Incentives such as those outlined above will be used to encourage non-stockists to take the brand into their stores.

Build retail inventory

In precisely the same way that the manufacturer might seek to encourage the consumer to purchase larger packages of the product, so he might also wish to ensure a deeper inventory on the part of the retailer. There are a variety of stock-loading techniques that will be discussed later and that may be employed for this purpose.

Maintain or increase share of shelf space

In a highly competitive market brands continually face challenges from both their existing competitors and from new entrants to the sector. The consequence is that shelf space, which is at a premium, may be squeezed in order to make space for those competitors. Promotions may be used to ensure that the brand maintains its level of presence and, in some instances, increases the number of facings that it receives in store.

To obtain display presence

In a similar vein promotions can be used to encourage the trade to feature the brand strongly. Sometimes point-of-sale material will be used to highlight the presence of the brand in its traditional location. Alternatively, it can be used to encourage the trade to feature the brand in other 'hotspots' around the store.

To reduce inventories

At certain times, the manufacturer may wish to ensure that there is effective pull through of his products and, thereby, reduce the level of stock held by the retailer. Such activity may be particularly associated with the introduction of a new product.

To counter competitive activity

Inevitably brands exist in a competitive environment. Often a brand is taken by surprise following the introduction of new marketing activity by one or more of the competitors in the sector. One great benefit of sales promotion over other forms of marketing communications is its speed of implementation. Certain forms of promotional activity can be introduced, literally, within days of determining the need. In order to minimize the effectiveness of competitive activity, particularly where it is difficult to mount a specific consumer offer within a limited time frame, incentives may be offered to retailers to ensure their continued support behind the brand.

Traffic building

Some techniques, particularly those that involve, for example, in-store sampling, may also serve to increase the volume of traffic for the retailer. Although the consumer will be motivated to visit the outlet because of the specific incentive, it is highly likely that he or she will make other purchases whilst in store, to the benefit of the retailer who participates in the promotion.

Obtain trade support for a consumer sales promotion

At times when the company seeks to introduce a sales promotion activity aimed at the consumer, it is imperative that it secures the active support of the trade. In order to achieve this objective a wide range of incentives might be offered to gain the necessary levels of support.

As noted above, the motivation of the sales force, dealers, etc., by the use of incentives (often linked to sales targets) is an important area of sales promotion activity.

Sales-force objectives

It must not be forgotten that the sales force represents a vital link between the manufacturer and the distribution chain. Unless it is able to sell in a promotion it is incapable of achieving the objectives established for it. By the same token the sales force itself may need some encouragement to achieve the targets established.

Sales promotion strategy

Sales promotions can and should be considered as having a significant strategic role. In many instances, such activity can achieve objectives that no other form of marketing communications can deliver. Importantly, sales promotion can improve the level of manufacturer profits because they permit price discrimination and because they can, in other ways, influence trade and consumer behaviour.

Price discrimination

Promotions enable manufacturers to operate a policy of price discrimination, by charging different prices to different consumers and trade accounts that vary in terms of price sensitivity. Recently, for example, the author failed to renew a subscription to a computer magazine. Shortly afterwards he received a mailing offering him a 'loyal subscribers' discount. Still failing to renew, he received yet another mailing with an even greater discount. Finally, he received a telephone call, offering him an even more advantageous price. Clearly, this system was established practice for the publication and, no doubt, previous subscribers were recruited at each of the differing price levels.

The same principles can also be seen at the retail level. Coupons and special prices are often aimed specifically at the price-sensitive consumer who will make the effort to obtain such discount offers. Sometimes, they will be accompanied by point-of-sale material, flagging the existence of the reduced price offer and inducing the consumer to go to the appropriate part of the store where the offer is available.

Certainly, it is apparent that different prices may be charged for the same product in different retail outlets. Designing promotions that enable more price-sensitive retailers and their consumers to pay less usually generates more contribution than if one price were charged to all. Using this approach, manufacturers can tailor their pricing to meet the particular needs of the retail outlets they serve. We have already seen that sales promotion activity can also enable the modification of manufacturers' effective prices over time without necessitating a change in the list prices. Short-term promotional price reductions can be used to reflect variations in consumer demand and minimize the impact of such fluctuations.

The following chart can be used as a simple check-list to establish the specific nature of a promotional technique to meet a defined objective. It must be remembered, however, that the list is not exhaustive and that, in some instances, several objectives may be combined.

Table 7.1

TECHNIQUE

OBJECTIVE	Money-off packs	Money-off coupons	Banded packs	Bonus packs	Free gifts	Free mailings	Self liquidators	Contests and competitions	Sampling
New product launch	**	*	*	*	*				**
Induce trial	**	**	*	*	*				**
Encourage new usage	*	*	*	*	*				**
Gain new users	**	**	*	*	*				*
Retain existing users	*	*	**	**		*	*	*	
Increase frequency of purchase		*			**	**			
Increase purchase size				**	*				
Increase distribution	*	*	*	*	*				*
Increase inventory	*	*	*	*					*
Reduce inventory	*	*							
Activate slow-moving lines	*	*	*	*				*	
Gain special featuring in store							*	*	*
Increase shelf facings	**			*	*				

* effective; ** very effective

Case study

KELLOGG'S NUTRI-GRAIN
Agency: Blue Chip Marketing

New brands flooding the marketplace had eaten into the brand share of Nutri-Grain, the pioneer of the healthy snacking category. Decisive action was required to develop an exciting promotion that would re-ignite trade and consumer support.

Targeting mums, dads and kids (12+) the strategy was to use an instant win mechanic offering a cash reward. 24Seven Cash Draw was the UK's first instant hourly free prize draw based on the latest SMS techniques.

Unique codes were printed on the inside of every bar. By texting the code, consumers were included in the next hourly draw to win £500. Winners were notified within 60 minutes and prizes delivered within 48 hours. The campaign was communicated on 30 million packs supported with TV, in-store displays, a launch mailer to store managers and a dedicated microsite.

The campaign lasted for 6 weeks with 24 winners every day giving consumers a genuine feeling that 'they really could win'.

More than half a million entries were received with over 50 per cent entering more than once. Sales increased by 32 per cent and household penetration grew by 13 per cent, both contributing to Nutri-Grain growing 50 per cent faster than the category.

The campaign was received a gold award in the Trial and Awareness section of the 2005 ISP Promotion Awards.

The above appeared in the Special Supplement to *Promotions and Incentives* magazine, June 2005.
The success of the promotion is indicated by the fact that the brand re-ran the promotion in 2005.

Questions

1 Why is it important to establish clear objectives for sales promotional activity?
2 What are the principles that guide the setting of objectives?
3 What consumer objectives can be established for sales promotion?
4 List the consumer objectives detailed in this chapter and identify a recent consumer promotion that corresponds to each of them.
5 What is the difference between consumer and trade objectives?

8 Consumer promotions 1 – financial incentives

Chapter overview

Even as there are many different objectives for sales promotion activity, so too are there a wide variety of executional techniques that can be employed to meet these objectives. This chapter deals with the variety of promotional incentives based on giving some form of discount to the consumer. In every instance the consumer is offered either immediate or delayed savings as an incentive to purchase the product or service.

Learning outcomes

- To consider the variety of financial incentives that might be offered to consumers
- To examine the advantages and disadvantages of financial incentives
- To examine the alternative approaches to money-off promotions
- To reflect on the implications of money-off promotions.

Reduced price offers

Money off

Money-off promotions, in their variety of implementations, remain the most commonly employed promotional device. Indeed, various trade estimates suggest that they may account for as much as 60 to 70 per cent of total sales promotion expenditures. Often referred to as price packs or reduced price offers (RPOs), these promotions offer the consumer the most powerful incentive to purchase: money! In essence, the promotion consists of a price reduction that is communicated either on or off the pack. The size of the price reduction will be determined by an assessment of the brand requirements and the competitive environment.

Most often, the offering consists of a flash on pack detailing the size of the price reduction, either as an absolute price or as a reduction on the normal price. However, it may be communicated to the consumer with a notice at the point of purchase. By providing an immediate price reduction, a manufacturer makes the most impactful offer. All consumers will be made aware of the offer and will receive the benefit at the time of purchase.

A study by Mulhern and Padgett (1995)[1] was designed to determine the relationship between regular price and promotion purchasing. They found a significant, positive correlation between regular price and promotion purchasing at the individual level. Over three-quarters of the shoppers identifying the promotion as a reason for visiting the store purchased one or more regular price items. Shoppers visiting the store for the promotion spent more money on regular price merchandise than on promoted merchandise.

This response makes such promotions extremely attractive to retailers. Indeed, according to Fearne *et al.* (1999),[2] over recent years promotions have gained importance within UK multiple grocers as a means of achieving competitive advantage. The significant decline in real (that is, inflation adjusted) levels of consumer expenditure during the early 1990s would certainly have helped to foster the image of promotions as a way of attracting price-sensitive consumers. Indeed, the evidence from consumer surveys supports the notion that consumers are becoming more aware of promotional activity and more active in seeking out promotional offers.

Retail price promotions have the effect of changing consumers' purchase decisions and retailers use price promotions more frequently to boost store sales. There are several ways to implement a retail price promotion. For example, retailers can present a price reduction in cash terms (money off), percentage terms (per cent off) or some combinations of these two methods.

Price promotions can be developed and presented using a bundling (e.g. buy a hamburger and large drink and get fries for an extra 50p) or unbundling tactic (item discounts provided). Even when the total amount of a discount remains constant, the format of the promotional discount can influence a variety of perceptions related to the attractiveness of the promotion. Bundled discounts aggregated into one large amount may be perceived as delivering a different level of value than those that are unbundled as several segregated discounts.

Madan and Suri (2001)[3] indicate that of the various forms of price promotions, short-term price discounts have been used by retailers to stimulate short-term demand for their products and services. Price discounts, compared to other forms of price promotion like coupons and rebates, are more popular with both retailers and consumers, as they are easy to execute and provide an incentive of an immediate price reduction (savings) to consumers. However, in a competitive market place, a pricing strategy involving price discounts has been suggested to have a few drawbacks. One of the drawbacks is that price discounts not only enhance the value of an offer (as described earlier), but also negatively influence consumers' perception of the offer by raising doubts about its quality.

Recently, there has been concern expressed about the negative consequences of retail price promotions, such as increased price sensitivity, weakening of brand franchise and the cannibalization of regular price sales. However, as Farris and Quelch

(1989)[4] describe, price promotions have numerous positive consequences, such as helping companies manage variations in supply and demand, inducing trial and enhancing the shopping experience. An additional benefit for retailers is that price promotions can attract shoppers who will also purchase regular price merchandise. They demonstrate that this behaviour does occur and, thereby, provides justification for the use of short-term promotions in retailing.

The advantages of money off

Money-off promotions can be speedily implemented. If the offering is a simple price reduction on shelf, the promotion can be implemented within a few days. Moreover, since most companies have built up considerable experience of the technique, there is little need for testing and the results can be predicted with a reasonable level of accuracy. Money off can be offered against regular stock by ensuring that the price reduction is indicated at the point of purchase. This involves negotiations with the retail trade to ensure that the discounted price is flagged to the consumer, often utilizing specially produced point of sale. Alternatively, money off can be carried on special packs that bear a flash or price mark indicating the size of the price reduction (e.g. 10p off) or the absolute price (now only £1 usual price £1.30).

The impact of the technique is considerable. It has a universal appeal and both the trade and the consumer like the promotion. Importantly, the promotional device is available to all manufacturers and service providers. Not only are there no specific economies of scale (which would otherwise restrict the use of the device to larger companies), a means of transmitting the offering to the end consumer is similarly available to all, i.e. the pack is not the only vehicle.

Because promotions have such strong effects on individual product sales, retailers can use them to build strong relationships with suppliers. Manufacturers and retailers can engage in strategic alliances that use price promotions to benefit both parties. For example, some retailers combine individual brand promotions with an overall store promotion, by providing a coupon worth money off a future purchase at that store to shoppers who purchase multiple units of a promoted brand. Equally, a retailer might offer a combination of a private-label product with a branded product at a reduced price. For example, Safeway (now part of Morrisons) offered free packs of spaghetti when the consumer purchases a jar of Dolmio (a pasta sauce).

Nijs *et al.* (2001)[5] consider a variety of the aspects of promotional activity:

1 Price promotion intensity. They distinguished between two components of promotional intensity in a product category: promotional frequency and promotional depth. Promotional frequency reflects the extent to which consumers are exposed to price promotions (e.g. the percentage of weeks with a price promotion), whereas promotional depth specifies the average size of the promotions to which consumers are exposed (e.g. cents off). Research at the brand level suggests that depth and frequency may have a distinct effect on promotional effectiveness.

2 Price promotion and advertising reactivity. For any given level of price-promotional intensity, the effect of price promotions may depend on competitive reactions. Competitors may react with the same weapon ('simple' competitive response) or with another marketing tool.

Their research indicates that in the short run, price promotions significantly expand category demand in 58 per cent of the cases over a dust-settling period that lasts, on average, 10 weeks. Moreover, in 60 per cent of the market categories they investigated, the initial impact of a price promotion is either not negated or is enhanced.

They argue that the frequent use of price promotions makes them a more important component in consumers' motivation to buy from a category, as they are conditioned to look for and rely on future promotions for a product purchase. However, this effect is completely dissipated in the long run. This indicates that, over time, the positive effect of price-promotional frequency on promotion effectiveness is offset by its negative side effects.

According to Gupta and Cooper (1992),[6] different brands have different price thresholds. On average, however, price reductions of around 15 per cent are required to attract a consumer to a sale. Generally, the level of discount required to attract consumers to a name brand are lower than for a store brand. Gupta[7] also found that the majority of promotional volume comes from brand switchers. Sivakumar and Raj (1997)[8] also found evidence in support of price promotions, but concluded that price reductions for national brands are more effective in attracting consumers away from low-quality brands than vice versa.

According to Blattberg *et al.* (1995)[9] temporary price reductions substantially increase sales. However, they assert that the frequency of deals changes the consumer's reference price. Moreover, the greater the frequency of deals, the less impact the promotion has. Price promotions on high-priced brands impact upon lower-price brands and private-label products disproportionately.

Similar conclusions are drawn by Garretson *et al.* (2002).[10] Recognizing that brands face increasing competition from retailers' own-label products they point to the fact that whilst value-consciousness is common amongst consumers who seek price savings, the perception of price in terms of its relationship to product quality had the opposite effect. For these consumers, the lower average prices of the private labels cause such products to be regarded as less attractive. It is likely that the low price on private labels signals inferior quality for consumers. In contrast, these same buyers viewed national brands on price promotion more favourably. For these consumers, price promotions may represent a way to achieve savings without feeling that quality was being sacrificed.

Research conducted by Srinivasan *et al.* (2002)[11] showed that whilst price promotions have little long-term effect, in the short to medium term promotions can have very strong positive effects. Moreover, a study by Helsen and Schmittlein (1992)[12] confirmed that in most cases promotional price cuts lead to purchase acceleration. Boulding *et al.* (1994)[13] argue that firms with high relative price use promotions to compete on price whenever necessary. When such promotions are used, price becomes a salient attribute.

An analysis of sales data generally suggests that there are no negative after-effects on brand sales from price-based promotions. The reason for generally expecting no negative after-effect is that most buyers of a brand buy it only infrequently. Promotions induce some of these buyers to buy the promoted brand on that occasion, rather than a competitor brand. The brand is also bought during the promotion by consumers who would have otherwise bought it at regular price. However, according to Ehrenberg (2000)[14] most buyers are also rather infrequent purchasers of a given category, whilst Gupta (1988)[7] and Bell et al. (1999)[15] suggest that promotions have comparatively minor effects on purchase acceleration or stockpiling compared to brand switching. Moreover, positive after-effects from a price promotion could occur if a promotion attracted some new users who repeatedly buy later. However, the evidence suggests no long-term favourable effects for established brands (Ehrenberg et al. 1994, Pauwels et al. 2002).[16,17] The prime reason is that price promotions attract mostly existing, albeit infrequent, buyers and that the small quantity of attracted new buyers have a low propensity to re-buy.

The disadvantages of money off

Against the above-mentioned advantages must be set the obvious disadvantages.

The first disadvantage to be considered is the fact that all consumers receive the incentive, despite the fact that some (the loyal users) would probably have purchased at the normal price. Equally, such promotional offers are easily and, potentially, speedily matched by the competition. Moreover, they lack distinction at the point of purchase since all products and services can offer money off.

A further dimension that mitigates against constant price promotions is that they are particularly easy for the competition to copy. The inevitable consequence is that profits for all players are reduced and, whilst the consumer may benefit in the shorter-term, the longer-term strength of the brand is eroded.

Possibly the most important disadvantage is the fact that frequent use of money-off techniques may result in a reduced price expectation on the part of the consumer (the reduced price becomes the norm) and may denigrate the image of the brand.

As Lichtenstein et al. (1997)[18] argue:

> A price reduction may erode a brand's equity, particularly if there is a strong and positive price–quality interference.

Winer (1986)[19] suggests that continuous sales promotions might train consumers not to purchase a brand when it is not on promotion. He also suggests that price promotions often cause consumers to reference price, which means that they will not be prepared to buy the brand when the promotion is completed.

This view is reflected in the comments of Mela et al. (1998),[20] who state that consumers who purchase within categories that have frequent price promotions may learn to anticipate when the next promotion will occur and may put off their purchase until that time, reducing profitability for the brand. Kalwani et al. (1990)[21] also demonstrated that brands that promote frequently have a lower price expectation.

Similarly, Kim (1989)[22] has shown that frequent dealing is also associated with lower brand equity, a view shared by Biel (1991),[23] who argues that: 'A company that constantly runs price promotions tends to reduce perceptions of quality, consumers feel that the brand is worth less because it is always on special.' Further, Diamond and Campbell (1988)[24] provided evidence that repeated discounting can decrease the reference price of the product. Extra product promotions do not appear to affect reference price.

Many authors are critical of the impact of the long-term use of price promotions. Mitchell (1999)[25] argues that there are significant problems associated with continually cutting prices as 'an item's price is pregnant with meaning and symbolism'. Similarly, Ambler (1999)[26] indicates that 'price promotions have a long term detrimental effect to the brand's acceptance in the market'.

Further research conducted by Smith and Sinha (2000)[27] indicates that consumers overwhelmingly preferred volume savings to money off. In their research, they tested three promotional executions: 50 per cent off; buy one get one free; and buy two get 50 per cent off. We will consider product-based offers in the next chapter.

Whilst Raghubir and Corfman (1999)[28] discovered that price promotions may affect pre-trial evaluations unfavourably, this only occurs when specific conditions obtain:

1 Offering a promotion is more likely to lower a brand's evaluation when the brand has not been promoted previously, compared to when it has been frequently promoted.

2 Promotions are used as a source of information about the brand to a greater extent when the evaluator is not an expert but has some basic industry knowledge.

3 Promotions are more likely to result in negative evaluations when they are uncommon in the industry.

However, they also point out that 'when consumers buy a product on a price promotion, they are less likely to repeat the purchase when the offer finishes.' There is no relationship being built and the product's value will not be enhanced.

Research conducted by Pauwels *et al.* (2002)[29] supports the notion that brand choices are in equilibrium in mature markets and that price promotions produce only temporary benefits for established brands. Because most consumers have already bought and experienced the brand, the learning effect from mere purchase is limited and easily offset by competitive activity. The opposite results hold for category incidence: although the immediate effects are smaller than those for brand choice, the short-term gains are reinforced rather than cancelled in the adjustment period. Price promotions can induce non-category shoppers to make a purchase and this expansion effect cannot be entirely explained by purchase acceleration. In other words, the incremental brand-specific sales (selective demand) are partly borrowed from sales in off-promotion periods, whereas the immediate boost in category incidence is largely retained for several periods.

Coupon promotions

Coupon promotions provide an alternative method of delivering a price reduction to the consumer and, as with direct money-off price promotions, offer an economic incentive to purchase a brand. The effect of coupon value predominantly has been demonstrated to be positive in terms of increasing perceived offer value, decreasing the intent to search and increasing the interest in a brand. Higher coupon values have been found to increase redemption rates.

In price-discount promotions, retailers reduce the sale prices and all buyers are eligible for the price reductions. Reduced sale prices in discount promotions may also lower the perceived quality of the promoted products. On the other hand, in coupon promotions, retailers maintain the regular price and only those buyers who hold coupons are able to reduce the actual payment by the face value of the coupons. The regular price of the promoted product in a coupon promotion is still the effective price paid by buyers without coupons. It is, therefore, unlikely that consumers will perceive a quality reduction on a coupon-promoted product. Accordingly, coupon promotions should also be more effective than discount promotions in maintaining the overall perceived value of the promoted product.

Coupon offers can be designed to have different impacts on the consumer.

- Coupons – this purchase

Some coupons are available for immediate redemption. Retailers both in the UK and elsewhere often provide money-off coupons on entry to the store that entitle the consumer to immediate reductions in the price of the product purchased. Clearly, these promotions are essentially similar to money off, although the means of communicating the offer to the consumer is somewhat different. They are highly effective since the consumer on picking up the coupon is made aware of the brand against which the offer is being made and are highly likely to take advantage of the offer.

- Coupons – next purchase

Many manufacturers offer coupons on their packaging that require to be removed before redemption can take place. Usually this occurs subsequent to purchase, once the consumer has returned home and has the means to remove the label or clip the coupon from some other part of the packaging. The nature of the incentive is to encourage subsequent purchase of the same brand. Such offers are sometimes referred to as a bounce-back coupon.

Where the coupon is designed to be redeemed at the time of a subsequent purchase, such offerings have a similar appearance of immediacy and impact, although in practice, many consumers forget to redeem the coupon! Hence money-off coupons may have a similar visual impact to that of an immediate money-off offer, but will represent a lower real cost, since the level of redemption will be lower. They thus represent an effective way of inducing sampling and because they can be transmitted via alternative carriers to designated groups of consumers, they are particularly effective in encouraging new users.

- Coupons – multiple purchase

An alternative is to motivate consumers to buy multiple packs of the same product. Although comparatively infrequently used, the motivation is to encourage the consumer to stock up with the product by purchasing several packs on a single purchase occasion.

According to the ASA,[29] over 60 per cent of all households use coupons on a regular basis as a useful and effective way of saving money and trying out new products at a discount.

Methods of coupon distribution

There are a number of different ways of transmitting a money-off offer to the consumer. Although the manufacturer's product is an ideal vehicle for carrying the coupon, there are many alternative carriers and means of communicating with the end consumer.

Couponing can be specifically targeted to reach particular groups of consumers. They are particularly useful in the context of new products, where not only can coupons create awareness of the existence of the product, but they can also offer an inducement to make the initial purchase.

- On pack – own product

  The most common method of coupon distribution is where the manufacturer includes the coupon on its own packaging. Whilst this application has immediate appeal, it may be restricted to current users of the brand since non-users may not be aware of the offer unless it is clearly signposted at the point of purchase.

  Obviously, on-pack coupons will take longer to implement, since the revised pack design containing the flash will need to be fed into the production pipeline. In addition, if another carrier is to be used, negotiations will be required before the offer can be implemented. Coupon offers are significantly more expensive and time consuming in terms of implementation. But sometimes they offer a particular benefit.

- In pack – own product

  Similar to the above execution, the manufacturer includes the coupon inside the packaging, either to prevent immediate redemption or because there is a restriction in terms of the label size.

- On or in pack – alternative product (sometimes referred to as a cross-ruff or cross couponing)

  In some instances the manufacturer will provide a money-off coupon with an alternative product from the same stable. This is commonly used to encourage consumers to sample a new product from the manufacturer or to enhance the perceived value of the carrier product. This has the dual advantage of providing an incentive to purchase product A, whilst encouraging trial of product B.

  On other occasions, a manufacturer will negotiate with another manufacturer to carry his coupon on their product. The alternative (non-competing) brand will be used to provide the consumer with a money-off coupon redeemable against the carried brand. This has a similar benefit to the carrier since the value of the purchase is enhanced. However, it may also ensure that the two products are related in the consumer's mind; for example, receiving money off toothpaste when you buy a toothbrush or money-off butter or jam when you buy bread.

- Door to door

  Coupons are often distributed on a door-to-door basis. Households may be specifically targeted as potential users of the brand and will be given an incentive to purchase the product (or service) by providing a discount against the regular price.

- Contained in advertising

  Either contained within brand advertising or as inserts in newspapers and magazines, coupons can be targeted to specific potential consumers based on the readership. Sometimes the device is used to enhance the level of noticeability and readership of the advertising by making an attractive offer to the consumer.

  According to Munger and Grewal (2001)[30] coupon advertising is a hybrid sales promotion tool with the characteristics of both ordinary coupons and advertising. In particular, coupon advertising often includes brand information (product characteristics, location, quality, guarantees, etc.) as well as information about regular prices. At the same time, it includes a coupon that offers a discount off the regular price.

- In-store

  As mentioned above some manufacturers provide retailers with special dispensers to enable customers to take a coupon. Equally, however, this may be the result of a retailer initiative to promote particular brands within their own outlets.

  The availability of electronic point of sale (EPOS) is increasingly being used to provide coupons to consumers at the point of purchase. Such coupons are printed at the till and can be used to reward an existing purchase or may be triggered by the purchase of a competitive brand to encourage consumers to buy the specified brand on the next purchase occasion.

  Heilman *et al.* (2002)[31] report on the newer types of coupon promotion: electronic shelf coupons, peel-off coupons on product packaging, etc. These coupons are specifically designed to target consumers at the point of purchase where the majority of brand-purchasing decisions are made.

  They cite Thompson (1997)[32] who reports that instant coupons can not only increase sales of a brand by 35 per cent, but also increase consumers' shopping baskets by 14 per cent. They argue that there are specific reasons for these findings:

- Monetary savings from the coupon may create an unexpected income effect.
- The surprise savings could indirectly increase spending by elevating the consumer's mood.
- The Internet has recently become a means of distributing coupons. Some manufacturers now issue e-coupons that can be redeemed at online retailers or in conventional outlets. Like some other forms of coupon distribution, these enable targeting of consumers, in this instance as the result of visiting a particular website or searching for particular items of merchandise.

The advent of Internet shopping has resulted in a new form of sales promotion. The nearly ubiquitous coupon has been transformed into a digital entity whereby shoppers are often prompted to 'enter a promotion code' during the checkout process. Unlike grocery-store programmes, promotion codes are almost invariably placed at the end of the online shopping experience when the total charges are displayed. If a valid code is entered, charges are amended to the reduced price. Most traditional retailers do not incorporate the query 'Do you have a coupon?' into the checkout process.

Oliver and Shor (2003)[33] indicate that in the on-line situation, consumers without the code and without the means to get one do not complete the purchase; a phenom-enon termed 'the shopping cart abandonment problem'. Estimates of the rate of shop-ping cart abandonment range from 25 percent to 75 percent. In the offline world, one generally obtains coupons by scouring local newspapers and unsolicited mail. In the online world, search is many orders of magnitude more efficient. Beyond newspapers, direct mail and other established coupon delivery vehicles traditionally controlled by the issuing companies, many websites are now devoted to locating online coupons. These repositories are independent of the firms whose promotions they advertise and many feature coupon listings updated daily and forums for users to exchange infor-mation on new promotions.

The advantages of coupon offers

There are a number of specific advantages related to coupon offers:

- Coupons enable the possibility of providing a discount to price-sensitive con-sumers whilst still selling the product at full price to other consumers.
- Coupons can encourage brand switching since, often, consumers who redeem coupons tend to be users of competitive products.
- Manufacturers can control various aspects of coupon distribution. They can deter-mine both the timing and the method of distribution enabling targeting to specific groups.
- Coupons provide the potential to encourage repeat purchases. Indeed, some exe-cutions of coupon offers can maintain purchases over extended periods of time: for example, the former Pedigree petfood company developed a highly distinctive coupon offer that was combined with a door-to-door drop. The leaflet dropped to households contained many part coupons redeemable against both cat and dog foods. In order to validate the coupon, the consumer was required to purchase a can of the appropriate petfood and to remove the label. Printed on it was a portion of the voucher that needed to be affixed to the one received on the leaflet. The coupon could then be redeemed against the chosen petfood on which would be found a further part coupon, and so on.
- In some instances, coupons can be used to encourage consumers to trade up to a more expensive product within the brand portfolio.
- Although most coupons bear an expiry date, some are undated with the result that the consumer is free to shop at the most convenient time at any outlet at which they can redeem the coupon. However, indicating an expiry date provides the man-ufacturer with some control over the duration of the promotion and, additionally, can create a sense of 'urgency' in terms of redemption.

Manufacturers can offer a price discount to all customers or only to those who hold coupons. In the case of coupon promotions, retailers can either make the coupons widely available to all customers or send them only to a sub-group of potential buyers.

Consumers' decisions to purchase a product are based on their perceptions of the product's value, defined as the trade-off of the product's perceived quality relative to its perceived price, i.e. the perceived monetary sacrifice. Retailers can reduce a product's perceived monetary sacrifice by offering a price reduction on the product. Assuming that price reductions do not affect a product's perceived quality, price promotions should enhance the perceived value of the product.

One of the associated difficulties of using money-off coupons is that of estimating the likely redemption levels. This is aggravated by retailers encouraging consumers to redeem coupons even though they have not purchased the specified product. In some instances, consumers simply misredeem. They mistakenly offer the coupon at the check-out despite having purchased an alternative brand. Whilst this problem is particularly apparent in the USA, elsewhere the levels of mal- and mis-redemption are at a much lower level.

It must be remembered that the costs of couponing not only include the face value of the coupon but, in addition, costs associated with printing and distributing the coupons, together with a charge levied by the retailer to defray the costs associated with handling the coupon. Remember, they are accepting the coupon instead of cash and there may be a considerable delay before they despatch them to the manufacturer (or the handling house or redemption centre acting on its behalf) in order to gain a refund.

The process of coupon redemption can be seen in the diagram below:

Figure 8.1

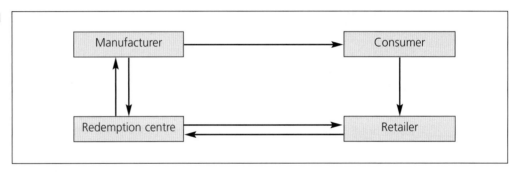

There is considerable evidence from academic research that couponing has an immediate impact on sales (Iron *et al.* 1983, Neslin *et al.* 1990).[34,35] However, these short-term sales improvements tend to be derived from consumers who switch temporarily from other brands to the coupon-promoted brand. Once the coupon promotion ends, these consumers tend to revert to their previous brand choice.

In a similar study by Sanjay and Hoch (1996)[36] they concluded that promotions in general were effective in increasing sales and profitability, but that for a given discount level, coupons generated greater incremental sales and produced higher profits for the retailer than bonus buys.

According to Raghubir *et al.* (2004)[37] nearly half of coupon redemptions are made by new customers and this percentage is increasing as face values are higher. Similar findings are demonstrated by Hahn *et al.* (1995)[38] who argue that coupon promotions represent an effective device for attracting users of competitive brands. From their investigation of coupon-based advertising they conclude that such campaigns may be most effective against loyal customers of competing brands, since such ads may provide the necessary incentive to induce trial.

Some companies use a format involving a 'bounce back' coupon that may be linked to a short redemption period at which time a new coupon is issued to the customer. Esso, for example, used a continuous, coupon-based, money-off promotion in a novel way. In order to instil some sense of urgency into the offer, they issued colour-coded vouchers to customers entitling them to a discount of 2p per litre of petrol. Each voucher bore a short expiry date (approximately 2 weeks) and customers were provided with a new voucher each time they redeemed. Esso used this device successfully to lock consumers in to their brand over an extended period of time.

This application is consistent with the findings of Inman *et al.* (1997)[39] who found that deals with restrictions such as two items per customer or offer good until a certain date, elicit more favourable evaluations from consumers than the same deals without restrictions.

In further research conducted by Shih-Fen *et al.* (1998)[40] it was found that coupon promotions were more favourably evaluated as well as more effective in changing subjects' purchase intentions than discount promotions. In a coupon promotion, consumers are not exposed to a reduced sale price. Further, price reductions with a coupon do not signal a quality reduction, nor is it likely that consumers will adjust their internal reference price of the promoted product downward. These factors contribute to the likelihood of a more favourable evaluation of a price reduction in coupon promotions than a similar price reduction in discount promotions. In addition, sending coupons to only a sub-group of potential (preferred) buyers may create a sense of exclusiveness for coupon users and their privilege of paying a lower price further enhances the value of the coupon savings.

However, Bawa and Shoemaker (1987)[41] demonstrated that coupons produce a short-term increase in the brand's purchase share resulting directly from redemption purchases. Nonetheless, they found only limited redemption amongst previous non-users of the brand and little increase in repeat purchasing.

Subsequent research conducted by the same authors (Bawa and Shoemaker 1989)[42] demonstrated that direct mail coupons lead to a significant increase in incremental sales and that, as might be expected, incremental sales are higher for higher value coupons. Most importantly, they found that, although coupon redeemers are the main source of these incremental sales, there is also what they call an 'exposure effect' resulting in the generation of incremental sales from non-redeemers as well.

Price expectations serve as an important frame of reference used by consumers in evaluating price information prior to purchase. Typically, the lower the price of the product, the lower the economic cost to the consumer and the higher the likelihood of purchase. A similar economic benefit is provided by a sales promotion tool such as a coupon. The higher the promotional discount, the higher the economic benefit and the higher the likelihood of purchase is. The reason manufacturers offer high coupon values is to increase the economic incentive to purchase a brand in the short term. If a consumer had a $1 coupon for a brand for which he or she expected to pay $4, he or she probably would be more likely to redeem it than a 50c coupon. In keeping with this logic, there is evidence that coupons with higher values are more likely to be redeemed than those with low values.[43]

Coupon redemption

Generally speaking, it is felt that three specific dimensions impact on the overall levels of coupon redemption.

- Price/saving
- Time/effort
- Pride/self-satisfaction.

Cotton and Babb (1978)[44] indicated that many consumers are more likely to respond to a coupon offer than an equivalent reduction in the price of the product.

Tat and Cornwell (1996)[45] found the following motives to be predictors of coupon usage:

- Perceived institutional barriers
- Self-satisfaction
- Perceived time and effort
- Price consciousness
- Interpersonal influence.

Moreover, particularly in areas where there is little real awareness of the actual prices of brands, a coupon offer is felt to be more meaningful to the recipient. Bawa *et al.* (1997)[46] argue that some consumers have a tendency to use coupons that interact with the intrinsic attractiveness of the product offered to determine their redemption behaviour.

The question remains as to why consumers respond more to an on-shelf coupon than to a similarly advertised temporary price reduction that offers the same monetary incentive. Chandon *et al.* (2000)[47] suggest that one explanation may be that coupons offer stronger value-expression benefits because collecting and redeeming coupons requires more skill and effort than buying products on sale. Coupon usage, therefore, more clearly signals the smart-shopping skills and values of the users; it may also enhance their social prestige and help them fulfil their personal values and moral obligations. The benefit congruency principle moderates this prediction by emphasizing that it would occur only to the extent that the value-expression benefits are important for the consumer or the purchase considered.

A further question to be answered is why some consumers switch brands because of a coupon but then do not redeem it. The failure to redeem the coupons responsible for the purchase decision may be due to these consumers valuing the convenience and exploration benefits coupons provide in the aisles at the time of the decision, but not the monetary savings they provide at the time of payment. For example, if consumers buy couponed brands because they reduce search and decision costs or increase the variety of products consumers buy by suggesting new alternatives, consumers may simply forget to use the coupon at the checkout. Alternatively, they may believe that the embarrassment of showing it to the cashier and the other shoppers is not worth the monetary savings provided.[48]

This is an important factor in costing coupon promotions. Unlike money off, which will be taken up by all purchasers, if some consumers fail to redeem coupons they have received, it reduces the effective cost of mounting the promotion.

The primary motive of coupon usage is saving money (there is a significant positive relationship between the consciousness toward saving money and the use of coupons) (Babakus *et al.* 1988),[49] suggesting that one's attitude toward price is an influence on consumer response to coupon promotions. Coupons increase the perceived value of a purchase through a temporary price reduction and consumers who are susceptible to coupons tend to be more price conscious. Because the overwhelming majority of coupons are offered for brand-named items, which are generally perceived to be better in quality than generics or private-label brands, consumers who use coupons can be considered 'value conscious'.

Babakus *et al.* also found that there is a significant negative relationship between people's value of time and their use of coupons. The time that it takes to search through media, collect and sort through coupons is a major obstacle to coupon redemption. In this regard, it can be expected that consumers who place a high value on their time are less likely to use coupons. Redeeming coupons requires an expenditure of time by searching through newspapers or magazines for desired coupons (Shimp and Kavas 1984).[50] Thus, people must engage in a screening-out process to find coupons that they are likely to use and screen out the unusable ones.

Whilst this is certainly true of the USA, in other countries where coupon usage and redemption is less widespread, these obstacles are not seen as being so difficult to overcome.

The disadvantages of coupons

According to Silva-Risso and Bucklin (2004)[51] the effectiveness of coupons as a promotional vehicle has remained a controversial topic for at least two decades. For example, practitioners who regularly analyse coupon promotions have characterized spending on coupons as a poor investment of marketing dollars (Bucklin and Gupta 1999).[52] In the mid-1990s, some consumer products companies attempted to eliminate coupons, lower the face value of coupons and shorten the time to expiration. These actions proved both unpopular and, arguably, lowered profitability. More recently the volume of coupons distributed has again been rising. Furthermore, coupons have become quite ubiquitous in online shopping. In light of the major role coupons play in the packaged goods marketing mix and the billions of dollars involved in spending, there is an ongoing need for improvements in the models available for assessing the effect of coupons on sales, share and profitability.

One concern expressed by managers is that coupons are redeemed predominantly by loyal consumers who would have purchased the brand in any event.

Everyday low prices

As an alternative to regular price promotions some manufacturers and retailers have implemented a policy of offering a continuous low price platform. Indeed, in 1991/2 Procter & Gamble instituted major reductions in individual promotional expenditures, developing in its place an alternative proposition: everyday low prices (EDLPs).

However, whilst this has proven to be an effective promotional format for a number of retailers, manufacturers have experienced less success with this device. According to Garretson and Burton (2003)[53] Procter & Gamble discontinued their non-coupon policy in various test markets five months ahead of schedule due to the ensuing consumer reaction. Moreover, both market penetration and share were adversely affected as a result of their adoption of the EDLP policy.

They argue that many consumers attracted to sales promotion may seek benefits beyond price savings. Such consumers enjoy the process of shopping as well as the final outcome of saving money. As such, they seek out products on deal to reinforce their self-image as 'smart shoppers'.

A similar argument is proposed by Chandon *et al.* (2000),[48] who suggest that sales promotions provide consumers with an array of hedonic and utilitarian benefits beyond monetary savings. As a result, EDLP cannot fully replace sales promotions without the risk of alienating consumers who value the non-monetary benefits that sales promotions provide. They argue that non-monetary promotions are more likely to create unique brand associations that can reinforce brand image.

Procter & Gamble attempted to operate an EDLP policy, although this subsequently backfired and sales dropped (Gardener and Trivedi 1998).[54] Despite the fact that the strategy would have saved consumers money, they perceived that they were losing out and turned instead to Procter & Gamble's competitors who continued to promote in the usual way. Gardener and Trivedi suggest that 'since P&G traditionally promoted their brands in a manner that stressed key attributes that commanded a premium price, a price cut actually signalled decreased value.'

The EDLP policy implemented by Procter & Gamble resulted in a decline in deal frequency of 15.7 per cent and coupon frequency by 54.3 per cent. As a result, the net price paid by consumers rose by approximately 20 per cent. Over the period of the EDLP activity Procter & Gamble lost approximately 18 per cent of its share across 24 categories.[55]

These figures are contradicted by Slater (2001),[56] however. Procter & Gamble were forced to abandon their EDLP experiment after considerable complaints from consumers who wanted the company to re-introduce coupon promotions. This was despite the fact that during the EDLP programme many consumers paid less for their purchases than previously. Slater reports that research indicates that coupons not only involve the consumer in the purchase decision, but they also give the consumer an element of control over the transaction. Many consumers feel that they are 'beating the system' and are 'smart shoppers'. Despite this, several retailers such as B&Q and others have continued with their EDLP programmes.

Price-matching promotions

Price-matching refund policies or offers by firms to match competitors' prices are common in both consumer and industrial marketing. An example of this is John Lewis's 'Never Knowingly Undersold' promise under which consumer may obtain a refund if they are able to purchase a product at a lower price than that offered by the store (within a defined time scale).

The following examples illustrate the type of price-matching refund policies that are commonly found in the marketplace:

> We promise to refund the difference if you find that you could have bought the same product cheaper locally at the time of purchase and call within 90 days.

In the unlikely event that you find an identical item that you purchased here for a lower price at another store, we promise to refund the difference.

Our price-matching policy guarantees you the lowest price – if you ever see a product for sale, anywhere, for a lower price, we will gladly refund the difference.

Both B&Q and their rivals Homebase offer similar money-back guarantees to their customers. Whilst Nationwide recently mounted a promotion on car insurance with the following offer: 'If you can find a car insurance quote for less within 28 days we'll refund the difference.'

As Jain and Srivastra (2000)[57] indicate, such price-matching refunds are a feature of both industrial and consumer markets. This provision ensures a long-term relationship between sellers and buyers, even in the absence of long-term contracts. Furthermore, it provides an assurance to buyers that should they be offered a lower price, the original seller will match that price, which thus protects the buyer from overpaying. In consumer markets, retailers (including electronic and appliance stores, grocery stores, hardware stores and major department stores) frequently offer price-matching policies.

Rebates

Some manufacturers attempt to encourage the consumer to make a purchase by offering some form of rebate. In some instances, rebates are used to remove the risk associated with the purchase of a new or unfamiliar product. If the consumer knows that they can get a full refund if they are dissatisfied with the product or service, they are more likely to purchase it in the first instance. Following the purchase of the product, the consumer sends some form of proof of purchase to the manufacturer who refunds part or all of the cost of purchase. An example of this is Schwartz spices for meat's rebate offer on a number of new products: 'Try me for Free'. The consumer is invited to send back the on-pack sticker plus their till receipt in order to obtain a full price rebate.

Rebates are commonly used by all types of manufacturer, from financial services to motor vehicles. They can be used to reduce the cost of purchase since the purchaser automatically qualifies for the rebate on making the purchase. Recently, some financial institutions have encouraged people to switch their mortgage on the basis of offering an immediate cash rebate once the transaction has been completed.

However, according to Tat *et al.* (1988),[58] some consumers fail to participate in rebate or money-back offers because of the perceived effort and time delay in getting their money back. They argue that rebates are an effective promotional tool in creating new users, as well as brand switching and repeat purchases amongst current users. Potentially, rebates can offer the consumer substantial savings. However, in many instances, the conditions attached to rebate redemption may be daunting:

- The complexity of the redemption process
- A short expiration date coupled with a requirement of multiple quantity purchase
- Difficulty in removing the proof of purchase from the package or container
- Rebate offers that require a greater volume of purchase than is required.

Kalwani *et al.* (1990)[21] point out that, in some markets, consumers expect prices to be based on some form of discount. For example, in the car market, incentives such as rebates, low interest rates, financing deals, trade-in incentive, etc., are taken as standard. According to Folkes and Wheat (1995),[59] rebates yielded price perceptions similar to those of the regular price.

However, results of research conducted by Munger and Grewal (2001)[30] indicate that consumers who were exposed to promotions that included something for free viewed them more favourably than promotions that involved rebates, which further resulted in more favourable purchase intentions. Providing promotions that emphasize free give-aways are likely to be more effective than a standard discount (e.g. 20 per cent off) or a rebate.

The implications of money-off promotions

Money-off promotions have important implications both in the determination of promotional effectiveness and for individual manufacturers. As noted earlier, a key consideration is the on-going battle between the brands and private label. The latter often have the advantage of lower prices to encourage consumer purchase. Some academics have argued that national brand promotions (particularly those that offer monetary incentives) are an effective way of combating the growth of store brands (Lal 1990, Quelch and Harding 1996).[60,61]

Research evidence suggests that gains by a promoted brand are primarily achieved at the expense of other brands, as a result of brand substitution (Gupta 1988).[7] In his study it was found that 85 per cent of the short-term effect of price promotions was brand switching and only 15 per cent was temporary category expansion. The temporary category expansion arises from purchase acceleration, which in turn comprises a shortened inter-purchase time and/or increased quantity at purchase. Similarly, Bell *et al.* (1999)[62] studied 13 different product categories and found on average 75 per cent of the short-term effect of price promotions was brand switching and 25 per cent was purchase acceleration.

A more recent study by Dawes (2004)[63] added to previous research on price promotions by isolating a particularly successful promotion and analysing its effects. It found that, despite its success, this price promotion:

- had no identifiable positive or negative longer-term effect on the volume for the brand that was promoted
- temporarily expanded the category for the duration of the promotion
- had an identifiable negative effect on the sales volume of one competing retailer chain in the period of the promotion, but not on the sales volume of the other two retailers
- did have a longer-term negative impact on category sales for the retailer that ran the promotion.

Over the longer term, the post-promotion decline was approximately 60 per cent of the initial sales increase. It is possible that this decline was, in part, the consequence of the fact that the promotion resulted in purchase acceleration or stockpiling by consumers.

One important dimension of consumer promotions, especially those which reduce the effective price of a product for a period (money off, extra product free, etc.) is that consumers tend to stockpile in order to take advantage of the price reduction. Most important, is the fact that such stockpiling tends to result in an increased rate of consumption on the part of the consumer (Assuncao and Meyer 1993).[64]

Similar findings are reported by Bell *et al.* (2002),[65] who indicate that price promotion can induce consumers to stockpile by purchasing greater than usual quantities. In some instances, this also leads to an increased level of consumption. It is important to determine whether this consumption effect is present, otherwise price promotions merely serve to bring forward consumer purchase resulting in an uneven pattern of demand.

As we have seen, temporary price discounting is a well-known merchandising technique whereby manufacturers, retailers or both, offer consumers an economic incentive to induce them to purchase a particular brand. Research into price discounting has concentrated on three key issues: the effect price discounts have on market share, brand-switching, and purchase quantity and timing.

Dodson *et al.* (1978)[66] concluded that price discounting increased the market share of the promoted product, at least in the short term. Furthermore, they suggested that a high discount led to a greater increase in market share than a low discount.

However, Shoemaker and Shoaf (1977)[67] concluded that consumers reverted to the purchase patterns they held prior to the promotion and suggested the market share gained from the promotion could be as temporary as the promotion itself. Thus they concluded that these promotions may have a limited effect because they serve only to disrupt consumers' short-term purchase behaviour, which eventually resumes its normal pattern.

Temporary price discounts may affect other aspects of consumers' purchase behaviour, such as the quantity of product they purchase and their inter-purchase intervals. Neslin *et al.* (1985)[68] and Gupta (1988)[7] concluded that these promotions may only displace sales that would have otherwise occurred at the product's usual price, thus delaying their subsequent purchase of it and competing brands.

One recent study that confirms the effectiveness of price-based promotional offers is that conducted by Anderson and Simester (2004),[69] in order to find out whether big discount strategies really prompt new customers to buy more items, more often? Or does promotional pricing actually undermine attempts to increase future spending among existing customers? A recent large-scale study of a US catalogue retailer investigated how discount promotion strategies ultimately affect the bottom-line business. Writing in the winter 2004 issue of *Marketing Science*, they concluded that heavy price reductions do in fact draw new customers and that these new customers spend more in the long run. However, the same discounts do not spur current customers to increase their purchasing. In fact, after receiving deep discounts, current customers buy fewer and less expensive items in subsequent purchases.

They demonstrate that price promotions raised short-term demand for items in the catalogue overall. Among current customers, the promotional catalogue generated 35 per cent more revenue than their research control, which lacked the deep discounts. Among each group of prospects, the differential was even higher.

Case study

CADBURY TREBOR BASSETT
Agency: Triangle Communications Ltd

Background

The chocolate confectionery market is estimated to be worth some £3602 million with Kit Kat being the market leader in the single bars market. The Cadbury brand is only slightly smaller, with the Mars Bar occupying third place.

Objectives

Cadbury needed a range promotion capable of driving brand penetration in a highly competitive market. Specifically the promotion was intended to sell through 70 per cent of promotional volume in 2 months and 100 per cent in 3 months.

Strategy

- To run two promotions a year over range of countline bars
- To ensure regular purchases are made across the range and that the Cadbury brand is top of mind
- Campaign to be designed to encourage both the trade and consumer to re-appraise the Cadbury range of count line bars
- Prime target audience to be 16–24-year-olds with mobile phones.

Campaign summary

Cadbury identified their target audience as 16–24-year-olds and built their campaign around the mobile phone culture and the spiralling popularity of text messaging. The promotion was communicated on 64.8 million packs of chocolate bar countlines encompassing 10 different Cadbury brands. Inside each wrapper there was a code and a network-specific mobile number.

Consumers were invited to text the code to the mobile number. An immediate reply was sent by return telling the consumer whether they had won a prize. If the entrant was a winner, the message also identified which prize had been won. £1 million worth of prizes were offered including £5000 cash and wide screen televisions. Lower value prizes were also of a technical nature to fuel the aspirations of the target group.

Over 260 different codes were used to encourage repeat play by consumers. When redemptions slowed down, registered players received a further text message reminding them to play again.

The promotion required no purchase, but anyone under the age of 16 needed to have written parental permission to take part in the promotion.

During the promotional period the brand offered a special price of four bars for 99p run as an overlay to the main promotion. This was used to help encourage cross-purchase over the promoted range.

To the author's knowledge, apart from the fact that this was possibly the first ever promotion to use SMS text messaging as the basis for sales promotion activity, it was also the first instance in which a promotion was cited in the company's annual report as being a major contributor to its profitability.

The promotion was the 2002 ISP gold award winner.

Questions

1 Why are money-off promotions so common within the retail environment?

2 Describe the advantages and disadvantages of offering money off to the consumer? What are the implications for brand profitability?

3 Outline the advantages of coupon offers as an alternative to money-off promotions.

4 Why did consumers reject the proposition of everyday low prices?

5 What are the merits of price matching offers and rebates?

9 Consumer promotions 2 – product-based offers

Chapter overview

As an alternative to the variety of money-off offers, many manufacturers provide incentive for the consumer with free product. This can take a variety of forms, such as extra product free, banded packs and product samples, together with a variety of free gifts that can be given away with the product.

The wide variety of incentive offers that come under this heading will be examined in this chapter.

> ### Learning outcomes
>
> - To appreciate the range of product-based offers that might be offered to the consumer
> - To examine the benefits and disadvantages associated with product-based offers
> - To consider the role of sampling activities
> - To consider the variety of free gift offers and their implications.

Peattie *et al.* (1997)[1] divide promotions into two types:

1 Value-increasing, price-based deals
2 Value-adding deals.

They argue that value-adding promotions have the potential to make a long-term contribution to the management of a brand beyond simple sales uplifts, whereas value-increasing promotions are likely to create benefits that only endure as long as the promotion itself and then only result in sales uplifts.

According to Leeflang and van Raaij (1995),[2] marketing resources allocated to promotional tools such as coupons, premiums, rebates, samples and the like represent a significant portion of a firm's total communication efforts. In many European countries, sales promotion expenditures are larger than advertising expenditures.

We will consider the wide variety of value-adding promotions in this chapter.

Bonus packs

Bonus packs provide the consumer with some extra product at the regular price for a smaller pack. The effect is to reduce the price to the consumer by changing the price–product relationship and providing additional value.

Since the cost of product is significantly lower than the equivalent price reduction, such promotions are attractive to the manufacturer. They enable them to offer a substantial reduction in the effective price without the same effect on their margins as would be the case with direct money off.

Moreover, apart from packaging changes (although these aren't always necessary), they avoid the complications of money-off offers (some of the rebate might be withheld by the retailer) or coupons (avoiding the costs associated with redemption).

For example, at the time of writing, Coke and Diet Coke are offering a 24-can pack for a discounted price of £6.75. Tesco is offering cut flowers with 25 per cent extra free.

The mega-deal in bonus pack promotions would be the 'BOGOF' (buy one get one free), as used by Nestlé on Aero, their Munch Bunch Yoghurt and Fanta drinks.

Typically, the amount of the bonus varies between 20 and 40 per cent; one-third more is most common, such as the offer by International Paints with their cans stating '33% extra free'. Although it may appear surprising to a consumer, offers of '80 per cent more' or '100 per cent more' are not uncommon. Indeed, at the time of writing, Disco's are offering 12 for 6 with an on-pack flash stating 100 per cent extra free.

Bonus packs can often generate large in-store displays that provide the brand with greater prominence. This is likely to generate increased sales of the product. Equally, by providing the consumer with additional product, these promotions extend the period during which the consumer has the product in-home and, consequently, the time before a new purchase will be necessary. This has the effect of delaying the possibility of competitive encroachment.

A disadvantage of these promotions is that they demand additional shelf-height from the retailer, which may not always be possible. Equally, they have the effect of reducing the retailer's margin and, hence, are not always attractive to the retail trade.

We can distinguish several forms of the bonus pack offer as outlined below.

Extra fill – extra product free

As noted, this provides the consumer with an enlarged pack size, although the price charged is that of the 'normal' pack that it replaces. In some instances, such packs are specially produced and provide the consumer with 10, 20 or more per cent extra product free, such as the offer by Miracle Gro Plant Food of 20 per cent extra. In other instances, partly to offset the additional manufacturing costs and difficulties, the manufacturer simply offers a larger size for the small size price.

In their 1998 paper, Gardener and Trivedi[3] identify that packs with 'buy-one-get-one-free' may be offered to the shopper at a regular price thus adding value to the product. However, such packs do not increase brand awareness before trial purchase because the customer will only come across the product once in store (unlike samples or coupons). However, the promotion is noticeable thus enabling brand recognition and brand recall for future purchases. Since an additional amount is given for free, consumers may be persuaded to buy the product if they feel it represents a fair deal that provides value for money. This means the consumer must compare and evaluate the additional quantity received with respect to any costs that may be incurred. For instance, the additional quantity may be inconvenient to the consumer due to lack of storage space thus resulting in a weak ability to convince the consumer to make a purchase. This can be overcome by advertising the promotional offer, which tends to make the offer more noticeable.

In the case of certain product categories such as detergent, bonus packs do sway consumers to purchase the product. However, in this product category and, possibly, others, consumers may take advantage of the offer and stock up on the item, reducing their future needs for the product.

Banded packs – same product

An alternative execution, especially important to manufacturers whose product format precludes the bonus pack offer, is that of the banded pack. Here, two or more packs are banded together at a reduced price: 'Save x per cent when you buy 2', '3 for the price of 2', etc.

Both promotional formats reflect the fact that there is a differential between the cost of the product and the consumer's perception of value. Indeed, such is the relationship that these promotions can sometimes offer greater consumer value at a considerably lower cost to the manufacturer. Both devices can encourage the consumer to increase the frequency of purchase or, in the case of the bonus pack, to trade up to a larger size. They obviously have a high perceived value and can offer considerable on-shelf impact.

The choice between the two devices will depend on manufacturing circumstances. Bonus packs require a flexibility of packaging and manufacturing, which is not available to all manufacturers. The latter requires minimal production changes, although it must be recognized that the process of banding may be both labour intensive and time consuming to implement.

The device is particularly attractive to retailers and several have run such offers on their own label merchandise. For example, Tesco ran a TV commercial offering 120 two for one offers. Similarly, Boots ran three for two on a range of Summer Essentials.

Bonus-pack promotions are rapidly becoming the accepted way for a company to boost sales. This technique saves the producer from having to reduce prices in order to gain a competitive edge. A price reduction may erode a brand's equity, particularly if there is a strong and positive price–quality inference. Also, with the bonus pack, the manufacturer can be relatively sure that the 'extra' product will reach the consumer rather than be absorbed as additional margin by the retailer. In most cases, bonus-pack promotions represent limited-time offers, designed to stimulate short-term sales and boost product awareness.

Marketing bonus packs can have drawbacks in terms of production capability, warehousing, shipping, inventory and shelving. Some oversize containers need significant modifications in the filling process. In some cases, the bonus pack bottle may be an inch higher or the 'buy on get one free' pack twice as big and will not fit on the shelf. Health and beauty care manufacturers frequently complain that grocery stores are reluctant to take bonus packs for this reason.

However, Ong *et al.*[4] suggest that:

> ... consumers view high volume bonus packs with scepticism. The higher the extra amount added 'free' the less believable the offer.

They add that 'occasionally, bonus packs offer 100 per cent more free. While offers like these may catch the attention of consumers and impress them, there is a chance that the manufacturers may be inadvertently sacrificing the credibility of their brands.'

Moreover, they also identified industry perceptions that bonus packs tend to attract current users of the products but not new users for the product category.

According to Guerreiro *et al.* (2004),[5] bonus-pack offers have potential drawbacks in terms of production capacity, warehousing, shipping, inventory, package design and size changes and shelf size limitations.

Similar research conducted by Smith and Sinha (2000)[6] indicates that consumers overwhelmingly preferred volume savings to money off. In their research, they tested three promotional executions: 50 per cent off, buy one get one free and buy 2 get 50 per cent off.

Banded packs – assorted products

A variation on the theme is where the manufacturer bands together two or more different products to enhance the offer to the consumer. In some instances, the products may come from different manufacturers. Such promotions achieve two different objectives, one for each of the participants. For the promoted brand, the attractiveness of the offer is enhanced by the provision of some free additional product (often associated with the product in terms of usage). For the carried brand it provides the opportunity to sample the product without the normal distribution costs.

In other instances both products are provided by the same manufacturer. The objectives are similar with the opportunity being provided to sample some form of variation on the original product or, alternatively, a new product from the same stable. Nestlé, for example, banded small packs of their Shredded Wheat Fruitful variation to the original Shredded Wheat packs.

Inman *et al.* (1997)[7] found that deals with restrictions, such as two items per customer or those that offer goods until a certain date, elicit more favourable evaluations from consumers than the same deals without restrictions.

Product sampling

Sampling is the process of providing the consumer with a quantity of a product at no charge to encourage trial. Whilst it is extremely effective in this respect, it must be recognized that it also very expensive.

Product sampling is a sales promotion technique used by companies to encourage trial of their products. It involves giving away a trial-size of a product to prospective customers in order to enable them to experience the product at little or no risk before making a financial commitment to its purchase. Tesco used the technique for a new range of desserts from Gü, offering samples outside the store. Consumers were given a discount voucher against their purchase from the range of products that were heavily featured inside the store. Additionally, to reflect the indulgent nature of the products, the brand ran a competition with a prize of 'a decadent night for 2 at the Ritz'.

The primary objective of product sampling is to generate product trial. Once trial has been achieved it is anticipated that consumers will purchase the brand. In one study by Costa (1983)[8] purchase rates following sample trial were found to be almost 60 per cent.

In certain instances manufacturers within the field of FMCG use sampling techniques distributing the product sample door-to-door or banded on an alternative product (own or alternative manufacturer) or, sometimes, banded to an appropriate magazine. Samples can also be provided in store or distributed at appropriate events.

There are several important requirements:

- It must be possible to produce a small trial size that does not cost too much to the manufacturer
- The trial size must be adequate to demonstrate the particular attributes of the product to the user
- Sometimes the sample is accompanied by a money-off voucher to encourage the consumer to trade up to the regular size
- The purchase cycle must be short so that the trialist does not forget the product before the next purchase of the category is made.

As noted above, there are several approaches towards sampling promotions:

- Door-to-door

  Small samples of the product are distributed on a door-to-door basis to enable potential consumers to try the product without risk or cost. Although the technique is highly expensive, it may overcome the resistance to purchase on the part of the consumer and, particularly if the product is found to have advantages in use, may result in purchases being made at the full price. In some instances, the door drop may be accompanied by a money-off voucher entitling the holder to make the subsequent purchase at a reduced price.

  The advantages associated with the door-to-door approach are that samples can be targeted to those households most likely to 'need' the product. Moreover, samples can be dropped on a local or regional basis to limit the overall costs of the operation or to enable the launch to be 'rolled-out' to areas progressively.

- Mail

  Similar to the above in terms of the ability to target consumers the mailed sample is dependent either on an existing database to ensure that samples are sent to named recipients or are simply sent to the 'householder'. As with door-to-door, the approach enables regionalization of the offer.

- Newspaper/magazine

  Using newspapers and magazines enables much more focused targeting, although the numbers involved may well be substantial dependent on the circulation of the title. Understanding the interests of the readers of specific titles is a key facet of the promotional technique, since products can be specifically targeted to consumers based on their readership profiles. Many magazines are used for this form of offer.

- On-pack

  The on-pack format has been mentioned earlier in this chapter. Often it enables a new product to achieve greater standing in the market place by associating it with another established product that is already in distribution. The image of the new product is thereby enhanced. It is, of course, dependent on the co-operation of the carrying brand and may take a considerable amount of time to negotiate. Sarson's vinegar ran an on-pack promotion offering a free portion of fish and chips.

- In-store

  Although relatively expensive, in-store sampling may provide the opportunity to provide a direct interface between the product and the consumer. Especially in those instances where the product is, perhaps, complicated to understand or new, the opportunity for a sales person to explain the functions of the product and to enable them to sample it may be very desirable. The trade likes such promotions since they generate in-store activity, which tends to encourage a higher level of all product purchases, not just the product that is being sampled.

  Many retailers provide regular samplings of products, sometimes in conjunction with the manufacturers, in other instances on their own initiative. Staff are deployed to specific points in the store where passing customers are invited to try a particular product. Often these sample tastings are accompanied by some additional offer (such as a reduced-price coupon) to encourage those who like the product to buy a regular size pack.

  According to Cook (1995)[9], in-store tasting is a valuable device for promoting sales. It has the potential to achieve penetration of a consumer base that may yet have to try the product. He provides a comparison of sales promotion activity for a brand to indicate the impact on weekly volume:

10% price cut with in-store display	+49%
Multibuy plus in-store display	+76%
In-store tasting	+133%

- Mobile – vehicles or street displays

  Some companies have created special vehicles to provide the means for sampling a new product. The vehicle is driven, perhaps, to a supermarket car park or to some other location where the opportunity is presented to offer free samples to passing consumers. Similarly, some manufacturers have specially erected displays in shopping precincts or railway stations to achieve the same outcome. In the USA Coca Cola utilized this approach to sample a new flavour, whilst Procter & Gamble sampled new variations of their Sunny D drink.

Historically, several cigarette manufacturers provided samples of their brands at sponsored events, although their use of the technique has diminished as a consequence of the agreement to limit promotional activity in the category.

● Trial offers

These are often used for expensive items to encourage consumers to make the initial purchase. If the consumer is dissatisfied with the product during use, they can return it to the manufacturer (or retailer) for a full refund of the purchase price. An example is that of the mattress that can be purchased by the consumer and used for 60 days, after which period they can return it to the manufacturer without penalty for a full refund of the purchase price.

Hunt and Jupe (1994)[10] argue that product sampling is a cost-effective way of communicating with potential consumers. Their effectiveness has been improved by new forms of data collection and processing, pre-screening and targeting of recipients and improvements in field control operations.

Their research indicates that 84 per cent of those interviewed claimed to have bought a different product than their usual one because they had received a sample to try.

However, subsequent research by McGuinness et al. (1992)[11] showed somewhat lower purchase rates at only 29 per cent across three brands of toothpaste, shampoo and dishwashing liquid.

In 2002, Gilbert and Jackaria[12] conducted research to specifically compare the effectiveness of four promotional tools, namely:

1 Coupons
2 Price discount
3 Product samples
4 Buy-one-get-one-free offers.

They found that 53.8 per cent of the consumers they interviewed have often been led to buy a product when there was a 'buy-one-get-one-free' promotion.

Their results indicated that not all consumers were influenced by the four promotional tools to the same degree. The respondents were asked on a three-point scale (often, sometimes and never) whether they had opted to purchase, based upon any one of the four promotional tools (i.e. coupon, discount, sample and buy-one-get-one-free), a product in the supermarket. This study found in reported behaviour buy-one-get-one-free received the highest rating 96.3 per cent (when the often and sometimes score were added), followed by discount 92.6 per cent, sample 67.5 per cent and coupon 65.6 per cent.

Free gifts

Among the variety of promotional tools, premiums (free gifts or give-aways) occupy an important place. A premium is a product or a service offered free or at a relatively low price in return for the purchase of one or many products or services. It may or may not belong to the same product category as the product or service that is purchased.

Many manufacturers seek to provide incentive for the purchase by offering a free gift item at the time of purchase. Once again, there is the advantage of immediacy in that if the consumer is attracted by the gift they are more likely to purchase the product. There are several distinct forms of free gift offer.

The Institute of Sales Promotion (ISP) in the UK defines six different types of premiums:

1   On-pack promotions
2   In-pack premiums
3   Extra product
4   Reusable packs

     all of which are considered in this chapter, together with:

5   Free mail-ins, with-purchase premiums
6   Self-liquidating premiums.

The last two types are considered in the next chapter.

According to Bertrand (1998),[13] in 1996 the reported sales volume of products used as premiums in the USA reached $9.5 billion. This represents a more than 18 per cent increase over the sales reported in 1995. The interest that marketers display in using premiums for promoting their products and services is exemplified in the growing number of annual trade shows such as the Premium Incentive Show (Goldsborough 1998) and the Motivation Show (Kaeter 1998). The trade shows focus on demonstrating the positive impact of premiums on customers' purchasing behaviour.

Although comparable figures for other countries are difficult to obtain, there is little doubt that premium offers represent a significant part of the promotional armoury. Research conducted by Mintel[14] for the UK market (2000) indicates that many categories use premium offers to provide incentive for purchase.

In their research, the five categories that were perceived to most use premium offers were:

1   Breakfast cereals   59%
2   Crisps/snacks   27%
3   Soft drinks   19%
4   Tea/coffee   16%
5   Chocolate   10%

On-pack free gifts

The on-pack free gift is any item of merchandise that is presented to the consumer by affixing it to the external surface of the product. The application of the technique is commonly seen in a wide variety of areas. A free spoon attached to a jar of coffee, for example, or a computer programme affixed to a magazine. Indeed, it is in the latter area where the promotional device is most frequently available. The obvious disadvantage is that of pilferage. If the free gift is missing, the consumer is less likely to purchase the promoted product.

Promotional items may gain value in the longer term. The NatWest pigs offered as incentives to young account holders are now collector's items and are worth considerable amounts of money!

In-pack free gifts

The in-pack free gift is used by a number of packaged goods manufacturers, with a description of the gift on the pack surface and the item only available once the packaging has been opened. Cereal products are regular users of this promotional tool. An obvious problem with this form of promotion is the possibility of contamination between the product contents and the free gift item and great care needs to be taken to avoid this occurring. Some manufacturers seal the free gift prior to its insertion into the pack, but this adds considerably to the price of the promotion. Kellogg's periodically run in-pack free gift offers, for example, the Horrible Histories audio book with breakfast cereals including Coco Pops, Frosties and Corn Flakes.

A similar promotion is Felix's 'Big Days Out', used to launch its multi-pack. Each pack contains 12 x 400g cat food cans with two-for-one activity vouchers inserted into packs. The promotion offers two booklets of vouchers to collect, the first of which offers 85 activity days out including paintballing, go-karting, and ten pin bowling. The second contains over 100 options including visits to theme parks, museums and wildlife parks. The promotion is designed to encourage people to trade up to the multi-packs.

Precision Marketing (1997)[15] reported that KFC ran a promotion offering plastic figures in their children's meals. Although the gift had been tested to see if there were any detrimental effects when placed in proximity to hot foods, they did not test whether young children might put the figures in their mouths, suck off the plastic and use the remaining wire frame to poke their eyes.

With-pack free gift

The with-pack free gift is an execution that relies on the co-operation of the retailer, since the free item of merchandise is not attached to the purchased item. However, it offers the advantage of not requiring any changes to the manufacturing process and is, therefore, available both to manufacturers of products and providers of services alike. The application of the technique is particularly popular within the cosmetics trade and free gifts of substantial value are frequently offered by the makers of perfumes and aftershaves.

In some instances, the perceived value of the free gift is enhanced by creating a themed offer to tie in with some other event. McDonalds has regularly offered their children's meals with tie-ins to current film titles. Similarly, Burger King has mounted a promotion that links to the release of the latest Star Wars movie. The promotion operates at two levels with Star Wars gift items given free with a purchase of a children's meal, whilst adults are offered the chance to enter a competition in order to win a variety of Star Wars themed prizes.

In one such offer, Sainsbury's offered a free cool bag (usual price £4.99) in exchange for five stickers from an identified own-brand assortment of products. This reflects the increasing tendency on the part of retailers to mount sales promotional offers against their own-label products, rather than simply relying on manufacturer/brand promotions to create in-store activity and excitement.

Pack as free gift

Another important area of free gift is the pack itself. Once it is recognized that the packaging, or some alternative presentation, may represent added value to the consumer, it can be appreciated that this is an area of considerable potential. This format has been used by a variety of packaged goods manufacturers, either with reproductions of previous packaging (history has value) or to present the consumer with some reusable container device that will be retained after the product has been consumed.

Several years ago, Ariel offered 2 kg of their soap powder in a reusable container. Once the contents have been used the consumer purchases a refill pack to be placed within the container. The promotion offers the consumer additional value at the initial time of purchase together with the opportunity to save money by purchasing refill packs rather than conventional packaging. A similar approach has been taken by Kraft Jacobs Suchard in France where consumers can purchase sachets of Carte Noire coffee at a lower price than in the conventional glass jars.

Most mustards in France, for example, come to the consumer in small glass containers that can be used as drinking glasses once the mustard has been used. Nestlé recently offered a series of reusable containers with its Nescafé instant coffee brand. Each canister bore a different legend, reinforcing the brand proposition of best beans, best blend and best taste. In this case, even after the product was consumed, the canister reminded the purchaser of the brand benefits.

Onken have taken the notion of the reusable container one step further with their Onkyblok yoghurt product. The child-targeted product is contained in packaging that can be used as a building block similar to Lego once the product has been consumed. So, the packaging has a collectable value since many of them are required in order to play effectively.

Free gifts offered with, on or in the product packaging are often attractive items that represent a high impulse level encouraging consumers to buy the brand. Sometimes the merchandise itself is branded, e.g. Coca Cola offered a free glass when a specified volume of the brand was purchased. Displays of the branded glasses were placed next to bottles of Coca Cola increasing their in-store presence and visibility.

All of these varieties of gift incentives have the attraction of immediacy and, if well selected, can add considerable value to the brand. Often their use serves to extend the brand values by a close association of the free gift with the primary product, for example, offering a tumbler with a bottle of spirits.

On-pack promotions offer free gifts or give-aways in an attempt to attract the consumer and alter purchase behaviour by adding to the perceived value of the product. There are several noteworthy factors operating here. First of all, such promotions are often left for the consumer to discover when they encounter the product in the store. Since the details of the on-pack promotions are often crammed into a small space and offered on the product itself, it gives rise to the possibility that the offer will go unnoticed. Even when shoppers do spot the offer, since the description tends to be small and wordy, they may disregard the promotion and make their purchase selection based on other criteria. This disregard on the part of the consumer may be further pronounced since the nature of the on-pack incentive and the consumer's attraction to the same may vary widely. In fact, this technique can actually prevent a purchase if consumers do not find the premium attractive. Although the offers are meant to entice consumers and can alter the purchase decision, the requirements for the consumer are somewhat demanding and the evaluation (understanding) process time consuming.

A variation of the theme is for the manufacturer to offer sequential free gifts over time, which serves to deliver loyalty over an extended period. These often take the form of a collectable series of gifts, which encourages the consumer to continue purchases of the promoted product in order to collect the set. The tea companies have long given away cards with each purchase, which are then placed in a collector album to encourage loyalty to the promotion. The gaps in the album induce consumers to continue collecting until they have completed the set.

Many companies mail homes with floppy disk or CD-Rom-based materials, accompanied by some form of incentive to encourage them to sign up to their service provision. This is particularly common amongst the Internet Service Providers who mail a free item of computer software together with their ISP access programme to encourage recipients to install the programme and, hopefully, adopt them as their ISP.

Collect promotions are not a new phenomenon. An early example of this promotional format was that of the Leibig company (now part of Brooke Bond Oxo). They offered a series of collector cards depicting a variety of themes as early as 1870. Indeed, the promotion was continued until 1956. Moreover, since the promotional items were available in a variety of languages (Italian, German, French and English) it is also an early example of a multinational promotional campaign.

Above all, all forms of free gift offer represent a distinctive form of promotional activity that will serve to differentiate the brand from its competitors. They have obvious on-shelf impact that may induce the consumer to purchase the brand ahead of its competitors.

The key problem associated with free gifts is that of identifying items of sufficient perceived value at an appropriate cost to the brand. Given the comparatively narrow margins available, the amount of money that can be allocated to such free gifts is somewhat small. Low-cost items may be of poor quality and value and, thus, serve to detract from the brand rather than add value to it. A good decision basis is to ensure that the quality of the free gift is perceived to be at least the same as that of the brand itself. The costs of a free gift promotion may be quite high if the quality requirement is to be met. Some degree of lateral thinking is required to identify a free gift that is both desirable, appropriate and can be obtained at an affordable price.

Simonson *et al.* (1994)[16] have argued that offering an unattractive premium (i.e. a premium that is perceived by customers as having little or no value) may negatively affect brand image and attitude toward the brand. In one of the studies they reported, giving consumers the (fictitious) opportunity to get a free subscription to the *Audio Video Interiors* magazine for the purchase of a JVC CD player led to significantly less choice (22 per cent) of the brand compared to a situation where no premium was offered. The authors argued that consumers develop negative reactions toward brands that resort to marketing gimmicks such as useless premiums in an effort to attract them.

Other disadvantages of the technique are associated with the different executions. As already noted, on-pack free gifts are subject to pilferage and this may annoy the real purchaser. Overcoming the problem by seeking to insert the free gift inside the packaging may require significant alterations to the packaging machinery and, particularly with food products, may themselves require additional packaging to avoid contamination of the contents. With-pack free gifts require a substantial level of trade co-operation, which may make their implementation more difficult to achieve.

Bannister *et al.* (1997)[17] writing in *Admap* state:

> The optimum is to devise a series of offers or a continuous offer which will not only attract present non-buyers, but also keep them with the brand for long enough for attitudes to change until that brand becomes the preferred brand. Loyalty is being built into the idea of a promotion rather than the brand.

It is important to note that this is especially true and evident in the case of petrol promotions. An example would be offers such as bonus packs (offering additional quantities of the product at a reduced price) or other forms of loyalty bonus: collecting proofs of purchase or 'points' in order to save for a gift may achieve the objective.

Many companies are involved in loyalty-building schemes, which can operate either in the short or longer term. Henri Wintermans offer a limited range of gifts in exchange for pack inserts. The consumer is free to choose how long they wish to participate in the promotion; that is whether to redeem a few vouchers for a small gift or to continue collecting until a large item can be redeemed.

In 1998, Pierre Chandon[18] chaired a special session to examine the responses to monetary and non-monetary promotions. Specifically it addressed questions such as why consumers react more to sales promotions than to price reductions and the effects of promotions on brand equity.

In a paper presented at the session, Chandon *et al.* (1998)[19] proposed that sales promotions can provide consumers with six different benefits:

- savings
- quality
- convenience
- entertainment
- exploration
- self-expression.

In their research, they demonstrated that monetary promotions such as coupons and money off are predominantly evaluated on their utilitarian benefits. Non-monetary promotions such as free gifts, competitions and sweepstakes are predominantly evaluated on the basis of their hedonic (pleasure-giving) benefits. In consequence, they hypothesized that non-monetary promotions are more effective for hedonic products, suggesting that promotions can have an intrinsic value for consumers beyond the monetary savings that they offer.

In a subsequent paper, the same authors (Chandon *et al.* 2000)[20] argue that a sales promotion's effectiveness is determined by the congruency between its benefits and those of the promoted product. In particular, because of the inherent differences between monetary and non-monetary promotions they are, respectively, more effective for different types of products.

They define the benefits of sales promotion as the perceived value attached to the sales promotion experience, which can include both promotion exposure (e.g. seeing a promotion on a product) and usage (e.g. redeeming a coupon or buying a promoted product). This definition implies that consumers respond to sales promotions because of the positive experience they provide or because of their customer value.

Increasing sales promotion effectiveness with non-monetary promotions

One of the major conclusions of the benefit congruency identified by Chandon *et al.* (2000)[20] is that marketers can increase sales promotion effectiveness by matching the type of promotion to the type of product being promoted. When this cannot be done, for example, when the promotion is offered across different brands or when the promoted brand is bought for a wide variety of benefits, the benefit congruency framework recommends using promotions that combine multiple hedonic and utilitarian benefits. Such multi-benefit promotions would appeal to the different benefits sought by the various segments of consumers that buy each product. They would also match the different benefits provided by the various brands promoted under a multi-brand promotion. They suggest that this can be achieved by designing promotions that combine monetary and non-monetary incentives (e.g. an in-pack coupon with an on-pack contest or a multi-pack refund with an in-store display that emphasizes new product uses). The effects of non-monetary promotions were always positive and were relatively more stable across product types. Non-monetary promotions are also more likely than monetary promotions to create unique brand associations that can reinforce brand image.

D'Astous and Jacob (2002)[21] conducted research in order to identify the appeal to consumers of various premium offers. They found that consumer reactions to a promotion offer were more positive when the premium was direct than when it was delayed: promotion that involved direct premiums were better appreciated and led to significantly less perception of manipulation intent.

There was also partial support for their hypothesis that the greater the quantity of product it is necessary to purchase in order to get the premium, the more negative the consumer reaction to a promotional offer. Consumer appreciation of a promotional offer was negatively associated with the quantity of product one needed to purchase in order to obtain the premium. Consumers liked promotional offers that indicated the value of the premium, but mentioning this value led to the inference that there might be some gimmick behind the offer. The greater the interest in the premium item offered, the more consumers appreciated the offer and the less the perception of manipulation intent.

According to Hiam (2000),[22] one fundamental element that must be considered in designing premium-based sales promotions is how well the premium is integrated with the brand's positioning. Sales promotion efforts typically pursue short-term sales objectives. It is important to consider the possible effects of the relationships between the premium, product and brand on the long-term variables such as brand image and brand equity.

D'Astous and Landreville (2003)[23] argue that the results of several different studies point to the importance of considering the fit between the product and its premium when evaluating the effectiveness of premium-based promotions. When the product–premium congruity is weak, the promotional offer is likely to be perceived as inconsistent and perhaps opportunistic. In addition, the perceived value of the promotional offer may be enhanced when the premium can actually be integrated with the consumption or utilization of the product (e.g. a glass offered with the purchase of a bottle of Bacardi rum).

With respect to consumer appreciation of sales promotions, they found that premium attractiveness played a significant role in shaping consumer evaluative reactions. Consistent with the findings reported in Simonson *et al.* (1994),[16] a promotional offer that included an attractive premium was better appreciated by consumers. Although consumers were generally more appreciative of promotional offers with attractive premiums, the results showed that the fit between the premium and the product category had a positive and significant impact on appreciation of the promotional offer when the premium was unattractive. That is, product–premium fit did not matter when consumers were interested in the premiums, but it had a significant effect on consumer appreciation in the case of less interesting premiums.

Case study

GLAXOSMITHKLINE – RIBENA

Research conducted by GlaxoSmithKline identified the fact that people drink more diluting soft drink when they keep it ready diluted in the fridge.

The objective was to exploit this finding to encourage households to keep bulk quantities of ready-to-drink Ribena.

The brand offered a free fridge jug, designed to fit into both the shelf and door compartments and was banded by a PVC sleeve to 2-litre bottles of Ribena Original, Light and Toothkind.

The promotion was mounted in the major supermarkets during the summer months of 2002. During the period of the promotion over 1 million jugs were given away to consumers and the brand achieved its highest level of monthly value sales for over 18 months, up nearly 37 per cent against the same period in the previous year.

The promotion was given an award for the best use of sales promotion 2002 by the Marketing Communication Consultants Association.

Questions

1 What are the advantages of offering free product rather than cash as an incentive to purchase?
2 When does product sampling represent an important marketing tool?
3 How can product samples be given to consumers? What are the advantages and disadvantages of each of the approaches?
4 Identify the difficulties associated with locating appropriate free gifts to offer to consumers.
5 Visit a local retail outlet and identify brands offering free gifts as an incentive to purchase. Evaluate their likely appeal to the presumed target audience.

10 Consumer promotions 3 – other consumer promotions

Chapter overview

This chapter deals with a variety of promotional formats that are comparatively inexpensive to implement. In most instances, they afford opportunities for extensive display to surround the brand and create an aura of activity without the expense of money off or free product. Moreover, they offer a wide variety of creative opportunities that can add excitement to the brand.

In addition we will consider those promotions that are designed to inject a degree to loyalty to the brand purchase by offering incentives over an extended period of time.

Learning outcomes

- To consider the variety of alternative consumer promotion techniques
- To examine the role of free mail-ins and self-liquidating promotions
- To consider the advantages and disadvantages of competitions
- To appreciate the benefits of loyalty-based schemes
- To assess the role of character merchandising.

Free mail-ins

An alternative to the free gift item offered at point of purchase is to invite the consumer to send in an appropriate number of proofs of purchase for a gift item. Although it is somewhat more complex in its implementation, the technique has a number of direct advantages.

Since the free gift may be occasioned by multiple purchases of the product, the gift item can be more expensive and, hence, more attractive to the consumer. As such, it may add to the differentiation of the brand from its competitors. There is an obvious loyalty aspect to the execution since the consumer will have to make several purchases in order to obtain the necessary proofs of purchase. In addition, as with some couponing techniques, although motivated to buy the brand with the intention of redeeming the free gift, many consumers forget to do so. In 2003, Kellogg's linked up with Amazon to run a joint free mail-in promotion. Consumers were offered a free best-seller in exchange for tokens from promotional packs of various cereal brands. The chosen book would be delivered by Amazon at no charge.

At the time of writing, the packaged drink product Capri Sun are offering a free mail-in linked to the Disney film *Madagascar*. Purchasers are invited to collect tokens from product packs to redeem a series of bendy character toys. Each toy representing a character from the film requires tokens plus 99p towards the cost of postage and packaging.

Similar problems are present with free mail-ins as with other free gifts in terms of the difficulty of obtaining suitable merchandise to offer. Additionally, however, it must be remembered that the extra costs of postage, packaging and handling may make the promotion too expensive to run.

The promotional device lacks immediacy and consumers will be far less motivated to buy the brand if they are expected to collect wrappers and wait to receive the free gift; to a large extent, this will depend on the nature and perceived value of the free gift being offered. Finally, the technique has relatively low appeal to the trade.

As with all forms of free gift merchandise, it is important to test the items both to ensure the level of acceptance of the gifts as well as to anticipate the likely levels of redemption.

Two further examples serve to illustrate the working of free mail-in offers. Heinz linked its Linda McCartney range of meat-free products with Kumala wine to provide a free mail-in promotion on 2.7 million packs. Consumers were invited to collect four tokens to send off for a free 75cl bottle of Kumala wine together with a wine and dine guide advising which wines go best with each meal.

Similarly, the sugar brand Silver Spoon offered a free mail-in on its low-calorie sweetener Sucron. An on-pack coupon offer invited customers to send off for a skipping rope with a digital calorie counter and a four-page booklet featuring tips on healthy eating and recipes featuring the sugar substitute. Both examples demonstrate the linking of the brand with an appropriate offer that extends the role and understanding of the brand positioning.

Prior to the government restrictions on smoking, the makers of King Edward, Castella and Panama cigars mailed a promotional offer to selected households. The mailer contained a free five pack of Castella mild cigars and information on a wide range of free gifts that could be redeemed by collecting pack fronts from the participating brands.

Self-liquidating offers

As the name suggests, these incentives are 'paid for' by the consumer. In effect, the manufacturer uses his bulk buying power to purchase gift merchandise, which is then offered to the consumer at cost. Obviously, depending on the item to be offered and the skills of negotiation, it is possible to offer such items at considerably less than their perceived retail value. The pack, or other promotional material, details the nature of the offer (for example, free cutlery set with a retail value of xxx, yours for only half xxx and proofs of purchase) and is thus attractive to manufacturers. The promotional costs of self-liquidating offers are low: the consumer bears the costs of the item themselves, whilst the brand bears the cost of distribution and display. They offer the opportunity to create an offer of apparent value without having to bear the associated costs. As such, they represent useful vehicles for the creation of a presence at the point of purchase and, as with other gift-based promotions, represent the opportunity to provide 'dealer loaders' where the manufacturer gives samples of the merchandise to retail staff in exchange for display space or some other consideration.

There are a number of aspects to consider with promotions of this nature:

- The item is offered at a reduced price to the consumer. The manufacturer uses his buying power to negotiate a significantly lower price for the item than the normal retail price.
- Both prices need to be displayed with the offer to indicate the saving that the consumer can make.
- The merchandise, if selected appropriately, can not only add value to the brand, it can inform consumers of additional uses for the product.
- Self-liquidating promotions offer the potential to create exciting point-of-sale displays.
- The items themselves can be used as 'dealer loaders': offered to members of the retail channel in return for their performing specific services for the brand. These might include providing special display, increasing shelf facings, etc.
- Comparatively few items will be redeemed by consumers so there is a potential risk of the company being left with large stocks once the promotion is over.

However, as a general rule, they are unlikely to generate major trade enthusiasm. Retailers are aware that self-liquidating promotions generate relatively low levels of consumer redemption and, hence, are not likely to create significant increases in sales volume.

An example is Homepride flour's offer of five new collectables featuring their cartoon character 'Fred', including an apron, a shopping pad and holder for 'points' from special promotional packs. All items are self-liquidators.

Recent years have seen an unusual application of the principle of self-liquidators. On a regular basis, media proprietors use the device of telephone-based competitions to reward participants in competition formats. Readers, viewers and listeners are invited to phone a dedicated phone line with the answer to a question. Although it is sometimes made explicit, in some instances the participant is not informed that the phone call will be charged to their account. The revenue generated will, often, more than cover the costs of the promotional offer.

Contests and competitions

A contest or competition is one in which consumers compete for prizes based on the exercise of skill and judgement. In addition, there is usually a tie-break to enable the judges to identify the winners in the event that several competitors have the correct answers. The entry form usually requires some proof of purchase and, in some instances, it forms part of the packaging.

In some cases, entrants are required to supply some personal details that can form part of a database for the manufacturer. One of the problems associated with the competition format is that, despite the attractiveness of the prize structure, there can often be a considerable delay between entering the competition and the winners being announced. This may act as a deterrent to entry. Equally, if the requirements for entry are perceived as being too difficult or daunting the resultant entry level is likely to be quite low.

A sweepstakes or lottery format differs in that the winners are determined solely by luck or chance. There are various executions of the sweepstakes format. Some manufacturers include a sealed element within the packaging, which instantly reveals whether the consumer has won a prize or not. In other instances the device is concealed beneath a ring pull on a can. Another execution is the scratch card where concealed elements on the card are revealed progressively to identify whether the card is a winner. However, in order to remain within the law, there can be no requirement for a proof of purchase. Accordingly, it is possible to submit an entry by post, with the manufacturer opening a pack on behalf of the entrant, who then wins the associated prize if the package is a winning one.

Some manufacturers require the consumer to compete over an extended period of time. 'Game pieces' are given away at the point of purchase (again with no requirement to make a purchase in order to qualify for entry) and the consumer is required to collect specific pieces in order to enter the draw. This device is used to promote extended purchasing and has been used widely by petrol retailers. One of the most famous executions is the Shell Make Money promotion in which consumers were given one half of a bank note in a sealed gamepiece and were required to match it with the other half of the same denomination in order to win the money. So successful was the promotion that many consumers ran ads in local and national newspapers, advertising the fact that they held one half of a high denomination note and were seeking the other half in order to share the prize. Other outlets such as McDonalds have used the sweepstake format in order to encourage potential consumers to visit their restaurants.

Both competitions and sweepstakes can be used to generate excitement around the brand. Often the prize structure provides exotic prizes including luxury holidays and expensive cars, both of which lend themselves readily to point-of-sales featuring.

This is an area that has enjoyed considerable growth over recent years, especially with the development of pseudo lotteries in which the consumer is, apparently, offered the opportunity to win a prize of sizeable value.

Contests and competitions are good point-of-sale vehicles as they represent an opportunity to add to the brand aura. The offer of a substantial prize fund in cash or merchandise is likely to attract the attention of the potential consumer. The chance to win, say, one of ten cars, or a luxury holiday will be likely to motivate considerable numbers of consumers to fulfil the competition entry requirements. However, set against the sales volume, the costs of such activities are relatively low.

A recent 'World Cup' promotion mounted by Coca Cola on a world-wide basis to reinforce their sponsorship activities of the event is a perfect example of the implementation of this form of pseudo lottery. The 'instant win' prizes were obtained by revealing the identity of the prize by removing the ring pull from the can. The rules of the competition provide, however, that anyone can enter the competition simply by sending in their name and address to the handling house who will open a can on their behalf.

The disadvantages of the promotional format is that they lack the immediacy of other forms of incentive. Once again, the retail trade is aware that they will often generate only low levels of consumer participation. In many respects, the success of the format will be dependent both on the creative treatment and the scale and nature of the prizes offered.

One word of caution, however, most countries require that participation in competition formats be dependent upon the exercise of some form of skill. The absence of inherent skill in a competition may render the promotion illegal. An alternative option is to remove the purchase requirement on the part of the consumer! Although this sounds less than sensible, the reality is that most consumers intending to enter the competition will continue to buy the brand as if it were a requirement of entry.

According to Peattie and Peattie (1995)[1] competitions offer several advantages:

1 Differentiation opportunities – by offering a range of interesting or exciting prizes, the brand can differentiate its offer from those of its competitors.

2 Link-up opportunities – to events, media, etc. In some instances, the prizes can be linked to some more widely publicized event, which itself provides greater impact for the offer. Cadbury Dairy Milk bars carried a flash on the front of the packaging that stated 'Win 2 seats at the best British events in 2005, instantly'.

3 Point-of-sale opportunities – by featuring the major prizes manufacturers can create exciting and different point-of-sale material that can be used to merchandise the brand at the point of purchase.

4 Quality cue appeal – competitions can offer relevant quality prizes. In a recent competition, Haribo – the German confectionery manufacturer – mounted a competition reminiscent of the Roald Dahl novel *Charlie and the Chocolate Factory*. Children were given the chance to take over the sweet factory for a day. Prizewinners were those who had written no more than 100 words on why they thought they were qualified to run the factory and become a sweet taster.

5 Demand smoothing

6 Consumer interaction – the consumer is directly involved with the promoted brand and in most instances the tie-break device used to identify the winners requires that the consumer complete some form of sentence that requires them to think more deeply about the attributes of the brand.

This latter point is reinforced by Ward and Hill (1991)[2] who indicate that promotional games provide opportunities for consumers to win a prize through luck or skill that are designed to promote a product by enhancing learning and/or involvement with the product or service.

An important aspect of prize-based formats is inevitably the perceived value and number of prizes. Often competitions and lotteries utilize a pyramid structure that is one major prize, middle tiers of prizes and a large number of lowest value prizes. Further, in some instances, the manufacturer includes a device to ensure that everybody 'wins'. Usually, this takes the form of a money-off voucher for a subsequent purchase of the brand. Although not of major value in itself, it helps avoid the dissatis-faction and disappointment associated with competitions in which the consumer makes multiple entries but does not win.

Lucozade, for example, mounted a competition to link with its sponsorship of the FIA World Rally Championship. Entrants were offered the chance to win one of 80 places to compete against the professionals. Consumers were invited to enter the on-pack prize draw online or by text. If they won one of the 80 places they were invited to compete in a series of UK heats where they received basic rally training. The five best entrants all received VIP treatment at the Finland stage of the rally where they underwent intensive training. The winner at that stage will take their place in the Australian rally in Perth. The promotion was backed with a roadshow, advertising and point-of-sale material.

Finish, the dishwasher tablet brand offered a top prize of £100 000 in a movie tie-in promotion. The brand linked up with the 20th Century Fox *Robots* film. The pro-motion centred on in-pack brochures that incorporated an instant win gamecard. As one of the film's characters is a dishwasher, Finish decided the brand and the film would work well together. A further 5000 runners up prizes of £1000 were also offered. To reinforce the film tie-up, packs featured eight collectable stickers showing characters from the film.

In a further paper by Peattie and Peattie (1994)[3] they describe several features of competitions that make them particularly suitable for financial services marketing:

- Differentiation opportunities. Competitions offer a useful source of differentiation. Although they can also be replicated, 'me-too' competitions risk failure if early com-petitions have exhausted the current supply of available competition-minded con-sumers.

- Link-up opportunities to above-the-line promotion or PR efforts. Abbey National ran a major national TV advertising campaign that featured its 'open an account and win a car' promotion.

- They add a tangible dimension to products. Services cannot readily be displayed but competition posters and leaflets provide opportunities for interesting, tangible and visible point-of-sale materials. Barclays have regularly used leaflets and posters high-lighting competitions and their prizes.

- Quality cue appeal. The intangibility of services prompts customers to look for sur-rogate 'cues' to judge service quality. The pursuit of 'quality cues' among financial services competition sponsors is reflected in their choice of prizes.

- Demand smoothing. The perishability of services means that demand fluctuations are the 'most troublesome' services marketing problem. Competitions can encour-age purchases during usually slack periods, or can support an attempt to bring for-ward seasonal purchases of products such as traveller's cheques.

- Consumer interaction. Interactive marketing is vital for services, but difficult to cre-ate through advertising, which is generally a unidirectional means of communica-tion, absorbed relatively passively by the potential consumer. Competitions can cre-ate real interaction and involvement between the customer, the service and the service provider. This may involve the customer analysing the service to answer questions or devise a slogan, sending away for information or meeting the service provider (thereby creating new service encounter opportunities).

- Cost certainty. Barring accidents, competitions involve predictable costs and are more cost-effective in maintaining perceived quality levels than 'give-away' promotions. This is because giving customers attractive 'freebies' that project a quality image can be prohibitively expensive. Give-aways can still be effective where the target group of customers is relatively small, the long-term business potential is good and the utility to the customer of a 'freebie' is high (children and students being good examples). Every year the major banks compete for the custom of the recent university intake. They offer a variety of tangible benefits to attract these students to open their accounts with the promoted bank. Offers include discounted rail cards, CDs and other items that are felt to be attractive to the target audience.
- Price/quality stability. A competition adds value by making use of awareness of a financial service a 'ticket' to enter the competition, without any need to alter the price or nature of the core service itself. This avoids any danger of sparking a price war, accidentally impairing perceived service quality or lowering the customer's reference price.
- Versatility. Competitions are associated with producing short-term sales boosts, but they can contribute towards a range of communication and other marketing objectives. Competitions can provide useful support for new product launches.

The significance of competitions can be seen in the following example. For the first time, the positive outcome of promotional activity was reported in the Cadbury Schweppes Annual Report, 2002. The company ran an on-pack competition inviting consumers to 'text and win'. The company received 5 million responses. According to John Sutherland, Chief Executive, 'It gave sales a big lift at a time when the confectionery market has been pretty flat.'

Peattie *et al.* (1997)[4] suggest that: 'Value adding promotions such as competitions, are being found to have the potential to make a long-term contribution to the management of a brand beyond simple sales uplifts.'

They also argue that competitions are able to achieve a number of important objectives:

- They can improve brand awareness and customer attitudes towards the brand
- They can help to smooth out seasonal demand patterns
- They act as a two-way communication channel, assisting with tasks such as gathering marketing information and developing customer databases
- They can link with above-the-line campaigns to reinforce advertising or can even provide the basis for advertising
- They can be used to reinforce efforts at the point of sale
- They provide the company with useful PR opportunities
- They can be used as a tactical weapon to try to negate or, at least, reduce the effectiveness of competitors' promotional efforts.

They concluded that promotional competitions represent a flexible marketing communications tool that can be used to achieve both strategic and tactical objectives.

Joint promotions

In the previous chapter mention was made of promotions involving two manufacturer participants in order to enhance the value of on-pack offers. In fact the development of relationships between manufacturers to jointly promote their products or services is becoming an increasingly important aspect of sales promotion activity.

An increasingly important area of promotional activity is that of joint promotions where two or more participants promote their brands together to obtain a mutual benefit. We have already seen that this form of promotional activity affords a major opportunity for close co-operation between brand manufacturers and retailer stockists.

There are a wide variety of joint promotions that encompass a range of different executions. Perhaps the most apparent are those promotions in which the brand proposition is advertised via other products and services. A free trial size of a new product, for example, banded to the packaging of an established brand. Such activity may offer significant advantages to both of the participants. For the promoter, the opportunity is to gain access to a group of new consumers who are encouraged to associate the product with another from a similar or related category. For the carrier, the promotion provides the opportunity to add value to the product in the form of a free gift or other incentive at a significantly reduced cost.

In some instances, such promotions are organized on an 'in house' basis, in which two products from within a company portfolio are combined to offer additional benefits to the consumer. Recently, Nestlé offered a free sample of its new breakfast cereal Shredded Wheat Fruitful banded to packs of other regular Shredded Wheat. The promotion served to introduce the new product to existing consumers of the core brand and, thereby, extend the appeal of the latter product.

For such activities to generate the maximum consumer impact and, therefore, benefit to the participants, several important factors need to be considered. Of these, it may be argued that the most important is the degree of image match between the participating brands. It is clearly important that the two products or services should have similar images; otherwise one might serve to denigrate the other. Equally, there should be a similarity in the target market profiles of the participants. There would be little value to the carrier if the audience for the promoted product was different from its own. That applies equally to the nature of the distribution patterns of the two brands. In the majority of instances, it is important that the two brands are available from similar outlets. There are exceptions, however, where the brands will be similar in other dimensions, but the promotion will be used to carry a product into a retail environment where it is not normally found.

For established brands, it is normally desirable for the two participants to be of similar status in the marketplace in order that each complements the other. However, it may be possible to trade off the quality of one product against the quantity of the other, particularly where there is a good correspondence of the audience.

Gala Bingo linked with Thomson holidays to provide a holiday-based promotion. The campaign included a nationwide door-to-door drop targeted against postcodes that fit with Gala consumers. Additionally there was a mailing to the Gala database of members. Both elements feature a prize draw offering a chance to win one of the 30 Thomson cruises. At the same time Gala members were offered a £100 discount on

Thomson cruises and a further £50 to be spent on board.

Joint promotions offer a wide range of advantages, as can be seen. Importantly, the costs involved in establishing the promotion, generating publicity and the necessary administration can be shared between the participants, both of whom will derive benefit from the activity. They enable the participants to build upon each other's customer base and, potentially, extend outwards to a variety of new customers. The participation of two players often results in greater visibility than if either of them promoted on a solus basis. Of course, the risks involved in the promotion can be shared between the participants. In many instances, the carrier brand may enjoy the benefits of a promotion at a very low cost or even totally free. Indeed, recognizing the power of their pack, some manufacturers charge for the privilege of being carried by them.

Against these can be set a variety of potential disadvantages. Great care must be taken to ensure that there is an image match between the participants since poor matches may be detrimental to the image of one or both partners. Such promotions are often both time consuming to set up, and relatively complicated to execute and administer. Particularly where the products are to be banded together, long lead times may be required and they suffer the potential danger of pilferage as with any other on-pack offer.

O'Connor (1993)[5] argues that linked promotions provide several benefits:

- They are highly advantageous platforms for brands to efficiently and cost-effectively extend market reach.
- They are a valuable endorsement from the co-promoter to their core loyal customer base.
- They have the potential to widen the impact of the activity through greater combined expenditure.
- They gain mutual and beneficial support from the positive brand equity of each party.

Further examples of linked promotions are those in which a manufacturer offers an incentive to visit the venue of one or more participants. Sometimes offered by newspapers, these promotions are also utilized by manufacturer brands. Often these operate to provide a free entry, for example, to a theme park for a child when accompanied by a paying adult.

The retailer Tchibo linked with the Tussauds Group to offer £60 off entry to the UK's top visitor attractions. In return for spending £20 in store, the retailer issued a voucher booklet offering discounts on entry to Chessington World of Adventures, Thorpe Park, Madame Tussauds, Warwick Castle and Alton Towers.

Similarly, Butlins and Kwik Save ran a joint promotion. Customers to the retail chain received a 'kids go free' day pass when they spent £10 in a Kwik Save store. The promotion was supported by a direct mail leaflet to 5 million homes.

However, a promotion allowing visitors to Alton Towers to gain free entry if they brought a garden gnome with them has resulted in a 'gnome mountain' with over 1000 visitors bringing a gnome with them. Most of the visitors left their gnomes behind and park officials are now inviting people to 'give a gnome a home'.

The linkage with theme parks is a common practice with the owners keen to increase visitor numbers to their venues. Apart from the examples given above, several other brands run such offers: Walkers Skip's offer of 20 000 theme park tickets to be won instantly and Dr Pepper, using an unusual format in that, whilst the offer is similar, details are obtained by visiting a dedicated website rather than on-pack.

In the same way, as the many examples throughout this book illustrate, several manufacturers link up with current film titles in order to gain additional benefit from the promotional activities given to the film itself. The resultant offers can take a variety of forms from free gifts to free mail-ins and competitions, all of which reflect the nature of the film and the characters within.

Continuity programmes

This is one of the fastest growing sectors of the promotional armoury. The desire to encourage brand loyalty over an extended period has encouraged many manufacturers and service providers to develop loyalty or continuity schemes.

Short-term collect promotions

The most common device is to use on-going incentives that involve the customer in sequential purchases, for example, the collect premium. The overall objective is to establish a pattern of usage in the mind of the consumer. Repeat buying may also be encouraged through various means such as short-term discounts on merchandise or reduced shipping charges.

Several of the major petrol companies mounted collect-based schemes featuring various themes, such as the Esso World Cup Coin collection or the Texaco Great British Regiments promotion. In these and other collect promotions, consumers received their item in a sealed envelope that, when opened, would be placed in a collector card. The customer was invited to collect a series of anything between 20 and 30 different items to complete the set which motivated repeat visits to the company's petrol stations. Moreover, since it was not apparent which item was received until opened, there was a strong likelihood that the more times the users visited the greater the chance of getting a duplicate. This part of the mechanic of the promotion ensured that the promotion would sustain over a longer period of time. However, to avoid disappointment towards the end of the promotion the envelopes were opened by the dealer and the customer was invited to select any missing item to complete the set. Several companies also operated a postal exchange facility to similarly minimize the levels of disappointment.

In the grocery sector, Kellogg's are past masters at the short-term loyalty collect scheme. On many occasions they offer collectable items, sometimes themed to wider events such as the Olympics, which can be found inside the packaging. Although the number of items will vary, the principle remains the same: to induce loyalty to the brand through encouraging consumers to complete a set of whatever is on offer. Moreover, they recognize the importance of targeting the consumer by utilizing themes that range from paperback books and CDs for adults, whilst plastic items of footballers, athletes, and film characters will be targeted at younger consumers.

However, it is important that such comparatively short-term promotions, which seek to generate momentary bursts in sales, should not be confused with loyalty-based marketing. Loyalty schemes should be carefully focused to identify customers who are likely prospects for long-term relationships. Short-term promotions are typified by the proliferation of loyalty schemes and discount cards, and managers often believe that loyalty can be bought by this kind of inducement. Whilst such initiatives can have a dramatic effect on sales, it is questionable whether, in isolation, they can maintain solid long-term customer support.

Loyalty programmes

Loyalty programmes have long been an important element of customer relationship management for firms in travel-related industries, such as airlines, hotels and rental cars. Information technology that enables firms to practise individual-level marketing has facilitated the spread of loyalty programmes into such diverse industries as gaming, financial services and retailing. Loyalty programmes that base rewards on cumulative purchasing are an explicit attempt to enhance retention. Such programmes encourage repeat buying and thereby improve retention rates by providing incentives for customers to purchase more frequently and in larger volumes.

Points schemes such as that operated by Shell are one form of a loyalty-based promotion. The consumer receives a point value against each purchase the points being collected for redemption against a catalogue of gifts. Other devices include airline frequent flyers rewards and hotels' frequent stayer programmes. Several sections such as the banks and the airlines often much longer-range continuity schemes. These are sometimes based on the provision of extensive catalogues offering a wide range of merchandise items (such as the Barclaycard catalogue) designed to encourage loyalty to the brand. Sometimes such programmes can encourage increased usage. In other instances, the objective is to ensure that as many of the purchases as possible are made of the particular product or service. BA's Airmiles scheme is unlikely to encourage increased usage. The cost of flying is simply too high to make this a realistic proposition. However, what it can and does do is to ensure that members of the scheme specify BA at all possible occasions in order to maximize their collection of air miles.

Frequency (loyalty) programmes that recognize and reward frequent customers have become one of the most commonly used marketing tools for retaining customers and stimulating product or service usage. In particular, evidence that customer retention is cheaper than acquisition and that some customers are more profitable than others, has led many companies to establish frequency programmes that both reward loyalty and increase the costs of switching for the customer. Loyalty programmes are currently employed by a wide range of consumer goods and service companies and are increasingly popular among business-to-business companies as well. Moreover, new technologies (e.g. smart cards, the Internet) facilitate the proliferation of such programmes by providing cheaper and more powerful solutions for managing customer relationships.[6]

The past decade has seen many firms (re)adopt a customer focus, often through a formal programme of customer relationship management (CRM). Recent advances in information technology have provided the tools for marketing managers to create a new generation of CRM tactics. One such tactic that thousands of firms have considered, and which many have adopted, is to establish a customer loyalty programme. Examples of these schemes can be found in Japanese retailing, US airlines and hotels, French banks, UK grocery stores, German car companies, Australian telecommunications, Italian fashion stores, US universities, and many other areas. Typically these programmes offer financial and relationship rewards to customers and in some instances benefits also accrue to third-parties such as charities. We will consider these charity-based promotions in some detail in Chapter 12.

When properly embraced, developed and implemented loyalty marketing strategies become inextricably linked to the product and go far beyond the provision of incentives. Some frequent flyer programmes provide special telephone numbers for service and queries, special check-in desks for members, access to upgrades or defined seating on congested flights.[7]

Various authors including Stewart and Gallen (1998)[8] suggest that consumer franchise building (CFB) is the basis of building strong brands. The basis is that the ratio of advertising to sales promotion is the major determinant of a brand's CFB ability.

Store-based loyalty schemes

Much focus has been created by the so-called loyalty cards developed by the retail supermarkets in particular and by other retailers in general. The success of such programmes is dependent on an understanding of consumer behaviour and motivational factors.

Davies writing in *Admap* in July 1998[9] commenting on card loyalty schemes says:

> The aim of these cards is that customers will visit more often and spend more money when they get there.

In the UK, several of the major retailers operate loyalty-card schemes. The following table overleaf illustrates how these schemes compare with each other.

According to Davies (1998),[9] there are in excess of 150 retailer card-based nationwide schemes currently in operation; to these can be added a myriad of smaller localized ones. All do the same thing: offer a commercial reward to the consumer for certain behaviour. It is estimated that the Tesco Clubcard was launched in 1996 at a cost of over £22 million. The *Times* article quoted overleaf suggests that Tesco spends a further £20 million each year maintaining the scheme. Boots made an initial investment of £52 million when it introduced the Advantage card and, similarly, spends about £10 million to sustain the loyalty-card scheme. Davies indicates that 80 per cent of households in the UK hold at least one card from the major grocery retailers.

As with other studies, he concludes that the real impact on true loyalty is comparatively slight. He supports the notion that, since most consumers possess multiple cards, they can maintain their promiscuity of purchasing, taking advantage of the price discount that these cards offer. He argues that there needs to be a distinction drawn between those cards that are, in effect, little more than rebate schemes and those that are designed to generate long-term consumer loyalty.

Table 10.1

Nectar		
Launched in 2002 with several retail members including Sainsbury, BP, Threshers, Vodafone, Debenhams, Hertz, ebookers.com amongst others.	Customers earn 2 points for every £1 spent, although the rate varies if points are earned through other participants. Points can be redeemed at Sainsbury at a rate of 2 points per 1p (1% discount) or can be exchanged for other rewards such as holidays or Argos vouchers.	13 million users
Boots Advantage Card		
Launched in 1997, the card also doubles as an NHS donor card.	Customers earn 4 points for every £1 spent, with each point worth 1p equivalent to a 4% discount.	14 million users
Tesco Clubcard		
Launched in 1995 by Tesco but now includes other participants such as MFI, Avis, Nationwide Auto, National Tyres, Marriott Hotels and Dollond & Aitchison.	Customers earn 1 point for every £1 spent, each point representing a 1% discount.	11 million households
Marks & Spencer &More Card		
Launched 2003 also acts as a credit card.	Customers earn 1 point for every £1 spent in M&S together with 1 point for every £2 spent elsewhere using the &More credit card. Equivalent to 1–2% discount.	2.7 million users
W.H. Smith Clubcard		
Launched in 1997.	1 point for every £1 spent giving a 1% discount.	10 million

Source: *The Times* [10]

The mechanics of card schemes

Each of these schemes utilize a card scanning system that records the purchases of the consumer as well as crediting them with the appropriate discount. In the USA, Wal-Mart has implemented a further development with a special 'card scanner' system designed to influence customers' buying behaviour. Customers swipe their card on entering the store allowing the terminal to produce tailor-made offers against previously stored data on previous buying patterns, as well as geo-demographic and life-stage information. Subsequent analysis of the Market Basket data that provide information on the outcome of the purchase visit enables promoters to evaluate the success or failure of a campaign immediately.

Mahoney (1999)[11] argues that the practice of sales promotion will be significantly enhanced with the advent of more sophisticated smart cards, similar to those being implemented by Wal-Mart in the USA. These are more efficient in enabling the retailer to both develop and analyse the response to sales promotion activity.

Gaudagni and Little[12] as long ago as 1983 identified the advantages of store data collection. Scanners directly record the sales of individual customers at the item level. They provide the competitive environment of the customer decision. Not only do they record what the customer bought and its price, but they also identify the other products, prices and marketing activities that impinged on the customer at the time of the purchase.

There are a variety of systems being used by retailers, suppliers and other organizations designed to engender loyalty. In the majority of instances the customer applies to join the scheme by completing an application form that is used to capture specific data about the individual. Subsequently, a membership card is issued with a unique number. This may contain a magnetic strip or be bar-coded and is presented to the sales staff at each purchase occasion. A reward is given to the consumer based on the scheme criteria. The details of the sales transaction and the customer number are logged and may contain details of the accumulated reward as well as purchase details.

Jacobs (1999)[13] reinforces the advantages of the new generation of smart cards. He stresses the benefits of gaining significant amounts of data about the customer and their potential for enabling the organizer to deliver a service that is individually customized to the customer.

He argues that customer relationships can be built by understanding the needs of individual shoppers, making them relevant offers and personalizing communications.

In a typical loyalty scheme, data can be derived from three principal sources:[14]

1   The registration details
2   Profiles – these are lifestyle data that can be overlaid against the original registration information to help identify preferences by geographic area
3   Activity data – constantly updated information captured on every occasion that the customer uses the loyalty scheme: frequency of visits, spending patterns, what is purchased, how much is redeemed and how individual shoppers respond to individual campaigns.

The objectives of loyalty schemes

The motivation behind these loyalty schemes derives from a recognition that it is easier and cheaper to enhance the value of existing customers than to attract and develop new ones. In the grocery retailing sector the requirement is more acute because there is a defined ceiling on the amount of money that consumers can spend feeding themselves and their families. If consumers cannot be encouraged to spend more, then the imperative becomes one of increasing the share of what is available.

Two aims of customer loyalty programmes stand out. One is to increase sales revenues by raising purchase/usage levels, and/or increasing the range of products bought from the supplier. A second aim is more defensive; by building a closer bond between the brand and current customers it is hoped to maintain the current customer base. The popularity of these programmes is based on the argument that profits can be increased significantly by achieving either of these aims. Loyalty programmes can have many other peripheral goals, such as furthering cross-selling, creating databases, aiding trade relations, assisting brand PR, establishing alliances, etc.

Uncles *et al.* (2003)[15] argue that where the focus is on individual customers, loyalty programmes can be seen as vehicles to increase single-brand loyalty; decrease price sensitivity; induce greater consumer resistance to counter offers or counter arguments (from advertising or sales people); dampen the desire to consider alternative brands; encourage word-of-mouth support and endorsement; attract a larger pool of customers; and/or increase the amount of product bought.

An important component of many loyalty programmes is the scope for cross-selling, in an attempt to increase share-of-spend, rather than market share. Loyalty-programme members are encouraged to buy products they would not normally have bought from that provider. In essence, the loyalty programme is seen as a brand extension aid. For example, through their respective programmes, United Airlines tries to interest customers in car hire and hotels, while Tesco attempts to expose its Clubcard members to high-margin wines, financial services and electrical goods, as well as lower-margin groceries. One issue is that many of the cross-selling opportunities are themselves in highly competitive markets (e.g. hotels, car hire, restaurants, financial services, etc.) and often these markets support other loyalty programmes.

Loyalty programmes are often set up to encourage customers to enter lasting relationships with an organization by rewarding them for patronage. Managers also hope to gain higher profits through extended product usage and cross-selling, to retain and grow high-value customers, and to defend their market position in the face of a competitor loyalty scheme.

Henry (2000)[16] argues that the high market capitalizations of America Online, Amazon.com and Yahoo are justified, in part, because their customer base has a high lifetime value based on their potential for cross-selling and low attrition.

Dowling and Uncles (1997)[17] argue that companies use customer loyalty programmes to achieve various objectives:

- To maintain sales levels, margins and profits
- To increase the loyalty and potential value of existing customers
- To induce cross-product buying by existing customers.

They argue that following the Pareto principle it makes most sense to concentrate promotional activities on the 'best' 20 per cent of customers.

O'Malley (1998)[18] extends the rationale for the development of loyalty programmes to include the following:

1   To reward loyal customers
2   To generate information
3   To manipulate consumer behaviour: to try new products or brands, increase multi-pack purchase or use the brand for increasingly diverse services
4   As a defensive measure to combat a competitive scheme – a number of supermarket schemes were launched following the introduction of the Tesco Clubcard.

Jacobs (1996)[14] argues that the validity of loyalty schemes derives from the benefits of loyal customers:

- They spend 30–50 per cent more per transaction
- They visit three times the average
- They spend four more times a year
- They account for over 50 per cent of sales.

Customer retention has a direct impact on profitability and past research has claimed that it can be five times more expensive to obtain a new customer than to retain one. Naturally then, considerable time and money is being spent in many organizations to develop strategies to retain customers. Traditionally, marketing has overemphasized the attraction of new customers, but today, well-managed organizations work hard to retain their existing customers and increase the amount that existing customers spend with them. On average it costs a firm five to six times as much to attract a new customer as it does to implement retention strategies to hold an existing one. The costs of attracting new customers include advertising and promotion, but loyal customers also act as word of mouth advertisers and will generally spend more.

Hallberg (2004)[19] argues that the premise underlying loyalty programmes is the belief that consumer buying behaviour can be modified in a manner advantageous to the marketer through a rational appeal: the more consumers buy, the greater the rewards. The issue as to whether such activities actually create loyal consumers to the brand is often considered of secondary importance. He argues that such evaluations fail to develop programmes to achieve their maximum potential. Developing a high level of emotional loyalty is, he suggests, an essential driver of brand leadership.

His analysis of more than 600 000 consumers confirms the impact of emotional loyalty to the brand on the sales of that brand. The greater the level of emotional loyalty, the more a consumer buys. Whilst that result might be expected, his findings indicate that those consumers holding the highest level of emotional loyalty buy at least twice as much as those who are less attached to the brand and often three to four times as much.

O'Brien and Jones (cited in Dowling and Uncles 1997)[20] suggest five elements that combine to determine a loyalty programme's effectiveness:

1 The cash value of the redemption rewards
2 The range of choice of those rewards
3 The aspirational value of the rewards
4 The perceived likelihood of achieving the rewards
5 The scheme's ease of use.

Dowling and Uncles (1997)[17] indicate a number of guidelines to improve the chances of loyalty programme success:

1 Design the loyalty programme to enhance the value proposition of a product or service. Too many programmes simply offer free gifts that are nice to receive but which tend only to provide a short-term incentive
2 Fully cost out the loyalty programme
3 Design a reward scheme that maximizes the buyer's motivation to make the next purchase. Davies (1997)[21] expresses the view that consumer segmentation is the key to developing loyalty programmes. Because different consumers have different purchasing patterns, he argues, it is important to both recognize and reflect these in promotional schemes.

However, as Hooper (1997)[22] explains, a loyalty scheme is not a panacea. It can only work when based on accurate knowledge of the customer, market and product. An issue with many schemes is that they generate loyalty to the promotion, rather than customer loyalty.

Many so-called loyalty schemes are actually incentives or reward schemes in disguise. They either reward customers for buying (but do not ask them why, or keep rewarding them) or they cajole them into buying with incentives and reduced prices. Too many schemes ignore many of the primary components of an integrated and effective long-term loyalty programme: customer service, excellence in production, packaging and distribution, value for money, reliability, etc. In fact these elements (they used to be called the marketing mix) work together to create real loyalty, by their influence on the shopper's psychology.

Similarly, most schemes concentrate on just part of the programme (the promotional mechanic, the production process and building a massive database) rather than taking the holistic approach that ultimately leads to true loyalty.

O'Brien and Jones (1995)[23] argue that too many companies regard rewards as short-term promotional give-aways or 'specials of the month'. Although such promotions create some value by motivating new or existing customers, they achieve only a fraction of their true potential. They argue that a company must find ways to share value with customers in proportion to the value the customers' loyalty creates for the company.

They establish a number of key principles for loyalty-building programmes:

● All customers are not created equal. In order to maximize loyalty and profitability, a company must give its best value to its best customers. As a result they will become more loyal and profitable.

● Value created must exceed the cost of the value delivered. The programme must provide incentive for real and long-term relationships that result in the customer increasing his or her spend with the company.

- Customer behaviour should drive value sharing. Customers must be given incentive to continue to participate in the programme rather than benefiting from the short-term incentive and then defecting.
- Long-term perspective is critical. With each additional year of a relationship customers become less costly to serve.
- Offers must target attractive customers.

O'Malley[18] also suggests some important guidelines:

1 Re-evaluate and clarify the objectives of the programme
2 Be realistic about the extent to which loyalty can be achieved
3 Identify the relative importance of data collection, customer reward, merchandise promotion, etc., within the scheme
4 Analyse and utilize the data generated by the programme
5 Supplement behavioural analysis with traditional research methods
6 Implement offers and communications that are relevant to individual customers
7 Be responsive and continually re-evaluate the value offered by the scheme especially in comparison with competing schemes
8 Ensure that the loyalty scheme is a coherent element of the company's overall strategy.

Any scheme to engender loyalty will only succeed when it has clear and defined objectives, focused on the customer. These have to be defined by the client, in terms of what is meant by loyalty: frequency of purchase, value of sales, share of spend, introduction of new customers, etc. Agencies have to refine how they are to achieve these objectives, in the light of the proliferation of media and disciplines that could be used. Research is needed, too, to elicit from consumers why they buy X or shop at Y: what motivates their choice and why does this selection appeal more than other options? It is specifically the psychology of the consumer that accommodates and gives rise to the possibility of a loyalty scheme. If customers cannot reveal why they are loyal and clients are not aware of what makes them loyal, it is impossible for the agency to find the communication conduit between them.

An important concept to consider when developing a customer loyalty programme is customer satisfaction. McIlroy and Barnett (2000)[24] suggest that satisfaction is a measure of how well a customer's expectations are met while customer loyalty is a measure of how likely a customer is to repurchase and engage in relationship activities. Loyalty is vulnerable because even if customers are satisfied with the service they will continue to defect if they believe they can get better value, convenience or quality elsewhere.

Customer care, too, is a key contributor to loyalty. It is a crucial part of servicing customers. The efficient and effective handling of complaints and tackling customer issues head on can add integrity and value to whatever loyalty scheme is in place, especially as programmes without this, such as most reward or incentive 'loyalty' schemes, look like dressed-up sales exercises. The key to loyalty lies in gaining commitment from customers and involving them to the point where it is hard for them to walk away. This self-same commitment helps to differentiate your brand from its competitors. Some short-term promotions may have many of the characteristics we would look for in a long-term loyalty scheme: repeated customer contact, customer response with related rewards, objectives that include enhanced loyalty (or at least repeat purchase).

The Internet is increasingly becoming part of promotional activity. Several Internet sites utilize the full range of sales promotion activity to encourage consumers (surfers) to visit their sites. The Internet provides a potentially important outlet for promotional activity. Van Doren *et al.* (2000)[25] have suggested possible uses of the Internet to promote brands.

Not all retail chains consider loyalty cards to be desirable or effective. Asda ran a 4-year pilot scheme across 19 of its outlets. However, it subsequently withdrew the scheme both as a result of customer feedback and independent research that demonstrated that customers preferred immediate discounts rather than points. Others such as Morrisons and Waitrose hold similar views. Various reports such as those from Mintel found that almost half of those interviewed preferred to have lower prices rather than points-based incentive schemes. In addition, a report from Verdict found that only 1 per cent of shoppers regard loyalty cards as an important driver of loyalty. The fact that many shoppers hold multiple cards appears to suggest that consumers use them to obtain the benefit from each store in turn without necessarily remaining exclusively loyal to any single chain of outlets.

Lewis (2004)[26] argues that, despite the proliferation of loyalty programmes in a wide range of categories, there is little research that focuses on the measurement of such programmes. The key to measuring the influence of loyalty programmes is that they operate as dynamic incentive schemes by providing benefits based on cumulative purchasing over time. As such, loyalty programmes encourage consumers to shift from single-period to multiple-period decision making.

For a frequency programme to be effective in increasing loyalty, it must have a structure that motivates customers to view purchases as a sequence of related decisions rather than as independent transactions. That is, the structure must give customers an incentive to adopt a dynamic perspective. O'Brien and Jones (1995)[23] suggest that the major factors that customers consider when evaluating programmes are the relative value of awards and the likelihood of achieving a reward. Furthermore, the likelihood of achieving a reward is a function of cumulative buying thresholds and time constraints. These design elements (e.g. thresholds, rewards, time constraints) combine with individual-level requirements and preferences to determine the customer's expected benefits of participating in a loyalty programme.

A special characteristic of loyalty programmes is that their attractiveness may change dynamically with a customer's decisions. As purchases are made, both the customer's investment in the programme and the customer's likelihood of earning a reward increase. Conversely, when a customer decides not to purchase in a given period, the likelihood of earning a reward decreases, because the customer moves no closer to the reward threshold and the time left to earn rewards shrinks.

The key to the successful adoption of relationship marketing lies in the building of client loyalty in dynamic business environments. In a business context loyalty has come to describe a customer's commitment to do business with a particular organization, purchasing their goods and services repeatedly and recommending the services and products to friends and associates. A loyal customer can mean a consistent source of revenue over a period of many years. However, this loyalty cannot be taken for granted. It will continue only as long as the customer feels they are receiving better value than they would obtain from another supplier. There is always the risk that a customer will defect when a competitor offers better value or a wider range of value-added options.

Character merchandising

Character merchandising has increased dramatically over recent years and, with it, the cost of negotiating deals with the owners of the copyright. A recent estimate of the value of the sector was prepared recently at the New York Licensing 98 show. It put the overall value in the region of £73 billion. However, that figure includes all forms of activity that could be classified as character licensing and includes the dominant portion of licensing for the production of toys and other merchandise. As an example, Typhoo Tea licensed the use of the Wallace and Gromit characters for use in an on-pack promotional offer. Consumers were given the opportunity to collect the characters as well as obtaining other themed merchandise, such as mugs, flasks, egg cups and salt and pepper pots.

Many companies used these characters as the basis of their brand proposition. Heinz has a range of child-oriented products featuring The Simpsons, Thomas the Tank Engine, The Tweenies and Fimbles. HP have a similar range of products linked to Bob the Builder, Postman Pat, Scooby Doo, and Action Man, amongst others.

The essential requirement is to ensure an appropriate fit between the chosen characters and the target market. Apart from adding value to the brand, the use of characters from television and films enables the promoting company to develop activity that has relevant topical interest.

As well as fictional characters, the industry is increasingly turning to real personalities from sport and music, to augment the offering of their brands. PepsiCo has used the form of activity over an extended period. As well as using characters in television advertising, the company's brands use them to develop on-pack offers.

According to Garretson and Niedrich (2004)[27] the use of spokes-characters has received increased media attention. This attention is not surprising given their prevalence both in historical and modern promotion campaigns.

The authors consider spokes-characters to be non-human characters used to promote a product or a brand. These characters aren't cartoons originally created for animated movies, cartoon programmes, and/or comic strips and then licensed by brands to appear in promotions. Rather, they are created for the sole purpose of promoting a product or brand. Since the late 1800s, hundreds of these non-celebrity characters have promoted brands, including the Snuggle Bear, the Poppin' Fresh Pillsbury Doughboy and Tony the Tiger. As suggested in television programmes, the popular press and academic research, these characters appear to benefit brands by establishing brand identity and favourable brand associations. Recently, the Jolly Green Giant character has re-emerged as the promotional vehicle for their corn products.

The results of content analyses of spokes-character commercials and print advertisements conducted by Garretson and Niedrich (2004)[27] reveal that:

- spokes-characters are used to promote numerous types of products and services
- specific types of spokes-characters are more commonly featured with particular products
- practitioners appear to consider the nostalgic qualities and relevancy of characters to advertised products (Callcott and Lee 1994; Neeley *et al.* 2000).[28,29] Furthermore, analyses of depth-interviews indicate that consumers notice character factors such as nostalgia, relevance to products and expertise (Callcott and Phillips 1996).[30]

For more than a century, marketers and advertisers have utilized spokes-characters in promotional campaigns and on-product packages. Some of the earliest characters include the Michelin Man and the Cream of Wheat Chef, both of which were created in the late nineteenth century and continue to appear in current campaigns. Exploratory research carried out by Garretson and Niedrich (2004)[27] indicates that consumers like spokes-characters and have even expressed their trust and respect for them. Consumers seem to evaluate characters and their qualities just as they do people.

They point out that there is a consistent pattern of spokes-character and product category pairings used in market categories. For example, animal spokes-characters are often paired with services and beverages. This consistent pattern implies that some types of spokes-characters might be better suited for and benefit specific product categories.

The above observation also suggests a more practical rationale behind marketers pairings of particular characters with products that might affect consumers' receptiveness or trust of spokes-characters. Perhaps marketers and advertising agencies contemplate the relevancy or 'match-up' of the spokes-character with the product at the initial inception of character development.

Their study demonstrated that spokes-character trust can be influenced by spokes-character characteristics. We found perceived expertise and nostalgia to engender spokes-character trust. Consumers appear to rely on spokes-character features as signals of this honesty and sincerity, as greater levels of perceived character expertise and nostalgic memories produced greater levels of trust. Regardless of consumers' brand experience, these character-specific features influence consumers' overall impressions of spokes-character trustworthiness.

This study also provides evidence that spokes-character trust mediates the relationship between spokes-character qualities on brand attitude. They can also reintroduce the nostalgic qualities of characters to adults, a strategy recently recognized in current campaigns. In sum, our findings show that efforts toward creating a trustworthy spokes character can be rewarded with more favourable brand evaluations since spokes-character trust favourably influenced brand attitudes.

According to Erdogan and Kitchen (1998)[31] there are several reasons why companies increasingly invest large sums of money to align their brands with celebrities:

- Celebrities are believed to possess dynamic qualities (attraction, sexiness, likeability) that can be transferred to products through marketing communications

- Because they are famous, celebrities can attract and maintain attention
- The positive impact of celebrities to stimulate actual purchase behaviour is well documented.

Sales promotion advertising

The point has been made earlier that, although many promotions stand alone, they are often incorporated into other aspects of a marketing communications campaign. Indeed, much advertising features specific sales promotional offers as an incentive to the reader to do more: to read the ad, to respond in some manner or to make a purchase of the advertised product.

Hahn *et al.* (1995)[32] indicate that as the sales promotion proportion of the total budget increases, there are a greater variety of sales promotion types being employed. Because of their strong potential for generating intensive product trial in a short period, consumer sales promotions are especially appealing for firms entering a new market or expanding their market share. They recognize that many promotions are advertised and have described such advertising as SPAD (sales promotion ads). They indicate that many examples can be found, especially in print media: a coupon contained within a magazine ad, a product sample attached to an advertisement, a competition or sweepstake entry form, etc.

In fact, SPAD appears in all forms of media. Dedicated television and radio commercials are used to announce major sales promotion campaigns, e.g. Fairy Liquid or Kit Kat (Kit Cash). Coupon advertising is a hybrid sales promotion tool with the characteristics of both ordinary coupons and advertising. In particular, coupon advertising often includes brand information (product characteristics, location, quality, guarantees, etc.) as well as information about regular prices. At the same time, it includes a coupon that offers a discount off the regular price.[33]

Moreover the range of opportunities to communicate promotional offers to the consumer is also increasing. Shopping centres, car parks, petrol stations, post offices and fast food outlets, including trolley advertising, take-away lids, floor advertising and carrier bags, all represent opportunities for promotional messages and are collectively defined as ambient media. A study conducted by Shankar and Horton (1999)[34] estimated the value of these ambient media channels in the UK at £24.2 million.

These all provide an opportunity to place a reminder message close to the point of sale or of a service available at a nearby retail outlet. In-store tastings, recipe cards and merchandising are all examples of communicating with customers close to the point of sale.

Case study

KIMBERLY-CLARK – ANDREX
Agency: SMP

Background

Toilet tissue is one of the UK's largest grocery product categories worth an estimated £815 million annually. Andrex has been the market leader for over 40 years and has enjoyed significant growth despite the market being low interest and price driven. Competitive promotional activity focuses on price reductions and free product.

Overall the Andrex strategy is to build brand equity with added value promotions, most often using the puppy device:

- The Andrex puppy which has appeared in almost 120 commercials has become inextricably linked with the brand, symbolizing the qualities of softness and strength that represent the core of the brand's proposition.

- As a brand icon, the puppy is also used in a variety of other marketing and promotional devices. This has included calendars, as well as joint activity with the Disney film *101 Dalmations*. The puppy has also been used as the basis of several soft toy offers.

- In 1999 the Andrex Puppy Appeal raised £110 000 for the National Canine Defence League which helped them care for over 11 000 dogs.

Promotional objectives

Several important objectives were established for the promotion:

- To achieve high awareness of the promotion both in and out of store.

- To run an added value promotion exclusive to Tesco that increases Tesco's share of the toilet tissue market.

- To prove the viability of added value promotions as an alternative to high-cost free product offers.

- To use the pack as the main communication vehicle without diluting core brand values.

Promotional strategy

- To target all toilet tissue purchasers.

- To exploit the universal appeal of the Andrex puppy.

- To communicate the promotion utilising all available below-the-line channels.

Campaign summary

Andrex produced 600 000 specially designed promotional packs in which the customary 'three free rolls' were replaced by an Andrex Puppy soft toy. The packs were priced at £5.99 of which £2 offset the cost of the premium. The pack was completely re-designed reducing the size of the Andrex brand name and logo to allow space for an 'actual size' image of the puppy adjacent to the bold statement 'I'm Inside'. The puppy was enclosed in a tube measuring the same as three rolls of toilet tissue. This was a tailor made promotion exclusive to Tesco.

Brand support

Extensive point of sale featured the puppy premium in his own perspex kennel allowing consumers to see the item prior to purchase. Shelf edgers, wobblers, banners, posters and header boards all contributed to gaining awareness of the promotion and gondola end displays. To create even more awareness a Puppy in Pack blimp (measuring 4 metres) floated above selected Tesco stores at a height of 70 metres. The Andrex website also carried details of the offer with a link to Tesco.com. 30 000 Tesco and Andrex consumers were sent an e-mail with the offer details and a link to Tesco.com enabling consumers to order packs for direct delivery. Ten thousand consumers were sent a viral e-mail featuring a virtual puppy.

To secure store involvement Tesco staff were able to enter a free prize draw to win £2000 to be put towards the staff Christmas party or donated to charity.

The promotion was the ISP Gold Award winner in 2003 for Communication On-Pack. It was also an ISP Silver Award winner 2003 in the Consumer Trial category.

(The above case study is adapted from articles that appeared in *Promotions and Incentives* magazine, September 2003 and May 2004)

Questions

1   How can a free mail-in gift be used to extend the value of the brand?
2   What are the benefits of self-liquidating offers?
3   Identify the roles played by competitions and lotteries as promotional devices.
4   Discuss the differences between short-term collect promotions and those designed to establish long-term loyalty towards the brand.
5   Why do some authors suggest that store based loyalty schemes tend to cancel each other out?

11 Promoting to the trade

Chapter overview

This chapter deals with promotions that are used to motivate the trade. Just as we have seen that a variety of promotional tools can be used to motivate the consumer audience, so too there are a variety of devices that are specifically targeted towards the trade audience. Most often these are related to some form of financial discount that serves to improve the trade margin, although there are other forms of activity, such as the provision of selling aids, sales force incentives and competitions, etc., all of which will be discussed in more detail below.

At the same time, we will consider the important interface between the manufacturer and the retailer – notably the sales force. They play an important role in ensuring that the trade provides the necessary support for all forms of promotional activity and are integral to the successful selling in of promotional activity.

Learning outcomes

- To consider the reasons underlying the growth in promotional activity directed towards the trade
- To appreciate the varying objectives of trade-based promotions
- To examine the benefits of trade promotions
- To investigate the types of trade-promotional activity
- To appreciate the important role played by point-of-sale material as a communication device
- To consider the role of the sales force.

Quelch (1989)[1] defines trade promotions as 'co-operative marketing activities offered by manufacturers to retailers and wholesalers to increase purchase commitments and build inventories'.

Trade promotions

The growth of trade promotions

Recent years have seen a tremendous growth in the amount of promotional monies spent on trade promotions. As a result, the phenomenon of manufacturer trade deals and retail-price promotion has received significant attention from both marketing academicians and practitioners. This interest is not surprising, as manufacturers are spending ever-increasing sums of money on trade promotions with the hope of providing incentives to retailers to temporarily lower the retail price or to provide other support for their brands. In some cases such expenditures have grown to the extent that they even exceed the advertising budget for the brand.

According to Ailawadi *et al.* (1999),[2] trade-promotion expenditures within packaged goods industries have steadily increased to the point where they represent more than twice the level of expenditure on media-based activities. There has been considerable debate regarding the validity of this approach, particularly from the standpoint of profitability. There is concern that trade deals such as everyday low prices (EDLPs) simply result in the retailer stockpiling product at the temporary low price and subsequently selling it at higher prices. However, they argue that well-designed trade promotions can not only increase channel profits but, additionally, increase the manufacturer's share of those profits.

Similarly, Kasulis *et al.* (1999)[3] carried out an investigation into the increasing level of trade promotions in the USA. They concluded that trade activity represents around half of all promotional expenditure by US packaged goods companies.

For a number of years, executives have been questioning whether the benefits gained from trade promotions are worth the increasing costs. Trade promotions can help a firm acquire not only short-term sales increases, but also crucial shelf-space and other advantages in merchandising and point-of-purchase activities. But low-margin sales don't generate incremental profits, and many marketers are watching sales erode because of trade-promotion activity.

Managers face a variety of pressures to increase trade spending. In addition to demands from retailers, competition from private-label and other manufacturers, and less brand-loyal consumers, marketing managers must deal with pressures from within their own firms to meet short-term financial and unit volume targets. For example, sales managers lobby for increased trade promotion budgets because they are rewarded for short-term sales, and the reward systems for brand managers encourage short-term volume and profit hits.

As Mohr and Low argue (1993)[4] retailers use their power to convince manufacturers to give them more and deeper discounts, better case rates, higher slotting allowances, and other concessions for distribution coverage and support. Their demands for payment are more exacting when manufacturers want shelf space for new products. If manufacturers don't pay, many retailers simply refuse to continue carrying the product. Threatening manufacturers with loss of distribution can be very effective, particularly when retailers can pit one competitor against another or emphasize private labels.

The major problem with trade promotions is that the retailers have become so powerful that there is no guarantee that the additional services desired by the manufacturer will actually take place.

The increased levels of competition between brands are evident from a study by Curhan and Kopp (1988).[5] They suggest that the average grocery retailer is offered 20 times as many manufacturer originated promotions as can be accommodated within the available store space. In return for these deal incentives, manufacturers expect retailers to perform certain activities in support of the promoted brand. These might include increased retailer inventory of the promoted brand, and retail promotional support.

It is a widely accepted fact that over the last 15 years there has been a rise in both the scale and frequency of trade allowances. Although these allowances usually specify retailers must temporarily reduce retail price, offer better displays and/or locally advertise the brand (usually by stating its price), there is often no direct link between the magnitude of the allowance and the actions taken by a retailer. For example, a retailer might order 4 or 5 weeks' supply of an item, receiving a discount on each unit purchased, and yet only promote the item for 1 or 2 weeks, selling the rest at the regular un-promoted price. More generally, Blattberg *et al.* (1995)[6] indicate that a substantial portion of trade allowances earmarked for retail promotion is normally pocketed by the retailer. Although estimates of the percentages pocketed vary somewhat, they generally are in the 30 to 50 percent ranges (Agrawal 1996).[7]

Murry and Heide (1998)[8] suggest that:

> Manufacturers currently tend to reward retailers for participating in promotional programmes. It is noteworthy, however, that though such methods may motivate retailers to agree to display programme materials, they may have limited effect on ultimate compliance because they offer the same rewards regardless of whether the agreement is honoured.

Manufacturers offer trade deals in a variety of forms, for example, off-invoice, billback, free goods, display allowances and inventory financing (Blattberg and Neslin 1987).[9]

The process of implementing a manufacturer-oriented promotion follows a number of distinct stages. Curhan and Kopp (1988)[5] depict this as follows:

Figure 11.1

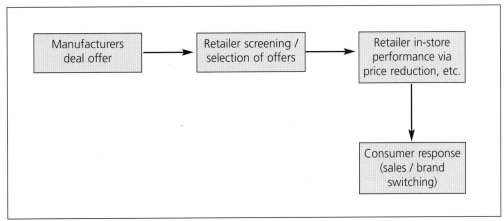

Objectives of trade promotions

- To obtain distribution for new products.

  A critical objective for any new product is to gain shelf space in retail outlets. Unless the product is widely available, volume sales cannot be achieved.

- To maintain trade support for existing brands.

  Similarly, existing brands need to maintain their in-store presence, not only to compete against alternative products from rival manufacturers but to offset the increasing levels of competition from private-label products.

- To encourage retailers to provide display and featuring for existing brands.

  Manufacturers not only wish to gain additional presence for their brands in alternative store locations, for example, but also to gain point-of-sale displays. Often these can only be achieved by offering the trade financial or other incentives to provide such support.

- To build retail inventories.

  In many instances, promotions provide the motivation to take in additional stocks above the normal patterns of trade purchase.

- Maintain or increase the manufacturers' share of shelf space.

  In any retail environment, shelf space is at a premium. In order to gain additional featuring for their brands, manufacturers will provide specific incentives to encourage retailers to provide additional facings for their brands.

- Obtain shelf space other than normal shelf locations.

  Increasingly, manufacturers seek to obtain presence for their products in various 'hot spots' located around the store. For example, many retailers maintain product displays at the store front, or at aisle ends. Because of their prominence retailers are aware that they can charge a premium.

- To reduce trade inventories.

  At times when, for example, the manufacturer is planning to introduce a new product, trade promotions will be used to ensure a rapid pull through of existing stock.

The benefits of trade promotions

According to Zerillo and Iacobucci (1995)[10] trade promotions can offer benefits to all channel members. Manufacturers benefit from higher sales and lower production costs because of economies of scale, reduced holding and inventory costs, increased support and relationship development with their channel partners and heightened consumer trial and value assessment.

Similar conclusions are drawn by Lucas (1996)[11] who adds that retailers may benefit from higher than normal brand margins and volume as well as increased customer satisfaction and store loyalty. Customers may receive increased product information from promotional displays and in-store assistance, as well as enhanced value as a result of promotional prices.

Chevalier and Curhan (1976)[12] suggest that the retail trade promotes to achieve one or more of three broad business objectives:

1   To maximize profits on the promoted item
2   To build store traffic and/or increase total store volume
3   To create a favourable store image amongst customers.

Blattberg *et al.* (1981)[13] sought to explain why retailers prefer to offer short-term price deals to consumers. They suggested a number of explanations:

- Retailers deal to attract customers from other stores
- Manufacturers offer trade deals that require price reductions from retailers in order to increase market share and to encourage non-users to try their products
- Dealing occurs because retailers have high inventory costs and seek to reduce their level of stocks.

Grewal *et al.* (1998)[14] state that a positive store image and good merchandise are key for retailers to achieve and sustain success in an increasingly competitive marketplace. They indicate that three dimensions are important to overall store success:

1   Store image, which encompasses the physical environment of the store and service levels. Stores continually adjust their positioning strategies and alter their image to remain competitive. Millions of pounds are spent each year by retailers designing, building and refurbishing retail outlets. One only has to see the process undertaken by Morrisons since its acquisition of Safeway to witness this process in action.
2   The quality of merchandise and brands sold
3   Prices and promotions are used to attract customers to a retail store and to generate an increased level of store traffic.

Sales promotions can influence the overall impressions of retail stores. If one outlet appears to be offering keen prices on favoured brands, the impression caused will be that the outlet offers keen prices across all of the products that it sells.

Research was conducted by Chevalier and Curhan (1976)[12] in order to identify the factors that determine whether a retailer is prepared to accept and implement a promotion offered by a manufacturer. These include:

- Item importance – brands that have a strong consumer reason for being are favoured by the trade.
- Promotional timing – the promotion must be planned to coincide with the retailer's own promotional timing schedules.
- Manufacturer's reputation, which can be enhanced by the activities of the sales force.
- Promotion wearout – brands that the retail trade consider as 'over-promoted' may lose their appeal as a short-term stimulus to sales.

- Sales velocity – the potential for the promotion to increase sales during the promoted period.
- Manufacturer support – the extent to which the manufacturer supports the promotion with other activities.

Promotions can also have an impact on distributor behaviour:

- Postponement effect – distributors know and demand to know the operations marketing programme of their suppliers and tend to defer purchases in order to stock up for sales promotions.
- Overstocking effect – when ordering at times of sales promotions, distributors tend to order as a function of their storage space, which decreases post promotion orders.
- Deviant ordering – some distributors only order when the products are on promotion and refuse to buy the product at full price. This is the attitude adopted by hard discounters who can then charge very competitive rates.

Murry and Heide (1998)[8] provide a strategic marketing fit model for retail promotions.

Figure 11.2

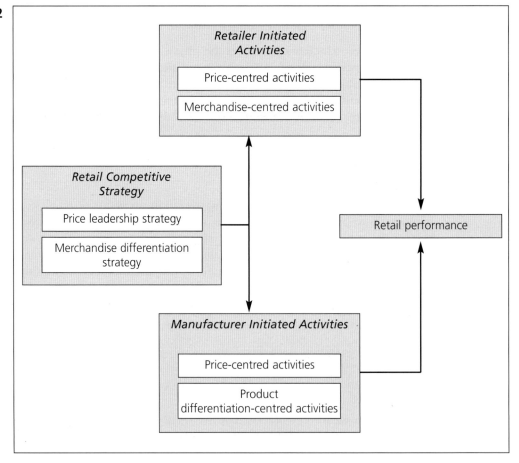

Types of trade promotional activity

There are a wide variety of trade promotions that are outlined below.

Trade trial promotions

1   New line fees or slotting allowances are cash payments made in return for stocking a new product for a particular period.

2   Price reductions are a direct reduction of the invoice price to the distributor. These may be linked to specific levels of volume, i.e. the price reduction increases as the distributor achieves pre-set levels or may operate retrospectively to provide an incentive to the distributor to attain set levels of sale.

3   Returns – the manufacturer agrees to take back unsold quantities of the product. Sometimes this operates on the basis of sale or return, in which the distributor only pays when the product is actually sold. This is common practice in many retail areas, designed to ensure adequate stock levels of products in which the trade might have limited confidence.

Buying allowances

Some manufacturers offer a discount on the regular price of products ordered during the promotional period. The 'special discount' is sometimes given in the form of an off-invoice allowance where the agreed discount is taken off the invoice. An alternative is to offer the retailer free goods in an agreed ratio when the retailer purchases items at the regular invoice price. In this instance, the retailer receives a number of additional cases of product alongside those that are paid for.

These promotions are widely accepted by the retail trade as they require little extra effort. Moreover, from the manufacturer standpoint, they are easy and speedy to implement. One problem that exists, however, is that not all of the reduced price will necessarily be passed on to the consumer. The retailer instead may take part or all of the discount as extra margin.

Indeed, research by Chevalier and Curhan (1976)[12] has suggested that retailers often absorb a substantial proportion of the promotional monies that they receive in order to lower costs and increase gross margins. It is suggested that, as a result, they only offer significant support to a small number of trade deals.

Promotional allowances

In some instances manufacturers provide special allowances in order to encourage retailers to perform specific tasks in relation to the brand. Most commonly these tasks relate to merchandising the brand: providing special in-store displays often away from the normal in-store positioning for the brand.

Trade repeat purchase promotions

1   Price-offs – these take the form of a discount against the normally invoiced price, usually on the understanding that part or all of the discount is passed on to the end

customer. An alternative form provides discounts in return for some additional service provided by the outlet, such as increased levels of display, advertising, etc.

2   Co-operative advertising allowances – the manufacturer provides allowances to fund all or part of the retailer's advertising to the end consumer.

3   Sales competitions or contests – often targeted to members of the retail staff who are invited to enter a competition to win prizes either in return for performing a specific service for the brand or to provide them with additional knowledge about the brand.

4   Sales education – manufacturers run seminars or training sessions to impart more detailed knowledge about the brand. This is common practice in high-tech areas where salesperson knowledge is an important factor in convincing the consumer to purchase the product.

Trade training programmes

An increasingly important aspect of sales promotion activity is to provide training forums for members of the trade. Staff at the retail level are given in-depth exposure to the product range. These sessions provide insights into nature of product, manufacture, special features or attributes, etc. Sometimes participants receive a certificate providing them with some form of qualification that enhances their reputation.

In some markets it has become popular to provide training for members of the retailer's staff. With the increasing complexity of some product categories, manufacturers provide special training in their use and application. They can provide staff with specific information relating to the product together with methods of communicating the benefits of the product to potential consumers.

In a highly competitive market sector, where staff have confidence regarding one of the products they are more likely to communicate this to end consumers, with the potential to increase sales.

Tailor-mades and account-specific promotions

A particular form of promotional activity is to provide promotions tailored to the individual requirements of the retailer. For a limited period of time, the retailer is provided with a unique promotional programme. These often take the same form as a national promotion but can only be found in the stores of the particular retailer.

Some manufacturers maintain 'war books' of promotional themes and outlines from which the retailer can select the execution most appropriate to their own requirements. Often, these are identified by objective so that the retailer can choose the promotional device that meets their needs. In the context of the competition between retailers such promotions add to their distinctivity.

Promotions may be offered by manufacturers to retailers and stockists via intermediaries. Recently, Coca Cola issued a book of vouchers to potential customers with an issue of Makro Mail. Makro are a Cash and Carry wholesaler serving independent retailers. Unlike consumer offers, which are usually redeemed against small quantities of the product, the vouchers offered savings against cases of Coca Cola and Diet Coke, Fanta and other beverages marketed by the company.

Demonstrators and tastings

A device designed to stimulate purchase of products is that of in-store demonstrations and tastings. Again, these are likely to be offered to individual chains rather than across the board and are welcomed by retailers as a means of increasing the levels of in-store activity. They serve to reduce the consumer's risk of purchasing a new or untried product.

Contests and incentive programmes

Manufacturers provide a variety of competitions or other forms of incentive programmes to encourage increased selling efforts and other support from resellers. Some of these incentives may be targeted towards reseller management, whereas others may target store staff.

Trade advertising

Many manufacturers utilize dedicated trade media to communicate, for example, the details of promotional offers. Given the volume of retailers that need to be contacted by the sales force at the time of new activity, such devices can be used to communicate the nature of promotional activity to the trade. Trade advertising often serves to augment the sales force effort, or may be targeted to reach specific outlets that do not receive regular sales force visits.

Co-op advertising

The manufacturer absorbs part or all of the retailer's costs involved in running an advertising campaign in return for his product or products being given prominent featuring in that advertising. Such activity is specifically designed to gain support from the retailer since the advertising appears under his banner. Whilst, for the most part, such advertising usually appears in local or national newspapers, it can encompass any form of media that is available: television, radio, posters, etc.

Often the manufacturer specifies the manner in which his products will be portrayed as well as other conditions. The overall costs and the proportion to be borne by the manufacturer will be agreed in advance of the campaign appearing. In addition, the rebate will be conditional on the retailer providing evidence of the advertising, in the form of tear sheets or some other tangible proof that the advertising ran.

In some instances co-op advertising may be used by the manufacturer to gain distribution. By agreeing to pay for part or all of the campaign, the retailer may be convinced to stock the product since the advertising will direct potential consumers to his retail outlets.

In some instances, retailers will secure support from a number of different manufacturers featuring all of their (usually non-competing) products and this is an important way for the retailer to defray his advertising costs.

According to Bergen and John (1997)[15] co-operative advertising is an important aspect of many manufacturers' promotional budgets. Co-op advertising is an arrangement whereby a manufacturer pays for some or all of the costs of advertising undertaken by a retailer for that manufacturer's products.

In many instances, retailers use deals negotiated with manufacturers as the basis of price-based promotional offers that appear in local or national newspapers. These are a common practice in which the 'special' price offered is compared with the 'normal' or 'usual' price. Grewal *et al.* (1998)[16] propose a model for the consideration of price comparisons:

Figure 11.3

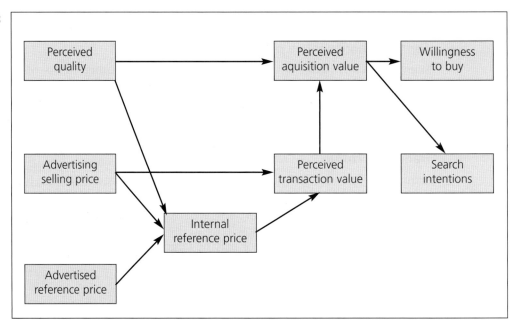

Co-op promotional programme

As well as co-operating in the costs of retailer advertising campaigns, some manufacturers will additionally develop co-op promotional programmes in which the manufacturer's brand is combined with a retailer own-label product for their mutual benefit.

This is a cost-sharing mechanism in a channel of distribution such that a manufacturer pays part of the cost incurred by a retailer who promotes the manufacturer's brand. It is known that such a programme can improve total channel profits, compared to a non co-operative situation.[17]

Provision of point-of-sale materials

Many manufacturers provide specially designed point-of-sale material to support in-store promotional activities. This has become such an important aspect of trade activity that it is covered in more detail later in this chapter.

Category management

Category management is an approach designed to develop relationships between manufacturers and retailers with the objective of increasing mutual profitability. The fundamental requirement is that the two parties work closely together to develop joint strategies. It is based on the assumption that co-operation is better than conflict. Clearly, manufacturers possess far greater knowledge of their own market category than retailers, who would otherwise need to possess detailed information about a wide variety of product categories. From the retailers' standpoint, there is a need to gain access to this information. In turn, manufacturers are provided with greater authority over the placement of products in-store.

The results of trade promotions

Murry and Heide (1998)[8] carried out a study to examine retailer participation in manufacturer-sponsored promotional programmes. Their findings reinforce previous studies that demonstrated that two factors are important in determining the level of participation. The first is the nature of the relationship between the company and the retailer. The second is the level of incentives offered to encourage participation. Of these, however, the second is far more significant.

However, a study by Rossiter and Percy[18] conducted in 1990 revealed that only 17 per cent of promotions accepted by retailers were profitable to the manufacturer.

Tomkins (2000)[19] identifies a two-level competition within the retail environment: first, amongst brand manufacturers and second, between brand manufacturers and private label.

Zerillo and Iacobucci (1995)[10] offer a similar viewpoint. Their work focuses on a misunderstanding that exists between manufacturers and retailers, often at the expense of consumers. Manufacturers want to win the inter-brand war by distinguishing their brands at the point of sale. Their focus is on brand share. Retailers, in contrast, are motivated by intra-brand considerations in terms of capturing their local trading area. Individual brands are simply a means of achieving that goal. Consumers search for the best deal during the shopping event itself, together with various shopping experiences.

In early 2004 ACNielsen[20] conducted its Trade Promotion Practices survey in the USA. The findings make interesting reading:

- Overall levels of trade spending showed an increase representing 12 per cent of gross sales on average.
- Thirteen per cent of manufacturers reported their spending investment on trade activities as being 'excellent/good' with only 18 per cent stating that they received 'poor value' from trade promotion spending.
- Category management was shown to be a strong element of trade-promotional practices. More than three-quarters of the companies contacted by Nielsen indicated that influencing decisions on their categories, optimizing their item mix, ensuring category leadership and creating positive relationships with retailers were the major motivations for these activities.

Zerrillo and Iacobucci (1995)[10] illustrate their work with a diagram that shows how manufacturers, retailers and consumers all benefit from promotional activity (see Figure 11.4).

Cooper *et al.* (1999)[21] have proposed a model for promotional planning from the retailer's perspective. They indicate that promotional planning is a daily task for both

Figure 11.4

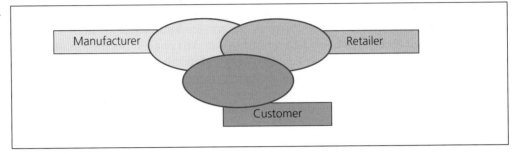

manufacturers and retailers. According to data in their paper, US retailers sold $48 billion worth of goods in 1997 with $13.3 billion (27.7 per cent) coming from sales on various promotions. They suggest that there are a variety of factors that need to be considered:

- The influence of promotional style
- The influence of an item's promotion history
- The influence of a store's promotion history
- Seasonality.

Category management

An important area of the relationship between manufacturers and retailers is the process known as category management. Category management is the process of developing a working relationship between manufacturers and retailers that shares market intelligence and develops strategies that are mutually beneficial. Category managers from both manufacturers and retailers work together to plan and execute merchandising programmes and promotional deals that are beneficial for both parties. The process begins with a strategic shift of the focus of management attention from the manufacturer's brands to the retailer's categories. A category is defined as a distinct manageable group of products that consumers perceive to be related and/or substitutable in meeting a consumer need (Blattberg 1995)[22] and a typical US grocer will have about 200 categories. Thus, category management is seen as a joint process of retailers and suppliers to manage categories as strategic business units. The intention is to produce enhanced business results by focusing on delivering increased consumer value. Category plans are jointly developed based on category goals, the competitive environment and consumer behaviour.

Category management theory argues that retailers' sales and profits will be maximized by an optimal mix of brands and pricing that is determined from the perspective of the consumer and is based on historical sales data. This mix is based on a systematic category review and it results in a category that is differentiated from competitors' categories in the 'eyes of the consumer'. Category reviews typically result in the elimination of several duplicate and poorly performing stock-keeping units (SKUs), the addition of a small number of category-enhancing SKUs, and adjustments in facings, pricing, promotions and organization of the category.[23]

The process of category management is attracting considerable attention as a means of generating manufacturer/retailer co-operation. In a recent paper by Johnson and Felice (1998),[24] the authors describe the growth of category management on a world-wide basis and outline the alternative strategies being pursued by participants. They stress the importance of understanding consumer purchase patterns and in-store dynamics to the success of such co-operative relationships.

This view is reinforced by Qureshi and Baker (1998)[25] who, similarly, both define and explain category management. Their study was based on an examination of a programme implemented by Unilever in conjunction with seven major UK retailers.

Category management continues to focus the merchandising, marketing and buying functions of suppliers and retailers in terms of identifying what the customers actually want. Ideally, it offers customers two benefits:

1 Providing the products consumers want or need in areas of the store where they can find them displayed in ways that facilitate such choice.

2 Developing the products consumers do not know that they want or need in areas of the store where they will come across them, displayed in ways that encourage purchasing.[26]

The process of category management utilizes 'efficient promotion' that ensures that the focus for the supplier's promotion activities is on selling through to the customer as opposed to being retailer-driven. Promotion strategies for the category providing the best mix of consumer-oriented promotions based on consumer demand, and taking account of the customers of individual retailers, offer substantial benefits in operations with much less inventory in the system. The ultimate aim is to ensure that the range at the point of purchase fulfils the needs of the target consumer, enhances profitability for the retailer and supplier, and benefits the overall health of the brand and perceptions of the retailer.[27]

Nielsen (1992)[28] indicates a series of stages that make up the process of category management:

1 Reviewing the category
2 Targeting consumers
3 Merchandise planning
4 Implementing the strategy
5 Evaluating results.

Harlow (1995)[29] suggests that category management is a fundamental aspect of a retailer pull strategy. He comments that category management is a strong vehicle for re-establishing beneficial supplier/retailer alliances, which have been progressively eroded by the combative nature of their relationships over recent years.

Hill (1998)[30] considers the importance of forging bonds between manufacturers and retailers, and emphasizes the need for the development of partnerships between them.

Dewsnap and Jobber (1999)[31] argue that category management is the ultimate expression of successful trade marketing. Apart from its ability to improve manufacturer/retailer relationships, they also contend that it provides an appropriate mechanism for improving the integration of sales and marketing activities.

The role of point of sale

The creation of impactful displays at the point of purchase is a major dimension of promotional planning. It provides the brand with an increased level of visibility and, particularly in impulse purchase situations, may be the necessary trigger to motivate a purchase of the promoted item. In the crowded retail environment, point-of-sale material may be an important element in distinguishing one brand from its competitors. Importantly, such material provides the opportunity to extend the brand proposition to the point of purchase and serves, for example, to remind the potential consumer of the key message from the advertising.

Point-of-sale promotions (referred to as PoS or Point of Purchase [PoP]) are a form of display that promotes a specific brand or category of merchandise. Displays are often located at the end of aisles, close to cash registers or at some other part of the store where they are likely to be noticed by consumers. PoS includes a variety of displays, signs and structures that can be used to promote a product. Importantly, PoS displays represent the last point in time that a manufacturer can reach the potential consumer. They can be used to create a specific impression about the brand before the purchase decision is made.

PoS augments the impact of the promotional proposition, which might otherwise be limited by, for example, the size of the pack, and allows for a more colourful and creative treatment. Whilst such material is comparatively expensive, it may avoid the greater costs associated with changing the pack design that, in turn, might reduce the consumer's recognition of the brand. Bearing in mind that the material is likely to be displayed in areas of the store other than where the product is displayed, it helps remind the consumer of the brand promotion.

Phillips and Cox (1998)[32] are strongly of the view that PoS material is a critical element of the consumer decision-making process at the point of purchase. They recommend that consideration of this element is an essential part of the marketing planning process.

Areni et al. (1999)[33] provide an alternative view. Following their experiments, they concluded that whilst PoS often results in reorganizing brands within the store, they do not always result in producing an increase in sales for the featured product.

However, Rachel Miller (1997)[34] reports on a survey conducted in the USA by POPAI (Point of Purchase Advertising Institute) in 1995. It concluded that three out of every four purchasing decisions are actually made in the supermarket. Consequently, brands are going to unprecedented lengths to attract the consumer's attention. She adds:

> Increasingly customers are making their decisions at the point of sale and marketers have to recognise that.

Similarly, Alan Toop (1994)[35] argues that:

> Point of sale is more successful than broadcast advertising. The message sent occurs at the period when the purchase can be made. The customer is not allowed time to forget the message.

The research by POPAI mentioned above and conducted over many years has consistently shown that up to 75 per cent of all purchasing decisions are made in store. Consumers have a profile of the brands that they will consider purchasing and the choice of which one to buy is made at the moment of brand selection inside the store. Displays at the point of purchase have a considerable impact upon the consumer's purchasing decisions. Making a brand stand out in-store at the moment they are about to make their brand choice can have a substantial effect on the actual decision. PoS displays not only raises awareness amongst consumers and stimulates the desire to purchase, but they also encourage consumers to touch, pick up and look at the product. Moreover, stores are where you can reach all of the people who are currently purchasing from the product category.

As Jones (1990)[36] asserts, retail stores have now become the newest battleground in the war of consumer goods manufacturers to win consumers. Manufacturers are discovering the need to reach potential buyers directly at the time and place at which the buying decision is made: the point of purchase.

In the same manner, Phillips and Cox (1998)[32] argue that point-of-purchase marketing is of significant importance since retailers are not simply passive channels of distribution.

Robin Cobb (1997)[37] suggests that the PoP industry generates a combined turnover of around £320 million. Their output ranges from short-term or temporary material, signage and similar items to more permanent fixtures designed to have a long life. Whilst many companies produce specific fixtures to present their range of products at the PoP, others produce equally permanent fixtures to assist the retailer in category management. Such items display many or all of the products within the category, but space is allocated proportionate to the market share. Often supplied by the market leader, the principle serves to reinforce the market leadership by ensuring that the company's products receive a dominant exposure. Special displays, price/promotions, demonstrations all create volume: they induce trial and encourage brand switching.

Manufacturers consider PoS as an attractive method of getting a brand more prominently displayed in front of customers. However, many retailers have introduced restrictions on the use of PoS material, requiring that permission be gained before the material is placed in store and, often, requiring that it conform to the design requirements of the store identity. Store space is often limited and retailers require material that does not take up too much space.

Many retailers now adopt strict design codes to minimize the confusion that would result from a wide variety of treatments appearing in their outlets. Most often, such material will need to be discussed at an early stage with potential stockists to ensure that the design is consistent with their own requirements. Importantly, this affords the opportunity to ensure the active participation of the retailer, who will enjoy the potential benefits of increased offtake of the brand through his outlets. Well-designed displays can be tailored to the size and style demanded by the individual retailer, creating a personalized offer while, at the same time, presenting a consistent image to the consumer.

Whilst some retailers have all but banned manufacturer PoS (especially retail grocery outlets), others continue to actively encourage it. The concern amongst the former is that it raises the level of in-store clutter and reduces the impact of store identity.

The difficulty in those instances is to convince retailers of the benefits that will follow from the use of such materials.

However, after many years during which manufacturers have been denied the ability to place PoS material in retail outlets, many retailers are beginning to again feature PoS. In part, this is a reflection of the increased competition on the high street. The somewhat restrictive approach adopted by many retailers resulted in their outlets becoming somewhat boring. Today, manufacturers are being encouraged to provide more support at the retail level to enhance the shopping experience and to increase the differentiation between retail brands. Banks and building societies, for example, are increasingly turning to PoS to enhance their retail branches as part of a recognition that their customers respond more positively to a less formal and impersonal environment.

An increasingly important aspect of PoS promotion, which follows on from the previous point, is the ability to 'tailor make' promotions with one or more retail chains. By developing material in conjunction with one or more retail groups, the promotion is more likely to achieve its desired objectives. Indeed, several retailers may be likely to insist, not only on personalized PoS, but also personalized promotional activity to provide them with a competitive advantage over other similar retailers.

Gordon and Valentine (1996)[38] have attempted to identify the wide range of cues that result in the split-second decision to purchase a particular brand. Their conclusions reinforce the findings of Connolly and Davison (1996).[39] They particularly stress the need to develop a stronger link between packaging and advertising.

Whilst much display creation originates from retailers, others derive directly from manufacturers. These may be sold or given to the retailers, sometimes in exchange for specific purchases of products from the manufacturer's range. The scale of PoS materials may range from the very small, including shelf strips or shelf talkers (these are attached to the shelf in the sector of the retail outlet featuring the particular brand) to large free-standing fixtures that feature the brand in a separate location within the store. Similarly, these may be of relatively low cost and short duration (such as cardboard dumpbins) or be both costly and durable (such as permanent in-store fixtures).

To be effective, PoS must communicate the product proposition or the promotional offer succinctly and clearly. The display should encourage the potential consumer to stop and look, perhaps pick up and examine the featured brand. All forms of PoS displays provide information to potential consumers. Some may be purely functional, providing the consumer with usage information. Equally, it is possible to provide persuasive messages that alert consumers to the existence of the brand. They can make the shopping experience easier for the consumer since well-placed PoS can help consumers to locate and purchase desired items.

Keeler (2004)[40] asserts that PoS enables marketers to maximize the effectiveness of the brand message. It carries the message from outside the store to achieve impact on the consumer at the moment of purchase.

Chevalier (1975)[41] indicates that aisle end displays are viewed by consumers as special bargains and often buy from a display products that they had no previous intention of buying. For the retailer, displays create in-store excitement and increase the average amount purchased. In an experiment featuring 64 FMCG products, displays featuring price reductions resulted in unit sales that were 572 per cent of regular weekly sales in the weeks preceding the experiment.

PoS material supplied by the manufacturer can be an important element of the overall promotion. One of the most prominent and, therefore, sought-after positions in a supermarket will be the gondola ends. These are invariably used by the retailer to promote specific lines and the offer may be enhanced by the provision of PoS material featuring the details of the offer.

Other items may range from shelf strips or 'wobblers' to posters and banners to counter self-merchandising material. The latter, usually placed close to the till, feature a specific manufacturer's products often impulse purchase items.

Types of point-of-sale displays

- Window and door signage
- Counter units
- Shelf units
- Floor standing units
- Mobiles and banners
- End of aisle display
- Dump bins
- Illuminated signage
- Moving displays
- Interactive units
- Trolley displays.

Customers may receive increased product information as a result of promotional displays and in-store assistance, as well as enhanced value because of lower prices.

One interesting feature emerges from a study conducted by Inman *et al.* (1990),[42] which further justifies the use of PoS material. They argue that the mere presence of a promotional signal such as a sign, marker or some other indication of a price promotion on a brand display may, in itself, be sufficient to convince some consumers to purchase the product. For those consumers who have a low awareness of the actual price of the product, the promotional signal may be sufficient to motivate their purchase, even though the saving may be very low. This is consistent with the findings of Dickson and Sawyer (1990),[43] who found that less than 15 per cent of consumers they interviewed after purchasing a price-promoted product knew the amount of the associated price cut.

A recent innovation that is likely to have a major impact on in-store display is the trial by Tesco of the in-store TV programme. For some time, retailers have been using small television monitors with video play-back machines close to the point of purchase. These have been used to demonstrate specific products making them more attractive to potential purchasers.

However, the Tesco experiment in conjunction with the media owner J.C. Decaux has a potentially more lasting effect. In the test, conducted in 10 stores, the company claims a 10 per cent uplift in sales of the 62 products advertised. Unlike conventional

PoS material that is static, the screens can be used to display moving images in colour, just like conventional television. They can also show conventional brand advertising linked to specific sales promotion offers. Moreover, the images can be changed readily to take advantage of regional opportunities, even down to the individual store level. The appointment of Decaux (one of the world's largest media owners) as the sales agency for Tesco TV is indicative of the serious nature of the project. In its initial roll-out, Tesco aims to have 300 stores operational, each with an average of 50 screens in-store.

In-store demonstrations

An extension of the principle of PoP display is the use of in-store demonstrations of a particular product or service. These can be stand-alone or work in conjunction with specially designed PoP displays sometimes of a permanent nature moving from store to store after a brief period.

Whilst some demonstrations are provided by human demonstrators and are particularly valuable in achieving sampling of a new product, for example, a food product when there might be reluctance on the part of the consumer to trial, especially where the cost and associated risk is high, it should be noted that such demonstrations are of high cost, requiring investment in trained personnel. However, some retailers are prepared to use their own personnel to provide in-store tastings with the proviso that the manufacturer bears the cost of the product consumed. Often such tastings are combined with a money-off voucher to encourage the consumer to make a purchase once the product has been sampled.

Anchor spreadable is mounting sampling events at 65 Tesco, Sainsbury and ASDA stores. The samplings feature costumed versions of the Cow and Moo characters from the TV commercial who will hand out samples of the spread on toast. Consumers will also receive 30p off coupons and helium balloons for their children. The brand is also repeating its link with the Tussauds Group after 18 000 people took advantage of the offer last year. Two million packs of Anchor spreadable will carry money off entry to Alton Towers or Thorpe Park and 500 000 cans of Anchor Real Dairy Cream will carry £7 off entry to Alton Towers or Chessington World of Adventures.

An alternative is the use of in-store video demonstrations that display the product and its applications. This is of particular value where the nature of the product is complex or its range of applications is significant, especially in the case of DIY products. These video displays also have the additional benefit of ensuring a consistent quality of demonstration.

New technology, such as computer-generated interactive displays, achieves high levels of consumer participation and may serve to highlight specific responses that are tailored to their individual needs. Several retailers provide mobile telephone displays, for example, which enable the potential customer to interrogate the database to identify a model that is best suited to their particular usage patterns.

An intermediate form is a display that invites consumers to trial the product themselves, for example, pens and pads in-store. Some of these displays serve to attract consumer attention and involve them in trying the particular product benefit.

Promoting to the sales force

Whilst the range of factors associated with the personal selling process are beyond the scope of this book, they are, nonetheless, an important facet of sales promotional activity. There are a number of excellent texts on sales-force management. This text will concern itself with those aspects of sales-force activity that are within the remit of sales promotion:

- Sales-force motivation
- Sales-force briefing
- The provision of selling materials (sales aids)
- The role of the sales force in achieving promotional objectives.

Manufacturers either have an internal sales force or use some form of third-party selling operation to communicate within the distribution channels. In the majority of instances, the manufacturer uses its own sales force to encourage the various intermediaries to promote the product range. However, some companies distribute via agents (who usually act on behalf of that company) or brokers (who represent several companies). They are both, usually, paid on the basis of commission, which might operate on a sliding scale.

In most organizations, the responsibility for the organization of sales-force motivational programmes rests with the sales department rather than the brand or promotional manager. However, there is inevitable overlap since the effective implementation of a sales promotion will be dependent on the level of support given to it by the sales force. Inevitably, therefore, there will be close co-operation between the sales department and the marketing department in the development of specific incentives designed to motivate the sales force to support a promotional programme.

Charles Wilson (1997)[44] suggests that the selling activities of UK companies cost more than £19 billion per annum: more than double that spent on advertising. He suggests that the typical annual cost of a salesperson is around £49 000. Of this sum, £28k goes on travel, communications and management. In addition, he estimates that only around 6 per cent of the time is actually spent on selling; the rest is consumed by travel, meetings and administration. The consequence is that a single sales call can cost anything from £27 to £200.

In a supplement to *Marketing* (1997) Nick Fennel[45] of CPM International argues that face-to-face communications is the only form of marketing communications that can take account of the complexities of the customer/supplier relationship. Sales calls play an important role within trade marketing. The sales force enable the company to monitor competition, provide feedback on data, evaluate the performance of activities at the point of purchase and, perhaps most significantly, establish and build relationships with new and existing customers.

Sales-force functions

The sales force can fulfil a variety of functions on behalf of the manufacturer, with the same tasks sometimes being fulfilled by agents or brokers. In those instances where the company is relatively small, the costs of maintaining a sales force may be prohibitive.

Accordingly, they may contract the selling function to other organizations. In many industries agencies or brokers operate on behalf of a number of companies, thereby reducing the costs to the individual organization. Moreover, they often have extensive contacts with the retail trade that can be exploited by the company rather than having to develop them on their own behalf.

However, many companies are examining ways of reducing the costs of maintaining contact with their customers. Direct mail, telesales and field marketing all provide lower cost routes to achieving the same goal. In those instances where the physical sales force is too small to ensure rapid contact with the trade, presentation materials can be mailed to designated buyers and influencers to outline the proposition.

New business selling

Most companies have the need to extend distribution, establish new retail outlets, etc. These objectives may be met either by maintaining a dedicated new business sales force or ensuring that the sales force devotes a percentage of its time to opening up new opportunities. These activities are sometimes referred to as cold calling or canvassing.

Missionary selling

Missionary selling overlaps with cold calling, but is especially relevant in the development of relationships within professional fields. Their function is often more closely associated with education than with achieving specific sales objectives. This may be seen, for example, in the pharmaceutical field, where the sales force will provide chemists, doctors, dentists, etc., with specific information relating to the products.

Technical selling

Some products/services, particularly those of an industrial or business-to-business nature, require an in-depth knowledge of the company operation and of the purchaser's needs. These sales staff require specialized training.

Trade selling

The sales force is an essential instrument in conveying information to the trade regarding promotional plans, as well as achieving specific sales objectives. Their ability to achieve objectives is often dependent on their establishing personal relationships with the distribution channels. The relationships established between salespeople and the retailer are a vital component of an effective marketing programme.

An important distinction must be made between the 'order taker' vs the 'order generator'. The former tends to fulfil only the most basic tasks and simply responds to specific requests for products from trade customers. The latter is the preferred type of sales person who creates additional sales for the company by increasing demand for the company's products.

Hardy and Magrath (1990)[46] argue that only the strong support of the sales force makes it possible to obtain strong support from retailers. This, in turn, makes it possible to gain strong purchasing activity from end consumers.

They argue that it pays to train the sales force in how to present promotions to buyers using both financial benefit arguments in addition to the promotion's creative and merchandising elements. Sales representatives must be capable of demonstrating that the promotion is likely to pay out for the retailer, which requires both the data and the skills necessary to make these presentations.

Sales-force remuneration and motivation

Most sales-force operations are dependent on the method of remuneration, which may be a composite of salary and incentive scheme. Many companies offer a comparatively low basic salary that is augmented by further income related to the volume of sales achieved. In many instances, sales forces are provided with specific (measurable) targets that can be used as the basis for reward schemes. The relationship between these two forms will vary considerably and reflect industry or sector custom and practice. Clearly, where the objective is to achieve something other than specific sales (as in the case of missionary selling) it is likely that the basic income level will be set somewhat higher.

A common practice is that a significant percentage of income derives from the achievement of sales objectives or targets to motivate. However, as well as direct monetary incentives, most sales forces are the recipients of other, non-monetary forms of incentive. These might include participation in special meetings (often held in exotic locations), specialized training programmes, sales competitions and contests to achieve a range of rewards.

Various incentive programmes are designed to motivate sales personnel to achieve a higher level of performance than usual. The motivating factor is some form of reward scheme that provides the sales force with extra income or gifts as a direct result of their achievement of specific and pre-determined targets. One such format is that of sliding scale rewards, where the benefit increases as the level beyond the established target is exceeded. The more the salesperson sells the greater the level of reward.

Although there will be considerable variation, sales-force incentives usually reflect three broad themes:

1 Contests or competitions – these will usually relate to a specific sales goal that must be met in order for the sales person to qualify for a prize. These might, for example, require the sales person to achieve specific volume sales, to achieve agreed distribution levels, to open new accounts for the brand, etc. Contests involve competition between individual members of the sales force in order to gain the limited number of prizes on offer.

2 Incentives – these similarly will be based on specific targets and may be of a sequential nature. On reaching each level of the target, the salesperson may qualify for a specific prize or other reward. In this instance, all members of the sales force may qualify for a reward, providing his or her targets have been met.

3 Financial rewards – here, rather than prizes, the sales person receives a financial bonus in the form of increased pay or additional cash for the achievement of targets.

It is important to note that the objectives of a sales incentive programme may be designed to achieve more than just additional sales volume. They may, for example, relate to identifying and securing new customers, achieving trade co-operation for increased product display, erecting PoS material, etc.

If any incentive programme is to achieve the established objectives, it is important to ensure that salespeople regard the targets as being achievable. If target levels are set too high, then it is likely that the programme will fail. Moreover, budgets must relate to the targets established. Most sales-force promotions have a wide range of prizes, usually following some form of tiered structure, to ensure that as many people as possible can qualify for a prize. There is little doubt that sales-force incentives that only reward the top salesperson generally fail. There will be many reasons for this, but since most participants will not see themselves as being able to achieve the best, they will give up early in the programme.

Key features of sales-force incentive programmes are that:

1 targets must be specific and measurable
2 they must be realistic
3 the conditions must be made clear from the outset
4 prizes must be attainable
5 prizes must be of sufficient value to be motivational.

It is impossible to be prescriptive concerning the nature of the rewards to be offered. However, most sales-force incentives consist of cash, gifts or travel. In some instances, the sales force is provided with a gift catalogue in order that they can choose their reward dependent on the level of achievement. This overcomes any difficulties associated with the offering of prize items that are not attractive to all members of the sales force or that duplicate items they already own.

Travel awards offer both excitement and attractiveness to the promotion and, in some instances, can be tied in to some corporate event, such as a visit to an appropriate location for a conference or to a manufacturing location in some foreign country.

Sales contests, special incentive programmes designed to motivate sales personnel to accomplish specific sales objectives, have become so commonplace in the selling environment that most sales managers are routinely engaged in their design and implementation, and most salespeople participate in them, often on an ongoing basis. Research conducted by Murphy and Sohi (1995)[47] indicates that most sales managers believe sales contests are effective at motivating salespeople, that certain contest designs, in certain instances, have been associated with attainment of contest goals. For example, travel incentives have been associated with greater gains in contest goals than either cash or merchandise awards, and managers believe contests produce increases in contest-related sales goals.

Once the objectives for the programme have been established, it is important to identify a theme for the programme. This serves to bring together the objectives of the programme together with the rewards themselves. Ideally, the theme should be simple to understand and easy to implement and should be challenging and motivational.

Sales aids

An important facet of promotional planning is the provision of specific materials designed to assist the sales force to sell in the promotion to retailers and others. Usually these take the form of small folders or portfolios that contain the key details of the promotional offer. Rather than rely on disparate presentations, many companies provide their sales teams with a variety of pre-prepared materials that guide the presentation. Some of these are very sophisticated.

These materials will provide a specific outline of the promotion, perhaps featuring the other support that the promotion will receive (in the form of advertising, PoS material, on-pack details, etc.). Usually such sales material will outline the benefits to the retailer with specific information on the likely performance of the promotional offer related to previous experience, etc.

Often other material will be used to maintain the interest of the sales force. This might consist of an invitation to a sales conference (particularly if the promotion is a major event in the brand calendar), periodic letters informing the sales force of the progress and achievements of the campaign, and specific details of how close he or she is to winning one of the incentives on offer under the scheme.

Case study 1

TOYOTA GB
Agency: Saatchi & Saatchi

Background

By 2001 the Toyota Yaris was in its third year of manufacture. Having been voted 'Car of the Year' during its first 12 months, the car was consistently coming top in trade and consumer magazine road tests. The result was that sales continued to grow.

Objectives

The promotion had two clear objectives:

1 To ensure that at least 10 000 people per show interacted or became aware of the car's presence.

2 To build a database of 20 000 potential targets to include personal details and car purchasing preferences.

Strategy

- To physically present the Yaris to the target audience of ABC1 females aged 25–45.
- To reflect the 'personality' of the Yaris emphasizing its style and image.

Campaign summary

Toyota undertook the sponsorship of The Vitality Show, a series of five 4-day 'healthy living' events, with an almost identical target audience to that of potential brand purchasers. These events took place in five major cities across the UK. The focal point was a Toyota Yaris surrounded by interactive screens. The consoles utilized a special technique that produces images of how the body 'feels' on the inside. This was combined with a specially designed computer-analysis programme that invited visitors to check out whether they had a 'winning aura' by placing their hand on a magnetic plate. The screen also displayed a general analysis of their personality derived from the aura reading. By association, the Yaris was seen to be delivering an activity entitled 'Beauty from within'.

Yaris promotions staff gave away branded 'colour healing' key fobs printed with heat-sensitive inks and invited visitors to enter a prize draw for a Toyota Yaris styled to their own specification.

Visitors to the stand could complete a hand-shaped entry form for the chance to win the Yaris and entries were posted in a box at the stand.

The Yaris promotion was the ISP silver award winner 2002 in the Trade Promotions Sponsorship category.

Case study 2

GUINNESS
Agency: The Triangle Group

Guinness has a long association with rugby and has always supported major events. In a declining beer market where consumers tend to default to lager, it needed a campaign to defend its sales.

The plan was to extend its support to non-professional, grass roots rugby where the bar is an active social centre.

The focus of the scheme was to drive loyalty by giving the clubs tangible rewards for every keg of Guinness purchased. All communication was targeted at the club rather than the individual. Points were awarded for each keg purchased and were redeemable against high quality merchandise ranging from rugby kit for the players to equipment for the bar. Eligible clubs were visited by a Guinness representative who explained the scheme and encouraged registration. Registered clubs received the 'Club Together' pack containing a Guinness kit bag, a rugby shirt and a desk notepad together with PoS materials to help to promote the scheme to members.

A total of 87 per cent of clubs registered, 50 of which had Guinness specially installed to enable them to participate.

The campaign received a gold award in the Loyalty Campaigns section of the 2005 ISP Promotion Awards.

(The above appeared in the Special Supplement to Promotions and Incentives magazine, June 2005.)

Questions

1 Why are there increasing concerns about the viability of trade-oriented promotional activity?
2 What are the benefits that might derive from promoting to the trade?
3 Identify the role of category management as a trade promotional tool.
4 Discuss the role of benefits of point-of-sale activities.
5 Why is the sales force an important element of effective promotional activity?

12 Trade shows, event management and sponsorship

Chapter overview

There are a variety of large-scale events designed to communicate the benefits of brands to the trade and consumer audiences alike. Increasing use is being made of trade shows and exhibitions to create 'events' that can be used to achieve cost-effective communication to members of the trade.

Equally, sponsored events are gaining momentum to extend brand values and communicate, in many instances, those values to a world-wide audience. A particular aspect of sponsorship that is considered in some detail in this chapter is the role of cause-related marketing, in which a company or brand links with a charitable organization to develop promotional activities.

Learning outcomes

- To consider the roles of trade shows and exhibitions
- To examine the functions of event marketing and sponsorships
- To appreciate the growth and scale of sponsorship activities
- To understand the increasing role and importance of cause-related marketing.

Trade shows and exhibitions

Many companies participate in trade shows, professional shows and other events that provide them with a forum to promote their products or services. Some events represent a major opportunity to establish and maintain contact with the trade, especially where the company's sales force is comparatively small. They are particularly cost-effective where the retailers of a product gather in a single location and can be invited to discuss their needs with members of the company staff, rather than have the latter visit the retailers in their own locations. Some shows additionally attract a consumer audience and again may provide a cost-effective direct channel of communications.

Despite the differences in the various words used to describe the events – trade shows, expositions, scientific/technical conferences, conventions – the basic function of the activity represents a major industry marketing event. Black (1986)[1] defines these activities as 'events that bring together, in a single location, a group of suppliers who set up physical exhibits of their products and services from a given industry or discipline'. According to O'Hara (1991),[2] trade shows rank second behind only on-site selling in influencing buying decisions of industrial purchases.

In the USA and the UK, trade shows are a multibillion-dollar business. De Kimpe and Francois (1997)[3] suggest that they account for about 10 per cent of the business marketing communications budget of US firms and more than 20 per cent of the budget for many European firms. Trade shows blend some elements of direct selling (there are usually sales personnel in the booth and, especially in Europe, some selling actually takes place on the show floor) and advertising. The booth generates awareness and can answer some key questions, even without involvement of the booth personnel. Display stands are specifically designed to convey information about the company and its products. Exhibitors have several objectives for participating in a trade show. Some are most interested in generating high-quality leads, others in promoting corporate image and still others in maintaining contact with current and prospective customers; many have multiple objectives.

Trade shows provide the opportunity to affect multiple phases of the industrial buying process in one location: they can create awareness in new prospects, reinforce existing customer relationships, provide product demonstrations for evaluation, establish relationships between vendors and prospects, and allow sales of products on the spot. Trade shows significantly influence the industrial buying process during the need recognition and vendor evaluation stages of the purchase process (Moriarty and Spekman, 1984).[4]

Pre-show promotion

Firms often announce well in advance that they will exhibit at a particular show. For example, they might send personalized invitations using their own customer or prospect list or the registration list made available by the show organizers. Other firms contact their customers by telephone or advertise in specialized trade magazines to announce their presence at an upcoming show.[3]

The advantages of trade shows

There are many benefits that derive from using a trade show. These include the following:

- A message delivered to a large number of qualified interested people (86 per cent of all show attendees represent a buying influence, are interested in a specific exhibited product or service and have not been called on lately by a sales representative).
- The introduction of new products to a large number of people. Many companies use major shows as the forum for the launch of new products, for example, cars are often launched at International Motor Shows, computers and peripherals at specialist events, etc.

- Trade shows provide the opportunity to identify potential customers. Often dealers and retailers specifically attend trade shows to gather information about new products, and meet sales personnel to obtain information and technical details. Most exhibitors maintain contact lists of visitors to their stands, often running prize-based competitions, entry to which is enabled by the provision of the individual's business card. These are subsequently used to compile a database of prospects and may form the source of information for follow-up calls by sales personnel.

- Enhancing goodwill. Equally, exhibitors use the opportunity to meet with existing stockists. Many show stands maintain a 'hospitality' facility where selected visitors can be invited for informal discussions regarding their relationships with the company.

- Gaining free company publicity. Media representatives often attend trade shows to gather information from which they can develop news stories. Features in national newspapers and specialist magazines publicize new products that will be available to consumers at a later date.

- Enhancing corporate image amongst competitors, customers, industry and the media. Presence at a major international show assists in positioning the exhibitor as a major 'player' in the field. Since the company is seen alongside other major organizations, it is likely that it will be considered as equivalent to them in scale and performance. This may also evoke pride amongst the company's staff.

- Gathering competitor information. Since the major competitors are equally present at trade shows and other events, companies use the opportunity to gather information on new products that they are intending to launch, advertising and promotional campaigns and other more general information about the company's activities that might not otherwise be available to them.

- Selling at show itself. Many companies use the opportunity to sell their merchandise at trade shows. Indeed, this function may well be particularly important for those organizations with small sales forces. The trade show represents an opportunity to meet with and to sell to a significant number of retailers. If the sales force is small, the opportunity to call upon retailers in their own outlets may, at best, be infrequent.

- Gaining access to key decision makers. Many companies send their senior personnel to trade shows both to gather information about competitive products and to meet with potential suppliers. They represent a unique forum in which the organization can inform potential stockists and others about their product range, philosophy and other aspects of the company.

- Disseminating facts about products, services. Trade shows provide a forum in which information about the company can be widely disseminated. Not only are potential stockists present but also representatives of the media. Many media titles provide coverage of trade shows extending the coverage of information received to a wider audience.

- Servicing current account problems. The opportunity to deal face to face with customers will often serve to alleviate problems that they may be having with the organization.

Other advantages inherent in participating in trade shows include noting that trade show activities can play a major part in vendor evaluation and recognition owing to their personal selling process elements of:

1 identifying prospects
2 servicing current accounts
3 introducing products
4 improving corporate image
5 gathering competitor information
6 selling.

Trade-show objectives

There are a variety of reasons that are cited by companies for their continued involvement in trade shows and exhibitions. Major objectives for participation are:

1 To enhance company/ brand awareness amongst trade audience
2 To introduce new products
3 To reach customers cost-effectively
4 To generate additional sales
5 To identify potential stockists
6 To identify sales opportunities/ leads
7 To enhance relationships with existing customers
8 To gain information about competitive companies.

In a trade-show bureau survey, objectives given for entering a trade show included: new product introduction and evaluation (60 per cent), leads/new contacts (83 per cent), sales goals/orders, sales training, new reps or intermediaries, and image building. Although 60 per cent of companies have defined exhibit guidelines, only 36 per cent say they set formal objectives (Donath 1980).[5] Another estimate is that only 56 per cent of exhibiting firms bother to set objectives and only 22 per cent have pre-show promotions (Mee 1988).[6]

The negatives of trade shows

Herbig *et al.* (1998)[7] suggest that trade shows have their downside. Tactical rather than strategic orientation might account for finding that only 23 per cent of executives think trade show effort is very effective. This poor opinion of trade shows by executives is often exacerbated by the fact that only 56 per cent of firms participating in trade shows have specific objectives before participating in a given show. Only 46 per cent of companies set goals before they exhibit, half are wishy-washy, and one out of three exhibitors do not set quantifiable objectives.

Few exhibitors do any pre-show promotion to ensure that their key prospects reach their booth. Booth personnel training has improved but leaves much to be desired, and lead qualification, tracking, and return on investment evaluation are functions unexplored by most exhibitors (only 14 per cent claim they track lead conversions to sales). Barely 17 per cent of all exhibitors provide their management executives with return on investment (ROI) data. Many firms have failed to measure quantifiably the return on their trade-show investment.

Other disadvantages with trade shows include taking salespeople away from their territories, the crowded, confusing environment found in large shows, labour problems and unions, proliferation and excessive frequency of trade shows, and a high proportion of sightseers. Bonoma (1983)[8] adds unknown effectiveness on return per dollar spent and difficulty of measuring efficiency, high and rising costs of participation.

To these must be added the costs of participation. In many instances costs can be extremely high. There is the cost of producing the company stand, maintaining a continuous staff presence to meet both existing and potential customers, the costs of providing hospitality, etc.

The evaluation of trade shows

According to Blythe (1999),[9] substantial sums of money are devoted to exhibitions. Trade exhibitions are, clearly, regarded as an important tool of marketing communications. Despite that, few exhibitors have an accurate way of evaluating the return on their trade-show investments.

He points out that only a minority of visitors to trade exhibitions have a purchasing role. Their attendance is predicated on information gathering, particularly about new products. He concludes that few exhibitors adopt a market-oriented approach towards their exhibition activities.

However, according to Gopalakrishna *et al.* (1995)[10] the measurement of trade show effectiveness is made more difficult as a result of a number of factors. First, a firm's participation in trade shows results in direct sales effects as well as attitudinal effects (creating product awareness and interest, building image and reputation, developing a favourable corporate image and handling customer complaints). Second, the trade show is typically combined with other communication activities such as direct marketing, advertising and personal selling. It is difficult to measure the contribution of each of the individual components.

White, Bryant *et al.* (1999)[11] consider a variety of the issues involved in the organization of both conferences and exhibitions. They suggest that there are a variety of methods for evaluating the effectiveness of such events, an area sometimes overlooked by participants.

Different participants have different expectations of the benefits of trade-show participation. Some are interested in generating leads; others in promoting their corporate image; whilst others seek to maintain contact with current customers.

According to Blythe (1999)[12] there is an anomaly in that few large firms making a large commitment to exhibitions actually use rigorous research to confirm the success of the exercise. In fact, it is smaller firms using exhibitions less frequently who are most likely to use market research, to use records of follow-up business and more likely to use records of contacts made.

It is clearly important to define precisely what objectives are to be met by participation in such events and how they are to be measured.

Faria and Dickinson (1986),[13] for example, rated 34 trade show selection criteria on a nine-point scale. Their results indicated the firms that exhibited were concerned primarily with audience quality, audience quantity, display location and logistical aspects in that order.

Another measure is exhibit efficiency: that is, the percentage potential audience that receives person-to-person contact at the company's exhibit. Other measures might include:

- personnel performance – the quality and number of exhibit personnel on duty at the booth
- product interest – the percentage of booth visitors who said they were interested in seeing the company's type of products/services
- buying influence – the percentage of an average exhibit's visitors who claimed a buying influence for its products/services
- buying plans – the percentage of an exhibit's visitors who said they were planning to buy the company's products/ services as a result of what they saw at the show
- memorability – the percentage of visitors who stopped at an exhibit and remember doing so.

Other measures of effectiveness generally used by companies exhibiting in trade shows include:

- the number of leads generated
- the quantity of actual sales that result from these leads
- the cost per lead generated
- feedback about the show given to sales force
- the amount of literature distributed at the show.

Event marketing and sponsorships

The term event marketing is used to describe a wide range of activities in which a brand is linked to some form of event. It is a moot point as to whether the category should be included within the framework of sales promotion. Certainly, for many organizations, such activity is an extension of their normal sales promotion planning. Elsewhere, however, it takes on greater significance, especially within the strategic framework of the brand and some companies have an individual or division specifically responsible for managing events in which the company is involved.

In some instances, this activity may be designed to associate the brand with a particular lifestyle and augment the brand image (e.g. V2000, The Stella Artois Tennis Tournament, etc.). When marketers associate their brands with events that already provide an emotional appeal, they may be able to associate these feelings with the brand. Moreover, by careful selection of the sponsored event, marketers can target activities that appeal to specific segments of the market.

Robinsons, which has long been associated with tennis, has mounted a roadshow to strengthen its ties. The play tennis roadshow, which coincides with the Wimbledon

Championships event, will run for 4 months. Players can test their serve at some 40 locations, including supermarkets and shopping centres with coaches on hand to give advice. A prize draw runs alongside the event with one participant at each event given the chance to win a tennis racket. One overall winner will receive £200 worth of tennis coaching.

Similarly, Strongbow cider is extending its presence at summer music festivals with its Strongbow rooms dance event. Now in its seventh year, it will be present at nine music festivals during 2005. These include V, Creamfields and Homelands. It will include product sampling at several of the events together with pouring rights at others.

In others, an event is created especially for the purposes of promoting the brand. When the firm creates its own event, it keeps control over exposure and organization. Many new public events are created in order to meet the needs of sponsors and this tendency is likely to increase in the future. Events will often be designed to entertain and reward members of the distribution chain or staff of the organization. These may be extended into some form of trade training activity. In many cases, firms invest in the sponsoring of pre-existing events that are conceived and organized by independent individuals and groups. One advantage associated with the sponsoring of existing events is that the sponsor can evaluate a priori the value of its investment. The sponsor is, however, constrained to play according to the organizers' rules.[14]

Often, these events are used for the purpose of distributing samples or information about the brand to potential consumers. Many companies use a wide range of merchandise items to promote their brand and these are frequently used as free gifts at events. Items include clothing, such as hats and t-shirts, balloons and other items, some of which are mailed to potential consumers and trade customers to direct attention towards the promoted brand. An extension of this principle is the provision of a range of branded merchandise, which is sold to the consumer (and sometimes used as a dealer loader). Some of these items develop a cachet of desirability. For example, Camel have moved into watches; Marlboro into clothing, etc.

Some events are designed to forge links with charitable organizations, others to commemorate specific moments in a brand's history, such as an anniversary, etc. An extension of the principle of event marketing is a new field often termed as experiential marketing. Whether in the form of a dedicated retail outlet or a permanent exhibition or visitor venue, manufacturers provide consumers with the opportunity to 'experience' the brand. Various companies such as Cadbury with Cadbury World, Levi's and Nike both with retail outlets and Lego with Legoland are examples of this new form of activity.

There are several issues that need to be addressed in the identification of an event:

1　Is the event compatible with the image (actual or desired) or the brand or the company sponsoring it?

Events can be used to reinforce a brand's existing image or to assist in the process of changing that image if it is felt to be inappropriate or out-of-date.

Sponsorship has its own characteristics that contribute to making it commercially attractive to corporations aiming to build favourable associations and identities for their brands. Quester and Farrelly (1998)[15] argue that it can be used to transfer positive image connotations from the event or athlete to the sponsors' corporate brand image.

Moreover, they argue, sponsorship may be influential if consumers perceive that marketing through a particular event is a less commercially biased approach than traditional advertising. Similarly, a sponsor's message may be more readily accepted if it is regarded as involving an element of patronage.

John Lewicki (1998),[16] however, argues that sponsorships should not try to change the perceptions of the brand. Rather they should improve these perceptions by linking the brand to an event or organization that the target audience already values highly. This can be maximized by intrinsically linking the sponsorship to traditional advertising.

2   Will the event attract an appropriate segment of the target audience?

Targeting of the appropriate audience is equally important. There is little point becoming involved with an event that is not appreciated by those consumers who purchase the brand (unless, of course, the objective is to attract new and different users).

3   Does it offer potential for trade entertainment?

As noted above, many events are used for the purposes of entertaining members of the trade or company employees. Sometimes, these events are used as rewards to members of the sales force who have achieved specific targets. However, in both cases it is important that the event can provide an appropriate environment for this purpose.

Many organizations spend considerable sums of money on entertainment facilities, usually employing an outside caterer to ensure that visitors enjoy the occasion.

4   Will the event provide exclusivity of association, or will it be shared with other sponsors (some of whom might be competitors)?

Many events attract significant numbers of sponsors. For example, Formula 1 motor racing will have guests from the sponsors of each of the teams racing, the tyre manufacturers, and many others who are less directly involved with the event. To these organizations exclusivity is not important. Indeed, given the nature of the event, exclusivity would be impossible to obtain.

However, some companies prefer to 'dominate' the event. Pedigree, the manufacturers of a range of petfood products, are heavily involved in events such as showjumping, dog shows, etc., all of which have direct associations with the products manufactured by the company.

One of the best ways to derive benefit from an event sponsorship is to be the title sponsor of the event. This automatically gives a company 'name' and 'advertising' recognition. Titling an event is a powerful tool for an organization or company whose objective is to generate awareness. Another objective of title sponsorship is to develop the event over a long period of time so the sponsor can help shape the event to meet multiple objectives.

5   Is it intended as a one-off or a long-term association?

The company must decide at the outset how long the association with the event will last. The shorter the association, the less likely it is that there will be a linkage established between the event and the brand. On the other hand the costs of a long-term deal will often involve expenditures of millions of pounds and these may not be affordable to the organization.

6   Will the event attract media interest and create publicity for the brand?

Whilst gaining publicity from involvement with an event may be important to some sponsors, others will be less concerned. Needless to say, the greater the prominence of the event, the larger the investment required to participate in it.

Moreover, a distinction needs to be made between those events that attract national attention and those which gain more local publicity. The latter may be particularly attractive to locally based organizations or that have a particular appeal to members of the target audience. For example, several manufacturers of farm products such as seeds and fertilizers will sponsor events that appeal to the local or regional farming audience.

According to Jonathan Hall, MD of RPM (Roadshows, Promotions and Marketing) the events industry has seen a proliferation of agencies over recent years. This has largely been driven by demand from clients, who have to use more targeted marketing tools and who, like drinks and tobacco, face advertising restrictions.

Sponsorship

A major area that is often included within the sales promotion armoury is that of sponsorship, although equally it could be considered as a discrete activity since there are an increasing number of specialist companies that deal with clients' sponsorship requirements.

Erdogan and Kitchen (1998)[17] define sponsorship as the practice of promoting a company's interests and its brands by tying them to a specific and meaningful related event, organization or charitable cause. It has become an increasingly popular medium of corporate communication especially among companies operating in consumer markets. Sponsorship is a versatile method of communications. It can be used to achieve a variety of objectives. It can persuade indirectly and by association. Many companies now sponsor events routinely as part of their promotional activities; however, in many instances the objectives tend to be vague.

Meenaghan (1991)[18] provides an alternative definition. He states that sponsorship is an element of the communications mix in which a firm provides some financial support to an entity, which may be an individual (e.g. sports), an organization (e.g. a humane society) or a group (e.g. an orchestra), in order to allow this entity to pursue its activities (e.g. a cultural event) and, at the same time, benefit from this association in terms of global image and consumer awareness of the firm's market offerings. He and others report that the practice of sponsorship is quite developed and has become a standard component of the marketing plan.

Although various definitions of sponsorship have been proposed, they all recognize that sponsorship is first and foremost a commercial activity. The definitions all identify that in return for support, the sponsoring firm acquires the right to promote an association with the recipient. There are, however, some differences between these definitions that affect the domain captured and hence the estimates of the global dollar amounts involved in sponsorship. Global estimates of spending, therefore, vary significantly depending on the exact definition used.

According to Dolphin (2003),[19] sponsorship (ambiguous or otherwise) has proved itself to practitioners and scholars alike as a cutting-edge marcoms activity, one with the potential to reach specific audiences and to reach them with sharply focused messages and themes; ones capable of achieving and sustaining real competitive advantage. Thus, sponsorship has become a global tool in an age when the global village has become a reality.

Sponsorship is often an extension of event management, although it may take on a variety of different forms. Usually, sponsorship activity manifests itself in some form of promotional programme to ensure direct association with the consumers of the brand. Sponsorship can take a variety of forms. Events can be local, national or even international. They can be used to target different audiences. Equally it is often used to support other promotional activities since it can provide synergy between other communications and enable exploitation in terms of public relations.

Sponsorship can be either philanthropic or commercial. Philanthropic sponsorship implies the support of a cultural or social cause. In this type of sponsorship, the sponsor's participation is generally less prominent. For some authors, such as Meenaghan (1991)[19] financial support of a philanthropic nature should not be part of sponsorship, since the firm is making a donation and does not expect any benefits in return. However, Fry *et al.* (1982)[20] have shown that corporate donation often represents a complement to advertising and is partly motivated by profit. Gardner and Shuman (1987)[21] and others consider that the support of humane, social or cultural causes is part of the domain of sponsorship.

Because it is associated with humane causes, philanthropic sponsorship is likely to create positive feelings among consumers. These positive emotional reactions would then extend to attitudes towards the sponsor or the brand.

In most situations, sponsorship is commercial, i.e. the firm associates itself with a public event in order to gain direct commercial benefits: increase in consumer awareness, improvement in image, sales, etc. Some, such as Armstrong (1988)[22] have suggested that when the objective is the improvement of corporate image, philanthropic sponsorship would be more efficient than commercial sponsorship. He notes, however, that the media coverage of philanthropic sponsorship is usually smaller than that of commercial sponsorship.

The scale of sponsorship activities

An event such as the Olympics represents a very large expenditure for corporate sponsors, but provides a superb marketing platform. Quester and Thompson (2001)[23] believe that the prominence of sports sponsorship is due as much to its flexibility as a communication vehicle as it is to the opportunities that it affords by its association with the commercially driven phenomena of sports heroes. Hoek (1997)[24] reports that figures like sporting celebrities have little to do with the function of a product but the presence of their photograph in close proximity to a brand name draws attention to the latter and creates certain connotations.

However it is used, there is little doubt that sponsorship is a rapidly growing area of activity. According to IEG Network (2004),[25] sponsorship is the world's fastest growing form of marketing, with $28.billion predicted to be the world-wide expenditure on sponsorship causes ranging from sports, financial services, education, the broadcast media and the arts. This represents an increase of 8.7 per cent over the previous year.

In the USA, expenditure is predicted to reach $11.14 billion in 2004, an increase of 8.7 per cent over 2003. Sports sponsorship continues to dominate the US sponsorship scene, accounting for some 69 per cent of the total. Other areas of sponsorship, whilst still representing substantial expenditure, are more fragmented and account for smaller percentages. In Europe, IEG estimate that total sponsorship expenditure will reach $7.9 billion, also up on the previous year by some 6.9 per cent.

At the other end of the spectrum some companies use local events in order to promote their products and services. Most countries have calendars that contain specific events related to gift-giving. Manufacturers often exploit such calendar events such as Valentine's Day, Mother's Day, etc., as a vehicle for the promotion of products and services that are considered appropriate as gift items.

Some manufacturers create 'events' that can be similarly used. Company birthdays, back-to-school, spring sales, etc., can be all used for promotional purposes. Retailers, similarly, create 'events' as vehicles for store promotion.

Sponsorship investment has been historically directed toward sports primarily because of its flexibility as a communication vehicle and because of the opportunity it affords for association with the increasingly commercially driven phenomena of sport and sports heroes. Importantly, consumers all over the world are enthralled by sports, as they increasingly seek leisure activities as a diversion from their daily work routine.

The arts, on the other hand, enjoy a significantly lesser public profile and a smaller share of the sponsorship dollar as they are perceived as less lucrative, deemed 'exclusivist' and 'inaccessible' by some corporations, and thought to preclude mass participation.[26]

The objectives of sponsorship

Javalgi (1994)[27] argues that sponsorship is the underwriting of a special event with the object of supporting organizational objectives by:

- enhancing corporate image
- increasing awareness of brands
- stimulating the sales of products or services
- leveraging corporate reputation.

These objectives might include brand awareness. Cornwell (2001)[28] suggests that generating brand awareness is something that accrues naturally from sponsorship. Perhaps the sponsor wants to achieve name recognition: raising the profile of the corporate brand. Maybe image association is the strategy. Long-term sponsorships may do much to enhance corporate image. Meenaghan (1991)[19] commented that sponsorship is highly regarded for its perceived ability to enhance corporate identity, awareness or image, but Javalgi (1994)[29] asks whether sponsoring an activity for handicapped children produces the same impression of a company as sponsoring the fine arts. Perhaps another objective is to form relationships with customers. Another may be simply the halo effect from developing local relationships and basking in reflected glory.

Smith (1996)[29] notes that analysts find sponsorship popular as a platform from which to build equity and to gain affinity with target audiences. Grimes and Meenaghan (1998)[30] report that the consumer is the primary public for corporate sponsorship activity. They report that a well-chosen sponsorship has the capacity to drive particular brand values. Amis (1997)[31] argues that sponsorship can become a distinctive resource: one capable of winning a sustainable competitive advantage. Sponsorship can inform customers of brand benefits, letting them know where and how to obtain the brand. Tripodi (2001)[32] reports that since the 1984 Los Angeles Olympics sponsorship has gained popularity amongst marketers as an effective brand equity-building strategy and, today, corporate sponsorship has become an increasingly visible element of the marcoms mix. Managers from a wide range of industries now appear to view sponsorship as an important part of the marketing mix.

Research by Pope and Voges (2000)[33] indicates that amongst those consumers who believe that a brand is involved in sports sponsorship there was a greater likelihood of purchase than amongst those who did not believe it.

Hoek *et al.* (1990)[34] provide the following ranking of objectives of sponsorship (from most to least important):

- Improving goodwill
- Enhancing image
- Increasing awareness
- Increasing profitability
- Management interest
- Staff recruitment.

Surveys conducted among American and European firms have found that sponsorship investments generally pursue two main objectives: increasing consumer awareness and improving corporate image. In one study investigating the impact of sponsorship on consumer awareness it was found that recall of the name of the sponsoring firm depends on the sponsor's degree of involvement, the amount of prior consumer knowledge about the sponsor and consumer interest in the sponsored activity. Wright (1998)[35] found that the association between the sponsor and the sponsored entity (and the activity or event) is long lasting, even when the sponsor withdraws. Consequently, there could be some sort of pioneering advantage associated with sponsoring, at least in terms of consumer recognition.

Sponsorship is often used as a vehicle to enhance the image of both companies and brands. A paper by Pope and Voges (1999)[36] suggests that prior usage of the brand is far more significant than sponsorship (in this case sporting activity) in the determination of the corporate image desired for the brand.

On an international level, sponsorship provides a medium that has a substantial non-verbal component. The values associated with the event often transcend national or cultural differences. Consequently, sponsorship may facilitate the building of multinational brands. Marshall and Cook (1992)[37] noted that sponsorship may be a catalyst for building corporate image and brand prominence on a global scale.

Evaluating the effectiveness of sponsorship

Surprisingly, few attempts have been made to understand the value and effectiveness of sponsorship. Several of the authors have commented that very little published empirical work examines the relationships between the goals and the results of sponsorship activities. Lardinoit and Quester (2001)[38] propose that the measure of sponsorship effectiveness is made more difficult by the fact that sponsors have sought to leverage their efforts with simultaneous investment in supporting communication activities. Thus, the need to develop and implement reliable evaluation methods becomes more urgent. Evidentially some organizations use tracking methods, others carry out attitudinal surveys, some measure impact on the market place, others the impact on stock prices.

Moreover, whilst it must be recognized that sponsorship is a potentially powerful marketing tool, many companies enter into sponsorship activities without having clearly defined objectives for the campaign. Even when objectives are identified, Otker (1988)[39] suggests that these are often inappropriate or deficient.

Cornwell *et al.* (2000)[40] similarly comment that, despite the rapid growth of sponsorship, little is known about its effectiveness. They report that this is changing and that there is a growing interest among marketers to quantify their sponsorship investment. McDonald (1991)[41] suggests that tracking measures have been used to measure the awareness, familiarity and preferences engendered by sponsorship.

This view is reinforced by Hoek (1999)[42] who found that surprisingly few companies rigorously evaluate the effectiveness of their sponsorship investments. Sadly, sponsorship evaluation remains a poorly defined art, and attempts to assess the effectiveness of such activities are typically ad hoc.

Research into sponsorship outcomes has produced equivocal results and there is considerable debate about whether sponsorships generate additional sales. Whilst an impact on recall, attitudinal and behavioural intention objectives has frequently been observed, behavioural effects such as sales have been much harder to identify in sponsorship activities. In short, sponsorship is normally conceptualized as a promotional tool that has stronger effects on awareness, image and attitudes, than on sales.

A study by Farrelly *et al.* (1997),[43] however, found that, certainly in the USA where companies have a greater experience of sports sponsorship management, an over-riding consideration was the fit between the sponsored event and corporate objectives. In their survey of US and Australian companies, almost 89 per cent of the former stated that the strategic fit was the most important criterion. Moreover, some 62 per cent were concerned to ensure that there was a complementary relationship with other marketing communication tools.

Kover (2001)[44] proposes that pay-off can be measured by:

- attitudinal effects
- direct market effects
- the impact on stock prices.

Stipp and Schiavone (1996)[45] similarly suggest three factors determine the effectiveness of a sponsorship campaign:

1 attitudes towards sponsorship
2 perceptions of the quality of leverage advertising
3 visibility of the campaign.

Various methods have been suggested for the evaluation of sponsorship activities. These include:

1 Monitoring the quality and nature of the media coverage obtained from the sponsored event.

   Whilst many companies involved in sponsorship activities quantify the levels of media coverage of the event and the sponsor's name, such measurement may not translate into positive changes in consumer perceptions either towards the brand or the company.

2 Estimating direct and indirect audiences.

   However, neither of these reflects overall recall or attitude change resulting from the sponsorship. Pham (1991),[46] therefore, argues that such methods are unable to provide information about the commercial effects of sponsorship.

3 Tracking techniques can be used to evaluate the awareness, familiarity and preferences engendered by sponsorship based on consumer surveys.[47]

   Some companies use pre- and post-research to establish levels of awareness, familiarity or positive connections with the brand. More beneficial are continuous tracking studies that reveal the trends more accurately and enable remedial action to be taken if appropriate.

Hoek (1999)[42] indicates that overall, while sponsorship clearly creates awareness, there is, as yet, no evidence that awareness, and the subsequent development of descriptive belief attributes, will prompt trial. She argues that frequent exposure of a particular sponsorship image, or repeated linking of an attribute with a brand, may lead respondents to associate those characteristics with the brand, but is unlikely to turn non-users into users of that brand.

She argues that there seems to be no reason why below-the-line techniques, which incorporate clear behavioural measures, cannot be integrated into sponsorship campaigns and used to provide direct behavioural evaluations. One such method would link the sponsorship directly to some form of sales activity. For example, Cadbury used special packaging on Moro bars to promote their Olympic sponsorship. Collection of a pre-specified number of packages has become a pre-requisite for entry into competitions, and entrants have been effectively conditioned to expect that they must attach bar codes to their entry. Use of these criteria may induce higher average repeat-purchase behaviour and may result in increased share of category requirements, at least for the duration of the sponsorship.

Where sponsorship has been associated with both an event and the media coverage of that event, sponsors have also run phone-in competitions, which have usually required entrants to display some knowledge of the sponsor, and for which the prize has been donated by the sponsor. For example, Fisher and Paykel used phone-in competitions to leverage their sponsorship of New Zealand netball.

Hoek *et al.* (1997)[48] describe the increasing use of sponsorship as a promotional tool. Although little research has been specifically conducted on the topic, they apply the Ehrenberg ATR model (1997).[49] They conclude that sponsorship may often generate somewhat higher levels of brand awareness than advertising and, additionally, may lead to the association of a range of new attributes to the promoted brand.

Although AIDA has been used extensively in the context of advertising theory, recent researchers have applied it to sponsorship management. Thus, Lee, Sandler and Shani's (1997)[50] modification of the AIDA model posits attitude towards the event, towards the promotion of the event, and towards behavioural intention as being at the core of sponsorship's effects on consumers.

Crimmins and Horn (1996)[51] used the AIDA model to argue that sponsorship fulfils a persuasive role, similar to the role of advertising. They claim that 'sponsorship improves the perception of a brand by flanking our beliefs about the brand and linking the brand to an event or organisation that the target audience already values highly'. Similarly, Javalgi *et al.* (1994)[52] noted the presence of operant conditioning (or reinforcement) when they noted that sponsorship may enhance corporate image 'if the company has a good image before the sponsorship'.

Ambushing

As official sponsorship becomes increasingly expensive, to some companies prohibitively so, some seek alternative routes towards associating their brands with major events. In some instances, companies purport to be the sponsors of an event without paying the fees associated with the event. Although the owners of events have strict policies to minimize this activity, they cannot eliminate it entirely.

By having a strong presence in the area outside of the event, for example, outside football stadiums or athletics tracks, manufacturers can associated their brand with the event taking place inside.

During the London Marathon, for example, Acsis paid to become the official footwear sponsor for the event. However, Nike ambushed the event by mounting a bus-shelter poster campaign along the route of the event.

Although the strategic use of sponsorship has been considered by a number of authors (Otker 1988, Cornwell 1995),[39,53] it is ambush marketing that has captured the attention of researchers.

Ambushing occurs when companies try to create the perception that they are associated with an event without actually being a sponsor (Sandler and Shani 1989).[54] It has evolved from a suspicious or even an illegitimate practice to an acceptable marketing strategy.

Meenaghan (1994)[55] distinguishes several types of ambush strategies. Among these are sponsorship of the broadcast of the event, sponsorship of sub-categories within the event, such as a specific team, or the development of significant promotions that coincide with the event.

At a conference on sponsorship following the Euro96 event, delegates were shown awareness figures for the participating brands. Each of the sponsors had paid £3.5

million to become involved with the event and, in return, was granted category exclusivity. Moreover, each of the participating companies had spent between twice and four times the amount on supporting their sponsorship involvement.

When the league table was published (headed by Coca Cola) it was observed that Nike was in seventh place ahead of brands like Fuji, Mastercard, Canon and Philips. This was despite the fact that the company was not an official sponsor of the tournament, but had spent around £2 million on press and posters around the event, convincing people that it was. Additionally, it distributed bags of give-aways to fans in the same way as the official sponsors. By handing out these bags and 'Just Do It' flags from vans parked outside the stadium premises, Nike was immune from prosecution.

Cause-related activities

Cause-related marketing (CRM) is an area of promotional activity that is receiving increasing attention and support. The purpose is to associate the company with some form of charitable activity in order to create positive attitudes towards itself through that association. CRM like sponsorship is commercially motivated and involves the 'giving' firm acquiring and leveraging the right to be associated with the recipient.

However, unlike sponsorship, CRM is defined in terms of the activities undertaken using these rights. CRM is the process of formulating and implementing activities that are characterized by an offer from the firm to contribute a specified amount to a designated cause when customers engage in revenue-providing exchanges that satisfy organizational and individual objectives.

Varadarajan and Menon (1988)[56] define CRM as a commercial activity in which profit and non-profit organizations form an alliance to market an image, product or service for mutual benefit.

Although the concept of CRM has become something of a buzz word over the last 10 years, it is not a new phenomenon. According to Adkins (2000),[57] CRM originates from the late 1890s, when William Hesketh Lever initiated gift schemes from America. More recently, Pringle and Thompson (1999)[58] traced CRM back to the 1980s when it first became popular in the USA and was widely accepted as a successful marketing tool.

It is undoubtedly clear that CRM has great presence in the world of marketing, and over the past few years it has arguably become a strategic element within the marketing of business organizations. Dupree (2000)[59] suggests that the rapid growth and interest in CRM is attributable to consumers growing increasingly socially conscious. Fellman (1999)[60] notes that companies are taking a more strategic approach to their community involvement efforts, and are seeking ways of benefiting community organizations whilst also satisfying business goals.

In a CRM programme, donations to the recipient are based on exchanges that provide revenue to the donor, that is sales. Hence, a specific objective of all CRM campaigns is to generate sales, and a promotion campaign (advertising, sales promotion, etc.) is undertaken to leverage the right to the association. Unlike the case of sponsorship there is a requirement for a donor to undertake specific activities and pursue specific objectives for the campaign to be classified as CRM. An additional distinction is that in both philanthropy and sponsorship, the amount donated to the recipient is normally negotiated in advance and fixed. In the case of the sponsorship, this represents the price of the right to an association. In the case of CRM, the amount donated can be variable, since the donation is on a per transaction basis, although in many cases the total donation is capped at predetermined maximum.

Recently, Fairy Liquid teamed up with the 'Make-A-Wish' charity to raise funds for fulfilling the wishes of children suffering from life-threatening illnesses. Target consumers (mums with children under 4 years old) were urged to take part in a one-mile Christmas walk on December 27th. They could either join one of four national walk events or hold their own walks with friends. Fairy pledged £1 for each registered walker. P&G donated £50 000 to the charity enabling it to grant wishes for 15 special kids in 2005.

A CRM-leveraged sponsorship involves the sponsor using the right of association as an input into a sales promotion campaign. To qualify as CRM, the sales promotion campaign must include an offer to the customer by the firm (the sponsor) to contribute a specified amount to the recipient organization when customers engage in revenue-providing exchanges, i.e. sales. For example, a manufacture may promote, both in advertising and at point of sale, the fact that it will give x amount for each unit sold to a worthy cause. Socially based CRM-leveraged sponsorship will, therefore, have as one of its objectives to increase sales of a given product. Beyond this, the sales promotion campaign can be implemented as the firm chooses.

In contrast, a CRM programme is normally conceptualized as a promotional tool that has stronger effects on short-term sales and that can also favourably impact on image and attitudes. A CRM programme provides the purchaser with a reason to change their purchase behaviour in favour of the sponsoring brand at the point of purchase.[61]

According to Till and Nowak (2000),[62] three-quarters of consumers say they will switch brands to a company involved with a charitable cause, if price and quality are equal. A business that demonstrates responsiveness to social concerns and gives proportionately more to charity than other firms receives higher reputation ratings by its public.

There is significant evidence to suggest that CRM campaigns distinguish business organizations in the eyes of consumers. For example, Bennett and Gabriel (2002)[63] found that consumers were more prone to purchase products that were affiliated with charities or that supported causes.

CRM activity can be either strategic or tactical. With tactical CRM activity, a brand may tie in with a cause for a limited time and for a fairly narrow purpose. On the other hand, some brands view the cause-related activity as a strategic component, the essence of the brand's positioning or personality.

CRM campaigns vary in their scope and design, the types of non-profit partners, and the nature of the relationships. The most common type of relationship may involve an organization donating a portion of each purchase made by a consumer during a specific period of time to a non-profit organization. However, there are several variations on this theme and not all campaigns channel money to non-profits, as in the case of this research study some engage in educational or awareness-building activities.

Whether the CRM activity is strategic or tactical, marketers must go to the customer to determine which causes will generate the desired consumer reaction. The importance of social and environmental issues varies with each target market, and only through careful research and concept-testing will a good match of customer, brand, and cause be ascertained.

Till and Nowak (2000)[62] establish a series of principles to guide the more effective use of cause-related alliances:

1   CRM alliances can affect consumers' overall attitude toward the sponsoring company or brand.
2   CRM alliances can affect consumers' cognitive knowledge about a brand.
3   CRM alliances will be more effective when used consistently over time.
4   CRM alliances will be more effective when the marketing communications focus primarily on the brand and the related cause.
5   Brands with smaller association sets are more likely to benefit from CRM alliances.
6   When selecting a cause-related alliance partner, select a cause that is not already associated with other brands.
7   The perceived fit, similarity, or belongingness should be an important consideration of a brand's selection of a cause alliance partner with which to pair.
8   Potential cause alliance partners should be tested among the target audience.
9   Alliances with a positive cause will be of greater benefit to less familiar brands.
10 A brand will benefit more from forming an alliance with a cause that is 'surprising' or 'novel' for consumers.
11 To gain the maximum value of a cause relationship, a brand should leverage the cause relationship in as many areas of the marketing mix as possible.

Pringle and Thompson (1999)[64] argue that it is the new values that the consumer is looking for in order for them to make their choices, instead of the usual functional, economic, emotional and psychological values.

The impacts of cause-related marketing

The marketing benefits of CRM can include:

● enhancing reputation and image
● making corporate social responsibility and corporate community investment visible
● increased loyalty
● building relationships
● aiding differentiation
● increasing sales
● generating awareness.

At the same time, from the charity or cause perspective, CRM provides the means for:

● generating additional funds and resources
● communicating and reinforcing new and existing messages

- developing awareness and loyalty among stakeholders.

Research amongst consumers conducted since 1985[65] has shown a growing level of support and interest amongst consumers for cause-related schemes:

- 81 per cent of consumers agree that, when price and quality are equal, they are more likely to buy a product associated with a cause they care about
- 66 per cent of consumers agree that they would switch from one brand to another, price and quality being equal
- 57 per cent agree that they would change retail outlet for the same reason
- 86 per cent of consumers agree that they have a more positive image of a company if they see that it is doing something to make the world a better place
- 67 per cent of consumers feel that CRM should be a standard part of a company's business practice.

The Profitable Partnerships report (2000)[66] indicates further benefits of these schemes:

- Almost 88 per cent of consumers are aware of a CRM scheme
- Companies that take part in CRM schemes are perceived as being more trustworthy and more innovative by consumers, both of which dimensions are key drivers of brand equity
- 77 per cent of participants were positively influenced at the point of purchase or decision making by the CRM programme
- 80 per cent of all consumers who have taken part in a scheme will continue to feel positive about the company.

The CRM partnership between Walkers and News International to provide free books for schools created a promotion that reportedly reached 80 per cent of the population. Free books for schools tokens were distributed free to consumers via Walkers Crisps packets and in various newspaper titles including the *Sun*, *News of the World*, *The Times* and *Sunday Times*. Consumers were encouraged to collect these tokens and donate them to schools. Schools, in turn, redeemed the tokens for books selected from a catalogue supplied by Walkers and News International, compiled with help from the DfEE. Over 5 million books worth an estimated £25 million were distributed to schools through the scheme.

Research from Business in the Community shows that over £200 million has been raised by business in partnership with their consumers for schools so far. Two promotions, Tesco Computers for Schools and Walkers Free Books for Schools, have alone raised over £100 million for schools.

Sainsbury's are running an 'Active Kids' promotion paralleling the Tesco computers for schools. The retailer provides vouchers with every purchase that can be donated to the school of the consumer's choice to be redeemed for a wide range of activity equipment. These include dance hoops, basketball nets and climbing walls. The promotion adopts the theme of the government's obesity campaign designed to promote a more active and healthy life amongst children.

Their report refers to consumer research amongst over 2000 UK consumers, which indicates overwhelming support for such promotional programmes:

- 98 per cent of consumers see the mutual benefit of partnerships between businesses and charities such as schools
- 67 per cent of consumers have taken part in a CRM programme
- 67 per cent of consumers also wanted to see more businesses engaged in partnerships of this kind.

Many other brands have participated in cause-related schemes: British Gas, Barclays, Cadbury, Trebor Bassett, Dollond & Aitchison, Lever Faberge amongst others benefiting partners such as the Alzheimer's Society, Help the Aged, Make a Wish Foundation, Mencap, Save the Children, etc.

There is no doubt that CRM schemes can build corporate and brand image and reputation. It can enhance customer loyalty and stakeholder relationships as well as generating sales.

Case study 1

TESCO COMPUTERS FOR SCHOOLS

Tesco was keen to develop a customer loyalty programme that would benefit the wider community. Research carried out amongst customers identified computers as the key requirement in schools across the UK, hence Tesco Computers for Schools.

The promotion

The Tesco Computers for Schools programme objectives were to reward customer loyalty, to strengthen community relationships, to attract new shoppers into stores and to help ensure the computer literacy of school leavers and potential employees.

The programme involves an annual voucher redemption promotion to help local schools obtain free computers and other information communication technology (ICT) equipment. During a 10-week promotional period customers were given 1 voucher for every £10 spent in a Tesco store. Schools could then collect these tokens and redeem them for computers and ICT-related equipment from a catalogue of equipment.

The outcomes:

- Increased sales
- Enhanced corporate profile in the community
- Reinforced brand values and improved customer loyalty
- Recognition as an innovative retailer
- Over £84 million worth of equipment given to schools nationwide (1992–2003)
- Over 50 000 computers and over 468 000 additional items of related equipment delivered to schools: equivalent to more than one computer for every school in the UK
- In 2003 alone, £7 million worth of equipment delivered to schools
- In 2003 over 1000 new schools took part and computing equipment was delivered to over 24 000 schools including over 3600 state-of-the-art computers, and over 74 000 additional items of computer-related equipment
- Approximately £100 000 worth of IT training provided for teachers.

This promotion was the winner of the Cause Related Marketing Award for Excellence 1998.

(Source: Business in the Community 2005)

Case study 2

AVON COSMETICS LTD – AVON BREAST CANCER CRUSADE

Avon is a company that reaches over a billion women through 4.4 million independent sales representatives in 143 countries worldwide. Its mission is 'to be the company that best understands and satisfies the product, service and self fulfilment needs of women globally'. The Avon Breast Cancer Crusade is a brilliant demonstration of this commitment.

The promotion

With 160 000 Avon Representatives in the UK and nearly 8 million customers, Avon sought to take action by raising money and awareness to address the number one health concern for women in the UK and launched the Avon Breast Cancer Crusade in 1992.

Eleven years on, the Avon Breast Cancer Crusade has now raised over £10 million for UK breast cancer charities. Over £ 8.4 million has been donated to their charity partner Breakthrough Breast Cancer, and Avon pledges to continue its awareness and fundraising work in 2004.

In 2003 Avon's fundraising continued with the development of the first ever fragrance 'Pink Suede' dedicated to raising money to help kiss goodbye to breast cancer. Other fundraising products, including limited edition Kiss lipsticks and lapel pins took Avon's total UK fundraising past the £10 million milestone.

The outcomes:

- Enhanced Avon's corporate reputation
- Reached women outside the Avon channel, particularly via the media
- Strong staff, sales representatives and customer support
- Avon acknowledged as a leading CRM practitioner, short-listed at the Marketing Effectiveness Awards 2003
- Over £700 000 raised in 2003, bringing the UK total raised to over £10 million since 1992
- Higher awareness and openness about the disease that was once only 'whispered' about, and this in turn is helping earlier diagnoses
- 50 of Avon's markets now support the breast cancer cause and global fundraising has now exceeded $300 million.

This promotion was the Joint Winner of the Cause Related Marketing Award for Excellence 2000.

(Source: Business in the Community 2005)

Case study 3

UNITED BISCUITS – MCVITIE'S
Agency: Catalyst Marketing

McVitie's 120 years of success had resulted in its name becoming synonymous with biscuits and many of its brand names had become generic. This, combined with the move to less traditional biscuits, led to own-label products gaining share at McVitie's expense.

To redress the situation, McVitie's needed to create a brand experience that would allow consumers to sample the top quality of its everyday biscuits.

The British passion for dunking inspired a 'Dunk for Britain' roadshow that visited 137 nationwide venues over an 8-week period. Promotional staff offered visitors the chance to put their feet up, have a cup of tea, and discover their favourite dunking biscuit by trying any of the McVitie's range. After casting their vote they were given coupons redeemable against McVitie's biscuits and PG Tips Tea. They could also visit a website and enter a competition to win a dunking trip to New York.

A total of 13 million people experienced the campaign and 1.2 million biscuits were sampled. The winning biscuit (McVitie's Milk Chocolate Caramel Digestives) was announced in the *Sun*. Most importantly, sales increased by 12 per cent year on year.

The campaign received a Silver Award in the Event Marketing section of the 2005 ISP Promotion Awards.

(The above appeared in the Special Supplement to *Promotions and Incentives* magazine, June 2005)

Questions

1 Identify the reasons for the growing use of trade shows and exhibitions.
2 What are the objectives that trade shows might fulfil?
3 What factors need to be considered in the development of event marketing?
4 Why is sponsorship considered to be an important aspect of promotional activity?
5 How can a manufacturer evaluate its sponsorship involvement?
6 What are the benefits that derive from cause-related marketing?

13 The evaluation of sales promotion

Chapter overview

Undeniably, the importance of evaluating sales promotion performance is the one area where many companies are remiss. Many promotions are mounted without a previous determination of their likely effectiveness. Similarly, many companies fail to assess whether a promotion has fulfilled the objectives established for it.

This chapter establishes both the need for appropriate evaluation of sales promotion activities and discusses the process of evaluation itself. It also considers the impact of failing to conduct the appropriate research both before and after promotions have been implemented. It also considers the broader role of market research in the context of the planning of sales promotion.

Learning outcomes

- To consider the need for promotional evaluation
- To examine the process of evaluation
- To discuss the contribution of sales promotion to the marketing plan
- To identify the techniques of research and evaluation that can be used to enhance understanding of promotional effectiveness.

Organizations need to systematically evaluate the outcomes of different types of promotions and the competitive conditions that prevailed in the target market. Such systematic evaluations will help identify how different markets respond to different types of promotions under different conditions and what types of promotions are the most effective in countering competitive moves in different markets.

It is essential that top management understand the role of sales promotions in their company's overall marketing strategy. When sales and profit goals are not met, managers often blame sales promotional strategies even though some other element of promotion or the marketing mix may be at fault. Sales promotion can not make up for a weak product, poor distribution, incorrect pricing or an ill-conceived positioning strategy. Moreover, managers should not expect that a one-time sales promotion will lead to a long-lasting impact on sales and profits. The impacts of sales promotions on brand sales have been shown in many instances to be short-lived. Managers must accept the reality that they need to regularly reinvest in sales promotions in order to succeed in the market place.

The need for evaluation

Businesses today are continually looking for ways to improve the effectiveness and efficiency of their operations. Coming under increasing pressure and scrutiny are promotional expenditures because they have long been among the most challenging marketing costs to analyse or justify on a profit versus cost basis.

Promotional expenditures are being examined closely by top management as one of the most promising areas left for cutting costs and increasing profits. This heightened scrutiny puts intense pressure on marketers to develop and implement promotional programmes that can add value to their organizations within the constraints of tighter budgets. Hence, there is a crucial need to re-examine how promotional monies are spent.

sales promotion expenditures are often the largest discretionary expenses in the promotional budget, so it is not surprising that chief executive officers (CEOs) are demanding a higher level of accountability than ever before for these expenditures. Irrespective of the type of sales promotion employed, marketing managers are looking for ways to better evaluate the effectiveness and efficiency of these diverse activities.

According to Pauwels *et al.* (2000)[1] the effects of promotional programmes on market and financial performance show that incentive programmes have uniformly positive effects in the short run: top-line, bottom-line and stock market performance all increase. The short-term success of promotions makes it attractive for managers to continue using them. In addition, because promotions are known to stimulate consumer demand only temporarily, they need to be repeated.

Evaluation and control systems are used in organizations to achieve two objectives:

1 To ensure that expenditures do not exceed budgeted levels
2 To evaluate the effectiveness and efficiency of the expenditures.

In evaluating sales promotions, however, managers need to consider several factors, including:

- profitability
- local market conditions
- effects on channel partners
- the synergy between different types of sales promotions
- competitors' promotional activities
- the role of sales promotions in the company's overall marketing strategy.

For example, in an article in *Business Week* (1996), coupon promotions were labelled as inefficient because the redemption rates of coupons had fallen from 4 per cent in 1985 to 2 per cent in 1995. At first glance, this indicator of the productivity of coupons might seem valid. However, a more in-depth analysis of the impact of coupons on brand performance reveals flaws in the logic of such a simple criterion. Maximizing redemption rates does not necessarily maximize a brand's profitability. For instance, if large numbers of existing customers who would have bought the product anyway end up redeeming coupons, then maximizing coupon redemptions might just maximize the cost of the couponing operation.

Beyond measuring the short-run profitability of sales promotions, it is also necessary to take into account the long-run value-added benefits attributable to promotions when conducting the cost-benefit analysis of the promotional activities. Success of the sales promotion in helping to push the product along the hierarchy of effects model, between unawareness and actual purchase, is seldom considered. In addition, different types of sales promotional tools can have different impacts on sales, profitability, and value added to the brand.

Promotional effectiveness, however, can't just be reduced to numbers. For instance, retailers and suppliers often have very different promotional objectives and it is vital that these are discussed and reconciled prior to the promotion taking place. As Hart (1997)[2] indicates, promotional objectives for a retailer may be to sell more, to generate incremental profit, to increase the size of the shopping basket, to increase footfall, to create in-store interest, to gain competitive advantage or to promote a best value image.

When judging the effectiveness of promotional expenditures, aggregate promotional spending is often compared with the sales generated by all promotional activities. But, just because different types of inducements (e.g. price cuts, coupons, sweepstakes and displays) are collectively identified as sales promotions, does not mean that the impact of all these different types of promotions can be lumped together and evaluated at the aggregate level. While some sales promotional activities may be profitable, others might be loss generating. Making decisions based on incremental sales from total spending (across all types of sales promotions) will invariably lead to the wrong conclusions.

Sales promotions impact upon brand sales in a number of different ways. These might be to cause brand switching, stockpiling, purchase acceleration and category expansion. However, not all of these effects need to be present for all types of sales promotions. In the case of a short-term shelf-price reduction valid only for a week, customers will have more incentive to quickly stockpile the product as opposed to a coupon promotion with a longer validity period. Therefore, generalizations like 'sales promotions cause stockpiling' are misleading and do not capture the differing impact that different types of sales promotions have on brand sales.

Evaluating the effectiveness of promotional activities requires an understanding of the costs and benefits of the different types of promotions. To be effective, the promotional programme must offer appropriate incentives for local market conditions.

Srinivasan and Anderson (1998)[3] assert that whenever manufacturers decide on consumer promotion they typically evaluate the impact of the sales promotion on their own sales and profitability but not those of their retail partner's. Similarly, whenever retailers promote products through retail promotional tools such as shelf-price cuts, they usually evaluate only the impact of the promotion on their own sales and profitability. However, sales promotions initiated by manufacturers also affect the sales and profitability of the retailers and vice versa. In some instances the total profits (sum of manufacturer and retailer profits) when a sales promotional programme is implemented might be higher than when the promotional programme is not implemented. However, these profits need not be equitably distributed between the manufacturer and the retailer. If one of the parties benefits from the promotion while the other party suffers a loss, conflicts are likely to develop between the manufacturer and the retailer. Sales and immediate profits are not the only concerns among channel partners. Brand awareness, comprehension, trial, enhanced brand equity and increased market share may also be areas in which channel members will need to co-operate and share the outcomes.

When designing sales promotions it is not only necessary for managers to understand the impact of different types of promotions on brand sales and profitability, but it is also necessary for them to consider the synergy between the different types of promotions. Often the impact of two or more sales promotions implemented jointly is much higher than the impact of these sales promotions implemented one at a time. For example, in the case of retailer shelf-price cuts and display/featuring activities, it has been established that the joint impact of simultaneously having a shelf-price cut and engaging in display/promotional activities is much higher than the sum of the impacts from each of these promotional strategies implemented separately. An in-depth understanding of the interaction between different types of sales promotions on brand sales and profitability is essential to design optimal value-creating joint sales promotions. Interaction effects call for creatively thinking through the promotional impact process.

Sales promotion activities are never going to be equally profitable to all players in the market place, but nearly all companies need to use sales promotions as either offensive and/or defensive tools in the never-ending battle for markets. Hoping that competitors will not use sales promotions seems futile, unless there is no surplus in supply of the product category. In developed economies, where supply generally exceeds demand, sales promotion tools can and will be used by those players who will benefit most from such strategies.

Historically, it has been extremely difficult to forecast promotional stock requirements. Vast under or over estimates of volume requirements have been commonplace. These either lead to out-of-stocks, lost sales and frustrated customers, or to warehouses packed with promotional stock that was never needed and, ultimately, had to be re-packed or destroyed incurring further costs. Pre-testing the promotional offer can go some way to remedy this problem.

The process of evaluation

When evaluating a promotion, it is important to consider the specific objectives since that will assist in the identification of the best approach. At the basic level there is a need to quantify the impact of the promotional device on volume and contribution.

The volume sold on promotion, multiplied by the reduced contribution per pack yields a contribution net of the cost of promoting. If there are any additional fixed costs, for example, the provision of point-of-sales material, dealer incentives, etc., these should similarly be deducted. The resultant figure can be easily compared with the expected contribution if the promotion were not run.

If the objective is one of profit growth, then it is important to identify the promotion that provides the greatest increase in contribution levels. If the objective is volume, then promotions that yield the greatest increase per pound invested will be required. If it is to increase penetration, then the key is to identify the return from each of the different approaches. In this context, it is important to consider the price elasticity of the brand. Understanding the price elasticity of a brand will help set appropriate discounts. Market leaders, more expensive brands and brands with very strong emotional benefits will tend to be less price sensitive than the market average. If such a brand uses price promotions, it is unlikely that it will be able to generate the necessary additional volume to get back the costs of the price discount. Strongly elastic brands that respond to price cuts are the likely beneficiaries of such promotional activity.

Cook (1995)[4] argues that in evaluating a promotion it is important to bear in mind the objective as that will determine the best approach. A simple evaluation should quantify, at the very least, the impact on volume and contribution.

Objectives should be clearly quantified, whether volume, penetration or contribution based.

In measuring the sales effectiveness of sales promotions, it is important to consider sales in both pre- and post-promotional period. Spillard (1996)[5] provides a graphic model for the consideration of sales promotional impact.

Figure 13.1

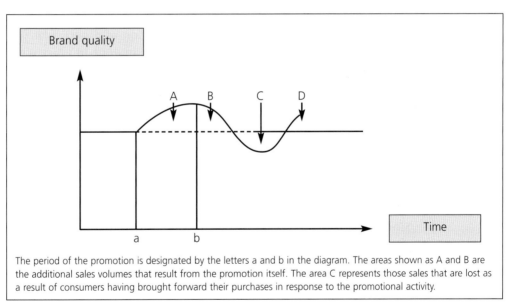

The period of the promotion is designated by the letters a and b in the diagram. The areas shown as A and B are the additional sales volumes that result from the promotion itself. The area C represents those sales that are lost as a result of consumers having brought forward their purchases in response to the promotional activity.

When a promotion is implemented, a quantity of product that would have been sold to the product's regular customers, even without the promotion, is sold at a discount. It is necessary to calculate the baseline of sales that would have occurred without the promotion in order to identify those sales that are directly attributable to the promotional activities. In order to calculate the true cost of a promotion, it is necessary to take the cost of these sales into account and add the costs of point of sale material, retailer support, merchandising materials, etc.

The volume a brand achieves when on promotion can be divided into two component parts:

1 Base sales: these are sales that would have happened irrespective of the promotional activity. One of the most common tools managers use to evaluate the profitability of their promotions is the measure of baseline sales. Using this measure to calculate the incremental volume attributable to a deal (i.e. promotional response), retailers and manufacturers can assess the profitability and effectiveness of in-store promotions such as discounts. The importance of this issue has inspired numerous studies of discount effectiveness and baseline sales.

Research conducted by Kopalle *et al.* (1999)[6] proposed an alternative method of calculating baseline sales. They suggest that managers can increase profits by as much as 7per cent to 31per cent over their current practices. Their paper argues that it is important to balance the trade-off between i) increasing sales arising in the current period from a given discount, and ii) the corresponding effect of reducing (baseline) sales in future periods.

2 Incremental sales: these are sales that are directly attributable to the promotional activity during the period. These derive from three consumer responses:
   a Competitor steal – where the promotion encourages switching from a competitor's brand
   b Brand cannibalization – where the promotion of a particular brand results in consumers switching their purchases from another product within the company's product portfolio
   c Category growth – where the additional volume derives from new customers who would not otherwise have purchased either the promoted product or one of its competitors.

Brand-sales models can be considered against a number of dimensions.

First, there is some evidence that estimates of baseline sales and discount effectiveness can be influenced by the history of promotions, as indicated below:

● Dynamics in baseline sales.
   Stockpiling is defined as the acceleration of a purchase in response to a price cut. If consumers accelerate purchases, their inventories increase. This can decrease sales in subsequent weeks. However, the effect may be difficult to observe in store data.

● Dynamics in price sensitivity.
   The increased use of discounts may affect price sensitivity as well as baseline sales, although the likely effect is less clear. On the one hand, consumers might become more price-conscious with an increase in the frequency of discounts, thus increasing price sensitivity. On the other hand, an increase in discounting may reduce consumers' reference prices, thereby leading to a lower level of utility for a fixed level of discount. This would imply that price reductions occurring immediately after discounts would yield a smaller increase in sales (suggesting lower price sensitivity).

Finally, changes in the baselines may make changes in price response difficult to predict because price elasticity is measured with respect to these changing baselines.

Marsden (1994)[7] identifies a series of dimensions that should be measured if the promotion is to be properly controlled and evaluated:

- Costs, translated into investment per unit, to set against gross margin
- Volume impact (how much extra was sold as a result of the promotion?)
- Media support (did we advertise the promotion and what was the media spend?)
- Competitive activity during the promotion period
- Changes in distribution patterns
- Changes in the levels of trade stocks and displays
- Results related to the type of promotion and distribution method.

The availability of scanner data in most markets coupled with the existence of substantial consumer panels enables sophisticated evaluation of promotional effects. Increasingly, modelling is being used to clarify results and to identify the contribution of each promotion whether separate from or in conjunction with other forms of communications activity.

This work enables marketers to refine the detail of their activity in a variety of ways. For example, they can help to optimize the timings of promotional activity, identify the scale of incentives necessary to achieve the desired effects, indicate the relationship between sales promotion and advertising, determine the balance of effort between retail chains, and isolate the relationship between sales promotion and advertising, etc.

Promotions inputs and outputs need to be measured in order that their effect and value to the brand can be assessed. The main measures will be quantitative measures of sales and other effects, but it may be desirable to measure effects on brand image as well. In addition, just as other communications can be pre-tested, technology is making pre-tests of promotions easier. [8,9]

The contribution of sales promotion

An estimate provided by ACNielsen[10] from a study published in 1995 provides some quantification of the contribution of promotions to annual brand volume. Across all of the brands examined by the company, promotions activity accounts for 11 per cent of annual sales.

Attitudinal research conducted by ACNielsen amongst a panel of 7000 households provides some important information on consumer attitudes towards promotional activity and their responses in terms of purchasing behaviour. In response to the question 'I will buy a brand I don't normally buy if it is on special offer', some 43 per cent of respondents agreed with the statement. Equally, 57 per cent stated that 'If I see a special offer I like, I will buy more than I need'. This is important in the context of bringing forward future purchases of the brand and encouraging brand switching.

The promotions-aware consumer

Seventy-four per cent of consumers interviewed by ACNielsen agreed that they look out for special price offers; 66 per cent look out for special displays and 56 per cent cut out coupons. These figures provide tangible evidence of the consumer impact of sales promotion activity.

Promotional impact in the impulse sector

The impulse sector includes soft drinks, snacks and confectionery. On average, amongst the brands studied by ACNielsen, a 10 per cent price cut generates a 30 per cent increase in sales volume; stores running a multibuy can expect a 112 per cent sales increase; extra fill boosts paid for volume by 27 per cent; and special packs, which include a multitude of offers, provides an uplift of 67 per cent.

In communicating the offer, a shelf talker will boost the effect by 13 per cent and secondary display by 44 per cent.

How long should a special pack last?

ACNielsen have provided information on four brand categories, one from each of the liquor, grocery, impulse and personal care sectors. The chart below shows the increase in volume from the first week when a special pack appears in store. The effect of distribution is removed and this, therefore, reflects genuine consumer demand.

Figure 13.2

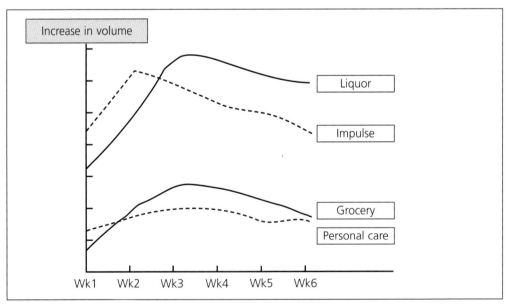

It is not uncommon for special packs to linger in the trade for a considerable time. In addition, whilst the shape of the curve undoubtedly varies by brand and by offer, the inference is that most special packs start losing their appeal after 3–4 weeks. Over production of special packs by manufacturers or over ordering by retailers is likely to be introducing unnecessary cost into special pack promotions.

ACNielsen suggest that in the evaluation of any promotional activity, several important factors need to be borne in mind:

1 Does the promotional concept fit well with the brand, its desired imagery and its target audience?
2 Is the recommended solution the most likely to achieve the desired objectives?
3 Is the promotion easy to understand and credible to the target audience?
4 Is it easy to participate in or does it create an unnecessary series of obstacles for the potential consumer to overcome?
5 Is the promotion likely to satisfy the needs of consumers? Ideally, promotional offers should not over claim, since this is likely to result in post-purchase dissonance. Rather they should ensure that the customer remains satisfied and, if possible, deliver more than is expected.
6 Is the promotion dependent on a particular fad or fashion (such as a tie in with a specific event) or does it provide a concept that can be repeated over time?

Based on their store level database, ACNielsen have provided an indication of the average uplift achieved from sales promotion tools.

Table 13.1

Promotion effectiveness: average uplift	
Promotion type	*Percentage uplift*
Shelf talker	10%
10% temporary price reduction	27%
Extra fill	28%
Display	44%
Multibuy	54%
Special pack	62%
Source: ACNielsen Modelling Database	

The company estimates that an average of 16 per cent of the shopping basket is bought on promotion. The breakdown of the promotional component, by mechanic, is as shown below.

Table 13.2

Breakdown of promotional purchases, by mechanic	
Temporary price reduction	34%
Additional quantity	13%
Price-marked pack	11%
Multiple purchase discount	13%
Send away	7%
Free item	5%
Banded pack	4%
Coupon	3%
Other	29%

Source: ACNielsen Homescan Panel

A similar report by Cook (1995),[4] also using ACNielsen's data, provides similar findings. The research in this instance examined the impulse sector – soft drinks, snacks and confectionery – with the results shown below.

Table 13.3

10 per cent price cut	+30%
Multibuy	+112%
Extra fill	+27%
Special pack	+67%
Shelf talker	+13%
Display	+44%

Research into sales promotion

Sales promotion is an area where market research can amply repay the investment made in it, although, sadly, comparatively little use is made of the techniques available. Given the scale of the potential problems that can result from a poorly constructed or badly implemented promotion, it makes a great deal of sense to ensure that all possible steps are taken to avoid the many pitfalls that might otherwise occur.

As Bowman (1997)[11] states: 'In the UK, 80 per cent of promotions don't work … as a whole, it's an area of the industry that still operates largely on gut feeling.'

The field of sales promotion is littered with examples of companies that have got it wrong. Hoover remains the outstanding example of the potential long-term damage that can result from a failure to understand the impact of the promotional mechanics on consumer demand. Customers who failed to receive free seats in the 1994 promotion continue to create adverse publicity for the company. As recently as 1997,[12] two customers were awarded damages in a move that opens up the way to thousands of other claims against the company, whilst *Marketing Week*[13] reported that a series of new legal challenges were due to be heard during the year.

However, other equally large companies have failed to ensure that the techniques they employ within the area satisfy the requirements fully. The *Daily Mirror*, for example, ran a scratch card promotion in July 1995 when, due to the poor construction of the wording, some 2000 readers thought that they had each won £50 000, representing a potential liability of some £100 million. Similarly, Pepsi ran a competition in which the consumer purchasing a bottle with the number 349 printed under the bottle cap would receive £26 000. However, some 800 000 'winning' caps were printed, representing a potential liability of some £19 billion!

The testing and evaluation of a sales promotion plan are an essential element of the management of the sales promotion activity. Only by assessing the outcome of a promotion will it be possible to identify whether the promotion has achieved the objectives established for it.

Many companies measure the success of a promotion on the basis of the levels of consumer response or participation. This might include, for example, the number of coupons redeemed or the number of free-mails requested. However, such information is not an adequate determinant of the promotion's success. What really matters is the level of sales volume achieved by the promotion.

Market research can provide an important contribution to the understanding of sales promotion in two broad areas:

1 testing
2 monitoring.

At the developmental stage the appropriate use of the available techniques can provide an insight into the identification of objectives. They enable focus and targeting of the offer to the desired consumer group, enable an informed choice between alternative executions, and assist in the refinement of a promotion concept into an effective and workable proposition.

The following chart sets out some of the important areas in which market research can contribute to the development of more efficient and effective sales promotion activities.

Figure 13.3

Desk research

Most companies already possess a considerable amount of information that can be used to assist the promotional planning process. In many cases, there will be a body of knowledge built up from past promotional experience. Some companies maintain comprehensive evaluations of previous implementations that will provide guidance on their likely impact if repeated. Importantly, such dimensions as redemption rates and consumer and retailer participation are often monitored and recorded and will provide a benchmark for the development of new executions. The same may apply equally to competitive activities. Understanding the way in which competitive brands respond to promotional activity may also provide a guide to how similar promotions might work on the companies' own brands.

Internal sources will be available including data on sales, shipments and levels of display. These might be augmented by specific collections of data related to the promotional activity. In this respect, the sales force can play an important role. During their regular visits to trade customers, they can collect information as to the progress of promotional activity.

Many companies subscribe to periodic data supplied by organizations such as ACNielsen or AGB. The former conduct regular retail sales audits in many different fast-moving consumer goods markets that can be used to monitor the impact of campaign activity. AGB conducts what is known as a 'dustbin' audit, with a panel of consumers recording purchases over a number of weeks.

Moreover, the increasing availability of EPOS data also means that the level of take-up of promotional activity can be rapidly monitored via retail outlets.

There are also a number of published sources that provide a valuable insight into promotional effectiveness. The annual Institute of Sales Promotion (ISP) awards provide details of a series of promotions that have demonstrated their effectiveness in the market place. Of course, the dedicated trade press in the form of magazines such as *Promotions and Incentives* regularly report on promotional activities.

Pre-testing

Pre-testing of a promotional execution is an important part of the determination of its likely effectiveness. Using a variety of simulation techniques, promotions can be assessed for their likely appeal, the propensity to generate consumer awareness and offtake, the potential for generating repeat purchase, perceptions of value for money, etc.

Consumers can be exposed to concepts indicating the nature of the promotional offer.

At this stage, it is possible to test a variety of different executions against each other and, where available, against a previously run promotion with a known outcome (to act as a benchmark). In this way some finite results can be obtained that will add to the ability of predicting the likely impact of the intended promotion. Equally it will help to eliminate those offers that either fail to appeal or have limited impact.

Qualitative research

Some organizations conduct specific research to monitor the outcome of sales promotions. As well as gathering sales data, this may provide them with important attitudinal data on how the promotion was received and what impact it had on consumers' regard for the company etc.

This is particularly important if the company is to understand how a promotion has affected the image of the brand. Whilst it is recognized that many promotions operate in the short term and may have little or no impact on brand image, some promotions, particularly those that discount the price of the brand, may impact negatively. Equally, it is increasingly realized that promotions may make a positive contribution towards the image of the brand.

Qualitative research methods can be used to assess such factors as the likely impact on the image of the brand of a particular range of promotional techniques. Identifying how consumers will react to an offer is important both in the tangible sense (how will it affect their propensity to purchase the brand?) as well as the intangible aspects (how will the promotion affect their overall perceptions of the brand?). Is a particular offer more likely to cheapen than improve the image, for example?

Quantitative research

Techniques such as 'Town Hall Tests', in which the purchase environment is simulated and the results of exposure to different consumer offers are monitored, can make a considerable contribution to the determination of the most effective incentive.

Similarly, quantitative techniques can be used in which consumers scale their preference for different forms of promotional offer. If possible, it is desirable to include some previous promotion for which results are known, as a benchmark against which the performance of alternatives can be assessed.

In some instances, especially where the scale of the promotion is likely to be large, it may be advisable to stage a 'mini test market'. By running the promotion in a small region of the country, it will be possible to gauge the impact of the offering in a live environment, where the brand has to compete with real competitors.

Monitoring research

The close monitoring of consumer response once the promotion is implemented is, similarly, an important part of the process. By maintaining a constant feedback from the market it will serve to alert the company to any potential difficulties, which may be avoided with a speedy response. It has to be said that these techniques are often ignored or overlooked in the context of sales promotion activity. Market research will provide some assurance that the particular technique chosen is the appropriate one to fulfil the task set and, most importantly, to provide some indication of the likely outcome of the activity.

Throughout the sales promotion process, as with other parts of the marketing communications mix, market research can provide valuable insights into the likely impact of the activity as an independent variable but, more importantly, in terms of the impact it will have on the brand as a whole. In this respect, a wide variety of research methods can be employed to gain additional knowledge about the brand.

Figure 13.4

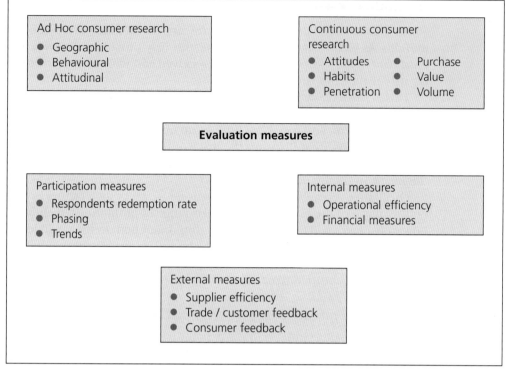

There are a number of key response areas that need to be considered:

1 redemption rates
2 displacement rates
3 acquisition rates
4 stock-up rates
5 conversion rates
6 product-line effects.

Redemption rates

It will be important to calculate both the total number and percentage of consumers likely to respond to the promotion. This, in turn, is likely to be influenced by the method of promotional distribution, particularly in the context of coupon activity.

In general, redemption rates will tend to be higher when:

- the product or brand is well established so that the value of the incentive is appreciated by the target audience
- the product is in wide distribution
- there is little effort on the part of the consumer to acquire the incentive
- the frequency of purchase is high
- the value of the incentive is high.

Displacement rates

Some of the sales achieved during a promotional period will simply replace sales that would otherwise have been made to regular buyers at the normal price. (Some studies suggest that as much as 75 per cent of coupon redemptions are made by consumers who already use the brand.) Understanding the degree of displacement will ensure that the promotional offer can be designed to minimize the level of unprofitable sales.

Acquisition rates

Some of the purchasers will be non-regular buyers who make a purchase as a direct result of the incentive offered. For most promotions, this is the underlying objective, since it is the incremental sales that are most important to the brand. These sales can derive from two groups of consumers: those who are regular purchasers of a competitive brand and those who do not normally buy from the product category.

The level of promotional redemption amongst these groups will tend to be highest when:

- the average level of purchase is high
- the perceived risks are low
- the incentive is specifically targeted towards groups amongst whom regular purchase is relatively low
- the method of distribution is specifically designed to reach these non-regular users.

Stock-up rates

If the incentive is sufficiently high, some of the sales achieved will be from those consumers who stockpile to take advantage of the offer and will serve to bring forward future intended purchases. The inevitable consequence is that the level of sales following the promotional period may suffer as a consequence of consumers bringing forward their purchases. This may be desirable if the brand intends to offset the impact of competitive activities, since once stockpiled, consumers will tend to withdraw from the market for extended periods. A further consequence, however, is that these promotional sales will be made at lower prices than normal and hence the level of contribution will be reduced.

Stockpiling will tend to be greater when:

- buyers are reasonably sure that they will use the extra amounts purchased
- buyers do not have a large amount of space or money tied up
- the risk of spoilage or deterioration is low
- promotions are directed towards regular buyers
- no limits on purchase volume are established
- the offer is of a short-term nature (i.e. expiry dates are short).

Conversion rates

Particularly when the promotional objective is to build market share, its role is to extend the customer base. In order to achieve this impact, specific promotions will be targeted to non-user groups or those that historically have been weak for the brand. In some instances, brands will have specific geographic weaknesses that such promotions will seek to overcome. Efforts will need to be made to estimate the volume of sales that will occur after the promotional period from users who have been attracted to the brand by the promotional offer.

Such conversion will tend to be highest when the promotion requires high degrees of customer effort in order to take advantage of the promotional offer.

However, it should be noted that conversion rates are somewhat difficult to calculate unless there is some historical experience on which to draw.

Product-line effects

Promotional success for a brand may have a negative impact on sales of other similar products within the company's portfolio. Hence, as much as attracting purchasers of competitive products, a promotion may equally attract regular consumers of products from the same company. For example, Kraft Jacobs Suchard manufactures a wide range of instant coffee brands. The parentage of these brands is unlikely to be apparent to the consumer. Accordingly, some consumers of, say, the Kenco brand, may be motivated to purchase additional quantities of Maxwell House as a consequence of a promotional offer. Although the latter will increase its sales volume, some of this increase will be a result of losses to the former. The extent to which a sales promotion is likely to cannibalize sales from other company brands needs to be considered.

Sampling

An imperative of a new product launch is the need to achieve consumer sampling of the product. Such activity is, potentially, expensive. Apart from the cost of the free product, there are the associated costs of placing the sample into the hands of the potential consumer. It is essential to define the target market as precisely as possible to ensure that samples of the products are placed into the appropriate hands. This can be achieved in a number of different ways:

- In-store sampling, enabling consumers to be self-selecting
- Attaching the product sample to a compatible product either in-house or from another company that is prepared to carry the product
- Through direct mail on a door-to-door basis
- Through media.

It is important to ensure that the customer receives sufficient product to conduct an adequate trial of the product. Whilst it is true that the greater the quantity of the product supplied free, the greater the cost, it is important that the consumer receive enough to ensure that they can subject it to a normal usage pattern, for example, enough free toothpaste, or enough soap powder to carry out a normal wash.

Measuring the effectiveness of competitions is not as simple as for other forms of promotional activity. Indeed, it is almost impossible to do so just by studying the competitions themselves. One obvious answer would seem to be to analyse sales patterns to determine the effectiveness of a promotion. However, this does not work for competitions where a purchase is not required (lotteries), and ignores the potential benefits of increased awareness or increased satisfaction among existing users.

Peattie and Peattie (1994)[14] suggest that one measure of competition effectiveness could be the 'marketing integration' of the competitions. Competitions vary in terms of whether either the prize, or the mechanics of the competition, relates back to the product or service being promoted. They consequently developed a method of classifying a competition according to its marketing integration as follows:

- Low – no link between product and competition or prize.
- Medium – a link between competition or prize and product.
- High – product, prize and competition all related.

Case study

RIBENA
Agency: Billington Cartmell

Ribena has an enviable and long-standing brand heritage, but recognized that to maintain saliency and relevance it needed to keep pace with a changing society.

The *Shrek 2* movie was expected to be a huge hit and, with its quirky humour, was identified as a perfect platform for Ribena. A unique and exciting campaign would be required to achieve its objective of £5.6 million incremental sales.

To achieve standout from other Shrek activity, Ribena focussed on the Donkey character with an on-pack instant win promotion featured across the entire product range. The top prize was a real live donkey (living in a donkey sanctuary) as well as thousands of cinema tickets and three-foot high inflatable donkeys. The winner of the top prize also received a £1000 travel allowance to visit their donkey at the sanctuary.

The promotion was supported with a fully integrated campaign of PR, cinema and TV advertising, viral, website and in-store activity.

'Win a Donkey' achieved all its objectives delivering incremental sales of £6.86 million: 22.5 per cent over target. A massive increase in penetration was also achieved with almost 60 per cent of participants being new to Ribena.

The campaign received a gold award in the Prize Promotions section of the 2005 ISP Promotion Awards, together with a further gold award in the Integrated Communications Section. It was also given the award for best communication campaign featuring sales promotion by the Marketing Communication Consultants Association.

(The above appeared in the Special Supplement to *Promotions and Incentives* magazine, June 2005)

Questions

1 Why is it important to evaluate the performance of sales promotional activities?

2 Identify the process of sales promotion evaluation.

3 Why is it important to consider the impacts of promotional activities on base sales separate from those of incremental sales?

4 What research approaches can assist in determining whether a promotion is likely to be effective against the defined target audience?

5 What are the possible impacts of sales promotion against consumers?

14 Integrating sales promotion activities

Chapter overview

One of the major issues in the field of marketing communications in recent years has been the debate surrounding integration. In simple terms, the process of integration is designed to ensure that all components of marketing communications communicate the same message to potential and existing consumers. The task is to eliminate the confusion caused by the variety of messages that are sent out by manufacturers on a regular basis.

This is particularly important in the context of sales promotion. Apart from the fact that many promotions are created as part of a total campaign, even in those situations where they stand alone, promotions must ensure that they contribute to the overall sustenance of the brand. This chapter discusses the development of the theories surrounding integrated marketing communications (IMC) and their application, and benefits within the arena of sales promotion.

Learning outcomes

- To consider the importance of IMC
- To appreciate the factors driving the need for integration
- To examine the benefits of integration
- To consider the process of achieving integration.

It is important in the planning of sales promotions to ensure the continuity of communication with other elements of the marketing communications plan. There is little point running sales promotion activities that only serve to confuse the consumer's expectations of the brand. In this sense, it is vital to ensure that there is a consistency of image and functional values before a sales promotion technique is employed and that it is fully integrated with other aspects of the marketing communications plan.

One of the problems associated with sales promotion is that the message provided to the consumer may not be consistent with other aspects of the communication campaign. Providing mixed messages to the consumer has the potential to damage the brand. It is necessary to ensure that the elements of any campaign are fully co-ordinated to ensure a consistency of message. The greater the level of consistency, the greater the potential impact of the campaign.

Flanagan (1988)[1] argues that promotions must be considered strategically to ensure that they do not conflict with and, potentially, detract from the image of the brand. Equally, he states that promotional activities must be fully integrated with other elements of the marketing communications mix.

Successful promotions invariably depend on thorough integration with the other tools of marketing communications. Often sales promotion activity is tied in with advertising or public relations campaigns to maximize the impact of the activity on potential consumers. As Parry (1994)[2] states: 'For sales promotion to attain its maximum effectiveness, it needs to be integrated with all the other relevant communications processes.'

The importance of integrated marketing communications

It must be remembered that sales promotion does not exist in isolation from the other tools of marketing communications. Whilst for many, advertising still remains the lead tool of the marketing communications mix (although even that position is being challenged by some, as alternative forms of communication become more important) there are few campaigns in which advertising is used on its own. More frequently, campaigns consist of a number of elements, such as public relations, sales promotion, direct marketing, used alongside advertising.

A subject of debate over recent years has been the significance of ensuring the integration of these marketing communications tools. A paper by Caywood et al.[3] in 1991 commenced a process of academic and professional discussion that continues today.

The study conducted by Schultz and Kitchen,[4] published in 1997, indicated that even then 75 per cent of all agencies in the USA devoted 25 per cent of their client time to IMC programmes. Interestingly, the smaller the size of the agency and, presumably, their client base, the greater the percentage of time devoted to achieving IMC.

In contrast to the opinions of Schultz and Kitchen (1997),[4] Duncan and Everett (1993)[5] suggest that IMC is not a new issue in that smaller communications agencies have been doing co-ordinated planning for their clients for years. Furthermore, on the client side, small marketing departments have also had a quasi-integrated approach by the mere fact that all of them knew what was going on because all of them were involved with major communications programmes.

IMC is significant to the consumer, although they are unaware of the concept. They recognize integration and see it logically as making it easier for them to build an overall brand picture. In essence, links between the media are seen as:

- providing short cuts to understanding what a brand stands for
- adding depth and 'amplifying' a particular message or set of brand values
- demonstrating professionalism on the part of the brand owner.

The blurring of the edges of marketing communications

Recent years have seen significant changes in the way that marketing communications campaigns have been developed and implemented. In the 1960s and 1970s, the primary source for the development of all forms of marketing communications activity was the advertising agency. At that time, separate departments within the agency provided their clients with advice in all of the appropriate areas.

Since then, two strands of change have taken place. Firstly, the wider appreciation of the techniques themselves, and the need for specialist personnel to develop them, have both resulted in the creation of specialist companies that deal with specific areas of marketing communications. The consequence has been a progressive fragmentation of provisions within the area. Initially, there was an emergence of specialists in each of the major fields of marketing communications, in areas such as sales promotion, public relations, direct marketing, etc.

Today, as we have already seen, those specialisms have been taken even further. Companies that deal with e-marketing, product placement, the organization of trade and consumer events, sponsorship activities, etc., now abound. Individual specialist companies can now provide clients with inputs in areas such as the design and production of point-of-sale materials, the creation of trade and consumer incentives, pack design and guerrilla marketing techniques, amongst many others. Even in the mainstream areas, agencies have become specialized in terms of youth or grey marketing, FMCG or retail marketing communications; dealing with pharmaceutical products or travel and tourism. Furthermore, the specialisms continue.

Secondly, and contradictorily, there has been an increasing tendency for this wide variety of specialists to provide inputs that encompass a range of executional devices. Today, several different companies will have the ability and expertise to develop campaigns utilizing a wide range of marketing communications formats. Moreover, few marketing communications campaigns utilize a single component or element. Rather, marketers will tend to employ several different devices that, previously, were the domain of dedicated and specialist companies.

The consequence has been a distinct blurring of the divisions between previous specialist practitioner areas.

> Discipline overlap is blurring long standing distinctions. It's becoming increasingly difficult to categorise work as sales promotion or direct marketing. Most direct marketing offers contain some form of sales promotion or vice versa. And with the growth of direct response press and TV advertising, direct marketing is moving closer to conventional advertising.

Cook (1994)[6]

The strategic challenges facing organizations

Marketing and, for that matter, marketing communications, are being re-addressed by major corporations to determine the values that they derive from the adoption of their principles. Indeed, the very nature of these principles is being challenged and re-evaluated to determine their relevance to the challenges being faced by companies at the start of the new millennium.

Nilson (1992)[7] suggested that marketing had 'lost its way'. Despite employing high-quality management, organizations have in many instances seemed unable to face the challenges that they face in the broader environment. Growth has come more from acquisition than brand development. The consequence of chasing niche markets has been the continued and growing failure of new products to attract substantial and profitable audiences. The continued growth of private-label products in a wide variety of market sectors evidences the fact that retailers are often more successful in their identification and satisfaction of consumer needs. New and innovative competitors have stolen share from the large multinational FMCG companies, despite their comparatively smaller scale, which should have precluded their entry into the market.

The essential requirement of the 'new marketing' approach is the development of a close customer focus throughout the organization that, in turn, demands an understanding of customers as individuals in order to appreciate their perceptions, expectations, needs and wants. The increasing availability of tools to enable the marketer to achieve this deeper understanding of the consumer similarly demands the re-evaluation of the ways in which the tools employed to communicate with those consumers are used.

Strategic marketing communications

Schultz *et al.* (1992)[8] argue that marketing communications often present the only differentiating feature that can be offered to potential consumers. By recognizing the fact that everything a company does is, in some form, a part of the communication that takes place between itself and its customers it becomes aware of the increasingly important role of marketing communications as a strategic tool

Just as the premise of the 'new marketing' places the consumer at the centre of all activity, so too marketing communications must be considered from the essential perspective of understanding consumer behaviour. This implies a consideration of more than just the content of the message itself. Close attention needs to be paid to the context of the message (the vehicle used to communicate with the target audience), as well as the timing and tone of the message. The underlying imperative is the need to identify clear, concise and measurable communications objectives that will enable the selection of the appropriate communications tools to achieve the tasks set.

By developing an understanding of the identity of the consumer, and their particular needs and wants, we can determine the nature of the behaviour that the communications programme will need to reinforce or change. In turn, we can determine the specific nature of the message that will affect that behaviour, and the means by which we can reach them.

The strategic role that marketing communications can play is increasingly evidenced by the impact of specific campaigns. These not only affect the way in which consumers think about the particular products and services that are offered to them, but also the very way in which they consider the categories in which those products and services exist.

The integration of marketing communications

A major contemporary issue in the field of marketing communications is the drive towards integrated activity. There are a number of reasons for this fundamental change of thinking that need to be examined.

The marketing methods businesses used in the 1980s and 1990s are no longer working and have lost their value as competitive weapons, such as the constant focus on new products, generic competitive strategies, promotional pricing tactics, etc. Today's marketing environment has been described as an age of 'hyper-competition' in which there exists a vast array of products and services, both new and variations on existing themes. A casual look in the supermarket will confirm this view. Take, for example, the 'cook-in-sauce' sector. The variety available to the consumer is little short of mind blowing, whole fitments devoted to ethnic and other varieties, and with each product replicated by several different brands.

Many of the fastest growing markets are rapidly becoming saturated with large numbers of competitors. In addition, each competitor has similar technology. The consequence is that, as Schultz *et al.* (1995)[9] put it, sustainable competitive advantage has been eroded away. In many categories new products and services are copied in days or weeks rather than years. Significantly, anything a company can do, someone else can do cheaper.

Consumers are searching for more than a single element in any transaction. Instead, they seek to buy into the array of relevant experiences that surround the brand. Successful marketing in the 21st century will require total consumer orientation. It means communication with the individual, creating long-term relationships, is quality driven, and the aim is customer satisfaction, not just volume and share.

Many writers on the subject, most notably Schultz (1999),[10] argue that IMC is the natural evolution of mass-market media advertising towards targeted direct marketing. Schultz sees IMC as a logical and natural progression within the field of marketing communications. As he describes 'it appears to be the natural evolution of traditional mass-media advertising, which has been changed, adjusted and refined as a result of new technology'. This author concurs with those who believe that IMC is significantly more than 'merely a management fashion' as attested by Cornellisen *et al.* (2000).[11] Many companies strive to achieve total integration of their marketing communications efforts, recognizing the undeniable benefits that are derived from the practice, not least of which is the ability to deliver consistency in their messages to their target audiences.

Proctor and Kitchen (2002)[12] argue that the brand is the hub of all marketing communications and depict this as the 'Wheel of Integration'.

Figure 14.1

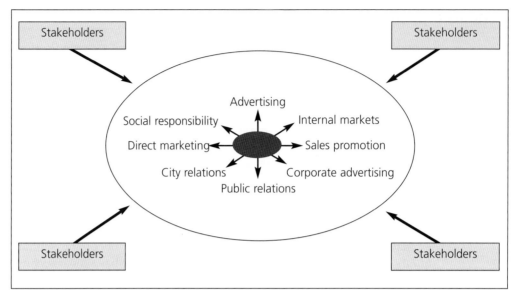

Defining integrated marketing communications

Much debate surrounds the very nature of IMC, with the consequence that several alternative definitions have been proposed. Cornellisen and Lock (2000)12 argue that one of the problems with the interpretation of IMC is the lack of a consensus decision as to what the phrase actually means in practice. They point to the fact that various writers have argued about the move away from the traditional distinction between 'above-the-line' and 'below-the-line' to 'through-the-line', and 'zero-based' communications. What they fail to recognize is that the practitioners within the field operate as brands and seek to provide a distinctive offering to their clients. Hence, the adoption of a variety of nomenclatures for the practice of IMC.

They argue that the theoretical concept of IMC is ambiguous and 'provides the basis for researchers to adopt whichever interpretation of the term best fits their research agendas at any given time'.

There appears to be discordance between academic thinking and practice in the market place. Schultz and Kitchen (1997)[4] argue that most marketing communications activities in the past have focussed on breaking down concepts and activities into even more finite specialisms. Few marketing communications approaches have involved integration or holistic thinking. Whilst it is acknowledged that the pace of change towards the adoption of a holistic approach has been relatively slow, nonetheless, many practitioners and clients have moved progressively towards a focus on IMC.

Schultz in Jones (1999)[10] defines IMC as 'a planning approach that attempts to co-ordinate, consolidate and bring together all the communications messages, programmes and vehicles that affect customers or prospects for a manufacturer or service organisation's brands'.

Jeans (1998)[13] provides greater clarity by proposing that 'IMC is the implementation of all marketing communications in such a way that each project, as well as meeting its specific project objects also:

- Conforms with the brand platform
- Is synergistic with all other projects related to the brand
- Actively reinforces the agreed brand values in any dialogue with the market
- And is measured by its short- and long-term effects on consumer behaviour.'

Shimp (1996)[14] suggests that 'the marketer who succeeds in the new environment will be the one who co-ordinates the communications mix so tightly that you can look from medium to medium and instantly see that the brand is speaking with "one voice"'. The one voice definition refers to an organizational effort to unify brand and image advertising, direct response, consumer sales promotions and public relations into a 'single positioning concept'.

Brannan (1995)[15] argues: 'Our communications are fully integrated when we identify a single, core message that leads to one great creative idea which is implemented across everything we do.'

However, perhaps the clearest definition of IMC is that of the American Association of Advertising Agencies (1993):[16]

> A concept of marketing communications planning that recognises the added value of a comprehensive plan that evaluates the strategic roles of a variety of communications disciplines and combines them to provide clarity, consistency and maximum communications impact through the seamless integration of discrete messages.

The important dimension of this definition is the recognition of the need for a comprehensive plan that considers the strategic aspects of each of the tools of marketing communications in a holistic manner, rather than the development of them as separate elements. This approach represents a substantial shift in the underlying planning process, since it aims to ensure cohesion and the delivery of a single-minded message to the target audience.

Paul Smith writing in *Admap* (1996)[17] states: 'Integrated marketing communications is a simple concept. It brings together all forms of communication into a seamless solution. At its most basic level, IMC integrates all promotional tools so that they work together in harmony.'

Key to the issue is the fact that the consumer does not see advertising, public relations, sales promotion and other marketing communications techniques as separate and divisible components. As the receivers of a variety of messages from an equally wide range of sources they build up an image of a company, its brands and its services (both favourable and unfavourable). As far as they are concerned, the source of the message is unimportant. What they will be concerned with is the content of the message:

> A surge of interest by marketers in integrated communications strategies, where promotional messages are co-ordinated among advertising, public relations and sales promotion efforts, brings with it the implicit acknowledgement that consumers assimilate data about popular culture from many sources.

Solomon and Englis (1994)[18]

Equally, according to Lannon (1994):[19] 'Consumers receive impressions of brands from a whole range of sources – first hand experience, impressions of where it can be bought, of people who use it or people who do not, from its role in cultural mores or rituals, from movies, literature, television, editorial, news, fashion, from its connections with events and activities and finally from paid advertising media.'

A parallel consideration is the fact that the communicator desires to achieve a sense of cohesion in the messages that the company communicates. If, for example, advertising is saying one thing about a brand and sales promotion something different, a sense of dissonance may be created with the consumer left in some confusion as to what the brand is really trying to say.

There is little doubt that marketing communications funds spent on a single communications message will achieve a far greater impact than when a series of different or contradictory messages are being sent out by the brand. With pressure on funds, marketers want to ensure that they are presenting a clear and precise picture of their products and services to the end consumer.

Few companies are specifically concerned with issues of whether to spend their money on advertising, sales promotion, public relations or elsewhere. They are concerned with ensuring that they develop a cohesive marketing communications programme that most effectively communicates their proposition to the end consumer. The particular route of communication is far less important than the impact of the message. In addition, in budgetary terms, companies need to consider where their expenditure will best achieve their defined objectives. The previous notions of separate and distinct advertising, sales promotion, public relations, and other budgets fail to appreciate that the considerations of the overall marketing communications budget need to be addressed as a matter of priority.

But, at the heart of the debate is the recognition that the consumer must be the focus of all marketing communications activity. If we consider the Chartered Institute of Marketing's definition of marketing, we can see that the primary need is the anticipation and satisfaction of consumer wants and needs. It is the development of an understanding of the consumer and his or her wants and needs that will ensure that marketing communications work effectively to achieve the objectives defined for it. This represents a fundamental change of focus: a shift from the functional activity of creating marketing communications campaigns to an attitudinal focus in which the consumer's needs are at the heart of all marketing communications planning. With it comes a change from a focus on the product itself to the ultimate satisfaction of the end consumer. Of course, there are functional implications.

Above all else, there is an increasing recognition that companies need to identify what position their product or service occupies in the minds of the consumer relative to that of other products or services. Only when they have gained that knowledge can they begin the process of planning marketing communications either to alter or enhance that position:

> As choice becomes an ever greater factor for consumers, both in the products they use and the way they learn about those products, it is increasingly clear that no marketer can rely on advertising alone to deliver its message. Integration permits us to focus the power of all messages. It holds the greatest, most exciting

promise for the future.

George Schweitzer (Senior Vice President, Marketing and Communications, CBE's Broadcast Group)

In general, some consistent themes may be drawn from prominent IMC definitions identified in the literature, including:

- A sound knowledge of the organization's stakeholders, acquired through two-way interaction with these parties
- The selection of communication tools that promote the achievement of communications objectives, are reasonable in regard to the organization's resources and are favourable to the intended recipient
- The strategic co-ordination of various communication tools in a manner consistent with the organization's brand positioning, and which maximizes their synergistic effect so as to build strong brands and stakeholder relationships
- The use of appropriate, timely and data-driven evaluation and planning to determine the effectiveness of this process
- Strong inter-functional and inter-organizational relationships with those responsible for implementing marketing communications campaigns
- Impact on customer relationships, brand equity and sales.

IMC is recognized increasingly for the strategic role it can play in managing the 'intangible side of business' through assisting in building relationships with customers and other stakeholders and in creating positive perceptions, attitudes and behaviours towards brands.[20]

One of the difficulties with many definitions of IMC is the narrow ambit that they suggest. For the most part, authors concentrate on the primary tools of marketing communications, rather than the broader aspects that impact on their target audiences. Since, to reiterate the notion of David Ogilvy,[21] that everything that a company does, communicates, then the notion of IMC should realistically embrace every dimension of company activity.

The impact of external factors on marketing communications

External and environmental factors have forced marketers to undertake a fundamental re-think both of marketing strategies and the positioning of products and this, in turn, must impact on the process of marketing communications.

Information overload

The discerning consumer

Changes in family composition

The ageing population

The green imperative

The changing face of media and the growth of narrow casting

The growth of global marketing

Value for money

Increasing pressure on organizations' bottom lines

Increasing client sophistication

- A disillusionment with advertising

  This has resulted in clients turning to other disciplines in the search to improve customer relationships and more sales.

- Traditional advertising too expensive and not cost effective

  There is an increased recognition that, for many companies, the use of traditional forms of advertising no longer provides the means of achieving cost-effective reach of their target audiences. As media costs escalate, many companies are turning to other forms of marketing communications to achieve their objectives.

- The rapid growth and development of database marketing

  The increasing availability of sophisticated database techniques has provided manufacturers and service providers alike with a more precise means of targeting consumers. The move away from traditional mass marketing towards closely focused communications techniques is a reflection of the increasing cost of traditional advertising techniques.

- Power shift towards retailers

  In most consumer markets, comparatively small numbers of retailers have come to dominate their respective categories. In the grocery field, for example, the major supermarket chains (Tesco, ASDA, Sainsbury and Safeway [now part of Morrisons]) account for a substantial part of the retail business. Together, these four companies account for over 50 per cent of retail sales. Inevitably, this has resulted in their taking the initiative in terms of the marketing to consumers. To a large degree, even major manufacturers have to bow to the demands of the retailers or face the prospect of their products being de-listed from their shelves.

- Escalating price competition

  As brands increasingly converge in what they offer to consumers, companies are striving to overcome the debilitating impact of the downward price spiral. The recognition that marketing communications is often the only differentiating factor between competing brands has led to an increased focus on how the tools can be used to achieve brand distinction.

The impact on marketing communications

We have already seen that marketing communications needs to focus on the end user rather than on the nature of the product or service provided. But it is suggested marketing communications needs to respond more rapidly to these underlying changes in the social and environmental framework.

If marketing communications is to be effective, it is vitally important that we move from a situation of specialization, in which marketers are experts in one area of marketing communications, to people who are trained in all marketing communications disciplines.

At the same time, as we have already seen, the process of change requires us to look at focused marketing approaches rather than adopt the litany of the 60s: that of mass marketing. With the recognition that all consumers are different and hence have different needs and wants, even of the same product or service, there is the need to ensure that we are able to communicate with them as individuals rather than as a homogenous unit. The increasing concern is the desire to communicate with ever smaller segments of the global market and, in an ideal world, reach a position where we can communicate with them individually. This desire manifests itself in the increasing drive towards direct-marketing techniques, the most rapidly growing sector of the marketing communications industry.

There needs to be a clear statement of the desired outcomes of marketing activity as a whole. This requires a totally new approach since most people working within marketing have been brought up in a disintegrated environment. Objectives need to be longer term and expressed more strategically than would be the case for the short-term objectives of more individual marketing tactics.

Schultz (1999)[26] argues that as the tools of marketing communications are progressively diffused into a variety of specialisms, there has been a natural inclination for those individual specialists to focus entirely within their own area; often to the detriment of the brand or communication programme. The consequence has been a natural drift towards less integrated, less co-ordinated, less concentrated marketing communications activities.

The task of IMC is to strategically co-ordinate the various elements of the promotional mix in order to achieve synergies and to ensure that the message reaches and registers with the target audience.

Novak and Phelps (1994)[22] have suggested that there are several important dimensions to the process of integration:

- The creation of a single theme and image
- The integration of both product image and relevant aspects of consumer behaviour in promotional management, as opposed to a focus on one or the other of these two
- The co-ordinated management of promotion mix disciplines.

Similarly, Low (2000)[23] identified four components that contribute to the co-ordination of marketing communications activities:

1 Planning and executing different communications tools as one integrated project
2 Assigning responsibility for the overall communications effort to a single manager
3 Ensuring that the various elements of the communications programme have a common strategic objective
4 Focusing on a common communications message.

The benefits of integration

Undeniably, the process of integration affords a great number of benefits to the companies that adopt it. Linton and Morley (1995)[24] suggest nine potential benefits of IMC:

1 Creative integrity
2 Consistent messages
3 Unbiased marketing recommendations
4 Better use of media
5 Greater marketing precision
6 Operational efficiency
7 Cost savings
8 High-calibre consistent service
9 Easier working relations.

Similarly, the Kitchen study (1999)[25] identified a series of benefits that could be derived from IMC programmes. These included:

- Increased impact
- Creative ideas more effective when IMC used
- Greater communications consistency
- Increases importance of one brand personality
- Helps eliminate misconceptions
- Provides greater client control over communication budget
- Provides clients with greater professional expertise
- Enables greater client control over marketing communications
- Helps eliminate miscommunications that result from using several agencies
- Enables greater control over budgets
- Provides clients with greater professional expertise
- IMC necessitates fewer meetings
- Enables client consolidation of responsibilities
- Agencies can provide faster solutions
- Provides method of effective measurement
- Reduces cost of Marcom programmes
- Greater agency accountability.

Consistency of message delivery

By approaching the planning process in a holistic manner, companies can ensure that all components of the communications programme deliver the same message to the target audience. Importantly, this demands the adoption of an overall strategy for the brand, rather than developing individual strategies for the separate tools of marketing communications. The avoidance of potential confusion in the minds of consumers is a paramount consideration in the development of effective communications programmes.

Corporate cohesion

For the company, IMC can be used as a strategic tool in communicating its corporate image and product/service benefits. This has important consequences both on an internal and an external level. As consumers increasingly gravitate towards companies with whom they feel comfortable, it becomes important to ensure that the overall image projected by the organization is favourably received. This demands, in turn, the development of a cohesive communications programme within the organization to ensure that all people working for the company fully understand the organization's goals and ambitions and, externally, to present the company in the most favourable light.

Client relationships

For the agency, it provides the opportunity to play a significantly more important role in the development of the communications programme and to become a more effective partner in the relationship. By participating in the totality of the communications requirements, rather than having responsibility for one or more components, the agency can adopt a more strategic stance. This, in turn, yields significant power and provides important advantages over competitors.

Interaction

IMC ensures better communication between agencies and creates a stronger bond between them and the client company. By providing a more open flow of information it enables the participants in the communication programme to concentrate on the key areas of strategic development, rather than pursue individual and separate agendas.

Motivation

IMC offers the opportunity to motivate agencies. The combined thinking of a team is better than the sum of the parts (and unleashes everyone's creative potential).

Participation

Everyone owns the final plan, having worked together on the brainstorming and implementation, avoiding any internal politics. Potentially, this can overcome the divisive nature of individual departments 'fighting their own corner'.

Perhaps the most important benefit is the delivery of better measurability of response and accountability for the communications programme.

The process of achieving integration

The task of developing and implementing marketing communications campaigns is becoming increasingly divergent. No longer is the task is one pair of hands. As the specialist functions develop further, the marketer must seek and co-ordinate the input from a number of different sources. Many organizations will retain an advertising agency, a public relations consultancy, a sales promotion company and, perhaps, even a media specialist. Ensuring that all of these contributors work to the same set of objectives and deliver a cohesive message to the consumer is a task that is an increasingly challenging one.

The key requirement is the establishment of a feedback mechanism between all elements of the strategic development process and, importantly, the consideration of all of the tools of marketing communications designed to fulfil the promotional objectives established for the campaign. It is the adoption of an holistic approach to campaign development that is at the heart of integration, a fundamental shift from the practice of developing each of the elements on a piecemeal basis.

'Integrated marketing communications offers strategic and creative integrity across all media' (Linton and Morley 1995).[24] This ensures that the company maintains a constant theme and style of communication that can be followed across all applications. In turn, this provides for a strong and unified visual identity in all areas of communication.

This does not imply that all material should have the same copy and visual execution; however, all items used must serve to tell the same story and to reinforce the overall message to the consumer. This enables each element of a campaign to reinforce the others and to achieve the maximum level of impact on the target audience. The best platforms for integrated campaigns are ideas that can be spread across the whole marketing communications mix, e.g. American Express 'Membership Has Its Privileges' and Gillette's 'The Best A Man Can Get' will work in any discipline.

Andrex has, for many years, used the image of a Labrador puppy in its advertising to symbolize softness. More recently, however, the device has been extended into other promotional areas; its 'Puppy Tales' campaign offered a series of books about the adventures of a puppy, which was featured on-pack and in television advertising. The promotion gained editorial coverage both for the promotion itself and by way of reviews of the author, Gerald Durrell. All of these devices reinforced the brand message.

An essential part of IMC is the process of ensuring that the message conveyed is consistent. Whereas this is achievable in the context of a single agency that produces all of the materials required by its client, in the vast majority of cases, companies will employ several different agencies, often independent of each other. Indeed, some of the material will be produced by the company in-house. In this instance, someone must take overall responsibility for ensuring the consistency of the various items to ensure that there is an overall coherence in what is produced. This means that the person or department must consider not only the obvious items such as advertising, point of sale and direct mail pieces, but everything else that is prepared to support the brand. This may include product leaflets and other literature, presentations and audiovisual material, sales training items, exhibition stands, etc.

A key area within the requirement of IMC is the need for recommendations that are without structural bias. Historically (and still to a large degree), it was inevitable that agencies promoted their own particular corners. Advertising agencies would often present advertising solutions; promotions companies would offer sales promotion responses, etc.

The move towards IMC has been hastened by the desire for agencies to become more accountable for their recommendations. Inherently, agencies have to be confident, as far as it is possible to be so, that the recommendations they make are those most likely to achieve the outcome desired by the client company.

At the conceptual level, integration is about capturing a single thought that expresses what we wish the brand to stand for and ensuring that this thought is expressed, whatever the medium. At the process level, it is about ensuring that the development and implementation of communications lives up to that brand thought, and drives forward the relationship between the brand and the consumer.

Integration is not just about execution. It is about the single brand thought that expresses the essence of the brand personality and then interpreting that thought for the appropriate audience without changing or denigrating it. Integration extends to the point where the client and agency work together as a single team. The total team across all communications requirements is fully integrated with the customer and brand requirements and that is what drives the focus of the team.

The consumer and integrated marketing communications

At the heart of the debate is the undeniable need to ensure the clear and effective communication of brand messages to consumers and others. The process demands a change of focus from share and volume to a detailed understanding of the extent to which the manufacturer can satisfy the needs and wants of consumers. The essential focus has to be on customers, relationships, retention levels and satisfaction.

Several authors have suggested that IMC, as well as benefiting the manufacturers of products and services, also works for the consumer. David Iddiols (2000)[26] suggests that IMC works on three levels for the consumer:

1 It provides short-cuts to understanding what a brand stands for
2 It adds depth and amplification to a particular message or set of brand values
3 It demonstrates professionalism on the part of the brand owner.

Integration and sales promotion

Increasingly, brands are seeking promotional devices that represent the achievement of integration. Various companies have ensured that the promotional offers made to consumers reflect other aspects of their communications programmes. Integration applies to sales promotion as much as any other marketing communications discipline. When the agency was briefed to come up with a promotion for Pepperami the proposal was a comprehensive communications package themed around a character called 'Fanimal'. This was an extension of the original Pepperami character in the form of a soccer hooligan. This enabled the brand to integrate its activity during the period of the World Cup in a manner that was consistent with previous activity.

Similarly, in the Jaffa Cake campaign, 'Save the McVitie's Jaffa Cakes from the Orangey Tangs', the company developed a campaign that integrated a variety of techniques to build a bond with its customers. The promotion commenced in 1997. According to Croft (1999),[27] the share for the brand had decreased from 55 per cent in 1994 to 42 per cent in 1997. After the promotion, it had risen to 47.2%: 'A number of customers have told us that the product tasted more orangey, although we haven't changed the recipe at all. That shows how we've successfully built up the brand values to the point where we have an effect on the consumers' perception of the product.'

Peattie and Peattie (2003)[28] writing in *The Marketing Book* put forward a model depicting the integration of sales promotion activity:

Figure 14.2

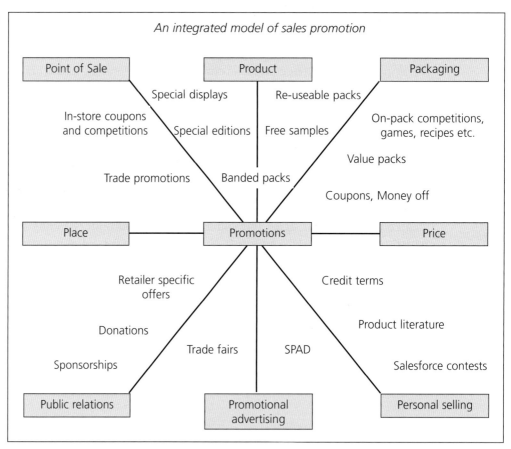

An integrated model of sales promotion

Parry (1994)[2] emphasizes the importance of integrating sales promotion with other aspects of the marketing communications programme. The author also identifies a series of measures for the measurement of promotional effectiveness, including brand awareness, sales volume, distribution, levels of trial, loyalty and the overall impact on brand image.

Of course, the adoption of a strategic approach to sales promotion does not preclude the tactical use of sales promotion techniques. Its purpose is to provide a framework in which tactical planning can exist and be improved.

Kevin Twitty (1999)[29] suggests that 'manufacturers which allocate £100,000 on an on-wrapper sales promotion and expect it to have an effect on the brand are in for a disappointment. It doesn't have the visibility, yet nine-tenths of sales promotions are unsupported. Their only means of communication is on pack and then it is to do with brand switching. We advise our clients to run promotional activities with media support to ensure that they enter people's consciousness and break the noise level'.

However, integration isn't always welcomed. According to Hugh Taylor,[30] CEO of Promotional Campaigns, advertising is seen as the most respected and glamorous in the heirarchy, whilst sales promotion is almost seen as a 'necessary evil'. Companies want to distance themselves from it.

Snudden quoted in Acland (1998)[31] indicates that integration will never work if the different elements of a campaign are separated into boxes. Beasley,32 quoted in the same article, indicates that the core idea needs to develop across all elements of the chain.

The benefits of sales promotion integration

Research conducted by Bemmaor and Mouchoux (1991)[33] indicated that promotions are more effective when used in conjunction with advertising. They found that elasticity increased from 20 per cent to 180 per cent when the promotion was advertised.

Similarly, Roberts (1996)[34] reports on research that shows that the sales effects of TV advertising over a 4-week period were between two and seven times greater when they coincide with promotions. The findings come from a survey of 21 different brands in eight consumer goods markets.

The trend towards integration offers added communication possibilities to the brand. In a paper by Bunyard (1999),[35] the example is given of an intensive sampling programme supported by a heavy weight of advertising.

Above all else, integration ensures that there is a consistency between the images created by sales promotion activities and those desired for the brand. It eliminates confusion on the part of the consumer and helps contribute to the long-term benefit of the brands they support.

Case study

NESTLÉ GOLD BLEND
Agency: Billington Cartmell

Gold Blend is one of the brands in the premium sector of the instant coffee market. Prior to the promotion the brand was achieving growth of only 3.4 per cent against the sector growth of 5.1 per cent. A fundamental objective was to remedy this under-performance without the use of price promotion.

The brand has a long history of 'romance' used as a device in its television advertising; hence, the link with the romantic comedy *Love Actually* to provide the basis for a fully integrated campaign.

Objectives:

- To increase base volume sales by 57 per cent
- To generate in-store display for the brand.

Strategy:

- The target audience for the promotion was identified as 25–34-year-old females considered to be most responsive to the 'romantic' proposition
- To counteract competitive tactical price cuts with a value-added promotion
- To reinforce the brand proposition with a link to the *Love Actually* film and using it as a communication platform for the brand.

The Promotion:

- The core of the campaign was an on-pack instant-win promotion carried on some 4 million jars, each with a highly visible, limited edition, gold wrap. Consumers were invited to 'Hug this jar' to reveal a win/lose message (printed with heat reactive inks) on the front label.
- Winners claimed their prizes by removing a perforated panel on the label and submitting to the offer address.
- Prizes were themed to reflect both the brand proposition and the film. These included a 'perfect romantic year' in which winners were given £50 000 to tailor their perfect life from a list of 50 choices. Additional prizes consisted of a Romantic Weekend in London that included a £500 spending spree in Harvey Nichols, a complete wedding package, bespoke jewellery and 10 000 *Love Actually* indulgence kits.
- The promotion was supported with television, radio, posters and in-store activity.

The Results:

- Sales increased by 71 per cent against base volume and by 33 per cent against a similar period of price promotion.
- The promotion received strong retailer support in the major outlets.

The campaign received a Platinum Award in the Integrated Promotions category and a Gold Award in the Prize Promotions section of the 2004 ISP Promotion Awards.

(The above case study is adapted from an article that appeared in *Promotions and Incentives* magazine, May 2004)

Questions

1 Why is a consideration of integration an increasingly important aspect of the planning of marketing communications activities?

2 Identify the factors driving the need for the integration of marketing communications.

3 Why is it considered important that the consumer is the focus of marketing communications?

4 Discuss the benefits that derive from integration.

5 Outline the process of achieving integration.

15 International sales promotion

Chapter overview

The moves towards international marketing have brought with them the desire to run common marketing communications programmes across a large number of countries. Whilst it may be possible to standardize some forms of marketing communications, such as advertising, the arena of sales promotion is fraught with difficulties. Many of these result from the diversity of rules and regulations that apply to the implementation of sales promotion programmes.

This chapter will discuss the relevant issues and outline some of the regulations that apply, although the cardinal rule will remain: before implementing any promotional activity across markets, it is imperative that its legality is determined before the event!

Learning outcomes

- To consider the process of globalization and the development of global brands
- To examine the factors involved in international branding
- To explore the influences on the international consumer
- To appreciate the role of international regulations on promotional activities.

The process of globalization

Since the Second World War there has been an increasing tendency towards the internationalization of brands. The term used to describe the process (globalization) is itself relatively recent. Increasingly, companies are recognizing that their competitiveness, even in domestic markets, is a reflection of their ability to develop their brands on a global basis. Their focus, progressively, must be to develop products that satisfy a wider range of consumer needs. With this growth come increased expertise, successive product improvements and economies of scale. As domestic markets have reached positions of virtual saturation, manufacturers have turned to new and often distant markets to ensure a continuation of their growth potential.

There are two different approaches to foreign markets that have significant implications for the determination of marketing communications strategies. On the one hand, the multinational company readily perceives the differences between the various markets that it serves. In general, it believes that its success is dependent on the development of individual marketing and marketing communications programmes for each of its territories. As a result it tends to operate through a number of subsidiaries that, for the most part, act independently of each other. Products are adapted or developed independently to meet the needs of the individual markets and the consumers within them. Equally, the other elements of the marketing mix, including sales promotion, are developed on a local basis. Although there may be some cross-fertilization of ideas through some form of central function, the primary aim is to satisfy the needs of the individual country markets, rather than identify the common elements that might allow for the standardization of activities. However, even within this framework there is some recognition of the need for local adaptation in order to respond to local pressures. The fundamental objective is to identify groups of buyers within the global market with similar needs and wants and to develop marketing communications plans that, as far as possible, are standardized within cultural and operational constraints.

As Kanso (1992)[1] states: 'Multinationals using a standardised approach believe that consumers anywhere in the world have the same basic needs and desires and therefore can be persuaded by universal appeals.'

Boyfield (2000)[2] states that the dramatic explosion in global marketing can be attributed to a variety of factors:

- The liberalization and privatization of former state monopolies
- The emergence of the internet as a new source of consumer information
- A relaxation of outmoded retail regulations
- The entry of new players challenging domestic incumbents
- Stricter competition rules adopted by national governments
- A wave of merger and acquisition activity.

The impetus for a more detailed examination of the implications of international marketing was provided by the seminal article by Theodore Levitt in 1983.[3] The thrust of his argument is that a variety of common forces, the most important of which is shared technology, are driving the world towards a 'converging commonality'. The result he argues is 'the emergence of global markets for standardised consumer products on a previously unimagined scale'. Levitt suggests that companies must learn to operate as if the world was one large market, ignoring superficial regional and national differences. However, this is far from being a universally accepted view. Philip Kotler (1994),[4] amongst others, considers globalization as a step backwards to the so-called production era of business, when organizations were more concerned about producing as many standardized products as possible, rather than worrying about satisfying individual consumer needs and wants.

Grein and Ducoffe (1998)[5] state that client companies are increasingly managing their businesses on a broad regional or global basis. They wish to use more standardized campaigns around the world that they consider easier to administer. The desire to identify a unified brand image and position around the world has increased the impetus towards the globalization of advertising agencies.

Whilst it is undeniable that cultural differences will continue to prevail, at least for some considerable time into the foreseeable future, so too are we witnessing the coming together of many attitudes and beliefs that enhance the potential for products and services that respond to those common and shared values.

Simon Anholt (2000)[6] suggests that several entirely new kinds of international business are now commonplace in a wide range of industries. These include:

- global start-ups
- small global businesses
- global businesses with one office
- global businesses based in developing countries.

In the past corporations only became global through the slow evolution from simple export marketing, via third-party licensee or distributor marketing, to global brand building directly from the country of origin. The process often took many decades. Indeed, many of today's multinationals began their international growth at the beginning of the last century.

Many of the new international businesses have little fixed presence outside their market of origin. They de-duplicate as many corporate functions as possible, centralizing such areas as NPD, finance, administration and, often, production. They use digital media to inform, distribute and sell. With Internet, WAP and database technologies, they can sell things almost anywhere. These companies are seldom inspired to build global brands merely because the notion appeals. They are compelled to, because in the new economy a global brand may be their only real asset. The window of opportunity for new products was always brief, but increased competitiveness means that the temporary monopoly enjoyed by new products might only last a few weeks before it is outperformed and under-priced by a crowd of imitators. Consequently, the only way in which these companies can achieve payback on their research and development efforts is by launching simultaneously in as many countries as possible.

The development of global brands

It is inevitable that the progressive standardization of products results in significant economies of manufacture that, potentially, lead to lower prices and a more competitive positioning for the brand. The high investment in product development will be rapidly amortized if the market for the resulting product is global and enormous rather than domestic and limited. Such developments, however, will not obviate the need in many instances to adapt the product to meet 'special' local needs, however these are occasioned.

Some manufacturers perceive the world of the future to be one in which global brands dominate. The perceived benefits of single world-wide brand identification outweigh those of country-specific products with separate brand identities. However, it is important to remember that, even here, it is not essential that the product delivered in each market is identical, only that the branding and the imagery associated with it are the same.

The arguments put forward in favour of global brands are widely known and compelling:

- They provide high economies of scale due to the standardization of product platforms.

- Technology that is now present in most products is itself an inescapable homogenizing force.

- The world has become a global village thanks to global media, CNN and the Internet.

- At the segmentation level there is much more resemblance between executive working women living in New York and Paris than between themselves and other groups within their own country. As a result, nations and countries are not considered relevant criteria any more for market segmentation. Moreover, there are an increasing number of open markets being created, such as the EU, aiming at the disappearance of all trade, legal and fiscal barriers in the Euro zone.

- At the consumer level, both common observation and recent empirical studies have shown that brands perceived as global induced better quality ratings, which in turn increased desire to buy.

- Lastly, as distributors themselves go global, they expect their suppliers to do the same.

According to Anholt (2000),[6] international branding is no longer a choice, it has become a necessity. The new global communications channels, the mobility of the consumer, the globalization of the economy, the Internet and the 'vigilante consumer' have ensured that no brand-building can ever take place in geographic isolation. It is no longer tenable for a brand to adopt different positioning in different territories, and a brand that fails to express its core values consistently from country to country will leak equity until it learns to be true to itself.

Few companies can afford fragmentation and inefficiency. The process of briefing, managing, co-ordinating and monitoring the work of many separate agencies is a major task, even for mature companies, with marketing offices in each country. For the emerging international marketers who sell direct to the consumer world-wide, or who rely on agents or distributors abroad, adequate management of brand communications becomes almost impossible.

International marketing in the 21st century is not about ignoring or over-riding cultural differences, but about understanding, accommodating and harnessing them in the service of global brand building.

Even where it is necessary to subjugate the current brand identity in favour of a single consistent world-wide brand mark, major manufacturers have determined that the long-term benefits are likely to outweigh the short-term losses. Despite enjoying considerable consumer acceptance in the UK with their Marathon brand, Mars opted for a standardization of the brand under the name of Snickers across all markets. The same policy has now been applied to Opal Fruits, renamed as Starburst. In a similar manner, Unilever have standardized the name of their household cleanser as Cif, replacing the brand names used in various countries such as Jif, Vif, etc.

However, the arguments in favour of the global approach are not accepted by all.

In March 2000, Coca-Cola's then CEO Douglas Daft announced the company's new 'think local, act local' marketing strategy. As Quelch (2003)[7] pointed out, having embraced Levitt's vision for decades, executives in America's global companies began to appreciate that they had taken their global-brand strategies too far. With their centralized decision making and standardized marketing programmes, they had lost touch with the new global market place.

As sales slumped, global-brand owners started to listen more closely to their local business partners about how to adapt product attributes and advertising messages to local tastes. They began delegating more authority over product development and marketing to local managers. They started developing and promoting local executives to take over from expatriates.

Meanwhile, some US multinationals like Philip Morris and Coca-Cola ramped up their acquisition of local brands, for the same reasons that investors diversify a stock portfolio. Today, two-thirds of Coca-Cola's sales in Japan are from local beverage brands, and the company now owns more than 100 local beverage brands world-wide. In some cases, the global-brand owners are financing totally separate companies. Unilever India, for example, has set up the free-standing 'Wheel' organization as a low-cost enterprise that markets quality, low-priced local brands to the mass market.

Byfield and Caller (1996)[8] argue that brands hold the same value in whichever markets they occupy. However, the reasons for purchase may differ. Klaus Wustrack (1999)[9] provides the example of Alcatel to illustrate this point. He found that customers for mobile phones had different reasons for purchase depending on their country of residence. Women in the UK purchased mobile phones as a means of security; middle-class consumers from China bought mobile phones as a status symbol; whilst those in South Africa found that due to the lack of fixed wire infrastructure, it was actually easier to buy a mobile.

Even the usage of the word 'brand' has to be re-interpreted in the international context. According to Mary Goodyear (1996),[10] Western marketers tend to focus on the product as brand; in Japan and Korea 'brand' tends to refer to the corporate entity. The consequence is that it tends to be evaluated over a much longer time scale. Individual 'brands' can come and go, but the total corporate share become the centre of long-term planning. Mitsubishi and Daewoo are good examples of this, with both companies maintaining diverse interests in a wide variety of, sometimes, unrelated markets.

It is important to recognize that, in developing countries, brands play a significantly smaller role in terms of the regular shopping process. Many products that have become brands in Western society (bread, biscuits, milk, sugar) remain as commodities that continue to be purchased loose.

As globalization is increasing, the scope and rationale for local differentiation is being reduced. In practice, the number of truly standardized global brands is limited: Burger King, BMW, Mazda, Coke and Pepsi. Many brands, like Kit Kat and Colgate, are global in name, but have shown significant differences in positioning, branding and packaging from country to country. The reality of globalization is that usually some decisions are standardized, whilst others are tailored to local needs. ClubMed attempts to standardize its villages, quality and advertising themes, but not its promotional activities and budgets; very often global brands co-exist with local brands. As Pawle (1999)[11] indicates: 'The attributes of brands are often common globally. It is remarkable how stable brand images often are in different cultures, despite somewhat different packaging in some cases and despite the lack of a global advertising campaign. There are, however, significant differences in the ways that people in different cultures respond to brand images, including how products are used.'

According to Aaker and Joachimsthaler (1999)[12] global brands are 'brands whose positioning, advertising strategy, personality, look and feel are in most respects the same from one country to another'.

Byfield and Caller (1996)[8] describe three distinct categories of global brand:

1 Long-term international brands (mostly American) that are exploiting a universal heritage
2 New products that have been developed with a global consumer in mind
3 Brands that have begun life in one or more markets and then have been exported to others.

They argue that the crucial issue is that brands hold the same values in whichever markets they are available. It is evident that brands can become irrelevant if their image is not kept in step with changes in society.

The proponents of globalization can demonstrate the enormous economies that are made when several local brands are replaced by one single world-wide offering. The opportunities to feature these brands in international media events such as the World Cup, the Olympics, Formula 1, etc., are undeniable.

Quelch (1999)[13] suggests that the degree of standardization of global brands will be dependent on the product category. In culture-bound categories like food, there will be larger cultural and national differences, but with a product like a PC the criteria are basically the same everywhere. He asserts that the impact of the Euro Zone will encourage further movement towards pan-European branding. The introduction of a single currency has made differential pricing across borders more transparent, with the consequence that brands will become subject to diversion, i.e. where parallel imports are made between high- and low-price countries. He suggests that the biggest consumers of global brands are the youth market: today, one teenager is much like any other, regardless of borders.

Duffy and Medina (1998)[14] suggest that as long as domestic environments remain fundamentally different to foreign environments, then there will be the need for adaptability.

Brand standardization is an international marketing strategy that consists of producing one product and selling it in the same way everywhere in the world, with the same specification and characteristics. Research carried out by Riesenbeck and Freeling (1991)[15] indicates that successful global marketers are those that ensure that they standardize the core elements of their brands. Their findings indicate that the companies that did not change or compromise the core elements of their brand, those that they consider to be at the heart of their business, proved most successful. Adaptation was implemented in other dimensions of the marketing mix to ensure global branding success.

Aaker and Joachimsthaler (1999)[12] suggest five guidelines to be effective in global-brand management:

1   It should include an analysis of the customers and brand associations that resonate with its competitors so it can differentiate itself from its competitors via its communication plan. Lastly, it should carry out an audit of the brand with its heritage, image, strengths and vision.

2   Fixation on product attributes should be avoided. The majority of strong brands go beyond functional attributes and deliver emotional benefits, through brand personality, user imagery, intangibles associated with the company, innovativeness or reputation for quality, and symbols associated with the brand.

3   Communication should be made effective internally throughout the company. Everyone should have a clear understanding about the company's objectives for brand building to be a success.

4   Brand equity, measurement and goals are very important; without these, brand building will be all talk and no real action. Brand equity should be measured in terms of customer awareness, customer loyalty, brand personality and associations that resonate with the public.

5   The process needs to tie in global brand strategies with country brand strategies, which can be done via a top-down approach beginning with a global brand strategy then country brand strategies following from it. The bottom-up approach would be global brand strategies built around country brand strategies. Country strategies are grouped by similarity, which can be based on market maturity or by its competitive context. Although there will be differences in brand strategies for these groupings, the global brand strategy should be able to find the common elements and, over time, should be able to capture synergies.

International branding considerations

In the development of companies, many find themselves forced to seek further opportunities to continue the process of brand expansion. In many cases, these opportunities exist by expanding into new countries. The benefits that can be derived from the economies of production and the apparent similarity of the markets in other countries have attracted some brands to expand beyond their original market places. The process of developing international brands is very similar to that adopted for national brands although, inevitably, it is both more complex and time consuming, especially if the underlying desire is to achieve parity of brand image in all of the markets in which the product is sold.

A series of fundamental questions must first be asked about how products in the category are expected to perform in different markets. The functional areas of a product may be different from country to country. The fact that many consumers in different countries all drink instant coffee, for example, should not suggest that their expectations of product performance are the same. Almost all of the Latin countries, for example, tend to drink their coffee much stronger than, say, in the UK. Offering the same blend to all markets might lead to acceptance in some, but would find rejection in most. The evaluation of the performance of washing powders might be the same in most markets (how white do they get my clothes?), but factors such as the way in which the product is used may have an important bearing. Is the penetration of automatic washing machines similar or do many consumers in some markets still wash by hand?

Understanding the brand personality is, arguably, even more important in the international context. We have seen that the dimensions of brand personality are, largely, perceptual. They relate to the images that have been created over time by the various aspects of marketing communications. Equally important, however, they relate to elements of consumer behaviour in the different markets. In some markets, the use or possession of a particular product may have no meaning beyond its functional purposes. In others, it may be regarded as a symbol of success or affluence. Setting, for advertising purposes, a product that may be viewed as aspirational in a mundane environment, though it may be a wholly appropriate setting for others, is likely to undermine the values associated with the brand. It is important to ensure that there is an adequate 'fit' between the positioning of the brand and the perceptions of the consumers in all of the markets in which it is to be sold.

Ultimately, of course, it may be possible to alter the underlying perceptions and reach a point at which all markets share a common view of the brand. Until that time is reached, however, it is important that the brand continues to deliver against the expectations of the consumers who purchase it.

Understanding the international consumer

If marketing communications demands a thorough understanding of the consumer and the environmental factors that surround them, this is even more true of marketing communications in an international context. Where we can reasonably expect to understand important facets of consumer behaviour in a domestic context, this is far less likely to be the case in different and separate markets where culture, tradition and other factors may result in vastly different meanings being attached to the communications message.

Language

Language is an obvious discriminating factor in the international context. It has been suggested that there are over 3000 different languages in current use. Some are indigenous to a single country or region; others are commonly spoken in several different countries. Many countries are multi-lingual. Canadian law requires that all product packaging be produced in both English and French. In Belgium, potential consumers may speak French or Flemish; India has over 200 distinct languages or dialects. Increasingly, packaging appears in multiple languages, which imposes restrictions on the length and nature of any promotional message that needs to be conveyed to the potential consumer.

Culture and tradition

A critical dimension of international marketing communications is the divergent nature of the cultures in which the activity will be seen. Culture, as discussed earlier, is that complex whole that includes knowledge, beliefs, art, morals, customs and the various other capabilities and habits that are acquired as a member of a particular society.

Arguably, this is one of the most difficult areas of multinational communications. Perceptions that are based on tradition and culture are extremely difficult to overcome. Fundamental areas, such as pack colours or symbols, may have totally different meanings resulting from cultural interpretation.

Culture is learned behaviour, passed on from one generation to another. Often it is a difficult barrier for the outsider to cross, substantially because we tend to observe other people in the context of our own cultural values. In many cases, the differences between societies are quite subtle and may not be immediately apparent. They may influence, for example, the ways in which people relate to each other; the roles of men and women within society; eating habits; relationships with authority; and dress habits, both within the working environment and in informal situations. Any of these elements may be a component of a marketing communications campaign that, in order to communicate effectively, must be considered within the context of the cultural values of the society in which the campaign is to be run.

When Disney introduced its theme park to Paris, it adopted the same style of operation as had been successful elsewhere. As in the USA and Japan, alcoholic drinks were banned. Subsequently, however, they were forced to change their policy when they recognized the French tradition of drinking wine with meals.

Equally, the nature of the individual purchase decision may vary as a result of cultural influences. The role of the family may, in certain circumstances, be more important in the final determination of which products and services to purchase. This is particularly true in parts of Asia. For example, the discretion over the use of income is heavily influenced by the expected contribution to the family. The tradition of deference to parental wishes affects patterns of buying in clothing, leisure expenditure, etc.

Perception

The perception of shapes, colours and symbols varies across cultures. White is the colour of birth and, in the West, it is usually associated with weddings; in China, Japan and India the colour symbolizes mourning. Green, a colour normally associated with freshness and good health in the West, is sometimes associated with disease elsewhere; the colour is favoured in Arab countries but forbidden in Indonesia. Black is often seen as the universal colour of mourning; however, in many Asian countries it is white, in Brazil it is purple, yellow in Mexico, and dark red in parts of Africa. Red suggests good fortune in China, but death in Turkey. In India the owl is a symbol of bad luck, the equivalent of the black cat. The stork, which in the West is associated with birth, symbolizes maternal death in Singapore.[16]

International marketers must gain a cultural understanding of the meaning of both colours and symbols in order to ensure that their packaging and product design and even advertising messages communicate the appropriate and desired values. As Jacobs *et al.* (1991)[17] comment, 'marketers in a particular nation often take colour for granted, having experienced certain colour associations all their lives, and do not even question whether other associations may exist in different societies.'

Signs (physical symbols that stand for something other than themselves) and rules and conventions (either implicit or explicit) are combined to form more complex messages. The successful combination of messages requires a common sharing of those same rules and conventions; the more we share the same codes, the closer our two meanings are to each other.

Motivation

Motivations are, similarly, different from one country to another, leading to difficulties in communicating aspirational 'norms' where such values either do not exist or have different parameters.

As Usenier (1996)[18] points out, it is important to consider the motivations to own, to buy, to spend, to consume, against the background of the intended market. He suggests that Maslow's 'Hierarchy of Needs' should be re-addressed in the international context. Importantly, whilst Maslow argues that needs must be satisfied at each level before moving on to the higher-order needs, this appears to be contradicted within specific societies. To some extent, the level of economic development exerts an influence. Clearly, in countries where the economies are somewhat less developed, the population, in general, tend to have more basic survival needs. In contrast, however, some of those same cultures encourage self-actualization in a manner that does not imply material consumption.

These factors apply equally to sales promotion. Several years ago, McDonalds mounted a worldwide promotion featuring the Snoopy character in a variety of national costumes. One character was given away free with every purchase and new characters were introduced at regular intervals. In most markets the promotional response was as might be expected. However, in the Far East, and particularly in Hong Kong, the promotion created mild hysteria. Consumers queued overnight prior to the release of a new Snoopy character and 'riots' took place when the outlets ran out of the new figures.

Learning and memory

The level of literacy is shaped by the education system. Prior experiences of product categories will have an important bearing upon the acceptance (or otherwise) of a new product launched into a foreign market.

The loyalty/purchasing environment

In most Western countries, consumers expect their 'favourite' brands to be available on a regular basis in the outlets they frequent. Elsewhere, factors of distribution may have an important influence on availability. In some instances, consumers become accustomed to purchasing from the product category, rather than expecting to be able to purchase any given brand. Similarly, the influence of salespersons may have greater or lesser importance in different markets.

Standards of living

Products that are consumed on a daily basis by some may be considered as luxuries by others, particularly if the relative cost is high. Cigarettes, for many purchased in packets of 20, are sold singly in some African markets, with the resultant difficulties of the lack of packaging to communicate brand values. Elsewhere, the incidence of fridges may preclude the sale of some packaged convenience foods, etc. However, it is evident that some developing markets often 'leapfrog' earlier stages of evolution that have been witnessed in the West. The mobile telephone market is evidence of this fact.

Market research will play an important part in identifying those areas of similarity in order to allow for the development of a single consistent message, if that is the objective. It should be clear that, in order to develop an effective multinational or global communications strategy, a number of 'new' dimensions will have to be considered, beyond those that would be appropriate for a single market communications strategy.

International regulations

The rules, regulations and codes of practice that govern sales promotion are far from being universal. Indeed, the application of the principles of sales promotion in the international context is fraught with difficulties. Free mail-ins, for example, are not permitted in Germany. Promotions designed to encourage consumer loyalty with the offering of collectors' schemes are similarly prohibited in Austria, Germany and some parts of Scandinavia. Self-liquidating offers may not be run in Norway and Switzerland, and special permission must first be obtained in Holland. The same problems exist with other forms of promotion and, whilst there are some movements towards common practices, at least within the EU, the situation for the moment remains somewhat confused.

It is imperative that any sales promotion planned for international implementation is checked for legal and other compliance on a country-by-country basis. It certainly cannot be assumed, as the examples above demonstrate, that simply because a promotion is 'legal' in one country, it will be equally so elsewhere.

The development of international sales promotion activity has been hampered by two important factors. Firstly, convention and usage and, secondly, the framework of legislation in which sales promotions operate.

Convention and usage

Whilst the broad scale application of sales promotional activity is commonplace in the UK and some other parts of Western Europe, different practices in each of the countries mean that the promotional tools will have greater or lesser significance. The offering of bonus packs with free product, often a standard format, is considered wasteful in countries like Japan. Similarly, free gifts tend to have less appeal in that country.

The legal framework

The single most important limitation on the development of global, or even pan-European sales promotion campaigns remains the diverse nature of the legislative framework in which such activity must operate. Several examples serve to illustrate the difficulties that confront the sales promotion planner.

In Italy, promoters are required to pay 55 per cent tax, in advance, on any prizes they intend to award in a competition. French products rarely offer extra product for free because the amount of free fill is restricted to 7 per cent. In Germany, there are no banded offers, such as three for two, as these are banned; similarly, cash discounts to the consumer are limited to 3 per cent in that country. The Grand Prix award-winning promotion for Cadbury in the ISP Sales Promotion awards offered an instant-win facility, but could not be run in Ireland where the interpretation of what constitutes a lottery rather than a competition is different from that in the UK.

The International Sales Promotion agency IMP (now Arc) developed a guide to the legal restrictions on sales promotion activity, which is reproduced below with their permission.

Table 15.1

	UK	Irish Republic	Spain	Germany	France	Denmark	Belgium	Netherlands	Portugal	Italy
On-pack price reductions	Y	Y	Y	Y	Y	Y	Y	Y	Y	Y
Banded offers	Y	Y	Y	C	Y	C	N	Y	Y	Y
In-pack premiums	Y	Y	Y	C	C	C	Y	C	Y	Y
Multiple purchase offers	Y	Y	Y	C	Y	C	C	Y	Y	Y
Extra product	Y	Y	Y	C	Y	Y	C	C	Y	Y
Free product	Y	Y	Y	Y	Y	Y	C	Y	Y	Y
Reusable pack	Y	Y	Y	Y	Y	Y	Y	Y	Y	Y
Free mail ins	Y	Y	Y	N	Y	C	Y	Y	Y	Y
With purchase premiums	Y	Y	Y	C	Y	C	C	C	Y	Y
Cross-product offers	Y	Y	Y	C	Y	C	N	C	Y	Y
Collector devices	Y	Y	Y	C	C	C	C	C	Y	Y
Competitions	Y	Y	Y	C	C	C	Y	C	Y	Y
Self-liquidating premiums	Y	Y	Y	Y	Y	Y	Y	C	Y	Y
Free draws	Y	Y	Y	N	Y	N	N	N	Y	Y
Share outs	Y	Y	Y	N	C	N	N	N	Y	C
Sweepstake/lottery	C	C	C	C	C	N	C	C	C	C
Money-off vouchers	Y	Y	Y	N	Y	C	Y	Y	Y	C
Money-off next purchase	Y	Y	Y	N	Y	N	Y	Y	Y	C
Cash backs	Y	Y	Y	C	Y	Y	Y	Y	Y	N
In-store demos	Y	Y	Y	Y	Y	Y	Y	Y	Y	Y

Y: Permitted; N: Not Permitted; C: May be permitted with certain conditions

Table 15.1
cont'd

	Greece	Luxembourg	Austria	Finland	Norway	Sweden	Switzerland	Russia	Hungary	Czech Republic
On-pack price reductions	Y	Y	Y	Y	C	Y	Y	Y	Y	Y
Banded offers	Y	N	C	C	C	C	N	Y	Y	Y
In-pack premiums	Y	N	C	Y	N	C	N	Y	Y	Y
Multiple purchase offers	Y	N	C	C	Y	C	N	C	Y	Y
Extra product	Y	Y	C	Y	C	C	C	Y	Y	Y
Free product	Y	Y	Y	Y	Y	Y	Y	Y	Y	Y
Reusable pack	Y	Y	C	Y	Y	Y	Y	Y	Y	Y
Free mail ins	Y	C	N	Y	Y	N	N	Y	Y	Y
With purchase premiums	Y	N	C	Y	C	C	N	Y	Y	Y
Cross-product offers	Y	N	C	C	N	C	N	Y	Y	Y
Collector devices	Y	N	N	C	N	N	N	Y	Y	Y
Competitions	Y	C	C	Y	C	Y	Y	Y	Y	Y
Self-liquidating premiums	Y	N	Y	Y	Y	Y	N	Y	Y	Y
Free draws	Y	N	N	Y	N	N	N	Y	C	Y
Share outs	Y	N	N	C	C	N	N	Y	Y	Y
Sweepstake/lottery	C	N	C	Y	N	N	N	Y	C	C
Money-off vouchers	Y	C	C	C	N	C	N	Y	Y	Y
Money-off next purchase	Y	N	N	C	N	N	N	Y	Y	Y
Cash backs	Y	N	C	C	C	Y	N	Y	Y	Y
In-store demos	Y	Y	Y	Y	Y	Y	Y	Y	C	Y

Y: Permitted; N: Not Permitted; C: May be permitted with certain conditions

Pan-European promotions

With the globalization of markets, marketers are striving for a common and consistent promotional message. Apart from the economies of scale to be gained, a consistent message can help to strengthen the position of the brand in those markets in which it is sold. However, the difficulties in achieving promotional consistency are significant, as a direct result of the legal and regulatory structures that are in place.

Pan-European promotional activity demands an even greater level of simplicity than would normally be applicable. The lack of a consistent regulatory framework means that any promotion must meet a diversity of different rules and standards.

According to a study by Havas (1998)[19] the use of sales promotion differs markedly between countries.

Table 15.2

Country	Share of promotion expenditures in communications budget (1997)	Expenditures in local currencies
Germany	15.7%	22,054 m DM
UK	17.2%	£2,965 m
France	15.9%	25,109 m FF
Italy	22.2%	7,735 bn IL
Spain	16.6%	212,217 m ESP
Netherlands	19.7%	3,096 NLG
Belgium	35.2%	60,694 BEF
Switzerland	19.5%	1,664 m CHF

Despite this, as Huff and Alden (1998)[20] argue, 'throughout the world, consumer sales promotions are an integral part of the marketing mix for many consumer products.'

They indicate that marketing managers use price-oriented promotions such as coupons, rebates and price discounts to increase sales and market share, entice trial and encourage brand switching. Non-price promotions such as sweepstakes, frequent user clubs and premiums add excitement and value to brands and may encourage brand loyalty. In addition, consumers like promotions. They provide utilitarian benefits such as monetary savings, added value, increased quality and convenience, as well as hedonic benefits such as entertainment, exploration and self-expression.

Burger King separately targeted adults and children in a global link-up with the release of the final Star Wars film, giving away 1 million prizes in the UK alone. The promotion, featured in 60 territories, consisted of a scratch card competition aimed at adults, with a kid's meals tie-in for younger customers. Every adult buying one of Burger King's meals got a free scratch card. Prizes included two Mitsubishi Colt cars, Virgin holidays worth £2500 and Sony Plasma televisions.

However, as Kashani and Quelch (1990)[21] suggest, sales promotion has, for a considerable period, remained a substantially local concern. They indicate that, even within large companies, local managers have retained a considerable amount of latitude in both the design and implementation of sales promotion programmes.

They cite Nestlé as being typical of the problems faced by many multi-national companies. Whilst the company maintained control of branding and packaging, most of the remaining decisions, including consumer and trade promotions, remained with the company's local operations throughout the world.

The consequence of this policy has been reduced brand profitability, contradictory brand communication and the potential for a dilution of the brand franchise with consumers.

Increasingly, many international companies are seeking to draw back control over this important area of activity. There are several reasons for their concern:

- The increased levels of promotional expenditure – For many major organizations, the combined cost of consumer and trade promotional activity now exceeds their investment in advertising. The cost of sales promotion has risen world-wide and with promotions now representing a major budgetary item, central management has been increasingly concerned to exercise control over how that money is spent together with ways of improving efficiencies and making savings.

- The increasing complexity of promotions – Many companies are concerned that their local management is not equipped to deal with the range of issues concerned with promotion design, execution and follow-up.

- Repetition of success – With central co-ordination, companies are recognizing that successful activities do not have to remain local. The knowledge gained from implementation in one area or country can often be replicated across entire regions or even the world (see MacDonald's example of the Snoopy promotion).

- Trans-national trade – As trade barriers are removed, many brands are being sold in different countries. This is a direct consequence of the desire on the part of transnational retailers to operate central buying policies. Satisfying these needs is, increasingly, a concern for the major companies, as is the requirement to ensure that promotional activity satisfies the wide variety of local regulations.

- However, the biggest concern is the impact of dissonant promotional activity on the brand personality. As multi-nationals strive to achieve constancy of brand communication, it is no longer tenable for their efforts to be undermined by local promotions that are inconsistent with the overall desired brand image.

It is generally agreed that for promotions to be effective they must be communicated clearly and simply. This is especially true when the work is implemented on a pan-European or international basis. There are inevitable problems related to the different interpretations that local communities place on the meaning of specific offers. Moreover, what is acceptable in one market may be regarded as being ill-suited to another.

Having said that, there remain a number of factors restraining the international development of sales promotion:

1 Economic development – limited purchasing power and lower levels of literacy in some markets pose particular difficulties. Expensive value-added promotions may put them out of reach of consumers in some markets.

2 Market maturity – given that products may be at different stages of evolution in different markets, implementing the same promotional solution may be inappropriate.

3 Consumer perceptions – consumer and trade perceptions of promotional offers may often be culturally inspired.

4 Regulations – these differ widely across countries. They govern both the types of promotion that are permissible and the manner in which they are presented.

5 Trade structure – this differs widely across nations. In some instances, retailing is highly concentrated; elsewhere it is far more fragmented.

6 There remains the need to deal with country-specific issues.

Case study

SRI LANKA TOURISM

In the early 1980s Sri Lanka was emerging as a significant island national destination with huge tourism potential, but subsequent decades of civil war and political conflict constrained the industry enormously. However, fortunes began to improve in 2002 with rising hopes for a resolution to the conflict.

By 2002, arrivals were some 400 000, an increase of 20 per cent over the previous year. The improvement continued into 2003 with a 30 per cent overall increase in March. However, the growth in the island as a tourist destination suffered a major setback following the tragedy in South-east Asia of the tsunami disaster at the end of 2004. Concern about the damage caused by the tsunami to the tourism infrastructure led to a dramatic decline in tourism throughout the region. The Sri Lankan airline saw a massive drop in bookings and was forced to fly well below capacity. It is estimated that Sri Lanka Airlines was running at less than 50 per cent capacity immediately following the tsunami and, bearing in mind that some of these passengers would be involved in business travel or visiting friends and relatives, the marked impact on tourism was immediately apparent.

Tourism to Sri Lanka represents the fourth largest generator of foreign earnings to the country. With receipts estimated to be worth $253 million in 2002. It was imperative that the decline in tourism should be arrested as soon as possible.

Immediately following the tsunami disaster the Sri Lanka Tourist Office determined to regenerate tourism to the country. To do so, it adopted a standard sales promotion technique: a two for one offer. Unable to incentivize consumers directly, it made arrangements for the offer to be made available through selected travel companies who were already established in the provision of trips to Sri Lanka. These included Kuoni and Voyages Jules Verne, amongst others.

The take-up of the offer was immediate and substantial. Significant numbers of tourists were attracted to the island. These would be significant in generating the important word of mouth recommendations to overcome perceptions that the country had been significantly affected by the disaster.

Unlike other tourist destinations that had suffered disasters that impacted on the attractiveness of their countries as tourism locations, the tourist office reacted rapidly. In fact, the offer appeared in selected newspapers within 8 weeks of the occurrence of the disaster.

Whilst signs of the disaster in the affected areas are still apparent, there remained a substantial amount of the country to be explored, including all of the important heritage and cultural sights and most of the nature reserves and wildlife sanctuaries.

Although it is too early to estimate the longer-term impact of the promotional offer, the significance lies in the fact that this is possibly the first time that a country has reacted so swiftly to recognize the importance of regenerating tourism. It is certainly to be commended as an example to other countries that suffer similar catastrophes, whether natural or the result of human actions.

Questions

1 Why are brands increasingly seeking to appeal to a global audience?
2 What factors must be explored in the development of international brands?
3 How will differences in international law and regulations affect the ability to develop international promotions?
4 Identify the factors constraining the development of international promotional activity.

References

Chapter 1

1 Van Waterschoot, W. and Van den Bulte, C. (1992), The 4P classification of the marketing mix revisited, *Journal of Marketing*, 56 Oct.

2 Mintel (1996), *Special Report on Sales Promotion*, April.

3 Mintel (2000), *Special Report on Sales Promotion*, Jan.

4 Lichtenstein, D.R., Burton, S. and Netemeyer, R. (1997), An examination of deal proneness across sales promotion types: a consumer segmentation perspective, *Journal of Retailing*, 73(2) Summer.

5 Mela, C., Jedidi, K. and Bowman, D. (1998), The long term impact of promotions on consumer stockpiling behaviour, *Journal of Marketing Research*, 35(2) May.

6 Wright, C. (1997), *Survey of Promotional Practices*, Carol Wright Promotions Inc.

7 Bateman, J. (1998), Winning the promotional race, *Marketing Week*, 5 Feb.

8 Ailawadi, K.L., Neslin, S.A. and Gedenk, K. (2001), Pursuing the value conscious consumer: store brands versus national brand promotions, *Journal of Marketing*, 65(1).

9 Buzzell, R. D., Quelch J.A. and Salmon, W. J. (1990), The costly bargain of trade promotion, *Harvard Business Review*, March/April.

10 Stewart, D. and Gallen B. (1998), The promotional planning process and its impact on consumer franchise building, The case of fast moving consumer goods in New Zealand, *Journal of Product and Brand Management*, 7(6).

11 Flanagan, J. (1988), Sales promotion: the emerging alternative to brand-building advertising, *Journal of Consumer Marketing*, 5(2).

12 Hardie, B. (1996), Who benefits from price promotion? *Business Strategy Review*, 7(4) Winter.

13 www.isp.org

14 Shimp, T.A. (2000), *Advertising Promotion*, 5th Ed, The Dryden Press.

15 Kotler, P., Armstrong, G., Saunders, J. and Wong, V. (1999), *Principles of Marketing*, 2nd European Ed, Prentice Hall.

16 Schultz, D.E., Robinson, W.A., and Petrison, L.A. (1992), *Sales Promotion Essentials*, 2nd Ed, NTC Business Books.

17 Direct Marketing Association (1994).

18 Toop A. (1994), *Marketing*, July 28.

19 Ehrenberg, A.S.C., Hammond, K. and Goodhart, G.J. (1991), *The After Effects of Large Scale Consumer Promotions*, London Business School.

20 Ehrenberg, A.S.C., Hammond, K. and Goodhart, G.J. (1994), The after effects of price related consumer promotions, *Journal of Advertising Research*, 34(4) Jul–Aug.

21 Jones, J.P. (1990), The double jeopardy of sales promotion, *Harvard Business Review*, Sept/Oct.

22 Blattberg, R.C. and Neslin, S.A. (1990), *Sales Promotion: Concepts, Methods and Strategies*, Prentice Hall.

23 Broadbent, A. (1998), *Marketing Business*, March.

24 Chandon, P. (1995), Consumer research on sales promotions: a state of the art literature review, *Journal of Marketing Management*, 11(5) July.

25 Gupta, S., Lehmann, D.R. and Mela, C.F. (1997), The long term impact of promotion and advertising on consumer brand choice, *Journal of Marketing Research*, May.

26 Peattie, S. and Peattie, K. (1994), Sales promotion, In Baker, M.J., *The Marketing Book*, 3rd Ed, Butterworth Heinemann.

27 Peattie K., Peattie S. and Emafo, E.B. (1997), Promotional competitions as a strategic marketing weapon, *Journal of Marketing Management*, 13 Nov.

28 Peattie, S. (2002), Applying sales promotion competitions to non-profit contexts, *International Journal of Nonprofit and Voluntary Sector Marketing*, 8(4).

29 Robinson, W.A. and Hauri, C. (1995), *Promotional Marketing Ideas and Techniques for Success in Sales Promotion*, NTC Business Books.

30 Gay, S. (1997), Promotional challenge, *Marketing Week*, 11 Sept.

31 Aaker, D.A. (1991), *Managing Brand Equity*, The Free Press.

32 Bunyard, J. (1999), If advertising alone fails to boost sales, developments in FMCG, *Admap*, 34(5) May.

33 Davis, S., Inman, J.J. and McAlister, L. (1992), Promotion has a negative effect on brand evaluations – or does it? Additional disconfirming evidence, *Journal of Marketing Research*, 29(1).

34 Raghubir, P., Inman, J.J. and Grande, H. (2004), The three faces of consumer promotions, California Management Review, 46(40).

35 Ingold, P. (1995), *Promotion des Ventes et Action Commerciale*, Vuibert.

36 Daugherty, P.J., Fox, R.J. and Stephenson, F.J. (1993), Frequency marketing programs: a clarification with strategic marketing implications, *Journal of Promotion Management*.

Chapter 2

1 Peattie, S. (1998), Promotional competitions as a marketing tool in food retailing, *British Food Journal*.

2 Blattberg, R.C. and Neslin, S.A. (1990), *Sales Promotion: Concepts, Methods and Strategies*, Prentice Hall.

3 Peattie, S. and Peattie, K. (1994), Promoting financial services with glittering prizes, *International Journal of Bank Marketing*, 12(6).

4 Ailawadi, K.L., Lehmann, D.R. and Neslin, S.A. (2001), Market response to a major policy change in the marketing mix: learning from Procter & Gambles value pricing strategy, *Journal of Marketing*, 65(1).

5 Ghosh, A.K. (1997), Targeted promotions using scanner panel data, *Journal of Product and Brand Management*, 6(6).

6 Chandon, P., Wansink, B. and Laurent, G. (2000), A benefit congruency framework of sales promotion effectiveness, *Journal of Marketing*, 64(4 Oct).

7 Ehrenberg, A.S.C., Hammond, K. and Goodhardt, G.J. (1991), *The After Effects of Large Scale Consumer Promotions*, London Business School.

8 Ehrenberg, A.S.C. (1994), An academics agenda for the nineties, *Admap*, September.

9 Jones, J.P. (1990), The double jeopardy of sales promotion, *Harvard Business Review*, Sept/Oct.

10 Anschuetz, N. (1997), Profiting from the '80-20' rule of thumb, *Journal of Advertising Research*, Nov/Dec.

11 Dodson, J.A., Tybout, A.M. and Sternthal, B. (1978), The impact of deals and deal retraction on brand switching, *Journal of Marketing Research*, 15(1).

12 Lattin, J.M. and Bucklin, R.E. (1989), Reference effects of price and promotion on brand choice behaviour, *Journal of Marketing Research*, 26(4)

13 Kalwani, M.U., Yim, C.K., Rinne, H.J. and Sugita, Y. (1990), A price expectations model of customer brand choice, *Journal of Marketing Research*, 27.

14 Bawa, K. and Shoemaker, R.W. (1987), The effect of a direct mail coupon on brand choice behaviour, *Journal of Marketing Research*, 24 Nov.

15 Hoek, J. and Roelants, L. (1991), Some effects of price discounting on discounted and competing brands' sales, *Marketing Bulletin*, 2.

16   Low, G.S. and Mohr, J.J. (1992), The advertising sales promotion trade-off: theory and practice, *Marketing Science Institute*, Report Number 92, October.

17   Doyle, P. and Saunders, J. (1985), The lead effect of marketing decisions, *Journal of Marketing Research*, 22(1).

18   PIMS website

19   Jorgensen, S. and Zaccour, G. (2003), A differential game of retailer promotions, *Automatica*, 39(7).

20   Davis, S., Inman, J.J. and McAlister L. (1992), Promotion has a negative effect on brand evaluations – or does it? Additional disconfirming evidence, *Journal of Marketing Research*, 29 (1).

21   Neslin S.A. and Shoemaker R.W. (1989), An alternative explanation for lower repeat purchases after promotion purchases, *Journal of Marketing Research*, 26(2) May.

22   Lambin, J.J. (2000), *Market Driven Management*, Macmillan Business.

23   Dekimpe, M., Hanssens, D. and Silva-Risso, J. (1999), Long-run effects of price promotions in scanner markets, *Journal of Econometrics*, 89.

Chapter 3

1.   Quelch, J.A. and Harding, D. (1996), Brands versus private labels: fighting to win, *Harvard Business Review*, 74(1).

2.   Buck, S. and Passingham, J. (1997), *Brands vs. Private Label*, TN AGB.

3.   Buck, S. (2000), The triumph of the premium brand, *Market Leader*, Winter.

4.   Sethuraman, R. (1992), Understanding cross-category differences in private label shares of grocery products, *Wall Street Journal*, 14 Feb.

5.   Garretson, J.A., Fisher, D. and Burton, S. (2002), Antecedents of private label attitude and national brand promotions: similarities and differences, *Journal of Retailing*, 78(2).

6.   ACNielsen (1993), Sales promotion and the information revolution, *Admap*, Jan.

7.   Ehrenberg, A.C.S. (1997), How do consumers come to buy a new brand, *Admap*, March.

8.   Ehrenberg, A.C.S. (1988), *Repeat Buying: Facts, Theory and Applications*, Charles Griffin.

9.   Ehrenberg, A.C.S., Long, S. and Kennedy, R. (2000), Competitive brands' user-profiles hardly differ, MRS Conference Paper.

10. Ailawadi, K.L. and Neslin, S.A. (1998), The effect of promotion on consumption: Buying more and consuming it faster, *Journal of Marketing Research*, 45(3) Aug.

11. Ailawadi, K.L., Lehmann, D.R. and Neslin, S.A. (2001), Market response to a major policy change in the marketing mix: learning from Procter & Gamble's value pricing strategy, *Journal of Marketing*, 65(1).

12. Mela, C., Jedidi, K. and Bowman, D. (1998), The long term impact of promotions on consumer stockpiling behaviour, *Journal of Marketing Research*, 35(2) May.

13. Fraser, C. and Hite, R. (1990), Varied consumer responses to promotions: a case for response based decision making, *Journal of the Market Research Society*, 32(3).

14. Anschuetz, N. (1997), Point of view: building brand popularity – the myth of segmenting to brand success, *Journal of Advertising Research*, 37(1) Jan/Feb.

15. Hooper, M. cited in Miller, R. (1998), Packing a real punch, *Marketing*, 5 Mar.

16. ACNielsen, (1997) Promofocus.

17. Fearne, A., Donaldson, A. and Normington, P. (1999), Pricing strategy and practice- the impact of alternative promotions on the spirits category: evidence from the UK, *Journal of Product and Brand Management*, 8(5)

18. Meer, D. (1995), System beaters, brand loyals and deal shoppers: new insights into the role of price, *Journal of Advertising Research*, 35(3) May/June.

19. Zeithaml, V.A. (1982), Consumer response to in-store price information environments, *Journal of Consumer Research*, 8 March.

20. Dickson, P.R. and Sawyer, A.G. (1990), The price knowledge and search of supermarket shoppers, *Journal of Marketing*, 54(3) July.

21. Vanhuele, M. and Dreze, X. (2002), Measuring the price knowledge shoppers bring to the store, *Journal of Marketing*, 66.

22. Schultz, D.E., Robinson, W.A. and Petrison, L.A. (1993), *Sales Promotion Essentials*, 2nd Ed., NTC Business Books.
23. Mintel (1996), Special Report on Sales Promotion.
24. Mintel (2000), Special Report on Sales Promotion.
25. Bawa, K. and Shoemaker, R.W. (1987), The coupon-prone consumer: some findings based on purchase behaviour across product classes, *Journal of Marketing*, 51(4).
26. Blattberg, R.C., Buesing, T., Peacock, P. and Sen, S.K. (1978), Identifying the deal prone segment, *Journal of Marketing Research*, 15 Aug.
27. Narasimhan, C. (1984), A price discrimination theory of coupons, *Marketing Science*, 3(2).
28. Feick, L. and Price, L. (1987), The market maven: a diffuser of marketplace information, *Journal of Marketing*, 51(1).
29. Lichtenstein, D.R., Netemeyer, R.G. and Burton S. (1990), Distinguishing coupon proneness from value consciousness: an acquisition-transaction utility theory perspective, *Journal of Marketing*, 54(3).
30. Mittal, B. (1994), An integrated framework for relating diverse consumer characteristics to supermarket coupon redemption, *Journal of Marketing Research*, 31 Nov.
31. Blattberg, R.C. and Neslin, S.A. (1990), *Sales Promotion: Concepts, Methods and Strategies*, Prentice Hall.
32. Griffiths, C. (1992), Brand as verb, *Admap*, July/Aug.
33. Lury, A. (1998), *Brandwatching*, Black Hall Publishing.
34. Biggest Brands (2003), *Marketing*, 25.8.2004 based on ACNielsen figures
35. Buzzell, R.D. and Gale, B.T. (1987), *The PIMS Principles: Linking Strategy to Performance*, Collier Macmillan.
36. *Financial Times* (1997), 23 June.
37. Brandt, M. and Johnson, G. (1997), *PowerBranding™: Building Technology Brands for Competitive Advantage*, International Data Group.
38. Biel, A.L. (1991), The brandscape: converting brand image into equity, *Admap*, Oct.
39. Bennett, P.D. (ed.) (1988), *Dictionary of Marketing Terms*, American Marketing Association.
40. De Chernatony, L. and McDonald, M. (1992), *Creating Powerful Brands*, Butterworth Heinemann.
41. Clifton, R. and Maughan E. (2000), *The Future of Brands*, Macmillan Press.
42. Sampson, P. (1993), A better way to measure brand image, *Admap*, July/ Aug.
43. Duckworth, G. (1996), *Advertising Works 9*, IPA/NTC.
44. Davis, S. (2002), Brand asset management: how business can profit from the power of the brand, *Journal of Consumer Marketing*, v19, i4.
45. Southgate, P. (1994), *Total Branding by Design*, Kogan Page.
46. Agres, S.J. and Dubitsky, T.M. (1996), Changing needs for brands, *Journal of Advertising Research*, 36(1).
47. Barnard, N., Ehrenberg, A.C.S. and Scriven, J. (1998), Branding and values, *Admap*, June.
48. Roth, M.S. (1992), Depth versus breadth strategies for global brand image management, *Journal of Advertising*, 21(2).
49. Park, C.W., Jaworski. B.J. and MacInnis, J.D. (1986), Strategic brand concept-image management, *Journal of Marketing*, 50.
50. Reynolds, T. and Gutman, J. (1984), Advertising as image management, *Journal of Advertising Research*, Feb/March.
51. Kotler, P. and Armstrong, G. (1996), *The Principles of Marketing*, 7th Ed., Prentice Hall.

Chapter 4

1. White, R. (1998), The blind alleys of recall, *Admap*, Jan.
2. Ong, B.S., Ho, F.N. and Tripp, C. (1997), Consumer perceptions of bonus packs: an exploratory analysis, *Journal of Consumer Marketing*, 14(2) Spring.

3.   Marklin, J. (1969), *The Psychology of Consumer Behaviour*, Prentice Hall.
4.   Henderson Britt, S. (1978), *Psychological Principles of Marketing and Consumer Behaviour*, Lexington Books.
5.   Stern, B. B. (1994), A revised communication model for advertising: multiple dimensions of the source, the message and the recipient, *Journal of Advertising*, 23(2).
6.   Chandon, P. (1995), Consumer research on sales promotion: a state of the art literature review, *Journal of Marketing Management*, 11(5) July.
7.   Strang, R., Marketing and sales promotions, special report, *Sales and Marketing Management Magazine*.
8.   Miller, R. L. (1962), Dr. Weber and the consumer, *Journal of Marketing*, 26.
9.   Peattie, S. and Peattie, K. (1995), In Baker, M., *The Marketing Book*, 5th Ed., Butterworth Heinemann.
10. Gupta, S., Lehmann, D.R. and Mela, C.F. (1997), The long-term impact of promotion and advertising on consumer brand choice, *Journal of Marketing Research*, 34.3 May.
11. Ailawadi, K.L. and Neslin, S.A. (1998), The effect of promotion on consumption: buying more and consuming it faster, *Journal of Marketing Research*, 35 Aug.
12. Guiltinan, J.P. and Paul, G.W. (1991), *Marketing Management: Strategies and Programs*, 4th Ed, McGraw Hill.
13. Lambin, J.-J. (2000), *Market Driven Management*, Macmillan Business.
14. Raghubir, P. and Corfman, K.M. (1999), When do price promotions affect pre-trial brand evaluations? *Journal of Marketing Research*, 36(2) May.
15. Mela, C.F., Gupta, S. and Lehmann, D.R. (1997), The long term impact of promotion and advertising on consumer brand choice, *Journal of Marketing Research*, 34 (2), May.
16. Ehrenberg, A.S.C., Hammond, K. and Goodhart, G.J. (1991), *The After Effects of Large Scale Consumer Promotions*, London Business School.
17. Gardener, E. and Trivedi, M. (1998), A communication framework to evaluate sales promotion strategies, *Journal of Advertising Research*, May–June.
18. Bawa, K. and Shoemaker, R.W. (1987), The effect of a direct mail coupon on brand choice behaviour, *Journal of Marketing Research*, 24, Nov.
19. Ehrenberg, A.S.C., Hammond, K. and Goodhart, G.J. (1994), The after effects of price related consumer promotions, *Journal of Advertising Research*, 34(4) Jul/Aug.
20. Gaudagni, P.M. and Little, J.D. (1983), A logit model of brand choice calibrate on scanner data, *Marketing Science*, 2(3).
21. Neslin, S.A. and Shoemaker, R.W. (1989), An alternative explanation for lower repeat purchases after promotion purchases, *Journal of Marketing Research*, 26(2) May.
22. Peattie. K., Peattie, S. and Emafo, E.B. (1993), Sales promotion – playing to win, *Journal of Marketing Management*, 9.
23. Jones, J.P. (1990), The double jeopardy of sales promotion, *Harvard Business Review*, Sept/Oct.
24. Huff, L. and Alden, D.L. (1998), An investigation of consumer response to sales promotions in developing markets, *Journal of Advertising Research*, 38 May/June.
25. St Elmo Lewis cited in Strong, E.K. (1925), *The Psychology of Selling*, McGraw-Hill.
26. Strong, E.K. (1925), *The Psychology of Selling*, McGraw-Hill.
27. Barry, T.E. and Howard, D.J. (1990), A review and critique of the hierarchy of effects, *International Journal of Advertising*, 9(2).
28. McDonald, C. (1992), *How Advertising Works, A Review of Current Thinking*, The Advertising Association/NTC Publications.
29. McAlister, L. (1986), *Continued Research into Sales Promotion: Product Line Management Issues*, Marketing Science Institute.
30. Pringle, H. and Thompson, M. (1999), *Brand Spirit: How Cause Related Marketing Builds Brands*, John Wiley and Sons.
31. Miller, R. (1997), Does everyone have a price? *Marketing*, 24 April.

Chapter 5

1. Jones, J.P. (1990), The double jeopardy of sales promotion, *Harvard Business Review*, Sept/Oct.
2. Ehrenberg, A.S.C. (1993), If you're so strong, why aren't you bigger? Making the case against brand equity, *Admap*, 28(10) October.
3. Mela, C.F., Gupta, S. and Lehman, D.R. (1997), The long term impact of promotion and advertising on consumer brand choice, *Journal of Marketing Research*, 34(2), May.
4. Buck, S. (2000), The triumph of the premium brand, *Market Leader*, 11, Winter.
5. Griffith, D.E. and Rust, R.T. (1997), The price of competitiveness in competitive pricing, *Journal of the Academy of Marketing Science*, 25/2 Spring.
6. Prendergast, M. (1993), *For God, Country and Coca Cola*, Phoenix.
7. Biel, A.L. (1990), Strong brand, high spend: tracking relationships between the marketing mix and brand values, *Admap*, Nov.
8. Ehrenberg, A.S.C., Scriven J. and Barnard, N. (1997), Advertising and Price, *Journal of Advertising Research*, 37 (3) May–June.
9. Mitchell, A. (1999), Technology breaks chain linking price with value, *Marketing Week*, Nov 11.
10. Ambler, T. (1999), Kicking price promotion habits is like getting off heroin, *Marketing*, May 27.
11. Light, L. (1998), Brand loyalty management: the new marketing basic, *Admap*, May.
12. Raghubir, P. and Corfman, K.M. (1999), When do price promotions affect pre-trial brand evaluations? *Journal of Marketing Research*, 36(2) May.
13. Campbell, L. (1996), *Promotions and Incentives Journal*, Nov/Dec.
14. Head, M. (1998), Define the strategy, *Admap*, May.
15. Schultz, D., Robinson, W.A. and Petrison, L.A. (1992), *Sales Promotion Essentials*, 2nd Ed., NTC Business Books.
16. Drake, M. In Bradley, U., *Applied Marketing and Social Research*, 2nd Ed., Chichester.
17. Davies, M. (1992), Sales promotions as a competitive strategy, *Management Decision*, 30(7).
18. O'Malley, L. (1993), Sales promotion and the information revolution, *Admap*, Jan.
19. Aaker, D.A. (1991), *Managing Brand Equity*, The Free Press.
20. Gay, S. (1997), Promotional challenge, *Marketing Week*, 11 Sept.
21. Peattie, K., Peattie, S. and Emafo, E.B. (1997), Promotional competitions as a strategic marketing weapon, *Journal of Marketing Management*, 13 Nov.
22. Lee, C.W. (2002), Sales promotion as strategic communications: the case of Singapore, *Journal of Product and Brand Management*, 11(2).
23. Flanagan, J. (1988), Sales promotion: the emerging alternative to brand-building advertising, *Journal of Consumer Marketing*, 5(2).
24. Biel, A.L. (1999), Long-term profitability: advertising vs sales promotion, *Admap*.
25. Stewart, D. and Gallen, B. (1998), The promotional planning process and its impact on consumer franchise building, The case of fast moving consumer goods in New Zealand, *Journal of Product and Brand Management*, 7(6).
26. Richards, T. (1998), Buying loyalty versus building commitment – developing the optimum retention strategy, *Marketing and Research Today*, 26(1) Feb.
27. Bunyard, J. (1999), If advertising alone fails to boost sales: developments in FMCG, *Admap*, 34(5) May.
28. Quester, P. and Farrelly, F. (1998), Brand association and memory decay effects of sponsorship: the case of the Australian formula one Grand Prix, *Journal of Product and Brand Management*, 7(6).
29. Davies, G. (1997), Loyalty is a gift – it can't be bought, *Admap*, 32(7) July/Aug.
30. De Chernatony, L. and Dall'Olmo Riley, F. (1998), Expert practitioners' views on the role of brands: implications for marketing communications, *Journal of Marketing Communications*, 4(2) June.
31. Davis, S., Inman, J.J. and McAlister, L. (1992), Promotion has a negative effect on brand evaluations – or does it? Additional disconfirming evidence, *Journal of Marketing Research*, 29(1) Feb.
32. Miller, R. (1998), Packing a real punch, *Marketing*, Mar 5.
33. Hallberg, G. (1995), *All Consumers are not Created Equal*, John Wiley and Sons.

34. Graeff, T.R. (1995), Product comprehension and promotional strategies, *Journal of Consumer Marketing*, 12(2) Spring.

35. Swait, J. and Erdem, T. (2002), The effects of temporal consistency of sales promotions and availability on consumer choice behaviour, *Journal of Marketing Research*, 34 Aug.

36. Hardy, K.G. and Magrath, A.J. (1990), Levering strategies for sales promotions, *Business Quarterly*, 54(3) Winter.

37. Ehrenberg, A.S.C, Hammond, K. and Goodhardt, G.J. (1991), *The After Effects of Large Scale Consumer Promotions*, London Business School.

38. McAlister, L. and Lattin, J.M. (1983), Identifying Substitute and Complementary Relationships Revealed by Consumer Variety Seeking Behaviour, MIT working paper, Sept.

Chapter 6

1. Ailawadi, K.L., Lehmann, D.R. and Neslin, S.A. (2001), Market response to a major policy change in the marketing mix: learning from Procter & Gamble's value pricing strategy, *Journal of Marketing*, 65(1).

2. Farris, P.W. and Buzzell, R.D. (1979), Why advertising and promotional costs vary: some cross-sectional analyses, *Journal of Marketing*, 43 Fall.

3. Low, G.S. and Mohr, J.J. (2000), Advertising versus sales promotion: a brand management perspective, *Journal of Product and Brand Management*, 9(6).

4. Connolly, A. and Davidson, L. (1996), How does design affect decisions at point of sale? *Journal of Brand Management*, 4(2) Oct.

5. Walters, R.G. (1989), An empirical investigation into retailer response to manufacturer trade promotions, *Journal of Retailing*, 65.

6. Krishna, A. (1991), Effect of dealing patterns on consumer perceptions of deal frequency and willingness to pay, *Journal of Marketing Research*, 28(4) Nov.

7. Gurumurthy, K. and Little, J.D.C. (1987), A pricing model based on perception theories and its testing on scanner panel data. MIT working paper.

8. Stewart, D. (1996), Allocating the promotional budget: revisiting the advertising and promotion-to-sales ratio, *Market Intelligence and Planning*, 14(4) Apr.

9. White, R. (2002), Sales promotion and the brand, *Admap*, April.

10. Zhang, Z., Krishna, K., Aradna, D. and Sanjay, K. (2000), The optimal choice of promotional vehicles: front-loaded or rear-loaded incentives? *Management Science*, 46(3).

11. Nair, S.K. and Taresewich, P. (2003), A model and solution method for multi-period sales promotional design, *European Journal of Operational Research*, 150(3).

12. Porter, A.L. (1993), Strengthening coupon offers by requiring more from the customer, *Journal of Consumer Marketing*, 10(2).

13. Tan, S.-J. and Chua, S.-H. (2004), "While stocks last!" Impact of framing on consumers' perceptions of sales promotions, *Journal of Consumer Marketing*, 21(5).

14. Feary, H. (1998), Watch your spending, *The Grocer*.

15. Stewart, D. and Gallen, B. (1998), The promotional planning process and its impact on consumer franchise building: the case of fast moving consumer goods in New Zealand, *Journal of Product and Brand Management*, 7(6).

16. Neslin, S.A. and Stone, L.S. (1996), Consumer inventory sensitivity and the post-promotion dip, *Marketing Letters*, 7(1).

17. Van Heerde, H.J., Leeflang, P.S.H. and Wittink, D.R. (2000), The estimation of pre-and postpromotion dips with store-level scanner data, *Journal of Marketing Research*, 37 Aug.

18. Polman, P. (1997), *Marketing Week*, 28 Feb.

19. Abraham, M.A. and Lodish, L.M. (1990), Getting the most out of advertising and promotion, *Harvard Business Review*, May/June.

20. Campbell, M. and Dove, B. (1998), Evaluating the impact of advertising on sales, *Admap*, Feb.

21. Strang, R. (1975), The relationship between advertising and promotion in brand strategy, Marketing

Science Institute Papers.

22. Ailawadi, K.L., Farris, P. and Parry, M.E. (1994), Share and growth are not good predictors of the advertising and promotion/sales ratio, *Journal of Marketing*, 58(1) Jan.

23. Hardy, K.G. (1986), Key success factors for manufacturers' sales promotions in package goods, *Journal of Marketing*, 50, July.

24. Low, G.S. (1999), Setting advertising and promotion budgets in multi-brand companies, *Journal of Advertising Research*, 39(1).

25. Cheary, N. (1997), Hoover fails to shake off free flight horror, *Marketing Week*, 1.5.

26. Sales Promotion League Table (2004), *Marketing Magazine*, 6 Oct.

27. Mishon, C. (1998), Remuneration in promotional marketing agencies, *Admap*, Oct.

28. Survey of Promotional Users (1994), *Campaign Magazine*, 25 Feb.

Chapter 7

1. Jones, D.B. (1994), Setting promotional goals: a communications' relationship model, *Journal of Consumer Marketing*, 11(1).

2. Crush, P. (2005), The hidden cost of success, *Promotions & Incentives*, Feb.

3. White, R. (2002), Best practice: sales promotions and the brand, *Admap*, 436, July.

4. Ehrenberg, A.S.C., Hammond, K. and Goodhardt, G.J. (1991), *The After-effects of Large Scale Consumer Promotions*, London Business School.

5. Ehrenberg, A.S.C., Hammond, K. and Goodhart, G.J. (1994), The after effects of price related consumer promotions, *Journal of Advertising Research*, 34.4 (Jul/Aug).

6. Chandon, P. and Wansink, B. (2002), When are stockpiled products consumed faster? A convenience-salience framework of post-purchase consumption incidence and quantity, *Journal of Marketing Research*, 34, Aug.

7. Gupta, S. (1988), Impact of sales promotions on when, what and how much to buy, *Journal of Marketing Research*, 25(3) May.

Chapter 8

1. Mulhern, F.J. and Padgett, D.T. (1995), The relationship between retail price promotions and regular price purchases, *Journal of Marketing*, 59(4) Oct.

2. Fearne, A., Donaldson, A. and Normington, P. (1999), Pricing strategy and practice – the impact of alternative promotions on the spirits category: evidence from the UK, *Journal of Product and Brand Management*, 8(5).

3. Madan, V. and Suri, R. (2001), Quality perception and monetary sacrifice: a comparative analysis of discount and fixed prices, *Journal of Product and Brand Management*, 10(3).

4. Farris, P.W. and Quelch, J.A. (1989), In defence of price promotions. In Quelch, J., *Sales Promotion Management*, Prentice Hall.

5. Nijs, V.R., De Kimpe, M.G., Steenkamp, J.-B. and Hanssens, D.M. (2001), The category demand effects of price promotions, *Marketing Science*, 20(1).

6. Gupta, S. and Cooper, L.G. (1992), The discounting of discounts and promotion thresholds, *Journal of Consumer Research*, 19(3) Dec.

7. Gupta, S. (1988), Impact of sales promotions on when, what and how much to buy, *Journal of Marketing Research*, 25(3).

8. Sivakumar, K. and Raj, S.P. (1997), Quality tier competition: how price change influences brand choice and category choice, *Journal of Marketing*, 61.

9. Blattberg, R.C., Briesch, R. and Fox, E.J. (1995), How promotions work, *Marketing Science*, 14(3).

10. Garretson, J.A., Fisher, D. and Burton, S. (2002), Antecedents of private label attitude and national brand promotions: similarities and differences, *Journal of Retailing*, 78(2).

11. Srinivasan, S., Pauwels, K., Hassen, D. and De Kimpe, M. (2002), Who benefits from price promotions? *Harvard Business Review*, 80(9).

12. Helsen, K. and Schmittlein, D.C. (1992), How does a product market's typical price-promotion pattern affect the timing of household's purchases? An empirical study using UPC scanner data, *Journal of Retailing*, 68(3) Fall.

13. Boulding, W., Lee, E. and Staelin, R. (1994), Mastering the mix: do advertising, promotion and sales force activities lead to differentiation? *Journal of Marketing Research*, 31(2) May.

14. Ehrenberg, A.S.C. (2000), Repeat buying – facts, theory and applications, *Journal of Empirical Generalisations in Marketing Science*, 5.

15. Bell, D.R., Chiand, J. and Padmanabhan, V. (1999), The decomposition of promotional response: an empirical generalisation, *Marketing Science*, 18(4).

16. Ehrenberg, A.S.C., Hammond, K. and Goodhardt, G.J. (1994), The after effects of price related consumer promotions, *Journal of Advertising Research*, 34(4).

17. Pauwels, K., Hanssens, D.M. and Siddarth, S. (2002), The long-term effects of price promotions on category incidence, brand choice and purchase quantity, *Journal of Marketing Research*, 39(4) Nov.

18. Lichtenstein, D.R., Burton, S. and Netemeyer, R. (1997), An examination of deal proneness across sales promotion types: a consumer segmentation perspective, *Journal of Retailing*, 73(2) Summer.

19. Winer, R.S. (1986), A reference price model of brand choice for frequently purchased products, *Journal of Consumer Research*, 13, Sept.

20. Mela, C., Jedidi, K. and Bowman, D. (1998), The long term impact of promotions on consumer stockpiling behaviour, *Journal of Marketing*, 35(2).

21. Kalwani, M.U., Yim, C.K., Rinne, H.J. and Sugita, Y. (1990), A price expectations model of customer brand choice, *Journal of Marketing Research*, 27 Aug.

22. Kim, D.H. (1989), The Role of Brand Equity in Modelling the Impact of Advertising and Promotion and Sales, doctoral dissertation,

23. Biel, A.L. (1991), The brandscape: converting brand image into equity, *Admap*, 26(10) Oct.

24. Diamond, W.D. and Campbell, L. (1988), The framing of sales promotions: effects on reference price chance, *Advances in Consumer Research*, 16.

25. Mitchell, A. (1999), Technology breaks chain linking price with value, *Marketing Week*, 11 Nov.

26. Ambler, T. (1999), Kicking price promotion habits is like getting off heroin, *Marketing*, 27 May.

27. Smith, M. and Sinha, I. (2000), The impact of price and extra product promotions on store preferences, *International Journal of Retail and Distribution Management*, 28(2).

28. Raghubir, P. and Corfman, K.M. (1999), When do price promotions affect pre-trial brand evaluations? *Journal of Marketing Research*, 36(2) May.

29. www.asa.org.uk

30. Munger, J.L. and Grewal, D. (2001), The effects of alternative price promotional methods on consumers' product evaluations and purchase intentions, *The Journal of Product and Brand Management*, 10(3) June.

31. Heilman, C.M., Nakamoto, K. and Wedel, M. (2002), Pleasant surprises: consumer response to unexpected in-store coupons, *Journal of Marketing Research*, 34, May.

32. Thompson, S. (1997), The scoop on coupons, *Brandweek*, 38, March.

33. Oliver, R.L. and Shor, M. (2003), Digital redemption of coupons: satisfying and dissatisfying effects of promotional codes, *Journal of Product and Brand Management*, 12(2).

34. Iron, K.W., Little, J.D.C. and Klein, R.L. (1983), Determinants of Coupon Effectiveness, Advances and Practices of Marketing Science – Proceedings of the ORSA/Tims Marketing Science Conference.

35. Neslin, S.A., Henderson, C. and Quelch, J. (1990), A market response model for coupon promotions, *Marketing Science*, 9 Spring.

36. Sanjay, D.K. and Hoch, S.J. (1996), Price discrimination using in-store merchandising, *Journal of Marketing*, 60(1).

37. Raghubir, P., Inman, J.J. and Grande, H. (2004), The three faces of consumer promotions, *California Management Review*, 46(4).

38. Hahn, M., Chang, D.R., Kim, I.T. and Kim, Y. (1995), Consumer response to coupon advertising, *International Journal of Advertising*, 14(1).

39. Inman, J.J., Peter, A.C. and Raghubir, P. (1997), Framing the deal; the role of restrictions in accentuating deal value, *Journal of Consumer Research*, 24(1).

40. Shih-Fen, S., Monroe, K.B. and Yung-Chien, L. (1998), The effect of framing price promotion messages on consumers' perceptions and purchase intentions, *Journal of Retailing*, 74(3) Fall.

41. Bawa, K. and Shoemaker, R.W. (1987), The effect of a direct mail coupon on brand choice behaviour, *Journal of Marketing Research*, 24 Nov.

42. Bawa, K. and Shoemaker, R.W. (1989), Analysing incremental sales from a direct mail coupon promotion, *Journal of Marketing*, 53(3).

43. Raghubir, P. (1998), Coupon value: a signal for price? *Journal of Marketing Research*, 35(3) August.

44. Cotton, B.C. and Babb, E. M. (1978), Consumer response to promotional deals, *Journal of Marketing*, 42(3) July.

45. Tat, P.K. and Cornwell, T.B. (1996), A motivation based model of coupon usage, *Journal of Promotion Management*, 3.1/2.

46. Bawa, K., Srinivasan, S.S. and Srivastava, R.K. (1997), Coupon attractiveness and coupon proneness: a framework for modelling coupon redemption, *Journal of Marketing Research*, 34 Nov.

47. Chandon, P., Wansink, B. and Laurent, G. (2000), A benefit congruency framework of sales promotion effectiveness, *Journal of Marketing*, 64(4).

48. Green, C. L. (1996), Ethnic responses to couponing: a motivational perspective, *Journal of Consumer Marketing*, 13(2).

49. Babakus, E., Tat, P. and Cunningham, W. (1988), Coupon redemption: a motivational perspective, *Journal of Consumer Marketing*, 5(2) Spring.

50. Shimp, T.A. and Kavas, A. (1984), The theory of reasoned action applied to coupon usage, *Journal of Consumer Research*, 11(4).

51. Silva-Risso, J.M. and Bucklin, R.E. (2004), Capturing the effects of coupon promotions in scanner panel choice models, *Journal of Product and Brand Management*, 13(6).

52. Bucklin, R.E. and Gupta, S. (1999), Commercial use of scanner data: industry versus academic perspectives, *Marketing Science*, 18(3).

53. Garretson, J.A. and Burton, S. (2003), Highly coupon prone and sales prone consumers: benefits beyond price savings, *Journal of Advertising Research*, 43(2).

54. Gardener, E. and Trivedi, M. (1998), A communication framework to evaluate sales promotion strategies, *Journal of Advertising Research*, May–June.

55. Ailawadi, K.L., Lehmann, D.R. and Neslin, S.A. (2001), Market response to a major policy change in the marketing mix: learning from Procter & Gamble's value pricing strategy, *Journal of Marketing*, 65(1).

56. Slater, J. (2001), Is couponing an effective promotional strategy? An examination of the Procter & Gamble zero coupon test, *Journal of Marketing Communications*, 7.

57. Jain, S. and Srivastra, J. (2000), An experimental and theoretical analysis of price matching refund policies, *Journal of Marketing Research*, 37(3) Aug.

58. Tat, P., Cunningham W.A. and Babakus, E. (1988), Consumer perceptions of rebates, *Journal of Advertising Research*, Aug/Sept.

59. Folkes, V. and Wheat, R.D. (1995), Consumers' price perceptions of promoted products, *Journal of Retailing*, 71(3) Fall

60. Lal, R. (1990), Manufacturer trade deals and retail price promotion, *Journal of Marketing Research*, 27(4).

61. Quelch, J.A. and Harding, D. (1996), Brands versus private labels: fighting to win, *Harvard Business Review*, 74(1).

62. Bell, D.R., Chiand, J. and Padmanabhan, V. (1999), The decomposition of promotional response: an empirical generalisation, *Marketing Science*, 18(4).

63. Dawes, J. (2004), Assessing the impact of a very successful price promotion on brand, category and competitor sales, *Journal of Product and Brand Management*, 13(5).

64. Assuncao, J.L. and Meyer, R.L. (1993), The rational effect of price promotions on sales and consumption, *Management Science*, 39(5) May.

65. Bell, D., Iyer, G. and Padmonbhan, V. (2002), Price competition under stockpiling and flexible consumption, *Marketing Research Journal*, 37 Aug.

66. Dodson, A., Tybout, A. and Sternthal, B. (1978), The impact of deals and deal retraction on brandswitching, *Journal of Marketing Research*, 15.
67. Shoemaker, R.W. and Shoaf, R.F. (1977), Repeat rates of deal purchases, *Journal of Advertising Research*, 17.
68. Neslin, S., Henderson, C. and Quelch, J. (1985), Consumer promotions and the acceleration of product purchases, *Marketing Science*, 2.
69. Anderson, E. and Simester, D. (2004), Long-run effects of promotion depth on new versus established customers: three field studies, *Marketing Science*, Winter.

Chapter 9

1   Peattie, K., Peattie, S. and Emafo, E.B. (1997), Promotional competitions as a strategic marketing weapon, *Journal of Marketing Management*, 13 Nov.
2.   Leeflang, P.S.H. and van Raaij, W.F. (1995), The changing consumer in the European Union: a meta-analysis, *International Journal of Research in Marketing*, 12(5).
3.   Gardener, E. and Trivedi, M. (1998), A communication framework to evaluate sales promotion strategies, *Journal of Advertising Research*, 38(3) May–June.
4.   Ong., B.S., Ho, F.N. and Tripp, C. (1997), Consumer perceptions of bonus packs: an exploratory analysis, *Journal of Consumer Marketing*, 14(2) Spring.
5.   Guerreiro, R., dos Santos Gisbrecht, J.A. and Soo Ong, B. (2004), Cost implications of bonus pack promotions versus price discounts, *American Business Review*, 22(2) June.
6.   Smith, M. and Sinha, I. (2000), The impact of price and extra product promotions on store preferences, *International Journal of Retail and Distribution Management*, 28(2).
7.   Inman, J.J., Peter, A.C. and Raghubir, P. (1997), Framing the deal; the role of restrictions in accentuating deal value, *Journal of Consumer Research*, 24(1).
8.   Costa, R.P. (1983), Product sampling – the personalised promo, *Progressive Grocer*, 62, Jan.
9.   Cook, R. (1995), So, what is sales promotion, ISP Effective Sales Promotion Conference, Sept.
10. Hunt, E. and Jupe, C. (1994), Product sampling as a medium, *Admap*, March.
11. McGuinness, D., Gendall, P. and Matthew, S. (1992), The effect of product sampling on product trial, purchase and conversion, *International Journal of Advertising*, 11(1).
12. Gilbert, D.C. and Jackaria, N. (2002), The efficacy of sales promotion in UK supermarkets: a consumer's view, *International Journal of Retail and Distribution Management*, 30(6).
13. Bertrand, K. (1998), Premiums prime the market, *Advertising Age*, 83(5).
14. Mintel (2000) *Special Report on Sales Promotion*.
15. *Precision Marketing*, (1997), 26 May.
16. Simonson, I., Carmon, Z. and O'Curry, S. (1994), Experimental evidence on the negative effect of product features and sales promotions on brand choice, *Marketing Science*, 13(1).
17. Bannister, L., Riley-Smith, P. and Maclay, D. (1997), Global brands, local context, *Admap*, Oct.
18. Chandon, P. (1998), It's more than the money: Hedonic and symbolic responses to monetary and non-monetary promotions, *Advances in Consumer Research*, 25.
19. Chandon, P., Laurent, G. and Wansink, B. (1998), Beyond savings: the multiple utilitarian and hedonic effects of sales promotion, *Advances in Consumer Research*, 25.
20. Chandon, P., Wansink, B. and Laurent, G. (2000), A benefit congruency framework of sales promotion effectiveness, *Journal of Marketing*, 64(4).
21. D'Astous, A. and Jacob, I. (2002), Understanding consumer reactions to premium based promotional offers, *European Journal of Marketing*, 36(11/12).
22. Hiam, A. (2000), Match premiums to marketing strategies, *Marketing News*, 34 Sept.
23. D'Astous, A. and Landreville, V. (2003), An experimental investigation of factors affecting consumers' perceptions of sales promotions, *European Journal of Marketing*, 37(11/12).

Chapter 10

1. Peattie, K. and Peattie, S. (1995), Sales promotion – a missed opportunity for services marketers, *International Journal of Service Industry Management*, 6(1).
2. Ward, J.C. and Hill R.P. (1991), Designing effective promotional games: opportunities and problems, *Journal of Advertising*, 20(3) Sep.
3. Peattie, S. and Peattie, K. (1994), Promoting financial services with glittering prizes, *International Journal of Bank Marketing*, 12(6).
4. Peattie, K., Peattie, S. and Emafo, E.B. (1997), Promotional competitions as a strategic marketing weapon, *Journal of Marketing Management*, 13 Nov.
5. O'Connor, K. (1993), Promotions – brand builders or killers? *Journal of Brand Management*, 1(2).
6. Kivetz, R. and Simonson, I. (2002), Earning the right to indulge: effort as a determinant of customer preference towards frequency program rewards, *Journal of Marketing Research*, 39(2) May.
7. Duffy, D.L. (1998), Customer loyalty strategies, *Journal of Consumer Marketing*, 15(5).
8. Stewart, D. and Gallen, B. (1998), The promotional planning process and its impact on consumer franchise building, the case of fast moving consumer goods in New Zealand, *Journal of Product and Brand Management*, 7(6).
9. Davies, G. (1998), Why loyalty cards alone will not build brand loyalty, *Admap*, 33.7 (Jul/Aug).
10. Butler, S. and Henerey, M. (2005), So, what is the point of loyalty? *The Times*, 4.6.
11. Mahoney, S. (1999), Interactivity: pressing the promotion button, *Admap*, 34/6 Jun.
12. Gaudagni, P.M. and Little, J.D. (1983), A logit model of brand choice calibrate on scanner data, *Marketing Science*, 2(3).
13. Jacobs, C. (1999), Relationship marketing with smart cards, *Admap*, 34/6 Jun.
14. Jacobs, C. (1996), The answer to a retail marketer's prayer? *Admap*, June.
15. Uncles, M.D., Rowling, G.R. and Hammond, K. (2003), Customer loyalty and customer loyalty programmes, *Journal of Consumer Marketing*, 20(4).
16. Henry, C.D. (2000), Is customer loyalty a pernicious myth? *Business Horizons*, 43(4) July.
17. Dowling, G.R. and Uncles, M. (1997), Do customer loyalty programs really work? *Sloan Management Review*, 38(4) Summer.
18. O'Malley, L. (1998), Can loyalty schemes really build loyalty? *Marketing Intelligence and Planning*, 16(1).
19. Hallberg, G. (2004), Is your loyalty programme really building loyalty? Why increasing emotional attachment, not just repeat buying, is key to maximising programme success, *Journal of Targeting, Measurement and Analysis for Marketing*, 12(3).
20. O'Brien and Jones cited in Dowling, G.R. and Uncles, M. (1997), Do customer loyalty programs really work? *Sloan Management Review*, 38(4) Summer.
21. Davies, G. (1997), Loyalty is a gift – it can't be bought, *Admap*, 32(7) July/Aug.
22. Hooper, M. (1997), Is there no such thing as loyalty? *Admap*, 32/7, July/Aug.
23. O'Brien, L. and Jones, C. (1995), Do rewards really create loyalty? *Harvard Business Review*, May/June.
24. McIlroy, A. and Barnett, S. (2000), Building customer relationships: do discount cards work? *Managing Service Quality*, 10(6).
25. Van Doren, D.C., Fechner, D.L. and Green-Adelsberger, K. (2000), Promotional strategies on the world wide web, *Journal of Marketing Communications*, 6.1 (March).
26. Lewis, M. (2004), The influence of loyalty programs and short-term promotions on customer retention, *Journal of Marketing Research*, 41(3).
27. Garretson, J.A. and Niedrich, R.W. (2004), Spokes-characters, *Journal of Advertising*, 33(2).
28. Callcott, M. F. and Lee, W.-N. (1994), A content analysis of animation and animated spokes-characters in television sommercials, *Journal of Advertising*, 23(4).
29. Neeley, S. M., Macias, W., Clark, T.M. and Lee W.-N. (2000), Advertising Spokes-Character Attributes and the Use Relationships, Proceedings of the 2000 Society of Consumer Psychology Conference.

30. Callcott, M.F. and Phillips, B.J. (1996), Observations: elves make good cookies: creating likeable spokes character advertising, *Journal of Advertising Research*, 36 (Sep/Oct).
31. Erdogan, Z. and Kitchen, P. (1998), Getting the best out of celebrity endorsers, *Admap*, 33/4, Apr.
32. Hahn, M., Chang, D.R., Kim, I.T. and Kim, Y. (1995), Consumer response to coupon advertising, *International Journal of Advertising*, 14(1).
33. Munger, J. L. and Grewal, D. (2001), The effects of alternative price promotional methods on consumers' product evaluations and purchase intentions, *The Journal of Product and Brand Management*, 10(3) June.
34. Shankar, A. and Horton, B. (1999), Ambient media: advertising's new media opportunity? *International Journal of Advertising*, 18(3).

Chapter 11

1. Quelch, J.A. (1989), *Sales Promotion Management*, Prentice Hall.
2. Ailawadi, K., Farris, P. and Shames, E. (1999), Trade promotion: essential to selling through resellers, *Sloan Management Review*, Fall.
3. Kasulis, J.J., Morgan, F.W., Griffith, D.E. and Kenderdine, J.M. (1999), Managing trade promotions in the context of market power, *Journal of the Academy of Marketing Science*, 27(3) Summer.
4. Mohr, J. J. and Low, G. S. (1993), Escaping the catch-22 of trade promotion spending, *Marketing Management*, 2(2).
5. Curhan, R.C. and Kopp, R.J. (1988), Obtaining retailer support for trade deals: key success factors, *Journal of Advertising Research*, 27(6).
6. Blattberg, R.C., Briesch, R. and Fox, E.J. (1995), How promotions work, *Marketing Science*, 14(3-2).
7. Agrawal, D. (1996), Effect of brand loyalty on advertising and trade promotions: a game. Theoretic analysis with empirical evidence, *Marketing Science*, 15(1).
8. Murry, J.P. and Heide, J.B. (1998), Managing promotion program participation within manufacturer–retailer relationships, *Journal of Marketing*, 62(1) Jan.
9. Blattberg, R.C. and Levin, A. (1987), Modelling the effectiveness and profitability of trade promotions. *Marketing Science*, 6.2.
10. Zerillo, P. and Iacobucci, D. (1995), Trade promotions: a call for a more rational approach, *Business Horizons*, 38(4) Jul/Aug.
11. Lucas, A. (1996), In-store trade promotions – profit or loss? *Journal of Consumer Marketing*, 13(2) Spring.
12. Chevalier, M. and Curhan, R.C. (1976), Retail promotions as a function of trade promotions: a descriptive analysis, *Sloan Management Review*, 18(1).
13. Blattberg, R.C., Eppen, G.D. and Lieberman, J. (1981), A theoretical and empirical evaluation of price deals for consumer non-durables, *Journal of Marketing*, 45 (Winter).
14. Grewal, D., Krishnan, R., Baker, J. and Berin, N. (1998), The effect of store name, brand name and price discounts on consumers' evaluations and purchase intentions, *Journal of Retailing*, 74(3) Fall.
15. Bergen, M. and John, G. (1997), Understanding co-operative advertising participation rates, *Journal of Marketing Research*, 34(3) Aug.
16. Grewal, D., Monroe, K.B. and Khrishnan, R. (1998), The effects of price comparison advertising on buyer's perceptions of acquisition value, transactional value and behavioural intentions, *Journal of Marketing*, 62(2) April.
17. Jorgensen, S., Taboubi, S. and Zaccour, G. (2003), Retail promotions with negative brand image effects: is co-operation possible? *European Journal of Operational Research*, 150(2).
18. Rossiter J.R. and Percy, L. (1997), *Advertising Communications and Promotion Management*, 2nd Ed, McGraw Hill.
19. Tomkins, R. (2000), Manufacturers strike back, *Financial Times*, 16 Jun.
20. ACNielsen (2004), 13th Annual Trade Promotion Practices Survey, 2003, ACNielsen.com/pubs
21. Cooper, L.G., Baron, P., Levy, W. and Gogos, M. (1999), Promocast trademark: a new forecasting method for promotion planning, *Marketing Science*, 18(3).

22. Blattberg, R.C. (1995), *Category Management, Guides 1-5*, Food Marketing Institute.

23. Dupre, K. and Gruen, T.W. (2004), The use of category management practices to obtain a sustainable competitive advantage in the fast moving consumer goods industry, *Journal of Business and Industrial Marketing*, 19(7).

24. Johnson, M. and Felice, P. (1998), Supporting category management, *Marketing and Research Today*, 27(4) Nov.

25. Qureshi, M, and Baker, J. (1998), Category management and effective consumer response: the role of market research, *Marketing and Research Today*, 26(1) Feb.

26. Johnson, M. and Pinnington, D. (2000), Supporting the category management challenge: how research can contribute, *Journal of the Market Research Society*, 40(1).

27. Johnson, M. and Felice, P. (1998), From identifying need states to testing in virtual reality: supporting category management, ESOMAR conference paper.

28. Nielsen (1992), *Category Management*, NTC Business Books.

29. Harlow, P. (1995), Category management: a new era in FMCG buyer-supplier relationships, *Journal of Brand Management*, 2(5) April.

30. Hill, S. (1998), Retailer brands, manufacturer brands and how they can live together, *Journal of Brand Management*, 5(3) Jan.

31. Dewsnap, N, and Jobber, D. (1999), Category management: a vehicle for integration between sales and marketing, *Journal of Brand Management*, 6(6) July.

32. Phillips, H. and Cox, J. (1998), Point of purchase marketing, *Journal of Brand Management*, 5(3) Jan.

33. Areni, C.S., Duhan, D.F. and Kiecker, P. (1999), Point of purchase displays, product organisation and brand purchase likelihoods, *Journal of the Academy of Marketing Science*, 27/4 Autumn.

34. Miller, R. (1997), Does everyone have a price? *Marketing*, 24 April.

35. Toop, A. (1994), Making more of alternative media: sales promotions that are cost effective and precisely targeted, *Admap*, 29(10) Oct.

36. Jones, J.P. (1990), The double jeopardy of sales promotion, *Harvard Business Review*, Sept/Oct.

37. Cobb, R. (1997), Variations on a theme, *Marketing*, Oct 23.

38. Gordon, W. and Valentine, V. (1996), Buying the brand at point of sale, *Journal of Brand Management*, 4(1) Aug.

39. Connolly, A. and Davison, L. (1996), How does design affect decisions at point of sale? *Journal of Brand Management*, 4(2) Oct.

40. Keeler, C. (2004), Editorial: branding in store – marketing in the 21st century, *Brand Management*, 11(4).

41. Chevalier, M. (1975), Increase in sales due to in-store display, *Journal of Marketing Research*, 12 Nov.

42. Inman, J., McAlister, L. and Hoyer, W.D. (1990), Promotion signal, proxy for a price cut? *Journal of Consumer Research*, 17 June.

43. Dickson, P.R. and Sawyer, A.G. (1990), The price knowledge and search of supermarket shoppers, *Journal of Marketing*, 54(3) July.

44. Wilson, C. (1997), *Profitable Customers: How to Identify, Develop and Retain Them*, Kogan Page.

45. Fennel, N. (1997), Field marketing, Supplement to *Marketing*, Oct 23.

46. Hardy, K.G. and Magrath, A.J. (1990), Levering strategies for sales promotions, *Business Quarterly*, 54(3) Winter.

47. Murphy, W.H. and Sohi, R.S. (1995), Salespersons' perceptions about sales promotions, *European Journal of Marketing*, 29(13).

Chapter 12

1. Black, R. (1986), *The Trade Show Industry: Management and Marketing Career Opportunities*, Trade Show Bureau.

2. O'Hara, B.S. (1991), *Evaluating the Effectiveness of Trade Shows*, South Eastern Louisiana University.

3. De Kimpe, M.G. and Francois, P. (1997), Generalising about trade show effectiveness: a cross national

comparison, *Journal of Marketing*, 61(4).

4. Moriarty, R.T. and Spekman, R.E. (1984), An empirical investigation of the information sources used during the industrial buying process, *Journal of Marketing Research*, 21.

5. Donath, B. (1980), Show and sell by the numbers, *Industrial Marketing*, 70(5).

6. Mee, W.W. (1988), Trade shows: this marketing medium means business, *Association Management*, 50(5).

7. Herbig, P., O'Hara, B. and Palumbo, F.A. (1998), Trade shows: who, what, why, *Marketing Intelligence and Planning*, 16(7).

8. Bonoma, T.V. (1983), Get more out of your trade shows, *Harvard Business Review*, 61.

9. Blythe, J. (1999), Visitor and exhibitor expectations and outcomes of trade exhibitions, *Marketing Intelligence and Planning*, 17(2).

10. Gopalakrishna, S., Lilien, G.L., Williams, J.D., and Sequeira, I.K. (1995), Do trade shows pay off? *Journal of Marketing*, 59(3).

11. White, S., Bryant, S. and Cohen, A. (1999), A case for the professionals: conferences and exhibitions, *Marketing Business*, 76 Feb.

12. Blythe, J. (1999), Exhibitor commitment and the evaluation of exhibition activities, *International Journal of Advertising*, 18(1).

13. Faria, A.J. and Dickinson, J.R. (1986), What kinds of business use trade shows most – and why? *Business Marketing*, 71(6).

14. D'Astous, A. and Butz, P. (1995), Consumer evaluations of sponsorship programs, *European Journal of Marketing*, 29(12).

15. Quester, P. and Farrelly, F. (1998), Brand association and memory decay effects of sponsorship: the case of the Australian Formula One Grand Prix, *Journal of Product and Brand Management*, 7(6).

16. Lewicki, J. (1998), Long term event sponsorship, *The Advertiser*, Aug.

17. Erdogan, B.Z. and Kitchen, P.J. (1998), Managerial mindsets and the symbiotic relationship between sponsorship and advertising, *Marketing Intelligence and Planning*, 16(6).

18. Meenaghan, T.A. (1991), The role of sponsorship in the marketing communications mix, *International Journal of Advertising*, 10.

19. Dolphin, R. (2003), Sponsorship: Perspectives on its strategic role, *Corporate Communications – An International Journal*, 8(3).

20. Fry, L.W., Keim, G.D. and Meiners, R.E. (1982), Corporate contributions: altruistic or for-profit, *Academy of Management Journal*, 25(1).

21. Gardner, M.P. and Shuman, P.J. (1987), Sponsorship: an important component of the promotions mix, *Journal of Advertising Research*, 16(1).

22. Armstrong, C. (1988), Sports sponsorship: a case-study approach to measuring its effectiveness, *European Research*, 16(2).

23. Quester, P.G. and Thompson, B. (2001), Advertising and promotion leverage on arts sponsorship effectiveness, *Journal of Advertising Research*, Jan/Feb.

24. Hoek, J. (1997), Sponsorship and advertising: a comparison of their effects, *Journal of Marketing Communications*, 3.

25. IEG Network (2004), IEG Annual Survey, www.sponsorship.com.

26. Quester, P.G. (2001), Advertising and promotional leverage on arts sponsorship effectiveness, *Journal of Advertising Research*, 41(1).

27. Javalgi, R.G. (1994), Awareness of sponsorship and the corporate image: an empirical investigation, *Journal of Advertising Research*, 23(4).

28. Cornwell, T.B. (2001), Exploring managers' perceptions of the impact of sponsorship on brand equity, *Journal of Advertising Research*, 30(2).

29. Smith, E. (1996), *Promo's Source Book*, Cowles Business Media.

30. Grimes, E. and Meenaghan, T. (1998), Focussing commercial sponsorship on the internal corporate audience, *International Journal of Advertising*, 17(1).

31. Amis, J. (1997), Achieving a sustainable competitive advantage: a resource based view of sports sponsorship, *Journal of Sports Management*, 11(1).

32. Tripodi, J.A. (2001), Sponsorship – a confirmed weapon in the promotion armoury, *International*

Journal of Sports Marketing and Sponsorship, Mar/Apr.

33. Pope, N.L. and Voges, K.E. (2000), The impact of sports sponsorship activities, corporate image and prior use on consumer purchase intentions, *Sports Marketing Quarterly*, 9(2).

34. Hoek, J.A., Gendall, P. and West, D. (1990), The role of sponsorship on marketing planning of selected New Zealand Companies, *New Zealand Journal of Business*, 12.

35. Wright, R. (1998), Measuring awareness of British football sponsorship, *European Research*, 16(2).

36. Pope, N.K.L. and Voges, K.E. (1999), Sponsorship and image: a replication and extension, *Journal of Marketing Communications*, 5(1) March.

37. Marshall, S. and Cook, G. (1992), The corporate (sports) sponsor, *International Journal of Advertising*, 11(4).

38. Lardinoit, T. and Quester, P.G. (2001), Attitudinal effects of combined sponsorship and sponsors' prominence on basketball in Europe, *Journal of Advertising Research*, Jan/Feb.

39. Otker, T. (1988), Exploitation: the key to sponsorship success, *European Research*, 16(2).

40. Cornwell, T.B., Relyea, G.E., Irwin, R.L. and Maignan, I. (2000), Understanding long-term effects of sports sponsorship: role of experience, involvement, enthusiasm and clutter, *International Journal of Sports Marketing and Sponsorship*, 2(2).

41. McDonald, C. (1991), Sponsorship and the image of the sponsor, *European Journal of Marketing*, 25.

42. Hoek, J. (1999), Sponsorship: an evaluation of management assumptions and practices, *Marketing Bulletin*, 10(1).

43. Farrelly, F.J., Quester, P.G. and Burton, R. (1997), Integrating sports sponsorship into the corporate marketing function: an international comparative study, *International Marketing Review*, 14(3).

44. Kover, A.J. (2001), The sponsorship issue, *Journal of Advertising Research*, Feb.

45. Stipp, H. and Schiavone, N.P. (1996), Modelling the impact of Olympic sponsorship on corporate image, *Journal of Advertising Research*, 36(9).

46. Pham, M.T. (1991), The evaluation of sponsorship effectiveness: a model and some methodological considerations, *Gestion*, 7(4).

47. Cornwell, T.B. and Maignan, I. (1998), An international review of sponsorship research, *Journal of Advertising*, 27(1).

48. Hoek, J., Gendall P., Jeffcoat, M. and Orsman, D. (1997), Sponsorship and advertising: a comparison of their effects, *Journal of Promotion Management*, 3(1) March.

49. Ehrenberg, A.S.C. (1997), How do consumers come to buy a new brand? *Admap*, 32/3 Mar.

50. Lee, M., Sandler, D. and Shani, D. (1997), Attitudinal constructs towards sponsorship, *International Marketing Review*, 14.

51. Crimmins, J. and Horn, M. (1996), Sponsorship: from management ego trip to marketing success, *Journal of Advertising Research*, 36.

52. Javalgi, R., Traylor, M., Cross, A. and Lampman, E. (1994), Awareness of sponsorship and corporate image: an empirical investigation, *Journal of Advertising Research*, 34.

53. Cornwell, T.B. (1995), Sponsorship-linked marketing development, *Sports Marketing Quarterly*, 4(4).

54. Sandler, D.M. and Shani, D. (1989), Olympic sponsorship vs ambush marketing: who gets the gold? *Journal of Advertising Research*, Aug/Sept.

55. Meenaghan, T. (1994), Point of view: Ambush marketing – immoral or imaginative practice? *Journal of Advertising Research*, 34(5).

56. Varadarajan, P.R. and Menon, A. (1988), Cause related marketing: a coalignment of marketing strategy and corporate philanthropy, *Journal of Marketing*, 52.

57. Adkins, S. (2000), *Cause Related Marketing: Who Cares Wins*, Oxford, Butterworth Heinemann.

58. Pringle, H. and Thompson, M. (2001), *Brand Spirit*, John Wiley and Sons Ltd.

59. Dupree, J. (2000) Review of brand spirit: how cause related marketing builds brands, *Journal of Consumer Marketing*, 17(5).

60. Fellman, M.W. (1999), Cause related marketing takes a strategic view, *Marketing News*, 26 April.

61. Polonsky, M.J. and Speed, R. (2001), Linking sponsorship and cause related marketing, *European Journal of Marketing*, 35(11/12).

62. Till, B.D. and Nowak, L.I. (2000), Toward effective use of cause related marketing alliances, *Journal of Product and Brand Management*, 9(7).

63. Bennett, R. and Gabriel, H. (2002), Charity affiliation as a determinant of product purchase decisions, *Journal of Product and Brand Management*, 9(4).
64. Pringle H. and Thomson H. (1999), At one level brands are very simple things, *Branding Strategy*.
65. Business in the Community (1999), The ultimate win, win, win.
66. Business in the Community (2000), Profitable partnerships.

Chapter 13

1. Pauwels, K., Silva-Risso, J., Srinivasan, S. and Hanssens, D.J. (2000), New products, sales promotions and firm value: the case of the automobile industry, *Journal of Marketing*, 68(4).
2. Hart, D. (1997), Minimising the risk of promotional failure, *Grocer*, Aug 16.
3. Srinivasan, S.S. and Anderson, E.R. (1998), Concepts and strategy guidelines for designing value and enhancing promotions, *Journal of Product and Brand Management*, 7(5).
4. Cook, R. (1995), So, what is sales promotion, ISP Effective Sales Promotion Conference, Sept.
5. Spillard, P. (1996), *Sales Promotion - Its place in Marketing Strategy*, Business Publications Ltd.
6. Kopalle, P.K., Mela, C.F. and Marsh, L. (1999), The dynamic effects of discounting on sales: empirical analysis and normative pricing implications, *Marketing Science*, 18(3).
7. Marsden, A. (1994), The cost effectiveness of sales promotion, *Admap*, 29(10).
8. Winiewski, K.J. and Phillip, A. (1996), Understanding Promotional Effectiveness and Profitability, ESOMAR conference paper.
9. White, R. (2002), Sales Promotion and the brand, *Admap*, 427 April.
10. ACNielsen (1997), *The Researcher*, Jan.
11. Bowman, J. (1997), In Hart, D., Minimising the risk of promotional failure, *Grocer*, Aug 16.
12. *The Times* (1997), Feb 28.
13. *Marketing Week* (1997), June 5.
14. Peattie, S. and Peattie, K. (1994), Promoting financial services with glittering prizes, *International Journal of Bank Marketing*, 12(6).

Chapter 14

1. Flanagan, J. (1988), Sales promotion: the emerging alternative to brand building advertising, *Journal of Consumer Marketing*, 5(2).
2. Parry, C. (1994), Designing the appropriate sales promotion, *Admap*, 29(10) Oct.
3. Caywood, C., Schultz, D. and Wang, P. (1991), Integrated Marketing Communications: A survey of National Consumer Goods Advertisers, Northwestern University report, June.
4. Schultz, D.E. and Kitchen, P.J. (1997), Integrated marketing communications in US advertising agencies: an exploratory study, *Journal of Advertising Research*, 37(5).
5. Duncan, T. and Everett, S. (1993), Client perceptions of integrated marketing communications, *Journal of Advertising Research*, 33(3).
6. Cook, W. (1994), The end of the line, *Marketing*, 24 Feb.
7. Nilson, T.S. (1992), *Value Added Marketing*, McGraw Hill.
8. Schultz, D.E., Tannenbaum, S.I. and Lauterborn, R.F. (1992), *Integrated Marketing Communications: Putting It Together and Making It Work*, NTC Business Books.
9. Schultz, D.E., Tannebaum, S.I., and Lauterborn, R.F. (1995), *The Marketing Paradigm - Integrated Marketing Communications*, NTC Business Books.
10. Schultz, D.E. writing in Jones, J.P. (1999), *The Advertising Business*, Sage.
11. Cornellisen, J.P., Lock, A.R. and Gardner, H. (2000), Theoretical concept or management fashion, examining the significance of IMC, *Journal of Advertising Research*, 40(5).
12. Proctor, T. and Kitchen, P. (2002), Communication in post-modern integrated marketing, *Corporate Communications*, 7(3).

13. Jeans, R. (1998), Integrating marketing communications, *Admap*, Dec.

14. Shimp, T.A. (1996), *Advertising Promotion: Supplemental Aspects of Integrated Marketing Communications*, Harcourt.

15. Brannan, T. (1995), *A Practical Guide to Integrated Marketing Communications*, Kogan Page.

16. American Association of Advertising Agencies, *Marketing News*, 18 Jan 1993.

17. Smith, P. (1996), Benefits and barriers to integrated marketing communications, *Admap*, Feb.

18. Solomon, M.R. and Englis, B.G. (1994), The big picture: product complementarity and integrated communications, *Journal of Advertising Research*, Jan/Feb.

19. Lannon, J. (1994), What brands need now, *Admap*, Sept.

20. Reid, M. (2003), IMC – performance relationship. Further insight and evidence from the Australian marketplace, *International Journal of Advertising*, 22(2).

21. Ogilvy, D. (1993), *Ogilvy on Advertising*, Prion Books.

22. Novak, G.J. and Phelps, J. (1994), Conceptualizing the integrated marketing communications phenomenon: an examination of its impact on advertising practices and its implications for advertising research, *Journal of Current Issues and Research in Advertising*, 16(1).

23. Low, G.S. (2000), Correlates of integrated marketing communications, *Journal of Advertising Research*, May.

24. Linton, I. and Morley, K. (1995), *Integrated Marketing Communications*, Butterworth Heinemann.

25. Kitchen, P.J. and Schultz, D.E. (1999), A multi-country comparison of the drive for IMC, *Journal of Advertising Research*, Jan/Feb.

26. Iddiols, D. (2000), Marketing superglue: client perceptions of IMC, *Admap*, May.

27. Croft, M. (1999), Orange fever, *Marketing Week*, 11 Feb.

28. Peattie, S. and Peattie, K. (2003), Sales promotion, in Baker, M., *The Marketing Book*, Butterworth Heinemann.

29. Twitty, K. (1999), Precision Marketing, 15 March.

30. Taylor, H. (1999), Precision Marketing, 15 March.

31. Snudden P. (1998), In Acland, H., Do's and don'ts of sales promotion, *Marketing*, 17 Sept.

32. Beasley, M. (1998), In Acland, H., Do's and don'ts of sales promotion, *Marketing*, 17 Sept.

33. Bemmaor, A. and Mouchoux, D. (1991), Measuring the short-term effect of in-store promotions and retail advertising on brand sales: a factorial experiment, *Journal of Marketing Research*, 28(2) May.

34. Roberts, A. (1996), What do we know about advertising's short term effects, *Admap*, Feb.

35. Bunyard, J. (1999), If advertising alone fails to boost sales, developments in FMCG, *Admap*, 34(5) May.

Chapter 15

1. Kanso, A. (1992), International advertising strategies: global commitment to local vision, *Journal of Advertising Research*, Jan/Feb.

2. Boyfield, K. (2000), Why survival will rely on branding skills, *Market Leader*, Winter.

3. Levitt, T, (1983), The globalisation of markets, *Harvard Business Review*, 61(3).

4. Kotler, P. (1994), *Marketing Management: Analysis, Planning, Implementation and Control*, Prentice Hall.

5. Grein, A. and Ducoffe, R. (1998), Strategic responses to market globalisation among advertising agencies, *International Journal of Advertising*, 17(3).

6. Anholt, S. (2000), Updating the international advertising model, *Admap*, June.

7. Quelch, J. (2003), The return of the global brand, *Harvard Business Review*, 81(8).

8. Byfield, S. and Caller, L. (1996), Building brands across borders, *Admap*, June.

9. Wustrack, K. (1999), One-touch sweeps the budget, *Admap*, Feb.

10. Goodyear, M. (1996), Divided by a Common Language, MRS conference papers.

11. Pawle, J. (1999), Mining the international consumer, *Journal of the Market Research Society*, 41(1).

12. Aaker, D.A. and Joachimsthaler, E. (1999), The lure of global branding, *Harvard Business Review*, 77(6).

13. Quelch, J. (1999), Global brands – taking stock, *Business Strategy Review*, 10,1.
14. Duffy, M. and Medina, J. (1998), Standardisation versus globalisation: a new perspective of brand strategies, *Journal of Product and Brand Management*, 7(3).
15. Riesenbeck, H. and Freeling, A. (1991), How global are global brands? *McKinsey Quarterly*, 4.
16. Copeland, L. and Griggs, L. (1986), *Going International*, Plume Books.
17. Jacobs, L., Keown, C. and Ghymn, K. (1991), Cross cultural colour comparisons: global marketers beware, *International Marketing Review*, 8(3).
18. Usenier, J.-C. (1996), *Marketing Across Cultures*, 2nd Ed., Prentice Hall.
19. Havas, (1998), Europub: le marché publicitaire européen.
20. Huff, L. and Alden, D.L. (1998), An investigation of consumer response to sales promotions in developing markets, *Journal of Advertising Research*, May/June.
21. Kashani, K. and Quelch, J.A. (1990), Can sales promotions go global? *Business Horizons*, 33(3) May/June.

Glossary

Above the line Any paid form of advertising (television, press, radio, cinema, posters) on which commission is paid by the media to the agency

ACORN An acronym for A Classification of Residential Neighbourhoods that enables consumers to be classified on the basis of the area of residency

Acquisition rates Those sales achieved from non-regular buyers who make a purchase as a direct result of the promotion

Affordability method The apportionment of a communications budget after deduction of the desired level of profit and all other costs

AIDA A model of personal selling subsequently used to explain the process of advertising but also applied by some authors to sales promotion

Appropriation The sum of money allocated to a campaign

Attention The process of arousing the interest of an individual in some activity

Attitude Knowledge and feelings (both positive and negative) towards a subject

Attributes The physical or emotional qualities that a product or service possesses

Audience The number of individuals reached by an advertising medium

Awareness The stimulation of knowledge about a person or object

Banded packs Consumer offer in which multiple packs are banded together at a reduced price

Baseline sales Those sales that would have occurred without any promotional activity

Beliefs A conviction regarding the existence or characteristics of something

Below the line Marketing communications activities that are not subject to commission being paid to the advertising agency

Benefit segmentation A grouping of consumers based on the specific benefits they desire from a product

Black box model A simple model of the communications process relating level of expenditure to sales effect

BOGOF Buy one get one free

Bonus packs Consumer offers in which the manufacturer provides additional product at no extra cost

Brand A name, term, design, symbol or any other feature that identifies one seller's goods or services from those of other sellers

Brand equity The assignment of a capital value to a brand. Sometimes used to describe the intangible benefits associated with the use of a brand

Brand image The total impression created in the consumer's mind by a brand and all its associations, functional and non-functional

Brand loyalty A measurement of the extent to which consumers are committed to a particular brand

Brand manager The person within the company responsible for the marketing of a specific brand

Brand personality The character of a brand expressed as if it were a human being

Brand stretch The ability of a brand to be extended to include products or categories beyond the original product

Brand switchers Consumers who alternate purchases between different manufacturers' products

Branding The process of creating a unique identity for the product or service

Budget The amount of money allocated to a campaign

Business to business The promotion of its products or services by one company to another

Campaign An all-embracing plan indicating the choice of media and other activities designed to support the brand within an identified timeframe

Cannibalization The consequence of taking share from another brand in the same company's portfolio

CAP Committee (Committee of Advertising Practice) Body responsible for producing the British Code of Sales Promotion

Case allowance Discount offered to the trade as a rebate against the number of cases ordered

Case rate method A method of budget calculation in which expenditure is calculated as a percentage of the sales value of a case of product

Category management The responsibility for co-ordinating the activities of all the company's brands within a particular market sector

Cause marketing (also referred to as cause related marketing) The process of sponsoring a charitable activity designed to achieve a positive impact on the brand image

Character merchandizing Promotions involving a character or device licensed from a third party organization

Clickthrough A measure of the effectiveness of Web advertising based on a measurement of the number of surfers who click on the ad

Clutter The surrounding messages that interfere with the comprehension of any form of communications

Communication The process of dissemination of information to establish shared meaning between the sender and the receiver

Competition Format in which prizes are distributed on the basis of skill or judgement

Complex problem solving Purchasing decisions in which the consumer will require additional information on which to base an evaluation of alternatives. Most often where the capital outlay is great or the risk is high

Comprehension The creation of an understanding about a product, service, object or person

Concept testing A research procedure in which outline ideas are exposed to current and potential consumers to learn about their response

Consumer behaviour The activities in which people engage in order to satisfy needs, wants and desires

Container premium Packaging item that can be reused by the consumer for some other purpose

Contest Competition format in which prizes are distributed on the basis of skill or judgement

Contingency A sum of money held in reserve to respond to unforeseen circumstances

Continuity promotions Format in which consumers are encouraged to develop loyalty to promoted brand as a result of regular purchase

Co-operative advertising A programme in which the manufacturer pays an agreed percentage of the retailer's advertising costs in return for the featuring of the manufacturer's brand

Core values The central values associated with a product or service

Coupon Promotional format in which the consumer receives a voucher to be redeemed against a subsequent purchase usually with a discount

Customer relationship management (CRM) Programmes based on the adoption of a customer focus

Database A computer-based listing of the names, addresses and other details of current and potential customers, which can be used for purposes of direct marketing

Database management The process of maintaining and refining accurate customer information

Deal proneness The extent to which consumers seek out promotional offers

Decision making unit Those individuals who participate in the purchasing decision process, usually in the context of company purchases

Decision stage That part of the process of consumer buying behaviour which results in an evaluative judgement about the alternatives

Decoding The means by which the recipient of a message transforms and interprets it

Demographics Groupings of individuals based on characteristics such as age, sex, race and income

Diffusion The spread of a new idea throughout a group of individuals

Direct mail The use of postal and other delivery techniques to communicate with a defined target audience

Direct marketing An interactive system of marketing which uses one or more advertising media to effect a measurable response and/or transaction at any location

Direct response A method whereby the company provides the consumer with a means of communicating directly with the organization

Direct selling The process of achieving the sales of products or services without the use of intermediary sales channels, such as wholesalers and retailers

Displacement rates The volume of sales that would have been made to regular buyers at the regular price

E-commerce The process of selling goods and services through the Internet

EDLP Everyday low prices

Emotional responses Those non-rational reactions to a proposition which are based on intangible benefits or associations which a product or service can induce

Encoding The process of putting information into a symbolic form of words, pictures or images

Endorsement The recommendation of a product or service by someone other than the advertiser

EPOS Electronic point-of-sale scanner technology

Ethics The principles that guide an individual's or organization's conduct in its relations with others, and the values it wishes to communicate

Evaluation of alternatives The consumer's consideration of the various options available to resolve an identified need or want

Event management The creation of activities in which the brand is linked to some form of occasion or experience

Event sponsorship The association of a company or brand name with a public activity

Everyday low prices (EDLP) A pricing policy adopted by some companies in which short-term promotional pricing is either reduced or eliminated and replaced by a consistent level of lower prices

External databases Computer-based records compiled from external sources that can be used for the purposes of direct marketing

Family life cycle A sequence of stages through which the individual passes over time

Feedback The process of ensuring an understanding of the recipient's comprehension of a message by the sender

FMCG Fast moving consumer goods

Focus group A qualitative group discussion structured to discuss specific issues

Free gift Item given away with purchase at no cost to consumer

Free mail-in Gift item given to consumer in return for a number of proofs of purchase

Frequency programmes Promotions designed to recognise and reward customer loyalty

Fulfilment house Organization that handles consumer redemptions of coupons and gift offers on behalf of the manufacturer

Geodemographic segmentation A method of segmenting the market using a combination of psychographic and geographic data

Geographic segmentation The identification of market or audience segments solely based on geographic factors

Generic branding A policy by which products or services are sold using their category name

Global branding Where the manufacturer utilises the same name and design in all markets

Global marketing The adoption of a common marketing strategy and implementation plan for all countries in which a manufacturer markets his goods

Gross margin The calculation of net sales value minus the cost of goods over a defined period

Guerrilla marketing The use of unconventional approaches that associate the brand with a sponsored event without gaining official recognition from the organizer

Image The creation of an identity for a product or service by its association with other values

IMC Integrated marketing communications

Impulse purchase Products or services bought without prior consideration, usually in response to some stimulus at the point of purchase

Incremental sales Those sales that can be attributed directly to promotional activity

Integration The process by which the tools of marketing communications are used in combination to reinforce each other

Internal databases Computer-based records compiled from internal records such as sales registrations, warranty cards and other sources for the purpose of direct marketing

ISP The Institute of Sales Promotion

Joint promotions Promotions in which two or more companies combine to offer an incentive to consumers

JND or just noticeable difference The amount by which a product or service needs to be changed to ensure that the change is observed by the consumer

Learning The process of change to an individual's behaviour resulting from experience

Licensing The process of using a third-party character for promotional purposes in return for a fee

Lifestyle The way in which a person lives, identified by his activities, interests and opinions

List broker An organization that provides mailing lists to companies

Local brand One that is marketed in a specific country

Look alikes Products that adopt the visual cues of another brand in order to facilitate the inclusion of the product within the category of choice

Lottery Promotional format in which prize winners are determined by luck or chance

Loyalists Consumers who exhibit a consistent purchasing preference for a particular brand

Loyalty promotions Incentives designed to reward regular purchase or involvement on the part of the consumer

Manufacturer branding The use of a manufacturer's name or logo to identify the products or services produced by the company

Margin allowance Discount offered to the retail trade

Market analysis Research that assists in the identification of markets for a product or service and which details information relating to consumer behaviour, competitive activity and similar factors

Market research The gathering and assessment of data and other information

Market segmentation The means by which the characteristics of homogeneous groups of consumers can be determined

Market structure The ways in which a market for any product or service can be defined or segmented

Marketing The management process responsible for identifying, anticipating and satisfying consumers, profitably

Marketing communications The process by which a marketer develops and presents stimuli to a defined target audience with the purpose of eliciting a desired set of responses

Marketing communications mix The combination of the various communications activities to create a sustained campaign of activity to support the brand

Marketing concept The process by which the marketer responds to the needs and wants of the consumer

Marketing mix The combination of the elements of the marketing programme, including product, price, place, and promotion

Marketing objectives The determination of specific and measurable goals to be achieved by the marketing programme

Marketing plan The formal document containing the information designed to guide the development and implementation of the marketing strategy

Marketing strategy Specific plans of action for the achievement of designated marketing objectives

Mass marketing An approach in which the advertiser attempts to appeal to the entire market using a single marketing mix

Mature market The stage at which a market for a product or service ceases to expand

Media The vehicles of communication by which a message is transmitted to its audience

Media mix The combination of two or more different media to be used to fulfil a media plan

Media plan The document embodying the specific media objectives, strategy and tactics designed to support a brand

Media planning The process of determining the means by which an advertising message will be communicated to a defined audience

Media schedule A graphic representation of the dates, times and media sources in which advertising is to be placed

Merge and purge The process of eliminating the duplication of names and addresses contained within two or more mailing lists

Motive An aroused need that directs behaviour towards a specific goal

Multi-branding A strategy adopted by some manufacturers in which the parent name is subservient to those of the individual brands which they produce

Needs The gap between a consumer's current state and the desired state

Noise The external stimulus factors in the environment which surround the communications message and inhibit its effective transmission

Objective and task method The nature of the task is determined and the cost of achieving the specific objectives is calculated and a budget allocated accordingly

Objectives The specific goals to be achieved during the timescale of a plan

Outcomes The results and consequences of any activity

Own label Products manufactured for and sold under the name of a retailer

Percentage of sales method A budgeting procedure by which the expenditure is calculated as a finite percentage of the sales value

Perception The process by which an individual receives, organizes and interprets information

Permission marketing The process whereby an individual agrees to receive communications from a company

Personal selling The process by which a salesperson communicates with one or more prospective purchasers for the purpose of making sales

PEST + C An acronym standing for the political, economic, social, technological and consumer factors used in the analysis of a marketing environment. Sometimes written as PESTI+C, the 'I' standing for International

Planning The process of anticipating the future, establishing goals and objectives

Point of purchase Promotional items designed to attract the attention of the consumer in those placed where the products are purchased, sometimes referred to as point of sale

POPAI The Point of Purchase Advertising Institute

Positioning Identifying the place in the market or the mind of the consumer that the company or product wishes to occupy

Post-purchase dissatisfaction A response to a purchasing decision in which the consumer feels that the product or service has failed to deliver the expected performance on some dimension

Post-purchase satisfaction A response to a purchasing decision in which the consumer's direct experience of the product or service matches or exceeds its expected performance

Premium Gift item offered to the consumer either with purchase or in return for a number of proofs of purchase

Private label Products manufactured for and sold under the name of a retailer

Problem identification The recognition of an unfulfilled want or need

Problem solving The process by which the consumer resolves an identified need

Product differentiation The process of creating a point of difference between the product and its competitors by identifying physical or emotional dimensions of the brand

Product life cycle A management technique in which a product is depicted as passing through a series of progressive stages

Product placement The inclusion or mention of products or services in films, television programmes or elsewhere, usually in exchange for a fee

Promotion That element of the marketing mix that includes all forms of marketing communications

Promotion management The process of determining and co-ordinating the elements of the promotional mix

Promotional mix The use in any combination of advertising, sales promotion, public relations, direct marketing and personal selling to achieve specific objectives

Proof of purchase Some element such as a sales receipt, voucher, bar code or some other item to prove that the consumer has made the necessary purchase to quality for a free gift or competition

Psychographics The understanding of the psychological profiling of prospective consumers

Publicity Any communication concerning a company, product or service that is not paid for or sponsored

Public relations All forms of planned communications between any organization and its publics with the purpose of establishing mutual understanding

Pull strategy A promotional strategy in which the manufacturer or supplier promotes a product or service to the end consumer with the aim of stimulating demand

Push strategy A promotional strategy in which the manufacturer or supplier promotes a product or service through a series of marketing intermediaries with the aim of pushing the product through the channels of distribution

Qualitative research Techniques used amongst relatively small groups in order to identify and evaluate subjective opinions

Quantitative research The collection of data from samples of the target population to enable quantification and analysis

Rational decisions Decisions based on the qualitative assessment of the performance of a product or service and relating to specific features, attributes and benefits

Rebate Money given to consumer to reduce cost of purchase after purchase has been made. Also used in the context of trade promotions once retailer has purchased a defined quantity of product

Receiver The target audience for whom a communications message is intended

Reference groups Those groups within society with which the consumer identifies and would wish to belong

Relationship marketing The process of getting closer to the customer by means of customer service and quality delivery

Remuneration The income received in return for the provision of services

Response rate The percentage of the target audience who respond to a direct response campaign or couponing activity

ROI Return on investment

Routine problem solving Situations in which the consumer possesses sufficient prior knowledge to take a purchasing decision without seeking additional information

Sales aids Materials such as brochures used by the sales force to inform retailers and dealers of a promotional offer

Sales promotion The use of short-term, often tactical, techniques to achieve short-term sales objectives

Sales quota A quantitative expression of a target to be achieved by a salesperson or team during a given period of time

Sampling The process of encouraging the consumer to try a specified product or service

Secondary research The use of information that has previously been compiled and published

Segmentation The process of dividing a market into smaller groupings based on an understanding of consumer needs and wants

Selective attention The process by which receivers only notice some of the messages to which they are exposed

Selective distortion The process by which receivers modify or change received information to fit in with existing attitudes and beliefs

Self-liquidator Promotional item offered to consumer at the cost paid by the manufacturer

Self-regulation The process by which manufacturers agree to abide by codes of practice without the force of law

Sender The person or organization transmitting a communications message

Slotting allowance Discount offered to the retail trade usually in return for displaying products

Social class An open grouping of people with similar social ranking

Social marketing Marketing campaigns that recognize the general 'good of society'

Source The sender of a message

Source credibility The extent to which the consumer believes in the trustworthiness of the source of the message

SPAD Sales promotion advertising

Sponsorship The connection of a company or product with a public event in which the manufacturer contributes part or all of the costs in return for the benefit of association. Sponsorship can also embrace popular personalities and media programmes

Stockpiling The process of purchasing quantities of a product on promotion for subsequent consumption

Stock-up rates The volume of sales that result in stockpiling by the consumer

Strategy The determination of the means by which longer term goals and targets will be achieved

Sweepstake Competition format in which prizes are determined entirely by chance or luck

SWOT An acronym standing for strengths, weaknesses, opportunities and threats used in the analysis of a company or brand's competitive position

Tactics Specific actions designed to implement strategies

Tailor mades Promotions mounted in conjunction with an individual retailer

Target audience The identification of a group of potential consumers who have specific characteristics in common

Target marketing The selection of specific market segments at which to aim marketing or marketing communications

Telemarketing A form of personal selling in which the communications process is conducted via the telephone

Test market An area or region selected as being representative of the market as a whole used to test elements of the campaign either individually or in combination

Tracking study A market research technique that analyses consumer response and buying behaviour over an extended period of time

Trade allowances Sums of money negotiated by manufacturers with distribution channels in return for the carrying out of certain functions or activities

Value-added promotions Those promotions in which the consumer receives an additional item to increase the value of purchase

Value-increasing promotions Promotions that are associated with a change in price, quantity or both

Index